PR TODAY

THE AUTHORITATIVE GUIDE TO PUBLIC RELATIONS

Trevor Morris

Visiting Professor in Public Relations, University of Westminster

Simon Goldsworthy

Senior Lecturer in Public Communication,
University of Westminster

First published 2012 by
PALGRAVE MACMILLAN

Palgrave Macmillan in the UK is an imprint of Macmillan Publishers Limited, registered in England, company number 785998, of Houndmills, Basingstoke, Hampshire RG21 6XS.

Palgrave Macmillan in the US is a division of St Martin's Press LLC, 175 Fifth Avenue, New York, NY 10010.

Palgrave Macmillan is the global academic imprint of the above companies and has companies and representatives throughout the world.

Palgrave® and Macmillan® are registered trademarks in the United States, the United Kingdom, Europe and other countries.

ISBN 978–0–230–24009–4

This book is printed on paper suitable for recycling and made from fully managed and sustained forest sources. Logging, pulping and manufacturing processes are expected to conform to the environmental regulations of the country of origin.

A catalogue record for this book is available from the British Library.

Library of Congress Cataloging-in-Publication Data

Morris, Trevor.
    PR today : the authoritative guide to public relations / Trevor Morris, Simon Goldsworthy.
        p. cm.
    Includes index.
    Summary: "A comprehensive textbook, from an established and high profile author team, which offers full coverage of PR theory and strategies, but also gives very practical guidance for anyone in a PR role. The broad coverage tackles the tough issues in the industry, and international case studies are used to demonstrate real-world scenarios" – Provided by publisher.
    ISBN 978–0–230–24009–4 (pbk.)
    1. Public relations. I. Goldsworthy, Simon. II. Title.
HD59.M644 2011
659.2—dc23   2011034397

10 9 8 7 6 5 4 3 2 1
21 20 19 18 17 16 15 14 13 12

Printed in China

CONTENTS

TABLES

FIGURES

PREFACE

If you want to work in, or even just understand, public relations – in any of its many forms – this book is for you. It brings together high-level experience, inside knowledge and scholarship.

We, the authors, have been teaching public relations for many years – to undergraduate and postgraduate students from all over the world at a range of well-known universities, and to professionals on training courses. This means we are made constantly aware of the popularity of PR as a career, something that is impossible to miss if – as we do – one has the privilege of working, teaching and training in London, the world's number one PR centre.

PR may have become a very popular career choice, but that makes entering the PR world increasingly competitive. If you want to break into the industry, to find (and keep!) the job you want, you have to prepare yourself properly.

This book is designed to meet this growing need. We know that many people who are studying PR and want to work in the industry, journalism students and journalists who want to break into PR, and people who want simply to improve their existing careers have been calling for a *single* PR textbook which covers all the ground effectively and in a compact form – explaining the PR industry, tackling in a frank and clear way the issues which concern PR practitioners, and at the same time telling readers how to practise PR successfully, wherever they want to work. It is a book that we believe all those involved in running the best PR courses will appreciate.

Until *PR Today* no such book existed. Our book, published alongside a dedicated website, is new in its style and approach and differs from other textbooks in the following ways:

- Too many PR textbooks lack the *real* authority that comes with high-level and wide-ranging industry experience. This book overcomes that weakness. Trevor Morris brings to this book the exceptional range of his experience in the

PR industry, which culminated in him becoming the Chief Executive of the UK's largest public relations group. Today he continues to work as a top PR consultant, alongside his international teaching and training work.

- We have also used our contacts throughout the industry, and around the world, to gather top tips and insights from leading practitioners and experts on a wide range of PR topics. We regularly host top experts from London and beyond on our courses, and now you too can benefit from their expertise. Their contributions can be found throughout the book.

- Top-of-the-range and constantly updated practical experience is indispensable, but so is our international teaching experience, which ranges from Westminster to the Sorbonne, Johns Hopkins University, and Tsinghua University in Beijing. We don't just know about PR. We know how to develop your knowledge and understanding of it. All those years of teaching countless PR students from around the globe, at all levels, have enabled us to relate this book to *your* needs.

- Our three existing books, each tailored to meet more specific needs, have won extensive praise from the very top – from Lord Tim Bell, Chairman of Chime Communications plc and Margaret Thatcher's former PR advisor; from Paul Taaffe, former Chairman and Chief Executive of Hill & Knowlton Worldwide; from journalists – including the editor of *PR Week* magazine; from distinguished university professors and academic experts in the UK and other countries; and even from Sheldon Rampton, co-author of *Toxic Sludge Is Good for You*, an activist who has made sweeping criticisms of the PR industry. We are proud that we have earned respect in these very different quarters. Our aim with this book has been to earn that acclaim again, but for a book which draws upon the strengths of our other books while meeting a universal need for a broad PR education.

- We know that you do not want a book which just theorises about PR. You need to know about the context in which PR is practised, and about the ethical debates which swirl around the PR industry. But it is also vital for you to know how to practise PR, from writing press releases, dealing with journalists and handling social media through to running complete PR campaigns. So we cover all aspects of what you need to know. And when we discuss how to become a successful PR person, we do so in a fresh way. For example, we describe how to do promotional work, but we also recognise something that most other PR textbooks draw a veil over – that the most successful PR people also spend time trying to suppress or minimise bad news on behalf of the organisations they represent. So we tell you about that too: it happens, and the skills are highly valued, so why dodge the issue or sweep it under the carpet?

- We are realists. We know from experience that PR is not undertaken in a perfect world, and that it is essential for you to read about PR as it is rather than develop woolly and unrealistic notions of what some people might like it to be. PR people always have to compromise – unless they want to lose their jobs very quickly! The exercises we provide throughout the book are designed to get you thinking about PR in a way that relates it to the real world. PR is a profoundly social activity: just as if you had a real PR job, to make these exercises meaningful you will have to bring your knowledge of different organisations and the outside world to bear.

- One of the great things that attracts people to PR is the sheer variety of jobs PR people do – from working with celebrities or music and fashion labels through to consumer PR and working for large companies, governments, politicians or charities and campaigning organisations. And PR has skill specialisms too – for example, financial PR, the best-paid sector of the industry; lobbying or public affairs; and corporate social responsibility (CSR). We look at all these – and more – areas of PR, and provide thought-provoking examples of all aspects of public relations in action from around the world.

- Ultimately PR is paid for by people outside the PR industry, and your ideal job will depend on the needs of others. Too many PR books ignore this simple fact. They are inward-looking, obsessed with the concerns of small groups of people who write about PR and generate theories about the PR industry which mean little to those who practise or pay for PR. We avoid excessive introspection and instead focus on generating a true understanding of what is a fascinating, dynamic but sometimes controversial industry. We want our readers to be able to have a sensible discussion with critics and those outside the industry, not to try to defend unsustainable ideas such as the notion that PR is free from bias or is about developing 'loving relationships'.

- It goes without saying that this book is up-to-date, with the latest developments in such areas as online PR covered, and highly international in its approach. A glossary is provided to explain the technical terms you will come across. But the PR world constantly evolves, so this book is backed up with a website, enabling us continuously to develop the learning resources available to you.

- We refer to PR's portrayal in popular culture – notably television series and films – not just because this is entertaining but for a number of serious reasons. Such depictions of PR are far more influential in establishing PR's wider reputation than any number of PR textbooks. As we shall see, they are one of the principal reasons young people want to join the industry in the first place. And finally, script and screenplay writers, without vested interests in PR, are sometimes able to offer refreshing and pithily expressed versions of the truth.

- This book is for people who want to find a PR job – or a better job than they have at present. The unique features listed above are intended to help you to become a well-informed, reflective, skilled practitioner. Our combination of informed insight into the industry and advice on practical skills is designed to help you track down and enjoy work experience, succeed at interviews and finally secure and thrive in the job you want. We keep that in mind, and towards the end of the book feature some top tips – from both ourselves and a wide range of top international practitioners – on achieving these career objectives.

We have always enjoyed teaching, so we really hope you enjoy and benefit from the book. We welcome your feedback via our website, www.palgrave.com/business/prtoday.

Good luck!

ACKNOWLEDGEMENTS

We are enormously grateful to the wide range of top practitioners and experts from a variety of fields who found the time in their busy lives to contribute their thoughts and advice, thereby enriching this book. Those who have helped in this and other ways include Richard Bailey, Jean-Pierre Beaudoin, Robert Blood, Paul Borge, Mark Borkowski, Hugh Burkitt, Duncan Burns, Simon Cohen, Sally Costerton, Nick Davies, Wang Hui, Francis Ingham, Barry Leggetter, Chris. MacLeod, Karen Myers, Paul Mylrea, Ashlea Reece, Philip Scheiner, Julian Vogel, Tom Watson, Adrian Wheeler and Lionel Zetter. Thankfully the world of PR embraces many views and is not boringly monolithic, so their views are their own. In the same way our views, as expressed in the rest of the book, are ours – and any faults are our handiwork and no one else's.

We would also like to thank many other people, too many to name, who have contributed to this book in other ways: as ever, the best insights into PR are gleaned at first hand. They include students and trainees of many nationalities, colleagues, journalists and people from throughout the PR industry and beyond. Some of the material in this book appeared in a modified form in our three earlier books: *PR – A Persuasive Industry?*, *Public Relations for Asia* and *Public Relations for the New Europe*, all published by Palgrave Macmillan. Once again we are indebted to the team at Newgen Imaging Systems for helping to produce this book, and to the doyenne of PR indexers, Alja Kranjec, for bringing her formidable skills to bear on the book's closing pages. Alexander Goldsworthy provided valuable assistance with the proofs. Finally we are deeply grateful to everyone at Palgrave Macmillan – especially in this case Martin Drewe and Ceri Griffiths – for publishing so much of our work with such professionalism.

FURTHER READING, ITS LIMITATIONS – AND HOW TO USE THIS BOOK

It is usual to offer plenty of suggestions for additional reading in books of this kind. We supply a list of books and other materials at the end of this book, and in the more theoretical chapters we mention or recommend particular books, websites and so forth. Some of these are stimulating works which offer real insights into the world of PR; a few are even entertaining. Indeed a well-written novel (and film) such as Christopher Buckley's *Thank You for Smoking* offers more food for thought about PR ethics than some textbooks.

We frequently cite examples from the real world of PR, often referring to events which may be familiar to you. Although we provide references to online information, clearly much more material is available. Tracking this down as you undertake our suggested exercises will help you cultivate useful research skills. As we mentioned, this book is accompanied by a website to which you may wish to refer: www.palgrave.com/business/prtoday.

Mental nourishment is vital, but it would be dishonest to suggest that most PR people, including top industry figures, perfect their skills by reading more and more books on the subject. There are fundamental skills you will need to get started, but thereafter experience comes to the fore. This book covers those essential skills comprehensively, but to make further progress there are plenty of things you can do for yourself. Close, daily study of the media will enable you to see PR in action all around you. Keep an eye on the PR challenges facing organisations you know or with which you are involved. At the same time, familiarise yourself with the PR industry. Read trade publications such as *PR Week* and some of the first-hand accounts of PR on our reading list (although it would be helpful if more senior practitioners were able to write about their experiences!); visit the websites of PR trade bodies and PR agencies; attend media and PR-related events and talk to fellow attendees; and – most important of all – get a range of work experience. Some PR books can be inward-looking, but PR is a profoundly social activity (one of its great joys) and, in the end, has to be lived in the real world!

ABOUT THE AUTHORS

Trevor Morris, FRSA, is Visiting Professor in Public Relations at Westminster University and a business consultant and PR trainer. He was formerly the high-profile CEO of Chime Public Relations, Europe's biggest PR group. He has regularly featured in the PR Week Power Book, is a fellow of the PRCA and a former chair of the judges for the AMEC media evaluation awards.

As an entrepreneurial businessman Trevor shaped and led the management buyout of QBO, a top UK PR consultancy, and then grew the business to achieve margins of over 30 per cent before selling it to Chime plc.

As a public relations consultant he led campaigns from crisis management to brand building and public information for blue chip commercial and government clients.

Former colleagues range from Lord Tim Bell (former Prime Minister Lady Thatcher's favourite PR man), David Hill (former Prime Minister Tony Blair's press advisor) and Rosie Boycott (journalist and broadcaster) through to Sophie Rhys-Jones (Countess of Wessex, the wife of Prince Edward).

He organised and chaired the controversial PR Week and University of Westminster debate 'PR has a duty to tell the truth' and took part in a follow-up debate on the same theme at the Sorbonne in Paris.

Trevor has a BA (Combined Honours) in History and Politics from Exeter and a Post Graduate Certificate in Education from the University of London. He has lectured at the University of Westminster, City University, Exeter University, the Sorbonne, Tsinghua University and Richmond, the American International University.

Married with two daughters, Trevor lives in Battersea, South London. He is a regular theatre goer, keen reader of literary fiction and lifelong supporter and season ticket holder of Fulham Football Club.

Simon Goldsworthy is Senior Lecturer in Public Communication at the University of Westminster. He has a first-class degree in History from the University of London, and was formerly a member of the UK's Government Information Service, undertaking press and publicity work for a range of government departments, including the Central Office of Information, the Department of Trade and Industry, the Department of Social Security and the Department of the Environment. His duties included advising government ministers on media handling. He subsequently worked both independently and for a number of PR consultancies, running PR projects for a wide range of public sector organisations, including an award-winning web-based campaign for the UK's largest science research council.

In 2000 Simon launched the first MA programme in Public Relations in London at the University of Westminster, adding an undergraduate programme two years later. Both programmes attract large numbers of students from all over the world, and benefit from excellent links with key figures in the PR industry, many of whom are guest speakers.

Simon has also set up and run courses for universities in other countries, including Johns Hopkins University in the USA; has lectured in China, including at Tsinghua University, as well as running a range of training courses for Chinese government officials; has served as a visiting professor at the Université Paris-Sorbonne; is an academic governor of the American International University in London; and has acted as consultant and external examiner for a number of PR courses at other UK universities. He has also published a number of academic articles on such subjects as PR education and ethics, the relationship between PR and advertising, propaganda and aspects of journalism.

Simon lives in Chiswick, West London. He is a keen traveller, cinema goer and reader of history. He is married, with a young son.

Trevor Morris and Simon Goldsworthy are the authors of three earlier books on public relations: *PR – A Persuasive Industry? Spin, Public Relations, and the Shaping of the Modern Media*; *Public Relations for Asia*; and *Public Relations for the New Europe*. All were published by Palgrave Macmillan in 2008.

THEORY AND ANALYSIS

CHAPTERS

1 UNDERSTANDING PUBLIC RELATIONS

2 PR ETHICS

3 THE MAKE-UP OF THE PR INDUSTRY

4 PR, MARKETING AND ADVERTISING

5 INTERNAL COMMUNICATIONS

6 LOBBYING, POLITICAL AND GOVERNMENT PR

7 PR IN THE ONLINE WORLD

8 CORPORATE SOCIAL RESPONSIBILITY

9 PR AND THE LAW

UNDERSTANDING PUBLIC RELATIONS

INTRODUCTION

Many people who seek to work in public relations want – understandably – to get on with it. The fact that anyone can embark on a PR career without years of training and exams is, after all, one of the attractions of the job. However for anyone intending to make a more serious commitment to a public relations career, it is worth pausing and reflecting a little on what PR is, how the discipline has developed, how it is seen by others, and the role it plays in society and – particularly – how PR relates to the media. This chapter explores these issues and offers some food for thought. Setting PR in a wider context in this way is not only an important part of good higher education courses, it can also help you see your own role more clearly. Who knows, it could even stand you in good stead at interviews!

LEARNING OBJECTIVES

- To review definitions of public relations and why defining PR has proved problematic
- To explore the origins and development of PR, and how it came to be valued as a means of securing third-party endorsement
- To review attempts to develop theoretical approaches to understanding PR
- To analyse PR's role in the information marketplace and its relationship to the mass media

WHAT IS PR?

If you are studying PR or have ambitions to work in the PR industry you probably feel you know what PR is. Public relations is talked about a great deal in contemporary society and your assumption is shared by many in the media and beyond who bandy around the term without bothering to explain it. Most PR practitioners happily carry on with their day-to-day activities without worrying too much about the issue.

But PR's own writers and educators, and many of those in PR's trade bodies, do not seem to find it so simple. In 1976 one public relations scholar identified 472 definitions of PR,[1] and the number keeps growing. As you will find as you read on we have added our own contribution. It is of course natural, particularly in an academic context, to define your terms before you proceed, but with PR there seems to be a particular difficulty.

How the industry defines itself

In 1988 the governing body of the world's largest PR membership body, the Public Relations Society of America (PRSA), adopted a definition of public relations which is widely used:

> Public relations helps an organization and its publics adapt mutually to each other.[2]

The definition devised by the UK equivalent of the PRSA, the Chartered Institute of Public Relations (CIPR), is different and makes particular use of the word 'reputation':

> Public relations is about reputation – the result of what you do, what you say and what others say about you.
>
> Public relations is the discipline which looks after reputation, with the aim of earning understanding and support and influencing opinion and behaviour. It is the planned and sustained effort to establish and maintain goodwill and mutual understanding between an organisation and its publics.[3]

One of the more interesting definitions was drawn up in 1978 at the first World Assembly of Public Relations Associations (also known as the Mexican Statement):

> Public relations is the art and social science of analysing trends, predicting their consequences, counselling organisation leaders and implementing planned programmes of action which will serve both the organisation's and the public interest.[4]

These three definitions, covering as they do the United States, the United Kingdom and the world, can be taken as representative of the official view. The problem with all of them is that they are not written by detached observers but by practitioners and members of trade associations who have a vested interest in promoting a positive rather than an objective view of the practice of PR. Whether consciously or not, they seek to protect and boost the status of an industry which they know has often been described by the media and members of the public in unflattering terms. Ironically, by defining PR in terms that many in the public might find unclear and unhelpful, or even disingenuous, they risk further damaging the reputation of that which they seek to protect.

All these definitions are marred by their failure to stress the reasons for public relations activity. For example, *goodwill and mutual understanding* (UK CIPR definition) may sound praiseworthy but are not ends in themselves; instead they are means to an end, whether it be getting people to follow the recommendations of a health campaign, making a workforce more productive, encouraging acceptance of a new development by a local community, or selling more goods or services. PR is a purposeful activity.

The British claim that PR is about *reputation* is also misleading. There are many factors which influence reputation that PR practitioners have little or nothing to do with. For example, PR seldom determines product performance or service delivery. So to assert that public relations is the discipline that looks after reputation is to exaggerate – it is more of an aspiration than a definition. Moreover there are PR campaigns where 'looking after an organisation's reputation' does not fully describe the objective – for instance, those encouraging changes in social behaviour (e.g. an anti-smoking campaign) or attacking government policy. And for many PR campaigns, brands or individuals may be the focus, not organisations. Moreover all these definitions seem to exclude negative PR – attacking the words and actions of others – although this is a staple of political PR, plays a huge role in the work of campaigning non-governmental organisations (NGOs), and is not unknown in the corporate sector.

Similarly, the American view that PR is about helping an *organization and its publics adapt mutually to each other* fails to describe how PR actually works and also glosses over the fact that public relations activity is generally undertaken to achieve objectives that are more specific and hard-nosed than mutual adaptation. Such language sidesteps the fact that PR is driven by those paying for it, not by its targets. PR is not about love of mankind, but about a desire to achieve something for its paymaster. Sometimes the aim may be one we can all agree is a noble one that benefits everyone (although surprisingly often this is awash with value judgements), but, for the most part, the benefit to society of any particular PR activity is open to debate.

The 'Mexican Statement' is strong on describing what PR does – or should do – at a strategic level – *analysing trends, predicting their consequences, counselling organisation leaders* (although relatively few PR people are paid simply to analyse, predict and counsel, and others do this sort of work too) – but loses focus when it says *and implementing programmes*. What sort of programmes? Building new factories? Creating an advertising campaign? In common with the other definitions it does not say *how* PR does what it is meant to do, nor does it acknowledge that the concerns of the organisation paying for the PR will always be weighed against the public interest.

A reluctance to admit the obvious

Most outsiders – and many insiders – associate PR with *persuasion*, even without giving the matter much thought. However *persuasion* is a word and an activity which is often viewed with suspicion. For this reason, throughout history many terms associated with the process of persuading fellow human beings to think or act in particular ways – from the techniques of rhetoric, sophistry and casuistry to propaganda – have acquired negative associations, although all were innocent to begin with. This has led to the word 'persuasion' remaining absent from most definitions of PR of which we are aware.

But most would probably accept the seemingly commonsensical proposition that PR is about persuading people to act (or not act) in particular ways: that is, after all, what people pay PR practitioners to achieve. Popular culture is often much pithier than formal definitions, and can often be down-to-earth or rude about PR, although the success of some of the popular portrayals of PR, from *Sex and the City* and *Gossip Girl* to *Sliding Doors*, *Bridget Jones's Diary* and *In the Loop*, suggests that they deal in recognisable stereotypes. Few outsiders have encountered the official definitions of PR, but millions around the world heard Edina Monsoon, the PR anti-heroine of the popular BBC TV comedy series *Absolutely Fabulous*, describe her work as follows:

> ❝ I PR things. Places. Concepts. Lulu. I PR them … I make them fabulous. I make the crap into credible. I make the dull into delicious …[5]

As the CIPR's definition makes clear, *reputation* includes what others say about you, so such portrayals of PR cannot be simply brushed aside. If you feel such descriptions of PR are exaggerated or inaccurate you need to be able to respond with credible counter-arguments.

Our definition of public relations

Public relations is the planned persuasion of people to behave in ways which further its sponsor's objectives. It works primarily through the use of media relations and other forms of third-party endorsement.

We have sought to be clear about the intent of public relations (*persuasion*), but our definition is also unusual in that it seeks to describe how PR attempts to go about this: *primarily through the use of media relations and other forms of third-party endorsement. Third-party endorsement* refers to getting the support and backing of independent voices: it is not about *you* saying you are good (a province dominated by advertising, which pays for its own space in the media and chooses what appears there), but about getting someone else, independently, to say you are good. Obtaining positive media coverage is the commonest way in which PR achieves this and it therefore seems odd to omit such a fundamental characteristic of public relations from the definition.

> ❝❝ All research I've seen says that editorial publicity is better than paid-for publicity.
>
> Sir Martin Sorrell, Chief Executive, WPP Group[6]

Relating PR to its sponsor's objectives and not just to goodwill or reputation means that the definition recognises that PR is purposeful, is not just about reputation and indeed may sometimes be negative and intended to undermine others. This aspect of PR is something of a taboo and hence falls outside most established definitions. PR is also a *planned* activity. This helps distinguish it, as a specialised discipline, from other persuasive activities in which we all engage, often unthinkingly, in our day-to-day life.

This definition of PR is controversial and continues to cause debate. Apart from those who dislike relating the word *persuasion* to PR, there are two main bones of contention.

First, some insist that PR does not just persuade people to go along with an organisation's objectives, but plays an active role in defining those objectives. As one prominent spokesperson for the UK industry put it, somewhat defensively: 'We're supposed to be strategists, advisers, working in the boardroom, helping companies get their policies right.' On the other hand, the former UK Prime Minister Tony Blair said of his long-serving Director of Communications, Alastair Campbell: 'Alastair likes to make out he ran the show... But the truth is I never ran any policy by him. Ever. I might have asked how something would play in the press, but never how to formulate policy.'[7] As this illustrates, too many claims by PR people are inward looking, and fail to take account of the perspective of those outside the industry who rely on PR advice. Their view of PR's role may not be quite as exalted as that claimed by public relations practitioners.

Clearly there is a distinction between policy formation and its presentation. But in the United Kingdom, according to a recent survey, fewer than a third of big businesses had communications directors on their main boards.[8] Most PR people communicate policy rather than decide it. However some proponents of PR like to portray themselves as sitting at the top table and like to claim as much power as possible, particularly as power equates to money and status. This perception is shared by critics of PR, and there has been much resentment in the

United States and the United Kingdom directed at the power wielded by political spin doctors.

Trusted PR advisors do have opportunities to exert influence – they sometimes, particularly in times of crisis, have more access to those they are advising than anyone else, and use that access to advise them on whatever are the most pressing and high-profile issues of the moment. Advice on presentation can blur into policy formation, as PR advisors urge particular courses of action on presentational grounds, so the issue remains a vexed and disputed one. However the truth remains that PR people seldom *lead* organisations – they *counsel* those who do.

Second, critics of our definition are reluctant to admit that PR's primary tool is media relations.

Some defenders of PR – and many who are simply trying to dodge some of its more negative connotations – hardly mention media relations. Some have even dropped the term 'public relations', preferring to call themselves 'communications experts'. Communication is of course one of those purr words that have overwhelmingly positive overtones – who's against it? – but the problem is that it is vague.

Communication can cover everything from a phone call between a receptionist and a customer to door drops and a million-dollar advertising campaign. It is now common to have the term 'communications' as part of in-house PR practitioners' job titles, but this could in itself be seen as just 'another PR stunt' or a 'bit of spin', designed to conceal what PR people really do.

One reason we have chosen to emphasise media relations is because it is the only persuasive technique which is the unchallenged preserve of PR. Almost every other technique used by the industry is sometimes undertaken – and can be claimed – by other disciplines. However, but for the rise of the mass media and the resulting need for media relations specialists, the PR industry in its current form would not have come into being. Although anyone may have dealings with journalists, doing so in a planned and deliberate way, and deriving one's income from so doing, is unique to PR. Making the call to a journalist, writing a press release, arranging a press conference or handling media enquiries are things the PR person does – and others are normally happy to leave it that way. The idea of speaking to a potentially hostile journalist and being quoted – or misquoted – to an audience of millions scares many people.

According to one survey in the UK, media relations work accounted for 37% of PR practitioners' time. Next came advising management (25%), brochure/video/ print production (14%), event management (10%) and research (9%).[9] Advising management is customarily seen as the most prestigious form of PR activity and therefore may well be over-reported. Moreover much of the advice given to management is likely to concern media relations: it would be odd if PR practition-ers' advice was not closely related to their chief area of activity. It is also likely that the research work and events management have media relations compo-nents. Moreover some of these functions could be carried out equally well – if not better – by non-PR staff. These findings were broadly confirmed by another UK survey which found that maintaining a 'positive image in the media' is seen by both in-house practitioners and consultants as the area in which PR is most effective.[10] None of this would surprise most outsiders for whom PR is forever associated with press releases, press conferences and talking to journalists.

But some PR practitioners remain troubled and uncomfortable about emphasising their role in media relations. Instead they prefer to stress other forms of communication and the overarching strategic role of PR (strategy being one of PR's most overworked words). Hence the omission of media relations from the other definitions of which we are aware. Indeed the so-called Father of Public Relations, Edward Bernays (see pp. 16–17), said, 'We've [speaking of him-self!] had no direct contact with the mass media for about fifty years.'[11] Similar statements may sometimes be true for those involved in financial or lobbying campaigns, but even they have to use the media as well as other third parties such as analysts and political insiders.

In the film version of *Bridget Jones's Diary*[12], Bridget Jones's boss tells her:

> You don't have the faintest bloody idea how much trouble the company is in. You swan in in your short skirt and sexy see-through blouse and fanny around with press releases.

As the quotation implies, one problem for some PR practitioners is that stress-ing their role in media relations is seen as diminishing their status: every disci-pline or profession has a natural desire for self-aggrandisement and wants to put itself at the centre of things. Too often media relations is seen as a set of tactical devices which are beneath the dignity of an industry with higher preten-sions; it is associated with *saying* rather than *doing*. PR practitioners, with an ill-defined role in the lives of the organisations for which they work, crave the kudos of a central decision-making role. A desire for more acknowledgement from the higher reaches of business can be found in many public utterances by PR peo-ple. They want to be more than a means to an end, and to be business gurus and management consultants rather than mere media handlers and intermediaries.

PR's often fraught relationship with journalism is another part of the prob-lem. One skeleton in the cupboard is that PR is partly descended from the role played by press agents, people who were often depicted as seedy huck-sters as they tried to sell their stories. To this day, public relations people face considerable public hostility from journalists, so it is understandable that some PR practitioners seek to play down the media relations aspect of their work.

This reluctance to admit the obvious is a pity and does PR no favours. Media handling – particularly in difficult circumstances – is a demanding art form which is highly valued by the senior people who hire PR talent. It is no accident that so many of the highest earners and most powerful figures in the PR field are known for their media handling skills, even if their work takes them into other areas of PR.

| What is your definition of PR? | You might want to consider using some of the following words: reputation, image, goodwill, brand, publics, stakeholders, influence, persuasion, management, relationships | Once you have prepared your definition try relating it to the PR activities of organisations you know. How well does the definition fit the reality? |

LESSONS FROM HISTORY

The history of public relations may sometimes seem to be of limited relevance to contemporary practitioners and we do not intend to provide an exhaustive version here. However, much of the knowledge which marks out successful PR practitioners is drawn from history, even if they have acquired the information informally and do not think of it as 'History'. There are few if any scientific laws in PR. Instead people learn from experience: much of what PR people do today and plan to do tomorrow is based on collective wisdom about what happened yesterday. Experienced PR people carry in their heads countless potted biographies of PR people, their employers and – not least – journalists. They also know the stories of the ups and downs of many PR campaigns, and are informal students of corporate history and much else besides – success in PR depends hugely on understanding unfolding events in whichever field you happen to work.

A number of significant themes emerge from the study of PR history which are particularly relevant to understanding the industry today. Our focus below is on those issues which seem most relevant to understanding the present and planning for the future.

In a sense PR is timeless, and has existed in all societies since the dawn of humanity. Political and religious leaders have always sought to win and retain support, and businesses have always sought to further their interests, so 'PR' has been a part of what such people do from time immemorial. However, PR as a specialist field with formal structures, to which people devote their working lives – and certainly the name 'public relations' – is a relative newcomer.

Professor Philip M. Taylor, 1954–2010

Any thoughtful PR person who wants a broader perspective on their field of work and seeks to put it in some historical context would do well to read some of the work of Philip Taylor, former Director of the Institute of Communication Studies at the University of Leeds in the UK and a great believer in the practical application of communications, not least in the military field.

Some PR people might baulk any connection between what they do and the title of Taylor's best-known work, *Munitions of the Mind: A history of propaganda from the ancient world to the present era*, but for Taylor, propaganda was simply:

the *deliberate* attempt to persuade people to think and behave *in a desired way*.

Public relations is a related communicative process designed to enhance the relationship between an organisation and the public and, as such, is a branch of propaganda, albeit a nicer way of labelling it.

Taylor's academic interest was in propaganda and all forms of communication. This means that his work is not infected with special pleading about PR. Instead he offers a very readable account of the role propaganda has played in history, particularly in the military sphere, from ancient times up to recent conflicts, where it overlaps with the activities of the rising PR industry.

In its current sense the term 'public relations' first surfaced just over one hundred years ago in the United States. At that stage – before the emergence of broadcasting – there was already a large network of newspapers and a well-established tradition of press agents creating publicity for their clients in the newspaper press, notably for circuses and other places of entertainment.

P. T. Barnum and the early days of publicity

The nineteenth-century American showman and circus owner P. T. Barnum is often seen as prefiguring the rise of PR as we know it today. Taking advantage of the emergence of cheap, mass-circulation newspapers in the United States, he displayed a mastery of the publicity stunt, ensuring constant coverage for his shows

and becoming a legend. General Tom Thumb, 'The smallest person that ever walked alone', and Jumbo the Elephant were among his creations, while he memorably described his circus as the 'The Greatest Show on Earth'. His crowd-pleasing willingness to use hype and hoaxes is often viewed with disdain by those who write about PR today.

Note: Scott M Cutlip, *The Unseen Power: Public Relations. A History* (Lawrence Erlbaum, 1994)

However it was the growth of major new companies in the United States in the late nineteenth century which created the need for corporate PR as we now know it. These companies operated in large and rapidly growing markets, with customers and interests spread across the North American continent and beyond. Gone were the days when companies could rely on local communities that they knew well and where they were well known. Instead today's global companies and brands were emerging from provincial America. Procter & Gamble was ceasing to be a small Cincinnati soap manufacturer and becoming the multinational we know today, while Coca-Cola evolved from a small-time medicinal drink manufacturer in the American South. Such businesses needed to start thinking about their reputations more carefully, and to start employing professionals to help them do it.

As businesses of this kind developed, they grew well beyond what an individual entrepreneur or founding family could control. Businessmen had traditionally been jacks of all trades, but increasingly companies came to rely on highly trained professional managers – often accountants, lawyers and engineers – people who respected specialist skills and subdivided work accordingly. Companies saw that they could gain competitive advantage and operate more efficiently by building on professional experience in this way.

The same process started to extend to marketing and publicity work. The US advertising industry began to take its modern shape in the nineteenth century, while the early twentieth century saw the gradual emergence of marketing as a distinct discipline and the birth of professional marketing bodies. Businessmen had always been interested in selling their own goods and services, but they were now able to do it in a more deliberate and planned way, using staff with special training and experience to help them. They also became used to engaging advertising agencies to help them accomplish their goals. This paved the way for PR as a specialist business discipline. Although PR had always been – and continues to be – part of the portmanteau of skills that marks out the successful founder of a business, it came increasingly to be entrusted to people with special skills and experience and became a career in its own right.

PR and politics

Some of the earliest users of professional PR techniques were politicians in the United States, and later in Europe. Of course political leaders, even dictators, have always been interested in trying to manage public opinion. However the advent of democracy and the rise of mass electorates created a different challenge. Millions of people had to be persuaded to vote for a particular candidate or political party when given a genuine choice in a secret ballot. Force and threats were no longer an option. PR has come to play an important role in the battle to secure people's votes, although it operates under a variety of aliases – most commonly, in the United States and the United Kingdom, people involved in such work are called by their detractors 'spin doctors', although they themselves tend to prefer to talk about 'communication' and dislike the implications of 'spin' (see pp. 131–132 for a fuller discussion of spin).

The two world wars of the twentieth century also gave an enormous fillip to the embryonic PR industry. The mass mobilisation and leadership of whole societies for total war, in circumstances of extreme crisis, not surprisingly required extensive communication efforts, and in democracies such as the USA and the UK with relatively free mass media the subtle techniques of PR came to be in demand. Many of the founding fathers of the US PR industry helped President Woodrow Wilson with the task of persuading a hitherto reluctant America when he took the controversial decision to intervene in the First World War in 1917, and they did not forget the skills they had honed when peace came. An even greater mobilisation of PR talent took place in the Second World War, and it is no coincidence that the Public Relations Society of America and the Institute of Public Relations (now the Chartered Institute of Public Relations) in the UK were both set up in 1948, with PR people with wartime experience among the founders, when memories of the uses of public relations in time of conflict were fresh.

PR, the rise of the mass media and third-party endorsement

Another factor contributed to the birth of modern PR – and indeed continues to shape its development to this day.

Late-nineteenth-century America experienced an enormous growth in print journalism, the only mass medium of the day. Many new newspapers and magazines were published, and their circulations soared. Aided by distribution on the railway network, for the first time large sections of the population across widely dispersed areas were absorbing the same news and information on a daily basis. Advertising boomed as companies paid to exploit the opportunities this created to reach large audiences in new ways. However, advertisements had inherent drawbacks: not only were they costly, but everyone knew who was behind them; however clever the ad, in the end it was just a company singing its own praises. A paid-for advertisement never has the credibility of a positive piece of independent media coverage.

Press agents, in many ways the precursors of PR in America, took advantage of the opportunities the media boom created. They recognised that journalists had needs of their own – that they wanted interesting, newsworthy material to fill their pages. Press agents made their living by supplying the material, ensuring that the resulting story contained a favourable namecheck, or mention, for the companies or individuals who hired them. Not only was this kind of publicity cheaper (the press agent had to be paid, but the journalist and the newspaper did not), but it also offered an additional advantage. Rather than appearing in the form of an advertisement, the information appeared on the printed page as editorial content, written by an independent journalist and bearing the independent authority of the publication in which it featured. As we all know, anyone can claim they are good at something, but it is much more credible if someone else – someone who is independent and appears to be objective (better still, with the authority of a well-regarded media outlet) – says they are. This special quality, called *third-party endorsement* remains the strongest unique selling proposition for PR. Advertising is like walking into a meeting and telling the people present, 'I am very good at what I do.' PR is like walking into that meeting and some of the people present telling the others you are very good at what you do!

Although the emerging mass media created new opportunities to put across favourable messages, they also represented a threat. The new newspapers with their huge circulations were competing with others to sell copies, and, as any journalist will confirm, bad news and stories about conflict and crises tend to outsell good news. Hostile stories not only made unpleasant reading for businesspeople but could also have more concrete consequences. This came to a head with the emergence of what were called the *muckrakers*, a group of what today would be called *investigative journalists*, who sought to uncover corporate abuses and greed. Their exposés could put the new breed of employee managers' jobs on the line, or cause a loss of custom, undermine share prices or lead to calls for government action to curtail business freedoms. By the early twentieth century, in an era of growing democratic accountability, US business felt increasingly beleaguered. The big new corporations, often headed by men who were labelled as 'Robber Barons', were obvious targets. Businesspeople started to feel it worth paying to try to halt – or at least minimise – negative press coverage. Ideally media interest in big business could even be turned around and transformed into positive coverage. It was perhaps this – a more sophisticated service than press agents could offer – that first gave rise to the modern PR industry.

If PR was born out of developments in journalism, it is worth noting that many early practitioners were themselves former journalists who were able to exploit their knowledge of how the media work. They understood what makes a good story, and what does not, and they knew the pressures under which journalists work. This established a tradition which continues to this day: many PR practitioners, including some of the most senior, formerly worked in journalism, and their understanding of the media is valued. PR continues to provide an alternative career for journalists, one which often offers better pay and working conditions.

Recent developments

Since the 1980s the PR industry in the developed world has enjoyed unprecedented levels of growth, much faster than the economy as a whole. Although it was affected by the worldwide recession in 2008/9, the effects of the economic downturn were not as severe for public relations as some feared: PR services still seemed to be very much in demand.

What are the reasons for the exponential growth of PR? One important reason can be traced back to the market liberalisation promoted by President

Reagan and UK Prime Minister Thatcher in the 1980s, which created enormous needs for PR services. The privatisation of state assets – nationalised industries – by selling shares involved expensive PR campaigns and gave an enormous fillip to the financial PR sector. Moreover the companies that emerged from the privatisation process proved to be much greater users of PR than their nationalised predecessors as they sought business in new, competitive marketplaces, while at the same time communicating with their shareholders. In place of direct state control came regulation, and this created a new PR requirement as companies needed to lobby government and the new regulatory bodies.

The boost this gave to PR quickly spread to all parts of the industry. Liberalisation led to economic growth and contributed to a sustained consumer boom. This created new opportunities for many kinds of PR as people shopped more, purchased more services (not least financial products such as savings, pensions and insurance), travelled more and enjoyed an ever wider range of expensive leisure pursuits. Branding, while not new, became more central to marketing as people spent lower proportions of their income on commodities such as basic foodstuffs and more on branded goods and designer labels. Here PR played a crucial role. While advertising continued (and continues) to play a vital part in promoting the sale of goods and services, spending in the evermore affluent societies of the West was increasingly lavished on big-ticket items – property, cars, luxury holidays, financial services – where relying on the advertiser's own words was not enough. People could not simply sample these goods and services at minimal cost and then decide whether to make a repeat purchase. Instead people seemed to want these products subjected to independent critical review by journalists, a trend reflected in the growing number of newspaper supplements and TV programmes covering precisely these product areas. Indeed the growing volumes of media content – ever thicker newspapers with more sections, more and fatter magazines, and increasing amounts of broadcast programming available around the clock, all produced without any commensurate increase in the numbers of journalists – created unprecedented opportunities for PR people in their role as content suppliers.

PR has also adapted and responded to the social changes in many western democracies which started to gather pace in the 1960s. The Civil Rights movement, the anti-Vietnam war campaign, feminism and the emerging Green movement – all of which made use of PR techniques themselves – were just some of the radical new features of that generation with which commercial and public sector PR had to contend. They proved to be the precursors of today's environmentalism and an increasing desire among well-educated publics to seek to improve the societies in which they live, a trend which has created new opportunities for PR. These days two of the biggest challenges facing many organisations are how to demonstrate to critical media and publics that they respect social concerns and that they wish to minimise their impact on the environment. This perceived need for businesses to be seen to be doing good – and not just doing good business – has led to the emergence of what is often called *corporate social responsibility* or CSR (see Chapter 8), an area which many in PR are keen to be involved in and profit from. This is of growing importance internationally as companies in all countries become subject to external as well as domestic pressure, for example from supranational bodies such as the European Union, which has its own environmental agenda, and from the opinions of consumers in the end markets for their goods. Increasingly the focus for these pressures on business is provided by NGOs – themselves major PR players – which feed their concerns to the media and hence public opinion.

Although not newcomers to PR, governments and the political parties which control – or seek to control – government have become ever greater users of PR. Effective communication is an important part of modern government, but PR is also used for direct political advantage and has become ever more central to political life. In the UK not only are large numbers of in-house PR people employed, but the past reluctance to use consultancies has been abandoned and government is now a significant user of agency services.

PR at the heart of politics

In the 2010 general election in the United Kingdom the electorate witnessed a struggle between the outgoing Prime Minister, Gordon Brown, who is married to a PR person and both of whose brothers are PR men, and his Conservative challenger, David Cameron, who formerly worked in commercial public relations. Cameron was often attacked – not least by Brown – for his PR background. The suggestion was that he was merely a slick salesman.

The election results were inconclusive. Two former senior Labour 'spin doctors', Alastair Campbell and Lord Mandelson, played a key role in the attempt to keep their party in power. In the end Cameron became Prime Minister, forming a coalition with the leader of the Liberal Democrat Party, Nick Clegg, who himself had worked briefly as a lobbyist. The new government included many people who had worked in lobbying and PR.

Edward Bernays: the Father of Public Relations?

It is impossible to read about the history of PR without encountering the figure of the American pioneer Edward Bernays. Bernays died in 1995 at the age of 103, and had been involved in PR work since before the First World War. He claimed that it was because of the odium which became attached to the word

'propaganda' in that war (he was directly involved in America's own propaganda campaign) that he started to use the title 'counsellor in public relations'.

Bernays made much of the fact that he was the nephew (twice over) of Sigmund Freud and sought to incorporate Freud's psychoanalytical ideas in his PR consultancy. He was one of the first to teach PR at a university, wrote many books on the subject, provided controversial

➡

quotes in ways in which most PR people are loathe to do, and was involved in some notable and much discussed campaigns, all of which gave him a high profile in an industry which is often deliberately self-effacing. Perhaps his main rival for the title of 'Father of PR' was Ivy Lee, a former journalist who first set up a corporate PR bureau in the USA in 1904. In many ways Lee's approach and methods were more comparable to the work of today's big consultancies, but he died relatively young, in 1934. He did not seek the limelight in the same way as Bernays, and at the end of his life was controversially linked to a client in Nazi Germany.

It is tempting to see Bernays as an all-powerful figure who was able to use the levers of power from behind the scenes – a view which certainly suits critics of PR, for whom he has become a convenient, sinister bogey man: every tale needs a villain! He was certainly a skilled self-publicist, but his achievements need to be kept in perspective. Many in the PR industry viewed him as an embarrassment. His consultancy did not survive the test of time (whereas other firms from his era are still around), and indeed the turnover rate among his clients seems to have been high. Nor have Freudian theory and psychoanalysis had much lasting impact upon PR practice: it is rarely among the skills that PR firms or departments

seek out in the marketplace. A general view of Bernays seems to have been that while he could 'talk the talk', he could not necessarily 'walk the walk'.

Perhaps the greatest legend associated with Bernays – and one of the most cited PR fables of all time – is that in 1929 he managed to break the taboo on women smoking by a single act, namely by getting debutantes to smoke publicly during that year's Easter Sunday March in New York and ensuring that this received extensive media coverage on behalf of his client, American Tobacco. The story has obvious emotional appeal, but does it have a rational basis or is it a piece of Bernays' personal PR to which, ironically, those with concerns about PR have succumbed? It has been pointed out that attitudes towards women smoking had been changing for some time, due to the changing social climate and the advent of milder cigarettes, and that advertising also played an important – and earlier – part in the process. In so far as PR contributed to the process, it is noteworthy that a firm headed by Ivy Lee started work for American Tobacco a year before Bernays, continued to work there for decades thereafter and was paid more.

Note: For a full and balanced account, see Larry Tye's *The Father of Spin: Edward L Bernays and the Birth of Public Relations* (Owl Books, 1998).

 Identify some long established PR consultancies and/or PR departments in your country and trace their development and changing roles. What does your research tell you about the evolution of public relations in your society? You could undertake this as a group exercise, choosing different agencies and departments, and then pool your knowledge and discuss what lessons can be drawn from it.

THE REPUTATION AND IMAGE OF PR

If public relations is closely bound up with the reputations of the organisations and people it serves – indeed according to some of the most common definitions it is about reputation management – then it seems only fair to pay some attention to PR's own reputation. Examining PR's reputation reveals what a complex and multi-faceted thing reputation is, as well as illustrating how hard it can be to pin down its source.

As a reader of this book it is likely that you are contemplating – if you have not already started – a career in PR. You are not alone. Public relations is now a hugely popular career. For university graduates in the UK it has come third, after journalism and teaching, as a career choice.[13] Large numbers of PR courses have emerged to try to cater to this demand, which has become truly global. Many more people seek to break into PR after starting their careers elsewhere. Above all, switching to PR has become an escape route for journalists. And as the PR industry continues to surge ahead, faster than the economy in many countries – it has been suggested that the *annual* growth rate in PR is over 30% in China, up to 40% in Russia, and up to 60% in Turkey[14]– this becomes more, not less likely.

Why does PR exert such fascination? The answer is an intriguing one.

Countless interviews with would-be PR students from many countries – at both undergraduate and postgraduate levels – reveal that while the PR industry is seen as glamorous and a desirable place to work, it is also surprisingly anonymous. Few can name more than one or two well-known PR practitioners – if that. The names of even the largest international PR consultancies are usually unknown. Most people have difficulty identifying PR campaigns, and, when they try, frequently confuse them with advertising and other forms of marketing. Few are aware of PR's trade publications or know much, if anything, about its trade bodies. If they have studied the media at school or college they tend to have barely touched on PR. In terms of real-life names, faces, facts and figures – even concepts – PR is largely a blank.

Nor do many of those interested in PR careers have direct experience or knowledge of PR in the way that is often the case for other careers. After all, students and graduates interested in teaching careers will have seen many teachers at work, and would-be journalists will have seen journalists reporting on television, heard them on the radio and read their stories in newspapers, magazines or online. They – or their families and friends – are likely to have direct dealings with people in many other popular careers. They will know – professionally if not socially – doctors, dentists, retailers, people working in financial services and perhaps lawyers too.

Not so with PR. Despite the title '*public* relations' PR people do not offer a direct service to members of the public in the way that many other occupations do. Instead they serve organisations, or occasionally rich or powerful individuals, and in the main operate indirectly, through the mass media and by other means. As the numbers of people working in PR grow people are becoming more likely to know someone working in the field. But the numbers are still not huge and so – beyond those circles which use PR services – the chances of direct contact remain relatively low.

In the USA, the home of the world's largest PR industry, there are perhaps 240,000 people working in PR. In the UK, by far the biggest centre of PR activity outside America, a PRCA/PR Week Census in 2011 suggested that just under 62,000 people work in PR.[15] But in most countries the number of PR people is in three or four digits – if that – and by contrast there are many more teachers, accountants, lawyers and doctors: the PR world's relatively high profile in the media can be misleading. Moreover the numbers for the PR industry often represent nearly all those working in the field, from receptionists upwards, whereas the social footprint of other occupations with their large numbers of related support staff is often much greater: even if one does not know a doctor it is hard not to know someone working in the health sector. The relatively small numbers of PR people are also disproportionately concentrated in major urban centres, further isolating them from the wider public.

If PR is often anonymous and seldom part of people's day-to-day lives, what drives so many people to seek PR careers? Since direct experience of PR is limited, the motive is indirect. There is an aura which surrounds PR, despite its relative anonymity, which enables it to exert a pulling power that transcends mundane facts and figures and first-hand knowledge of the industry. PR often has a high profile in the media, where the handful of real-life PRs who are well-known break surface, with frequent references to 'spin', PR and PR stunts. Moreover journalists know that if they want case studies to illustrate almost any positive story – from personal finance or beauty treatments to property and leisure pursuits – a PR practitioner will happily appear in person in the hope of promoting a product or at least pleasing a journalist: many of the namechecks for PR in the media are a result of this.

❝ 'Scumbags.' 'Insensitive, manipulative charlatans.' 'Sleazy ... disingenuous.'

The above words come from a media evaluation company's report into UK newspaper coverage of the PR industry. The insulting language is supported by the rest of the report's findings, which showed that only 9% of articles contained positive mentions, and that the position was actually getting worse.[16] In the USA, PR people are similarly disdained by journalists and labelled as 'flacks'. US research found that 83% of media references to PR were negative and only 7% positive.[17] A recent book by two American academics puts the following question on its first page: *When was the last time you heard public relations referred to in a way that did* not *imply something negative?*[18]

Despite this tradition of journalistic hostility towards PR people, and despite the fact that this is ordinary people's main source of information about PR, PR's attraction as a career choice remains and grows. Those attracted include countless journalists, for whom a lucrative second career in PR often beckons. PR's reputation is both ambiguous and nuanced – in itself an object lesson in the complexities of reputation for those setting out to be reputation managers!

PR is also prominent in popular culture, where fictional characters with PR jobs – some of whom have swept the world and have become international icons – exert an immense influence on the image of PR. From *Sex and the City*'s Samantha Jones to Bridget Jones, from Gwyneth Paltrow's Helen Quilley in *Sliding Doors* to Edina Monsoon in *Absolutely Fabulous*, the popular depiction of PR has spilled over into real life in programmes such as reality series *PoweR Girls*, *The Hills* or *The Spin Crowd*. PR people often find the characterisation of PR in film and television embarrassing and demeaning. They want their industry to be taken seriously. However, successful satire has to have some recognisable basis in fact. Although the satirists may have their own prejudices, they have often worked as journalists or in the media and have acquired some knowledge of PR. As the original producer of *AbFab* put it:

> At least when we started, maybe not now, they were written out of hate really, maybe not hate, anger certainly... A... way of Jennifer [Saunders – the actress playing Edina Monsoon] letting off steam and looking at all these terrible people in fashion and PR and now it's kind of taken over the world because it seems now that the world is fashion and celebrity mad... worrying and a note on the decline of western civilization.[19]

This version of the PR world is largely female, the milieu of 'PR girls'. The PR activity is typically lightweight, revolving around fashion, clubs and restaurants, and involving parties and celebrities. The work may seem trivial but is varied and fun.

Three reasons why there are so many women in PR

Karen Myers, Corporate Communications Director IPC Media, the consumer publisher

Statistics suggest that over 60 per cent of the PR profession is female. Why? For me, the appeal of PR is gender neutral, and stereotyping around characteristics such as 'women are good with people' or 'women are good at doing more than one thing at once' isn't very helpful. But I believe women are particularly attracted to PR because:

1 There is constant opportunity – in personal progression; in engaging with new audiences; in addressing new challenges; or in the case of consultancies, in winning new clients.

2 A vibrant and engaging personality is a help, not a hindrance. PR doesn't limit how individual you can be – conforming in a pinstripe suit is not the passport to success.

3 It is possible to 'have it all', both personally and professionally. While finding work–life balance can be challenging when there are demanding colleagues, clients or media needing your attention at 10 pm, there is the opportunity to work flexibly. And you can be successful whether your skills are in persuasion, creativity or logistics. From media relations to events; from public affairs advice to speech writing; from issues management to long-term strategy, it's a life of infinite variety.

Popular culture also depicts another, very different and overwhelmingly male version of PR – the world of 'spin doctors' who work for political parties, governments, large companies or powerful commercial interests. Such representations include the PR man helping to cover up problems in the nuclear industry in the film *The China Syndrome*; inventing a war for political advantage in the film *Wag the Dog*; defending the seemingly indefensible in the novel and film *Thank You for Smoking*; dealing with day-to-day political life in the television series *Spin City*; and the foul-mouthed and aggressive prime ministerial press aide Malcolm Tucker in the BBC series *The Thick of It* and the film *In the Loop*. Even Stieg Larsson's international best-seller *The Girl with the Dragon Tattoo* adds a journalist-turned PR to the cast list at the outset, and portrays the character in a negative light. Today any political or corporate-based drama would seem incomplete without a – often sinister – spin doctor.

Here much more is at stake than is the case in the world of 'PR girls'. Spin doctors are shown wielding considerable influence over the fates of powerful people and large organisations and are at the centre of things as they respond to fast-moving events. The PR techniques they use are often Machiavellian, ingenious, cunning and brutal.

The upshot of all these portrayals of public relations in the media and popular culture is that PR seems to have the last laugh. Despite – or even in part because of – these depictions it remains a growing industry which many people want to join. 'Official' PR – some of PR's trade bodies, authors of other PR textbooks and PR educators – may decry these representations of their occupation (we are not immune to it ourselves – following a review of our book *PR – A Persuasive Industry?* in the newspaper *USA Today*, one member of the Public Relations Society of America blogged: 'I have not seen the book … but I already hate it'!), but their reaction often seems humourless and misses the point that reputation is nuanced and multi-faceted. The same thing can be seen in different ways by different people at different times: parents' ideas of a good job are not necessarily the same at those of their children, and work which seems safe and respectable can also be seen as dull and predictable, while on the other hand riskier and less 'respectable' career paths can seem exciting and fun.

Taken together, portrayals of public relations in the mass media and popular culture point to a number of explanations for PR's popularity as a career choice:

- Notwithstanding its relative anonymity, PR manages to have a high profile and, as a young industry, retains novelty value. Indeed PR's anonymity perhaps works in its favour as it has meant that it has developed a certain mystique and has acquired curiosity value.
- PR is perceived as glamorous. Its practitioners are depicted as working alongside celebrities, the wealthy and the powerful, and are in constant contact with

well-known mass media outlets, programmes and personalities. In the background lurks the suggestion that some of the glamour and success will rub off on people joining the PR industry.

As Samantha Jones, the New York PR woman in the *Sex and the City* TV series (and now films), puts it, she 'never missed a major fashion show'.

In one episode she handles the opening of the 'hottest new restaurant in Manhattan'. As she turns away people at the door she mentions that some are actually crying. The restaurant has the hottest chef in New York: 'Did I mention I'm sleeping with him?'[20]

- Public relations is closely associated with whatever is newest, freshest and most fashionable – and often with what is most successful (and indeed is, disproportionately, a young person's industry). PR's role in promoting new products and repositioning old ones has reinforced its cutting-edge and contemporary image, and, unsurprisingly, whatever is currently in the news or in vogue tends to be closely associated with PR.

- PR also adores novelty for itself. It is hard for PR people and PR consultancies to differentiate themselves and seek competitive advantage (they are selling an intangible service and ultimately the difference is about personalities, but this is notoriously hard to articulate convincingly). To get round this problem they like to show themselves keeping abreast of new technologies, new media, and new social, political and style developments – and advancing new PR techniques to respond to new needs. Although hard to quantify, this aspect of the industry is undoubtedly attractive.

- PR work may often be depicted as superficial, but is rarely viewed as dull. It is – and certainly likes to be seen as – a creative industry. In popular culture PR is often portrayed as consisting of thinking up ideas for events or parties – and then attending them. Even the most grudging PR person would have to admit that PR work can involve lunches, receptions, events and parties which include meeting many different people at a range of locations – and this is readily exaggerated for the small or large screen. For glamour and excitement this compares well with routine office work – and may be one of the reasons film and TV producers favour PR settings.

- Public relations is at the heart of the things. When 'spin doctors' feature in the media or in popular culture they are usually shown working closely with the most important people in the organisation and tackling the most pressing issues, reflecting the fact that senior people in all walks of life pay close personal attention to relevant media coverage.

Some are attracted by the suggestion that PR wields immense but sinister and often hidden power. The opening words of one of Edward Bernays' books sum this up well, as well as demonstrating why many in the PR field found it embarrassing to be associated with him!

The conscious and intelligent manipulation of the organised habits and opinions of the masses is an important element in democratic society. Those who manipulate this unseen mechanism of society constitute an invisible government which is the true ruling power of our country.

Bernays, Edward L., *Propaganda*, Horace Liveright, 1928. See pp. 16–17 for more details on Bernays.

- The PR industry is easy to enter – anyone can set up a PR consultancy with minimal resources (although whether they will succeed is quite another matter). This puts PR in marked contrast to the established professions, where prolonged study and on-the-job training are formal requirements, and other business sectors where much more start-up capital is required.
- PR offers – and is portrayed as offering – the prospect of earning a great deal of money. In popular culture the lifestyle of 'PR girls' and 'gurus' are often displayed as opulent – a vision backed up by the underlying reality that the PR industry is booming and PR skills are in demand.
- PR also offers an appealing variety of work. One of the great attractions of a PR career, which is brought home in coverage of PR in the media and portrayals in popular culture, is that PR people can work almost anywhere – and do a great variety of things, not just media relations work. Indeed PR seems to offer would-be practitioners the chance to decide what interests them, do the PR for it and get paid into the bargain. This is reflected in student interest in fashion, sports, music and celebrity PR. The variety does not stop there. The peculiar structure of the PR industry means that practitioners can not only work for innumerable organisations – of all kinds – in-house, but can also work for PR consultancies – which themselves vary considerably – where they might work for a range of clients. And of course they can set up their own consultancies.
- PR people personify the modern, metropolitan lifestyle. Big cities – particularly London and New York, and sometimes Washington DC – are the principal settings for representations of PR in popular culture. These are the locations where 'PR girls' work (and more generally enjoy life), and they are also where 'spin doctors' cluster, in seats of government, corporate headquarters and financial centres.
- PR epitomises self-assured, modern womanhood. One of the common characteristics shared by the 'PR girls' who feature in popular culture is that they have well-paid, interesting jobs, or are able to set up and run their own businesses.

Many of the PR people who have been central characters in films have run their own businesses. Edina Monsoon, the central character of the long-running BBC comedy series *Absolutely Fabulous*, who is modelled on a real-life London PR woman, Lynne Franks, runs her own agency (as did Franks). As Samantha Jones says in the TV series *Sex and the City*: 'Hey, I'm as good looking as a model and I own my own business'.[21]

The London PR woman played by Gwyneth Paltrow in the movie *Sliding Doors* goes on to set up her own agency after being sacked from the firm where she worked at the start of the film. As another character says to her, 'Do you want to spend the rest of your life working for other people?'[22]

The attractions of PR have to be put into context, as no one considers their career options in a vacuum without comparing them with possible alternatives. Established professions not only require considerable commitment and long periods of training, but can also seem dull and stuffy, involving monotonous work. Within its own media and marketing services sector PR has growing attractions. Compared with journalism the prospects are better: it now offers more jobs at higher salaries and with better working conditions. In the United States and the United Kingdom public relations has overtaken advertising as a source of employment,[23] and is rightly regarded as offering more varied career opportunities. Compared with marketing, which is sometimes perceived as a somewhat dry discipline, PR is often seen as offering more human interest and more scope for intuition: PR remains an art and not a science and thus appeals to the creative.

| What attracted you to public relations in the first place? How do your initial ideas match up to what you now know? | (You can extend this exercise by asking others the same questions.) | What challenges does its reputation pose for the PR industry? What if anything can or should be done about it? |

THEORISING ABOUT PUBLIC RELATIONS

You will not get far in most PR courses without people mentioning 'theory'. The term is slightly ambiguous. It is used to describe two things: ideas about how to undertake public relations work better – how to plan, deliver and evaluate PR; and more abstract academic theorising about PR, its ethical implications and its wider social meaning. All PR practitioners are amateur theorists of the first kind, as they draw upon their own experiences to draw lessons for the future. However they would seldom recognise this as 'theory', and indeed very few PR practitioners – including the most senior and the best known – have bothered to read books about PR or study PR 'theory' of any kind in any formal way. (A survey we conducted within one of the world's largest PR firms found that few if any employees recalled reading any books about PR, and the offices from which the PR industry is controlled are not exactly bedecked with well-thumbed copies of PR textbooks!) This situation has only begun to change with the emergence of more PR courses in higher education.

> ❝ 'I think there are people who try and make PR sound fantastically complicated when it's really quite simple – why try and use long words to make it sound more important than it actually is, and I don't like people who demonstrate their ignorance by trying to sound like they're highly intelligent when they're not.'
>
> Lord Tim Bell, Chairman of Chime Communications plc[24]

It is not surprising that the production of both kinds of theory is expanding to meet the growing needs of PR education and training. Public relations is now well established as an academic discipline, and courses require textbooks – and theory. PR's own academics also seek a theoretical base which enables them to hold their heads up with other academics in the universities in which they teach and which provides a foundation for academic research and teaching. PR academics, writers and those active within its trade associations – the industry's public intellectuals – are well aware of the criticisms heaped upon PR, and often use theory defensively as a way of demonstrating PR's moral value and its seriousness and importance. But before we look more specifically at PR theory, it is important to understand that there are some special reasons underpinning PR's search for its own theory:

• Within universities PR is a new discipline and is often seen, whether fairly or not, as a lightweight one, lacking the solid academic foundations of traditional subjects. In so far as universities tolerate it, there is a suspicion that they do so simply because it attracts students and hence generates income. It remains true that many of the world's most prestigious universities do not deign to teach PR. Understandably some of the growing number of PR academics are uncomfortable with this, and see the generation of academic theory as a way of boosting their status. Many of those who teach PR work alongside those teaching theory-rich subjects such as mass communication. If they were closer to other disciplines, such as history, there would probably be less pressure to develop theoretical underpinnings. Among other things, less emphasis on the holy grail of abstract theory might allow more appropriate weight to be given to the more interesting role that individual personalities continue to play in the development of PR.

Jacquie L'Etang

Jacquie L'Etang is perhaps the most prolific academic writer on PR in the UK. Based at the University of Stirling she writes, as she says, 'within the European context from the periphery of Great Britain (Scotland)'.[25] She is frank about how PR is often perceived within higher education:

> public relations as an academic discipline is often poorly (and unfairly) regarded within universities, often seen as a convenient cash-cow to attract students, but ideologically unsound and intellectually impoverished.[26]

L'Etang has written extensively about PR theory and is not afraid to be critical of some prevailing views. She laments the way in which media scholars, while critical of PR, fail to engage with its literature. Perhaps her most valuable contribution to PR scholarship is her thoroughly researched account of aspects of the development of PR in Britain, in which she also describes the longer history of antipathy towards public relations.[27] As the discipline developed in the 1960s, a group of leading journalists semi-humorously formed a 'Society for the Discouragement of Public Relations', while Harold Wilson, Labour Prime Minister of the UK for most of the decade, described PR as 'a rather squalid profession'.

L'Etang describes how some within the PR industry sought professional status, partly in response to these slights. The first PR course was established at London's Regent Street Polytechnic in 1956 but although she describes the difficulties surrounding the course, she does not elaborate on what ultimately became of it (the Polytechnic was the precursor of the University of Westminster, and PR was not resurrected as a standalone course until 2000). Despite the ambitions of some, many of PR's leading lights were uninterested in professional status. As she comments, notwithstanding its lack of formal professional status, the PR industry has flourished.

It would be useful to see more books of this kind, exploring the development of PR in different societies, and indeed different organisations. Since PR is often relatively new to the scene, and in many countries early practitioners are often still available for interview, this is a subject which lends itself to student dissertations.

- Teaching PR alongside study of the media and mass communication presents further problems. This part of the academic world is still overshadowed by the Frankfurt School, established by those left-wing German social thinkers who fled Nazi Germany for the USA. For them Nazi propaganda might have been a terrible abuse of the opportunities presented by mass communication – but the world of advertising and PR they encountered in the US was little better. It is not surprising that PR is at best viewed with suspicion by many academics. Their emphasis upon the way PR bolsters the interests of big business is coupled to a general hostility towards the commercial world, the most conspicuous user of public relations (although the same academics seem to accept that their own universities and the publishers of their academic books are enthusiastic users of PR!). It is easy to see why PR's own writers and thinkers feel a need to respond defensively. Unfortunately the PR theory they have sought to develop has attracted little interest or respect beyond the PR's own small academic field.

- Linked to this is the search by a vocal minority within the PR industry for a higher, more professional status for themselves and their industry. They are particularly anxious about portrayals of PR as trivial, or immoral and even sinister. They welcome theory of all kinds in the hope that it will correct this impression.

- PR is often taught in universities which also teach journalism. Journalists have traditionally viewed PR in a critical and even disdainful way. One purpose of PR theory is to try to present PR in a way which counters or avoids such criticisms. It is striking that so much of PR's own self-analysis seeks to play down the way in which media relations lies at the heart of PR activity.

Noam Chomsky and the Propaganda Model

Public relations features strongly in the influential 'Propaganda Model' developed by the American writers Edward S Herman and Noam Chomsky in their book *Manufacturing Consent: The Political Economy of the Mass Media*.[28] They describe how PR in all its guises is used to ensure that the media serve, and propagandise on behalf of, the powerful interests in society which control and finance them.

- It is also worth bearing in mind that many other subjects have taken time to establish themselves at universities – even degrees in history and modern literature, let alone social sciences – and to build up their own academic expertise and bodies of literature. By definition, those schooled in well-established subjects tend to dominate university governance and this can act as a brake on change.

- Finally – and this has more of a bearing on theoretical approaches relating to the delivery of PR services, although it can overspill into pure theory – PR is taught within some (but not usually the best-known) business schools. It has to fight for its place as it is often looked down upon for lacking the rigour of other business-related disciplines, not least because of its failure to put in place agreed and robust systems of financial measurement (see pp. 224–233). Here too PR needs to demonstrate its serious credentials.

Of course for most people these debates represent storms in teacups. Not only do they not concern the overwhelming majority of people in the PR industry, who get on cheerfully with their jobs (and are usually ignorant of 'PR theory'), but they demonstrably do not seem to bother those who employ ever more PR people around the world (and are almost invariably ignorant of 'PR theory'). Nor do they put off the large numbers of people who want to work in PR.

James Grunig and the four models of public relations

Professor James Grunig

James Grunig is an American PR educator and writer who is now Emeritus Professor at the University of Maryland, where he taught for many years. Readers may also come across the work of his wife, Larissa Grunig, who also taught PR at the same university, and, among other subjects, has written about the role gender plays in the public relations field.

Grunig is renowned in PR academic circles for the four models he developed, initially with Todd Hunt (see below). His list of publications is extensive, but he is probably best known for editing and contributing to *Excellence in Public Relations and Communication Management*,[29] a 666-page work which represents the fruit of a project sponsored by the International Association of Business Communicators, an industry trade body.

As its title suggests, the work makes great play of 'excellence', although the term is somewhat vague. Grunig puts it thus: 'Excellent public relations are defined as those that are managed strategically in order to maximize the contribution of communication programs to organizational effectiveness'[30], but few PR people would admit to doing anything less! He claims to draw upon 'sociology, psychology, management, marketing, women's studies, philosophy, anthropology, and communication' in developing the book's ideas, but notably omits history.[31] He asserts that they 'have produced the first general theory of public relations – a theory that integrates the many theories and research results existing in the field'. However he admits that the book is only the first stage and '[w]e may have a different theory when the research is completed'.[32]

Despite the book's links to a trade association, and attempts to turn theoretical thinking into material with practical value (for example a final chapter of estimating the value of public relations offers a series of algebraic equations for evaluating PR), there is little evidence of the industry buying-in to the book and the ideas it seeks to propagate. In essence it remains a massive *piece justificative* for the PR industry and its academy.

As any student of propaganda could tell you, the strongest foundations for intellectual movements are books. From the ancient, sacred texts which underpin the world's religions to *Das Kapital* or *Mein Kampf* in more recent times, there are countless famous and infamous examples. Lesser intellectual movements have their own, less widely known, texts. Sometimes the writings concerned are not read by many people, but nonetheless they are studied and quoted. In some quarters at least they are deeply respected and revered; at the very minimum they provide an intellectual focal point. The growing but still limited field of PR education is no different.

The dominant theory among PR's educators and theorists is derived from the ideas of James Grunig and his co-author Todd Hunt, originally expounded in *Managing Public Relations*. Grunig and Hunt[33] – the former went on to develop the ideas in further books (see above), identified four models of public relations which are summarised in the Table 1.1.

It is hard to overstate the influence of these models. They are cited in countless PR textbooks, and no alternative theory has enjoyed anything like their success. Perhaps the main reason for their success is that they play brilliantly upon the industry's insecurities which we have outlined above. In their relative

Table 1.1 Grunig and Hunt's four models of public relations

Model	Characteristics	Where practised and examples*
Press agentry/Publicity	The purpose is propagandistic, and providing the complete truth is not essential. The communication model is simply source to recipient, and little research is involved.	Showbusiness is the archetypal arena for this type of PR. Grunig and Hunt cite the American circus owner and user of PR stunts and celebrities, P. T. Barnum see p. 11. It has been suggested that Max Clifford see p. 89, the British publicist, is an heir to this tradition.
Public information	The aim is the dissemination of information. Truth is important. The communication model is simply source to recipient, and research is limited.	Grunig and Hunt say this is practised in government, the not-for-profit sector and in business. They cite as example Ivy Lee (see p. 17); other examples include early government public information services.
Two-way assymetric	The purpose is scientific persuasion. The communication is two-way but is not balanced.	This is seen as applying to almost all sectors of PR work. It has been associated with the work of Edward Bernays (see pp. 16–17) and many others in government and the private sector who seek to persuade people.
Two-way symmetric	The purpose is mutual understanding. The communication model is two-way and balanced. This kind of PR is based on negotiation, compromise and understanding. Sometimes described as the ideal for public relations.	Grunig suggests there are few examples of this kind of PR and that this approach is largely theoretical. Perhaps, it is argued, that as PR people study this model it will become more prevalent.

Note: *Grunig has pointed out that organisations often use more than one model.

simplicity they seem to provide PR with the theoretical foundation some writers and academics feel it needs, while dealing with many of the moral issues which trouble some practitioners. By filling an intellectual vacuum they force other writers on PR to take issue with their theories, thereby giving them further publicity (as we are doing here!) – even if their models add little to any real understanding of PR.

There are other attractive features of the four models theory. Although the use of the different models may overlap, they are essentially seen as part of virtuous path, with crude and selfish press agentry eventually giving way to virtuous two-way symmetrical communication, in which self-seeking is replaced by a search for mutual understanding. Grunig and Hunt's most favoured model also distances PR from the intricacies of media relations, and particularly those activities for which journalists are wont to criticise PR people.

Grunig's theories, which have been subsequently embellished, may exert considerable control over academic theorising about PR, but his empire consists of small and scattered outposts. Outside the confined world of PR academia his ideas – and indeed the ideas of other PR theorists – have attracted little interest.[34]

The vast majority of the PR practitioners we have ever encountered are unaware of the four models. Nor – significantly – has the theory aroused much interest in neighbouring disciplines. There are several weaknesses in Grunig and Hunt's theory:

- There is at least a suspicion that their models are self-serving – a way of wishing away the industry's reputational problems and providing a bedrock of theory to underpin the academic teaching of PR – rather than serious attempts to engage with the realities of PR work. Thus they are more about advertising PR than a serious analysis of it.

- They offer no proof or hard evidence to back up their claims (a common problem besetting PR theory). Much of what they describe is vaguely defined and open to question. It can, admittedly, be hard to furnish hard evidence for PR work, but what they describe does not ring true to practitioners' day-to-day experience of PR reality – as the authors can attest.

- As they themselves acknowledge, individual organisations often use a combination of their models, but where does one model stop and another start? What about a government agency using a PR stunt to highlight health concerns? A single event of this might bring together the *publicity model*, *public information* culled from medical research, and *two-way communication* as market research is employed to establish current thinking on the issue.

- It is hard to think of 'pure' *public information*: the facts and figures provided by public authorities are usually provided with some persuasive intention, even if the intention is a laudable one, such as an anti-smoking campaign. That persuasive intent inevitably has some bearing on how the information is presented. What information should be included and what should be left out? Will words, phrases and images with loaded meanings be used? When is the information to be made available? All of these and other factors mean that one person's public information is often another person's propaganda.

- All effective PR contains some elements of *two-way communication*. PR people have to find a way of 'listening' to their target audiences – not necessarily for moral reasons, but because they need to know what their audience already thinks and how their thinking is changing if they want to get across their messages properly. As we show elsewhere (see pp. 224–233), evaluating PR has always been fraught with difficulty and many PR people have traditionally relied on gut-feeling and anecdotal evidence, not least because of the expense involved in two-way communication. Ironically dictatorships, which use a blend of coercion and persuasion, and for which money is no object, spend far more time monitoring the views of their publics in much more 'scientific' ways: this is always one of the main subjects of secret police reports! Anyone who reads Dr Goebbels's diaries can see how much time he devoted to thinking about the public mood, while today many repressive regimes pour consider-able resources into monitoring people's online activities.

- Finally, even for Grunig and his champions, the final model, *two-way symmetric* communication is more an ideal than a reality. Nonetheless, terms such as 'mutual understanding' have become popular components of some official definitions of PR. It is hard to see how PR could ever be described as balanced in this way when it is paid for by one side. The PR people for any company will want to consider carefully the views of its different stakeholders, but ultimately the reason they do so is to serve the company's interests better: two-way *a*symmetric communication. The same is true for charities and politicians. To pretend otherwise is disingenuous and does not answer PR's critics: people smell a rat.

As we can see, the dominant theoretical models within academic PR may be well-meaning but are seriously flawed. This further isolates the discipline within academia and does not strike a chord with the industry. The truth is that PR is not dominated by theoretical models and that practitioners – including the most senior ones – are instead heavily reliant on practical experience. Outsiders, including media scholars, have played surprisingly little attention to the role of the PR industry, but for those seeking insights into the important role PR plays in contemporary society, it is PR's role in relation to the media which offers the richest pickings.

Kevin Moloney

A refreshing, distinctive and critical view of PR is offered by Kevin Moloney, a former UK PR practitioner turned long-serving academic, in his book *Rethinking Public Relations: PR, Propaganda and Democracy*[35] (he has also written about lobbying[36]). His book is marked by a clear, direct style, unlike many others in the field. Few punches are pulled. It is striking that although he cites PR literature, his most acute observations are often derived from personal conversations and direct experience. For Moloney PR is 'weak propaganda'. His book is guided by two key concerns which he seeks to put right.

First, 'if the PR academic has any claim on the role of public intellectuals, it is to speak out about the impact of their subject on democracy', a concern which he feels most PR literature ignores.

His second concern is that 'the academic study of PR has got stuck ... in a conceptual paradigm (the Grunigian one) that needs to be challenged'. It overemphasises PR's virtuous nature and 'takes the PR academy into a neverland of perfection'. Moloney's analysis is clear-eyed and realistic: PR is not necessarily virtuous, or bad, and is here to stay.[37]

Having diagnosed the problems, the first part of the treatment he prescribes is eminently sensible. As he suggests, citizens in modern societies would benefit from greater PR literacy – which could be provided through the educational system. Sadly, as the present authors can attest, there is little sign of this happening in practice, and with few exceptions PR remains a black hole in the field of media studies.

His second step is to find mechanisms for offering 'communicative equality' to resource-poor causes, with funding provided to ensure that 'a public system of communication would exist alongside a public system of justice, both

➡

predicated on ideas of fair and equal treatment.'[38]

Unfortunately it is here that Moloney himself enters a neverland. In the unlikely event that funding could be secured (another tax on big corporations?), how could agreement ever be reached on how it should be allocated? Equal funding for pro- and anti-abortion groups, for example? (Inevitably some 'resource-poor' groups will have deeply controversial aims, and may use objectionable tactics as well.) Although it is nice to imagine worthy causes receiving money – one's favourite charity, for example (although in practice charities manage to carry out their PR pretty well under existing arrangements) – it only takes a moment's thought to see how unworkable and unlikely such a scheme will always be.

Books every public relations practitioner should read

Professor Tom Watson, Professor of Public Relations,
The Media School, Bournemouth University

The first book that I recommend is one whose core arguments I don't entirely agree with. It is, however, one of the most searching discussions of public relations, its practise and ethical dimensions. My colleague Kevin Moloney's *Rethinking Public Relations*, 2nd edition (Routledge 2006) is the work of a loving critic and critical thinker who sees the value of public relations in a liberal democracy but recognises its failings in delivery and practise. Dr Moloney makes challenging arguments which every student and practitioner should be aware of.

My second book is one that I constantly use. Every research student of mine is given chapters to read and a strong recommendation to borrow or buy it. It is *Qualitative Research Method for Public Relations and Marketing Communication* by Christine Daymon and Immy Holloway (Routledge 2002). It is a very readable and indispensable introduction to qualitative methods for novice researchers. It guides them through the array of 'qual' methods that are so rich for academic and professional research in the PR field.

The third book is my idea of the 'bible of PR research' – Robert Heath's *Handbook of Public Relations* (Sage 2001). Shortly to be succeeded by a much-revised second edition, it covers all major thinking on public relations. Although 10 years old, it has all the big names and is frequently quoted in academic articles.

Finally, every PR practitioner, who considers themself to be working in international or multi-cultural public relations, must have a copy of Krishnamurthy Sriramesh and Dejan Verčič's *The Global Public Relations Handbook*, revised edition (Routledge 2009). It has 44 chapters which cover every topic in world PR.

PR and the shaping of the modern media: alternative ways of viewing PR

Looking for a grand theoretical model for public relations may well be a wild goose chase, not least because PR cannot really be looked at in isolation. As we shall see, it is scattered in thousands of penny packets across the economy, political life and society. It offers a set of tools which can be, and is, used to serve the very different purposes of its users: a means to an end and not an end in itself. PR people's role as paid persuaders is an important one but is perhaps best looked at in terms of the arenas where PR people do battle. Although PR people do more than deal with journalists – we look for example at the important areas of lobbying and internal communications elsewhere – the main battleground for PR is media relations, an arena which is played down in industry definitions. In fact anyone who is seriously interested in how the media operate needs to pay attention to PR, and would-be journalists would surely benefit from studying PR (one of their professional weaknesses is that usually they do not!).

Media scholars often debate the nature of *media effects* – how far and in what ways media coverage does or does not affect people's thoughts and actions. The debate swings around and becomes muddled. All concede that the relationship is a complicated one. However most experts agree that in some circumstances some coverage *can* have an impact (a piece of accepted wisdom which forms the basis for many of the restraints on media content, including advertising, which all societies put in place). However indisputable evidence of media effects is hard to come by.

PR – and indeed advertising – cast an interesting light on this vexed issue. The growth of PR, and its expansion to cover almost every area of international life, is a powerful sign that the people running all kinds of organisations judge that it is worth spending scarce resources on trying to influence media coverage. Their investment demonstrates that such people, seldom PR practitioners themselves, think that in some circumstances positive coverage can have a worthwhile effect – and that negative coverage can be harmful, perhaps even fatal, to an organisation's interests. PR people and their paymasters have worked this out for themselves in blissful ignorance of the academic 'media effects' debate!

PR is perhaps better looked at not in a purely abstract way but with reference to the realities of history. As we have seen, PR was in large part a by-product of the rise of the modern media. Now times have changed. The mass media may seem more dominant than ever, but while numbers of journalists have grown the increase has failed to keep up with the exponential growth in media production. Not only do we now expect media organisations to broadcast around the clock via an infinite number of channels, but we expect bigger newspapers with more pages and more supplements, and more and fatter magazines. We also expect the same media organisations to maintain extensive websites, Twitter feeds and Facebook links.

This has contributed to the increasing pressure upon media organisations, but the other crucial factor is loss of revenue. Paid-for newspaper circulations in the developed world are dwindling. In many countries advertising revenue is migrating away from traditional media while the fragmentation of advertising-funded broadcasting means that many more channels have to be paid for out of a similar-sized, or shrinking, pot. Public sector broadcasters such as the BBC face pressures of their own as their right to raise funds through what amounts to taxation – in the BBC's case the licence fee – is increasingly challenged. Meanwhile the search for successful payment models for online news media continues: people overwhelmingly expect to access information online for free, and advertising does not make up the shortfall. The jury on whether people can be made to change their ways is out. This pressure on income has exacerbated the struggle to control the media's costs of production. Specialist journalists with many years of experience have lost out to less experienced but cheaper general reporters. Sub-editors have become a costly luxury. Sending journalists out to investigate stories is expensive, and offers no certainty of a return on expenditure. Keeping journalists in the office, tied to their computers, makes it easier to assess their productivity. It has been calculated that in the UK journalists now have to produce three times as much copy as they did 20 years ago.[39] 'Citizen journalism', potentially written by anyone and self-published online, is often talked up as the future for journalism, and can merge seamlessly with other forms of online content (see Chapter 7). It may be free at the point of use, but it is far from clear that it can match the work of salaried journalists working for leading media brands in terms of the resources available, the range of coverage or the breadth of its reception and the level of authority it attains.

All of this has coincided with PR's growth and its emergence as a prominent and still swelling industry. In the United States, the world's most advanced economy, there are more PR people than journalists, and the same is now true in the United Kingdom.[40] However the relationship between journalism and PR, one that is so fundamental to the modern media, remains underexplored. Wise PR people do not want to boast about their achievements; journalists seldom want to admit the extent to which they are reliant on PR; and scholars – even if so minded – find the subject difficult to investigate.

Put in nutshell, what has happened is that the power balance has shifted. Journalism, with shrinking resources, is losing the ability to generate its own news content and cross-check what it is being told. In contrast PR people now increasingly have more resources at their disposal than their counterparts in journalism. PR also benefits from its clarity of purpose. Notwithstanding what some people try to say, PR is about persuading people to act in particular ways to further the aims of the people who pay for it: its objective is clear. The situation for journalists is much more problematic. What is often portrayed as a crusade for truth is trapped within the commercial imperatives of business: journalists like to talk about objectivity and the importance of investigation, but have to work within the constraints of mounting anxiety about circulation and ratings, sales and advertising. Many journalists recoil from the notion that they work in an entertainment industry, yet to a considerable extent they do.

This is an arena where PR people can and do help them. Altogether an enormous proportion of what appears in the media originates in the hands of PR people, while PR also has a big impact on what does *not* appear in the media. PR's influence on what we read, see and hear spills over from news and current affairs into entertainment and drama. The media's modes of production and, critically, their costs of production assume the existence of a well-resourced PR industry which is able to supply or, at least, help with the production of, media content.

Studies of the subject sometimes offer suspiciously rounded percentages for the proportion of newsprint derived from PR, with 80 per cent towards the upper end.[41] But another way of approaching the subject is to pose a different question: *if journalists do not get their stories from PR then where do they obtain them?* Clearly a journalist may witness a newsworthy event, but for increasingly desk-bound journalists this is even less likely than a police officer on patrol chancing upon a crime. Sometimes an individual with a story may approach a news organisation directly, although more and more they are likely to seek PR advice first. Again, some journalists frequent venues which are likely to generate news – parliaments and law courts for example, although for reasons of cost this has become rarer – and even in such places PR people make their presence felt. In practice if a journalist witnesses a newsworthy event it is usually because he or she has been alerted to it, and this can often be traced back to PR.

Much of what journalists write and broadcast comes from elsewhere in the media, or from news agencies, or information exchanged among media colleagues. Such material is no longer obviously PR-related, but if it is traced back to its source that is often what it is. A successfully managed piece of PR can snowball its way through the media, appearing in different news outlets and re-emerging in the comment and feature pages, gossip columns, and elsewhere. As the snowball grows the original press release, briefing or tip-off will be lost to view. The PR practitioner may no longer need to intervene. Ideally – from a PR perspective, given the craving for third-party endorsement – the media will feel they own the story.

PR's role as a content supplier to the media has been termed *information subsidy*. There is no such thing as a free lunch, and the material supplied by PR people is prepared with a persuasive purpose in mind. The cumulative effect of this has led some to point to the *PR-isation* of the media, raising the spectre that the media will lose the reputation for independence and objectivity which made them such a valuable vehicle for PR people in the first place. This might be a particular danger in those pages, supplements and programmes which cover not traditional 'hard news' but fashion, food, property, leisure, sport, culture, travel, personal finance and so on. It is hard to imagine the emergence of such media content without PR (and related advertising), and it is here that PR has most obviously shaped the modern media.

As we show elsewhere in this book, PR also plays an important role in seeking to block or downplay bad news about the organisations it serves. Largely informal pressures and inducements are used to try to suppress unwanted coverage. The British scholar Aeron Davies, in his study of corporate PR, found that up to 50% of activity was devoted to lowering the profiles of organisations or blocking journalists.[42] The scale of this activity reflects the fact that, for the most part, journalists find bad news – stories about scandals, problems and arguments – more enticing than good news.

There is little evidence, however, of public awareness of the extent to which PR shapes content in the media, and journalists have the last word on what appears, so two important qualifications must be borne in mind. First, even if most news media content is PR-driven, most PR fails to feature in the media. An oversupply of 'news' from a well-resourced PR industry means that most press releases are simply discarded, calls from PR people are frequently not acted upon, and many press conferences are thinly attended. Critics of PR tend to focus on the PR associated with top ranks of government and big corporations, but most PR is far more humble and much more readily ignored. Second, even if there is coverage, no PR person can ever be wholly certain of its extent and nature: the story may appear, but all too briefly, without the hoped-for prominence; or the journalist may include other information and comments, often gleaned from rival PR people, which undermine the original message.

In his best-selling book *Flat Earth News*, first published in 2008,[43] the award-winning UK journalist Nick Davies commissioned research on the sources of UK news stories in Britain's most prestigious national newspapers. The research found that 60% of stories comprised wholly or mainly PR material and/or news agency copy. Overall PR material found its way into 54% of the stories. In 8% of cases the source was unclear. Only in 12% of cases was the material generated by the reporters themselves. He also found that although staffing levels had declined slightly over the previous 20 years, the amounts of editorial space had trebled. Davies fears that the predicament of journalism is 'terminal'.

PR and the information marketplace

In public discussions of PR's role journalists usually have the last word. PR lacks much of a public voice other than the one it finds through journalism, and its embryonic academic theory seems unconvincing and lacks impact.

However when journalists trade information with PR people, each side holds some high value cards. PR people act as gatekeepers to the inner sanctums of information and comment and can provide the exclusives that the media crave. Journalists hold the keys to media coverage and preserve some independence: powerful media organisations cannot be easily pushed around. Investigative journalism may be under threat but is not extinct. No PR person, even those working for the most powerful organisations, can be wholly certain about the way a client or organisation will be reported: coverage can be massaged, but not fully controlled. In recent years, despite lavish expenditure on top PR advice, all governments in developed countries have been at the receiving end of hostile coverage, as have many business leaders and big corporations.

But the pressures outlined above mean that news stories increasingly reflect PR battles fought between rival organisations (sometimes even dissident PR *within* organisations is involved): the media simply report and comment upon the conflict. Journalists rely on – or are, arguably, used by – the different PR people as suppliers of content. So political parties' spin doctors do battle with each other, companies' PR departments combat the PR activities of NGO campaigners and so on. Amid such clashes journalists perform the not unimportant role of judges when summing up at the end of a court case: they summarise the evidence advanced by the various PR people, and highlight strengths and weaknesses. They also offer their own opinions. Occasionally they will be able to go further than this – but this is the exception rather than the rule, as they seldom have the resources to carry out extensive research themselves.

Critics of PR often mistakenly view the PR industry as monolithic. This could not be further from the truth. Healthy debate is actually fostered by rival PR people in a way that the media themselves can rarely afford, even if it is the media which provide the forum. Indeed today PR people in many big corporations are more exercised about the threat posed by vigorous, well-resourced campaigning NGOs than they are by media organisations themselves. NGO PR is a major supplier of fuel to the modern media.[44] The debate will never be perfectly balanced – what debate is? – but neither was journalism ever able to report the world perfectly. The rise of PR may be unstoppable but it is not necessarily harmful. Indeed, given that journalism is unlikely to recover its past resources, the current paradox is that the best hope for the media and for informed debate may be more PR for more voices on all sides of the debate.

Three things about PR I'd like to see changed

Nick Davies, Award-winning journalist and author of Flat Earth News[45]

No more mass emailings where press releases are sent round to hundreds of random journalists, clogging up our in-boxes and making us wish that the PR industry would go bankrupt immediately.

The complete and global collapse of any PR company which works for dictatorships and/or generates falsehood and thus not only pollutes news coverage but inflicts fundamental damage on the image of all PR people.

And, most important, albeit beyond the reach of the PR industry, a revival of the financial and editorial strength of news organisations so that legitimate PR activity takes its place as one of numerous sources of information from which journalists would select stories according to news values and not simply in search of something quick and safe to fill some space.

Think of PR work of which you are aware and try to relate it to Grunig and Hunt's four models.

Select some news media coverage at random and analyse it carefully, sentence by sentence and image by image. What sources do you think the journalists use?
Take a newspaper and try to estimate what percentage of the content has been generated by or sourced from PR.

Hill & Knowlton: case study of a global PR firm

Hill & Knowlton would be the epitome of a large US PR firm – but for the fact that it is now owned by the British WPP group, headed by Sir Martin Sorrell. Its origins go back to the early days of PR, and it was the first of the major US firms to develop a large international network. While rankings change from time to time, Hill & Knowlton has often featured in the league tables as the largest PR consultancy in the world.

The company's founder was John W. Hill, who set up a 'corporate publicity office' in 1927 in Cleveland, Ohio. He was already 37 and had formerly worked as a journalist, but had also dabbled in publicity work, creating a newsletter for a company which became one of his new business's first clients. Other clients included Otis Steel, United Alloy Steel, Standard Oil of Ohio and Republic Steel.

During the Depression, Hill took into partnership Donald Knowlton, the public relations director of a failing client. In 1934, Hill moved his headquarters to New York, in order to serve as public relations counsel to the American Iron and Steel Institute; Knowlton remained in Ohio and ceased to be involved with the company's development (although his lasting impact on the company's name is not untypical of the industry: traditionally firms often liked to have two names over the door even if there is – or was – one dominant founding personality).

Hill & Knowlton experienced steady growth within the United States. Although originally dependent on the steel industry, it adjusted to changing times. In the post–Second World War era the firm worked for aircraft manufacturers and became instrumental in cultivating the idea that air power was the solution to America's strategic problems. In the 1950s, Hill & Knowlton

was the firm the tobacco industry turned to as it faced the first evidence of a link between smoking and tobacco. Hill & Knowlton recommended the establishment of the Tobacco Industry Research Council (see p. 56).

Hill & Knowlton was an important industry pioneer in other respects. In the 1950s, it led the way with a network of international offices, designed to service the needs of US business overseas. Today its London office also serves as the headquarters of its Europe, Middle East and Africa network, with 27 offices. In 1985, it opened an office in Beijing, the first international PR firm to do so in the post-Mao reform period.

Hill & Knowlton was also active in other areas of PR activity from an early stage. It worked with schools and teachers on behalf of its steel industry clients, and set up an Environmental Health Unit in 1966, while John Hill emphasised the importance of community relations as early as 1963. It also blazed a trail with innovative business methods, developing a system of standard fees and staff-time charges to replace its former, haphazard methods in the 1940s. It borrowed from advertising the idea of testing copy in the 1950s, and used computers from the 1960s.

Hill managed the firm until 1962 and remained active within it until his death in 1977: in this Hill was like many PR people, and particularly its founding fathers (there were few women in leadership roles in the early days of PR), who remain wedded to the industry well beyond normal retirement age. In 1980, Hill & Knowlton was acquired by the J. Walter Thompson (JWT) advertising group, a name as iconic within American advertising as Hill & Knowlton was in the PR world. The JWT group was in turn acquired by WPP in 1987.

Hill & Knowlton's historian, Karen Miller, explains how, under pressure to demonstrate improved financial results, both growth and income, the company's new chief executive, Robert Dilenschneider, engaged in self-promotion, which included publishing a book, *Power and Influence: Mastering the Art of Persuasion*, a tactic which emulated Ivy Lee and, particularly, Edward Bernays. Clients were accepted on a project basis, not just the long-term counsel upon which Hill had insisted. The agency's policy of refusing political and religious accounts was also discarded, and the Church of Scientology was taken on as a client (leading to the loss of Hill & Knowlton's important SmithKline Beecham account).

Following Iraq's invasion of Kuwait in 1990, Hill & Knowlton undertook probably its biggest project of all time, when it assisted the Kuwaiti Government in exile in its bid to persuade the world – and particularly American opinion – to back a campaign to liberate their country (see pp. 60–61). Although the account was high profile and lucrative, it marked a watershed in Hill & Knowlton's history. In 1991 Dilenschneider left, as did his successor the following year. The Hill & Knowlton star was descending. The agency undertook research to find out what was going wrong and found that potential clients were put off by the way its large size seemed to denote high costs, insensitivity and slow responses. The reforms included a move towards greater specialisation reflecting contemporary needs including, for example, marketing communications groups for gay and lesbian audiences.

Today a much revived Hill & Knowlton is still owned by WPP group, which also owns 4 other major PR groups along with advertising agencies and other marketing services firms. It is ranked among the top 5 PR firms in the world with over 2000 staff and 72 offices in 41 countries. Its restored fortunes can be seen as pointing towards the maturing of the PR industry; once personality-led, its largest firms now demonstrate an ability to reform themselves and thrive long after the departure of their founders. Hill & Knowlton's size and success attracts criticism from the likes of CorporateWatch and hyperbole from likes of Wikipedia which said of the company: 'Its reach and control over mass media allows the firm to have direct impact on world events, public policy and shaping news events.'[46]

- There are hundreds of definitions of public relations, but few are specific about what it is that PR people do, or meaningful to outsiders. They are more concerned with elevating PR's status and sidestepping criticism. Our definition seeks to address these weaknesses:

    Public relations is the planned persuasion of people to behave in ways which further its sponsor's objectives. It works primarily through the use of media relations and other forms of third-party endorsement.

- PR developed in its current form in response to the emergence of the modern mass media and the opportunities and threats the media presented to businesspeople, politicians and others. Events throughout the twentieth century accelerated the rise of PR, particularly in newly emerging democracies and free market economies towards the end of the century.
- PR may be subject to frequent criticism but is little studied. PR academics' own attempts to examine the industry frequently fall short. Too often they are unable to penetrate the veils which obscure the realities of high-level PR activity and instead theorise about what they think PR *should* be rather than what it *is*.
- One casualty of the relative neglect of PR in academic circles is a failure properly to assess the huge and growing role PR plays in shaping the modern media. PR is the main content supplier to the news media in an increasing number of countries, a fact that has important consequences for all media outlets and journalists.

Imagine you have been invited to return to your old school to give a short presentation. They want you to explain to the senior students what PR is, and to provide a little historical background on the development of PR in your country. Many of the students are interested in the media, so the school has also asked you to explain PR's relationship to the media and to give one or two examples.

Prepare the key points for a short presentation. Think about what questions they might ask you afterwards. How would you respond?

Some reading suggestions

For more coverage of all the above issues: Morris, Trevor and Goldsworthy, Simon, *PR-- A Persuasive Industry? Spin, Public Relations, and the Shaping of the Modern Media* (Palgrave Macmillan 2008).

For a general, critical American-focused history of PR: Ewen, Stuart, *PR! A Social History of Spin* (Basic Books 1996); a critical equivalent by British authors is Miller, David and Dinan, William, *A Century of Spin: How Public Relations Became the Cutting Edge of Corporate Power* (Pluto Books 2008).

For a summary of how UK PR educationalists see these matters: Theaker, Alison (ed.), *The Public Relations Handbook* (Routledge 2008).

For a thoughtful account of the role of persuasion in our societies: Taylor, Philip, *Munitions of the Mind: A History of Propaganda from the Ancient World to the Present Era* (Manchester University Press 1995).

PR ETHICS

INTRODUCTION

Some textbooks treat PR as though it is a branch of moral philosophy. Such an approach leaves most PR practitioners bemused and is of limited practical use. While there is no evidence that PR people are more – or less – moral than anyone else, they confront particular ethical challenges in their day-to-day work and have to make up their minds about what to do. Frequently such decisions have to be made swiftly, when the practitioner is subject to all kinds of competing pressures. It is those challenges upon which we have sought to concentrate. Often there is no 'right' answer: we have included exercises to stimulate thought about the issues presented by these challenges. Discussion of these issues leads naturally to a wider debate about whether governments and professional bodies need to regulate PR activity, and if so how.

LEARNING OBJECTIVES

- How to recognise and assess for yourself the main ethical issues affecting PR work
- How thinking about ethics can be applied to day-to-day PR activity
- To consider in what ways, and how far, PR can be regulated

PR'S ETHICAL DILEMMAS

Ethics is defined by the *Shorter Oxford English Dictionary* as 'the moral principles by which any particular person is guided' and 'the rules of conduct recognised in a particular profession or area of human life'. Obviously this overlaps with the law (see Chapter 9) and indeed one way of looking at the law, particularly in a democracy, is that it represents the settled ethical view of an entire society, even if at any given time most of us regard some laws as outmoded or running counter to our personal views.

In this chapter the focus is on aspects of PR activity which are legally permissible but ethically questionable, although it is worth noting that – as we shall see – some PR people working for NGOs proudly and openly make the law take second place to their ethical concerns.

Most occupations have particular ethical issues which concern them. In the case of public relations the issue is particularly sensitive for two reasons. First, the critical way in which PR is often depicted in the media and in popular culture (see Chapter 1) puts PR on the defensive and in the ethical spotlight, not least because of the PR world's fraught relationship with journalism. Second, some PR people aspire, as practitioners of a relatively new discipline, to be taken more seriously and attain the coveted status of membership of a profession, akin to doctors or lawyers. Addressing ethical concerns is a key stage to achieving that goal.

The ethical dilemmas of PR must be seen in this context. They fall under two main headings: first, those arising from the organisation or person for which the PR practitioner works – if the purpose is unethical any PR activity associated with it is by definition unethical; and second, the way in which the practitioner works – just because a cause is ethical you do not have *carte blanche* to do as you please.

The purposes for which PR is used

In our view PR is amoral: it comprises an approach and a set of techniques which can be applied to any cause and can be and is used by heroes and villains. This may be a difficult thing to say – people tend to like to claim the moral high ground – but is easy to illustrate. Early PR pioneers such as Ivy Lee and Carl Byoir worked for the Nazis before the Second World War,[1] and indeed PR firms continue to be hired by repressive regimes to this day, particularly when they need to cultivate opinion beyond their borders and can no longer rely on the more brutal forms of persuasion they use at home.

Few would now seek to defend Lee and Byoir's decisions – although of course we benefit from hindsight – but often there are more difficult judgement calls: is it realistic to refuse to work for *any* government or its state-owned companies unless the country is fully democratic and has an impeccable human rights record? Such things are difficult to determine and indeed any country and its government can be criticised in some respects. Similarly companies can be criticised and are not necessarily paragons of virtue. In practice PR people cannot expect to find moral perfection, and to a large extent have to take the world as they find it. They can legitimately argue that good PR can play a part in opening a country – or indeed a company – up to external influences and new ways of thinking, but even that argument can be self-serving and it is not always true – it failed to work in the case of Lee and Byoir for example.

PR is also used by everyone's favourite charities and campaigning groups, but that can create its own moral hazards, because PR techniques are used by all NGOs, including what may be one's least favourite: for instance one cannot simultaneously support pro- and anti-abortion groups, or be pro- and anti-hunting. Once again PR is available to heroes and villains, even if we often disagree on who is who. Just because such groups are not-for-profit does not necessarily make them morally perfect. NGOs compete with each other, individual careers and incomes are at stake, and the imperative of fund-raising means that there is always a temptation for them to do the *popular* rather than the *right* thing.

The 3 most important ethical standards to which PR needs to adhere

Simon Cohen, founder and Managing Director
Global Tolerance

Powerful questions

Persistently pose powerful questions of yourself, your colleagues and your clients. What are our values and how do we live them? Under what circumstances would we say 'no' to a client or turn down new business? Is it ever okay to lie to a journalist? Progress in PR lies not in ethical answers, but in our courage to pose powerful questions and being open to challenge our own and others' views in the ensuing debate.

Communicating solutions

Every time you communicate a problem, communicate a potential solution. When PR spreads problems alone, it fails to live up to its ethical role and responsibility in society – spreading fear rather than hope is no noble profession. Bill Clinton recently said, 'We are now in the age of how.' Can solutions sell in today's PR world? Three words: Yes We Can.

Personal relations

Think of PR as personal relations, not public relations. This applies to how we represent our clients and ourselves. If you are generally a decent person, and you unswervingly reflect your personal ethics in your professional PR life, you will rarely go wrong. PR is fundamentally a people industry: treat colleagues and clients with dignity, humility and respect.

www.globaltolerance.com

Even if one broadly supports the *cause* espoused by an NGO, one may think that its specific campaigning objectives are wrongheaded and even dangerous. For example anxiety about feeding the world's growing population is a shared concern not only of the leading environment groups which oppose genetically modified foods, but also of many people who support the development of GM foods and believe they are the only realistic way of supplying the nutritional needs of the earth's inhabitants. Neither side is necessarily more 'moral' than the other.

Many critics of PR focus on its associations with big business. After all PR as we know it came into being a hundred years ago to manage the relationship between corporations and the emerging mass media – and beyond that the public (see Chapter 1). It follows that people who do not like or are suspicious of business and capitalism do not like, or are suspicious of, PR. Indeed many attacks on PR are really thinly disguised attacks on the business world. If advertising is frequently pilloried as the public face of capitalism and the main motor behind consumerism, PR practitioners and lobbyists are often depicted as the sinister special forces of the big corporations and their allies in government, operating behind enemy lines and using a variety of unfair, clandestine tricks. Yet the same critics tend to remain silent about the vigorous and ingenious campaigns of NGOs such as Greenpeace.

Objecting to PR on the basis of the causes it serves leads into a *cul-de-sac*. PR can serve the interests of any company, large or small, from the most hated multinational to innocuous local businesses, or indeed wholesalers and others who have little contact with the public: unless one repudiates business altogether it is hard to object to the use of PR as such. Typically therefore people object to the use of PR in particular, unpopular business sectors. The problem with this is that no two people can agree on which businesses are acceptable and which are not – different societies often view these issues in different lights, and even one's individual perceptions alter over time or in response to particular events.

This can be readily illustrated. Some might object to the arms trade altogether on pacifist grounds – indeed one major PR agency head in the UK boasted that he would never work for an arms company.[2] More might object to the sale of particular kinds of weapons, or arms sales to particular regimes, but it would be impossible to reach a consensus on which weapons and which regimes are acceptable. Some might see providing arms, for example to fight someone *they* view as a tyrannical dictator or brutal aggressor, as deeply moral. Even those who object outright to arms sales are caught in a trap, due to the interconnected nature of the business world: companies which do not make weapons themselves may be supplying goods and services to those that do.

Alternatively, take the growing consensus about climate change and the threat of global warming. As we have seen with NGOs, general agreement about the problem does not mean that there is necessarily common ground about solutions. Some urge more use of nuclear power, others strongly oppose it. Some favour wind farms, others disagree. Some back the use of biofuels, while others see this as counterproductive. Tree planting to offset air travel has been fashionable in some circles, but is not backed by some of the largest environmental NGOs. Encouraging food exports from developing countries may seem positive and uncontroversial, but what about the air miles used up when they are flown to marketplaces in the developed world? In the case of the environment, even if people can agree on a destination, they rarely agree on the route to it: with limited time and expertise at our disposal, we all try and find our own way through the shifting sands of ethical debate, sometimes – it must be admitted – placing more weight on the evidence which suits our prejudices and interests. And yet the environment is but one example: the list of controversial businesses and moral dilemmas is endless. From gambling to tobacco, from alcohol to 'unhealthy' foods, from pornography, intensive farming, animal testing and the use of fur, to marketing directed at children and much more besides, most people have ethical qualms about some legal forms of business activity.

In their role as the messengers for the world of business PR people are sucked into all these and other debates. The reality is that, just like PR, business is amoral. It may create the wealth and products which we all need to survive – it is worth bearing in mind that those who attack business tend to sidestep the fact that people's jobs depend on it, and that in a competitive market companies depend upon us as their willing customers. However successfully meeting human needs and desires is not necessarily a moral activity, and so individual areas of business are not of themselves moral. There can also be a temptation to attempt to align one's morals with business advantage. For example, one's point of view on whether biofuels are a good thing might be influenced by the prospect of well-rewarded work for a biofuel company, even if one tries hard to convince oneself that one has reached the decision independently! Moreover some decisions which are trumpeted as moral ones may not be all they seem at first glance: a PR firm which refuses to work for tobacco companies may be doing so because of fears it might upset existing or potential clients or employees rather than for strictly ethical reasons.

Lawyers, who like PR people can also act as professional persuaders, have traditionally seen it as part of their professional duty to act for the most disreputable of clients. By and large the need for this is accepted by society, and lawyers who defend unpopular individuals or companies are seldom pilloried. But there is no right to have PR representation, and the stakes are lower – losing a PR battle cannot in itself lead to imprisonment. For all these reasons, coupled perhaps with a little prejudice against PR, particularly on the part of journalists, there is little comparable acceptance of the right of PR people to represent all comers.

Can PR people be passionate about their work all the time?

It is often said that PR people should only work for purposes they passionately believe in. This sounds good and hence hard to dispute – but the concept deserves a little scrutiny.

In theory a PR person could work exclusively for organisations and products about which they are passionate, but in reality that is rarely the case. When working for a PR consultancy no one can be sure that the brands they are working on will be their favourite products, and, even if that were true at the outset, products change and new decisions are made which not everyone can be enthusiastic about. The same is true working in-house; it is impossible to agree with everything a big organisation does and says.

It is certainly difficult to do PR work for something you are passionately opposed to – in such circumstances it might well be time to reconsider your position. However the real world of PR is about compromise: working for people and purposes about which one may occasionally be enthusiastic, but which are at least bearable. In any case there are advantages to being dispassionate. PR people need to retain some objectivity to work effectively. They need to empathise with their target audiences – something which is hard to do if they are swept away by their own feelings. Why does this point need stressing? Because too much talk about 'passion' sounds implausible and does PR a disservice: it makes PR people sound as though they are morally supple, can push aside the realities described above and express passion to order.

Discussion points

- What, if any, lawful activities would you not be prepared to undertake PR work for on ethical grounds – and why?
- List some controversial areas of business activity. Are they viewed differently in different societies around the world, and if so, why?
- You are working for a PR agency which is offered the opportunity to work for a large state-owned company from a foreign country. The country is not generally regarded as a democracy and has faced criticism over its human rights record. What – if any – ethical considerations would you need to weigh up before accepting or declining the potentially very profitable account? (You may choose to relate this to one or more actual countries.)

Consider depictions of PR in films, on television or in novels (see Chapter 1 and the further information section at the end of the book), or news stories involving PR. What, if any, ethical issues do they raise?

Corporate social responsibility and ethics

One of the more talked about developments in PR work in recent years has been the rise of corporate social responsibility (CSR – see Chapter 8). This may be defined as the notion that companies – and indeed other organisations – have responsibilities which go beyond profitability and seeking to maximise the value of shareholders' investments. Instead CSR emphasises wider duties to society and, often, to what is one of the highest-profile concerns of our time, the environment.

Champions of CSR often emphasise rather glibly the way in which it achieves 'win-win' results for the organisation they serve: society benefits, but so does their paymaster. This may be the case (public displays of CSR have become familiar marketing tools), but it poses the question as to why such an approach is particularly 'responsible': surely the most ruthless business person would be in favour of maximising his or her profits, and if acting in a 'responsible way' is one way of achieving that, so be it.

❝ *A principle is not a principle until it costs you money.*
> Bill Bernbach, American ad man.

CODES OF CONDUCT AND PR TECHNIQUES

Whether the causes served by PR are legitimate may be forever open to question, but PR's trade bodies tend to focus more closely on the techniques which PR people use. They have done this by developing their own codes of practice, or adopting international ones. Leading examples can be found on the websites of the Public Relations Society of America (www.prsa.org), the European Public Relations Confederation (www.cerp.org), the International Public Relations Association (www.ipra.org), and the UK's Chartered Institute of Public Relations (www.cipr.co.uk), but trade associations in most parts of the world have their own codes. Below we have taken one general example and paraphrased IPRA's Code of Venice (so-called after where it was agreed), adding our own commentary on its implications.

A general duty of fair dealing towards clients and employers, past and present

This may sound straightforward and unexceptional, but the difficulty lies in determining what constitutes 'fair dealing'. The term can be quite flexible and there is a danger of interpreting it in a self-serving way. However it is usually counterproductive to flout the accepted rules of the community in which one operates (not least because it makes it difficult to find other people prepared to deal with you in future), so a knowledge of what is and is not acceptable is crucial. This is one reason why, when operating internationally, local PR experience is so often crucial.

One general problem which can and does arise is when a client or employer insists on a course of action which in the PR practitioner's opinion is unwise – although in itself perfectly ethical. The PR practitioner certainly has a professional obligation to explain why the course of action is inappropriate and to suggest alternatives, but how far is it realistic for them to press their point if their paymaster continues to insist, given that their only alternative is to resign the account or quit their job?

Personal views v. corporate interests

In the UK, in 2009, the head of sustainability (a concept closely related to corporate social responsibility) at large property company won the right to appeal against his dismissal. He claimed that his beliefs about the effects of climate change and the need for urgent action to combat it put him at odds with the company. A hearing found that his views could amount to a philosophical or religious belief which is protected by legislation.[3]

Hypothetical

The drinks company you work for is promoting Bourbon whiskey from the southern states of America in another country. They want to run a promotion, including PR, which features the flag of the southern states. You point out that this flag is also seen as the confederate flag or flag of slavery and may be offensive to many, particularly black people, and that the media may pick up on it. Your boss says it caused no problems when used in the US and tells you to get on with it. What do you do and why?

Not representing conflicting or competing interests without their consent

This generally accepted principle is one PR shares with the advertising industry. It would clearly be difficult – if not impossible – for a PR practitioner to do their utmost for two rivals, and there would be a risk of sensitive information passing into the wrong hands. Historically both PR consultancies and advertising agencies have resigned profitable accounts in order to take on even more lucrative business for rivals. Indeed one reason the big international marketing services groups such as WPP or Interpublic include more than one PR consultancy or advertising firm is so that they can serve competing businesses. Since it is hard to hide the identity of clients (and publishing one's client list is often a requirement) this principle is generally adhered to. Problems may arise if the conflict of interest is not obvious, or the competition is indirect: here commonsense and a sense of judgement are required.

Safeguarding confidences of clients and employers

Confidentiality is an important feature of most professional codes and goes well beyond PR – it is, for example, what we expect of doctors or lawyers. PR people cannot expect clients or employers to speak to them frankly unless they know their confidence will be respected. However an issue might arise if there were legal or regulatory reasons for revealing what a client or employer is doing or planning to do – or if the PR practitioner feels that there are public interest issues at stake (see the point on public interest below).

Not attacking other organisations

At first glance this sounds uncontroversial – PR practitioners should only say positive things about the organisations which they represent, and never attack others. It often makes practical sense as well: big organisations and brands are understandably reluctant to draw attention to rivals; to appear negative or undignified; or to start slanging matches which might drag the sector in which they operate into disrepute. But these are self-serving, not ethical, reasons and do not necessarily reflect the customer's interests. Indeed stifling negative PR in the commercial world can be seen as anti-competitive: within the law there is nothing wrong with attacking a rival if it offers consumers more information upon which to make informed choices. Drawing attention to poor products and bad service – or high prices – could serve the consumer's – and hence the public's – interest. In practice what happens is that attacks on rivals take place but are often indirect and subtle – perhaps the rivals' names are not even used.

It is also worth noting that, beyond the commercial world, large areas of PR would all but disappear if this rule was applied rigidly. Major NGOs such as Greenpeace or Amnesty International put much of their PR effort into attacking large corporations and/or governments, and much – some would say most – political PR is negative as parties and their leaders use their PR machines to attack each other. This is a timeless and inevitable part of public life. We cannot see anything wrong in principle with PR contributing to public debate in this way.

Payment by results should neither be proposed nor accepted

It is noteworthy that this stipulation does not appear in all PR codes. Where it does – as here – it is partly driven by the desire of PR people to be seen as comparable to other professions, where the client accepts that the professional they hire applies their skills as best as they can but payment is due regardless of the outcome. Thus doctors are paid even if patients do not recover, and lawyers were traditionally paid irrespective of the outcome of the case (this is changing in some countries with the advent of no-win no-fee agreements). Understandably many PR people would like to enjoy a similar, high level of trust.

But some business people like to tie their payments to PR people to concrete achievements, such as particular volumes of media coverage, and in a competitive market some PR people are prepared to accept this rather than forego the business. Aside from the issue of whether this undermines PR's claim to professional standing, the main problem is determining the degree to which PR is responsible for any outcome (see pp. 224–233). Marketing PR, for example, is usually used in conjunction with advertising and sales promotions and so singling out the achievement of PR is difficult and tends to be a matter of judgement. In crisis management, despite the best efforts of PR people, the organisation concerned may still be harmed, but PR may have diminished the amount of damage: how is that relative success to be measured? Similarly, it would be tempting but untrue for PR people to take the credit for every success story.

Max Clifford is perhaps the UK's best-known PR person and a controversial figure in public life (see p. 89). His work often involves helping people who are embroiled in scandals to sell their stories to popular newspapers, and typically he will be paid a percentage of whatever he negotiates. It is unusual for PR people to be paid in this way.

Conducting professional activities with respect to the public interest and individual dignity

Many PR codes contain a general statement of this kind, but defining what is meant by the public interest is fraught with difficulty and will always tend to come down to the individual conscience. The Public Relations Society of America, for instance, defines 'public interest' as conforming to the US Constitution but this is rather stating the obvious: all PR people are subject to the law. As we have seen, whether a cause is in the public interest is debatable and whether the techniques used to further it are in the public interest can also be a matter of opinion. For example even the sternest critics of corporate and government PR techniques seem unfussed about campaigning NGOs which set out flagrantly to break the law for publicity purposes.

Lord Melchett, then a Director of Greenpeace, and 27 other Greenpeace activists appeared in court in the UK charged with criminal damage to a field of genetically modified maize. Melchett told the court he felt a 'strong moral obligation' to act as he did, although he was later acquitted.
   Melchett later severed his connections with Greenpeace and undertook work for the corporate social responsibility practice of the PR giant Burson-Marsteller.[4]

Giving priority to the public interest could clash with those areas of the code (see above) which emphasise duties to the client or employer. At the very least a PR person who felt that the public interest was threatened might feel obliged to resign the account or leave his or her job and might even feel obliged to break his or her obligation of confidentiality. In practice PR people compromise: few enjoy the luxury of never disagreeing with their paymasters, but, equally, few continue working for people with whom they are completely at odds.

As more and more PR is conducted across borders PR practitioners also have to familiarise themselves with different ethical notions in different societies. What may seem to be in keeping with public interest and individual dignity at home can look very different in another country.

Hypothetical 1

You work for The Explosive Vodka Company. In your own country the company is careful to abide by the regulations on promoting alcohol. These forbid portraying it in a glamorous way. The company is now entering new less regulated markets and is offering you a sizeable pay increase to manage the PR. The promotions they plan to use include highly sexualised images of young women and wet T shirt competitions in night clubs. What do you do and why?

Hypothetical 2

You are working for an environmental NGO which is strongly opposed to genetically modified foods. They plan to break into a warehouse belonging to a well-known supermarket chain and spray a large consignment of GM food with paint. They want you to participate and help publicise this activity. What do you do and why?

Not engaging in practices which tend to corrupt the integrity of public communication

Making payments or gifts to journalists or others in the media in return for coverage is traditionally a taboo area for PR people. While journalists set great store by their independence and objectivity, PR people pride themselves on their ability to secure the right kind of coverage without money changing hands. However there is ample evidence that in many societies corrupt practices do exist, and it is difficult for a lone practitioner to buck the trend.

Within the same country the approaches of different sectors of the PR industry may vary. In political or high-level corporate PR the very notion of gifts for journalists – beyond meals, hospitality and entertainment (although of course these can become lavish and questionable in themselves) – may be unthinkable. Most would consider the idea of media workers being given privileged access to government services, such as healthcare, outrageous. But in other areas of PR accepted practice is different. Free holidays for journalists are a staple of travel PR, and free samples and gifts are often offered in fashion and lifestyle PR. Indeed these and other valuable and sought after perks have become essential elements of modern media production. While such benefits may not be explicitly tied to media coverage, it would be foolish to deny that the relationships thus cultivated (not least the prospects of future benefits) can help tip the scales. The treating of journalists may involve giving them goods and services of a considerable value but this tends to be regarded as socially acceptable, whereas if they were given a lesser amount in cash it would be seen as blatant corruption. Even if journalists are not 'bribed' in this sense, they can be, and are, provided with exclusive stories. These are valuable in their own right as they can lead to promotion and salary increases for the journalists involved. Similarly advertisers may exert direct or more subtle pressure over editorial coverage in the media outlets in which they advertise, a process in which PR can become involved (see p. 276).

Research in which the Polish Public Relations Consultancies Association participated revealed that 'communication leaders in Poland are most concerned with indirect media bribery, such as publishing a news article in exchange for advertising, or providing free samples or attractive discounts to journalists'. Overall 'less than half of public relations professionals and only a third of journalists believe that public relations is practiced in an ethical manner in Poland.'[5]

Not deliberately telling lies

This might seem simple and uncontroversial at first glance, and is not just an ethical matter as passing on untrustworthy information can be counterproductive. If it comes to be known that a PR person is not a source of reliable information then journalists and others will look elsewhere for facts and comment. Therefore lying about specific facts and figures is usually a bad idea, and in some contexts may be illegal. But beyond that social attitudes to lying vary. No-one likes to admit to being a liar, but in practice few of us tell the truth all the time.

This means that no one – including journalists – expects PR people to tell the full truth about the organisations they serve. Nor can PR people always avoid difficult issues by refusing to comment on bad news stories; such a refusal can imply you are not denying the story – which usually you would if it were untrue. Real disputes and problems will frequently have to be glossed over or even denied, but in most societies such 'lies' are normally considered socially acceptable. Colleagues have to pretend to like and respect each other even if they do not – and PR people have to participate in such white lies. PR people who sought to tell the full truth in such circumstances would probably find themselves without a job. Indeed politicians and others who admit the full truth to journalists are seen as more naïve than praiseworthy by the media. (It is worth noting that although journalists often rail against PR people for lying, in reality their own position is more nuanced. Sometimes the end justifies the means. For example major news stories are often the result of journalists operating undercover and adopting a false identity. In such cases journalists are, by definition, lying but justify their deceit by claiming that it is only in such ways that they can secure information which the public deserves – or would like – to know.)

Immanuel Kant and telling the truth

Writers on public relations ethics often cite the ideas of the German philosopher Immanuel Kant (1724–1804).

Kant denied that there was a moral right to lie in any circumstances and, when challenged, famously argued that it would be wrong to deceive a would-be murderer about the location of his intended victim. Although in his view one was under no obligation to help the would-be murderer – one could refuse to answer him or even challenge him – it would not be right to lie. This attitude towards telling the truth at least has the advantage of intellectual consistency, but one hopes most of us would shy away from putting such thinking into practice, even in less extreme situations![6]

The issue continues to be hotly contested – not least because it is seen as having a critical bearing on the reputation of PR. Unlike many of the ethical issues outlined above it directly concerns PR's relationship with journalists. In 2007, following a major debate in London organised by us and sponsored by *PR Week* magazine, the audience – made up of PR practitioners and students – voted by a small majority that PR people did not have a duty to tell the truth. When we restaged the debate at the Sorbonne in Paris the vote went the same way – but much more decisively. One irony was that while many PR practitioners were prepared to vote discreetly with the majority, we had much more difficulty getting PR people to speak in the debate and admit publicly to the need, on occasion, to tell lies.

Nor do these dilemmas only apply to relations with the outside world. A senior internal communications person might be aware of possible redundancies long before they become general knowledge, but might be under instructions to deny that they might take place if asked. Refusing to comment could simply lead to even more suspicion.

One of the authors handled the launch of one of the UK's largest online banks. Prelaunch secrecy was vital as the new bank wanted to maximise its competitive advantage by maintaining control over the timing of the announcement. However, as is often the case, a journalist heard rumours about the preparations and rang up to enquire.

Telling the truth would have meant losing control over the announcement before the bank was ready, leaving competitors with a free hand. Obfuscation and refusal to comment was not an option: the journalist already had the germ of a story and if it was not denied it would probably be published in some form. The option chosen was to tell a direct lie. The journalist was told that the new facilities were simply a new back office for the bank's existing branch network: untrue, but effective and, most would argue, harmless.

Using the PR ethics map below consider the ethical issues for each of the four groups when related to:

1 Manufacture of alcohol
2 Manufacture of arms
3 Manufacture of cheap clothing

Sometimes it can be difficult to satisfy the conflicting ethical requirements of all 4 groups.

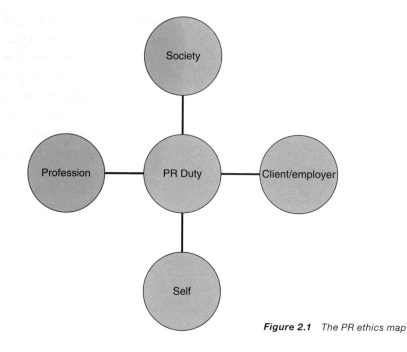

Figure 2.1 *The PR ethics map*

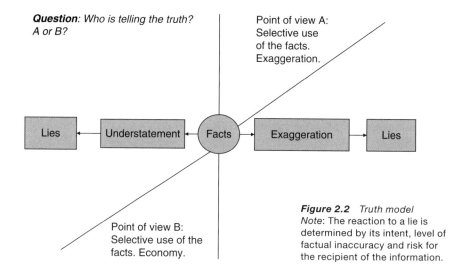

Question: *Who is telling the truth? A or B?*

Point of view A:
Selective use
of the facts.
Exaggeration.

Point of view B:
Selective use of the
facts. Economy.

Figure 2.2 *Truth model*
Note: The reaction to a lie is
determined by its intent, level of
factual inaccuracy and risk for
the recipient of the information.

 Divide into two groups. One group should construct and write up the most persuasive argument they can for the legal obligation to carry national identity cards. The other group should meanwhile construct and write up the best argument they can against mandatory national identity cards. Each group should then examine the others using the truth model above for examples of exaggeration or understating the 'truth'.

Giving a faithful representation of the organisation which the PR person serves

This overlaps with the points on lying above. The organisation is paying for the service, so no one should be surprised that the PR person accentuates the positive and minimises the organisation's negative aspects when portraying it to journalists and others. A truly faithful representation would have to include detailing all an organisation's faults. After all, when you go for a job interview the prospective employer does not expect you to lie, but nor do they expect you to volunteer a complete list of all your shortcomings!

A similar point applies to the popular concept of 'transparency'. This term, with its positive overtones, is much talked about, often in a rather unthinking way. There is some information which every organisation has to reveal, and even more that it is hard to conceal – so it may be better to reveal it yourself in a controlled way rather than allow it to emerge in a way and at a time which is not of your choosing. However we know of no organisation which allows itself to be fully transparent (for example, by disclosing full records of all its internal discussions).

Not creating or using organisations which serve the undisclosed interests of the organisation the PR person serves

Businesses often have an interest in issues which can affect their ability to carry on or develop their activities. This might include permission to build new plants, regulations affecting their workforce, environmental controls, or their ability to promote and sell controversial products.

Businesses have long realised that their voice in such debates will be undermined if they are simply seen as furthering their commercial interests. To counter this, many business organisations have set up, or contribute towards, what are called *front groups* – business-sponsored lobbying groups which disguise (or do not publicise) their business links.

One of the key issues here is whether any deception is used. If an organisation is clear about how it is funded and controlled it is for the media and others to take that into account. Certainly the media should ask more searching questions about every organisation which contributes to public debate: How many people does it represent? What are its decision-making processes? How is it funded? What are its qualifications for offering a view? Do its ideas make sense? Does it have any ulterior motives? Much of this information is normally available for commercial organisations, but the fact that the media place more trust in not-for-profit organisations makes it irresistible for some companies facing controversy to imitate them.

However, whilst in the past there have been clear examples of what is called *Astroturfing* (fake grassroots movements), exposure of such practices seemed to have led to a decline in their use – or perhaps they are just better concealed.

Front groups in fact and fiction

In the 1950s, faced with mounting evidence that cigarette smoking can cause cancer, the American tobacco industry sponsored the establishment of the Tobacco Industry Research Committee (TIRC), which later became the Committee for Tobacco Research. The TIRC hired Dr Clarence Little, a respected former managing director of the American Society for the Control of Cancer, as its director. The Committees focused on publicising inconclusive or contradictory information about the harmful effects of tobacco smoking, producing a booklet entitled 'A Scientific Perspective on the Cigarette Controversy' which was mailed to doctors, politicians and the media. However, despite a promise to sponsor independent research, less than 10% of the two Committees' budget was spent on scientific projects.

Another important voice in the debate was the National Smokers' Alliance, which sought to protect the rights of smokers. Ostensibly a grassroots organisation bringing together millions of smokers from across America, it received millions of dollars from the tobacco giant Philip Morris.

These organisations illustrate how front groups can work – by claiming or implying academic or scientific expertise and independence (in the case of the Committees); or asserting that they represent the views of ordinary people (in the case of the Alliance, a classic 'Astroturf' movement). In all cases front groups seek to put some distance between themselves and the business sector which funds them, while putting a positive gloss on the sector's activities, and playing down any problems. They choose their titles and their spokespeople carefully, and thereby hope to achieve greater credibility.

An excellent fictional example of this is the Academy of Tobacco Studies, for which the main character of Christopher Buckley's hilarious novel (now also a feature film), *Thank You for Smoking,*[7] Nick Naylor, acts as spokesman (or *smoke*sman). Buckley brilliantly satirises the world of front groups: Naylor's friends and acquaintances include spokespeople from the Society for the Humane Treatment of Calves (representing the veal industry); the Friends of Dolphins (formerly the Pacific Tuna Fisherman's Association); and the Land Enrichment Foundation (formerly the Coalition for the Responsible Disposal of Radioactive Waste).

For more on this, see also Robert Jackall & Janice M. Hirota's excellent *Image Makers: Advertising, Public Relations, and the Ethos of Advocacy.*[8]

PR people working with new media may face a particular temptation to pose as disinterested parties on social media and even when preparing entries on Wikipedia. The temptation arises because by appearing to be ordinary members of the public they will have much greater independent authority than company employees would have. However, aside from issues of PR ethics, such practices are contrary to the strongly held views of the online community and, if uncovered, may cause outrage and adverse publicity. In the UK contributing to online media in this way, without declaring an interest, may also be illegal.

Not injuring the professional reputation or practice of other PR practitioners

This is clearly intended to stop unseemly attempts to undermine rivals in a way which would run counter to the behaviour expected of a proper profession and could damage the standing of the PR industry. Of course attacks on business rivals can circumvent this by using a little subtlety: other people's ways of doing business can be belittled without naming the practitioners. It might also be argued that this part of the code is anti-competitive, serving the industry's own interests and clashing with the injunction to respect the public interest: what if a PR practitioner felt that he or she could offer a better service, or that the work of another had serious shortcomings?

Not seeking to supplant other PR practitioners in their work by poaching their clients or their jobs

Again, this has much to do with PR's desires for professional status, making it more similar to medicine or law than commerce. Most PR people would avoid doing this in too obvious a way – it would be unattractive and often counter-productive – but as suggested above the supplanting of rivals can be achieved in subtle ways that are hard to stop. Once again it could be argued that this restriction is more about protecting the interests of the PR industry than the public interest: it is in the interests of users of PR to be made fully aware of the options available to them and then to choose.

Cooperating with other practitioners to uphold the ethical code

As we shall see, upholding and enforcing codes of ethics has proved to be very difficult. This requirement also sits uneasily with the need to avoid injuring the professional reputation or practice of other practitioners: PR practitioners are generally reluctant to launch attacks on their rivals.

PROBLEMS WITH ENFORCING CODES OF PR ETHICS

There are many codes of PR ethics and they are occasionally revised and added to. Indeed individual PR practitioners may be bound by more than one code if they are members of both national and international PR bodies; they may also be subject to specialist codes – for example, governing lobbying. However it has proved very difficult to enforce such codes. There are various reasons for this.

One major problem for would-be PR regulators is that much of the most controversial PR work takes place behind the scenes and involves private conversations and meetings between protagonists who know each other well. The process can be a subtle one, with many things left unsaid. Moreover journalists have a long tradition of protecting their sources. This makes it peculiarly difficult to prove beyond doubt that someone has breached the PR code. So PR scandals often revolve around PR people's conversations being tape-recorded without their knowledge; misunderstandings about whether they were speaking off the record to journalists; or their failure to realise that email, despite its convenience as a means of communication, leaves a permanent record. Thus in the UK the Queen's daughter-in-law, Sophie Wessex, who ran a PR consultancy, was forced to step down after an embarrassing conversation with a newspaper journalist posing as a potential client was tape-recorded and published (and, for the same reason, her business partner became a rare example of someone who was forced to leave the UK's Institute of Public Relations). In contrast it is much rarer for the more public face of PR – press releases and press conferences – to be called into question on ethical grounds.

Another problem is that membership of PR organisations in most countries is voluntary. In most societies anyone is free to practise PR (whether they will succeed is quite another matter), and organisations of all kinds are free to employ whomsoever they wish to carry out public relations duties; quite often they hire people without PR backgrounds (most typically, ex-journalists). This openness is likely to remain the case and is arguably one of PR's positive characteristics, enabling the industry to grow and adapt itself to changing circumstances by taking on talented individuals with a range of experience.

Attempts to impose statutory regulation would not only be restrictive and undermine PR's essential dynamism but would be difficult to put into practice. What exactly would be regulated? There is no universally accepted definition of PR and as we have seen (pp. 4–10) those which are in widest circulation are both general and vague (for example, saying PR is about reputation management) and hence would not be of much value to a regulator. Moreover the duties of PR people can overlap with those of other communication and management disciplines.

In practice there are two main ways which can be used to restrict entry to a profession. Often some combination of them is used.

First, certain duties can be specified as ones only members of a professional body can perform. For example, only a doctor can prescribe certain drugs, or only a lawyer may have the right to represent others in a court of law. However it is hard to know which exact duties could be reserved for PR people. Offering advice on reputation management is too vague and general – it is something all kinds of people are involved in. On the other hand, more specific tasks undertaken by PR people are often undertaken by others – we all may speak to journalists, on our own behalf, on behalf of friends, or for the organisations for which we work. Saying that only PR people can contact, or be contacted by, the media would certainly not be acceptable to journalists, would be all but impossible to enforce, and would indeed flout most ideas – and laws – concerning individual freedom. Similar problems apply to other areas of PR work. In the case of lobbying or public affairs, citizens in many societies enjoy a cherished right to approach politicians and administrators with their concerns – and to get other people to help them to do so. Most would consider restricting that right to registered lobbyists outrageous.

Second, people can be denied the right to use the profession's name and job title to describe what they do – just as an ordinary person cannot set up a lawyer's office or doctor's surgery. If this approach was applied to PR, PR people would have to be members of a professional body before they could use the term 'public relations' in their company names, or on their stationery or websites. In theory this would be quite straightforward: transgressors could be readily spotted and dealt with. The difficulty with applying this to public relations is that many PR people already prefer to use other job titles and descriptions and often avoid using the term: for them being forced to drop references to PR would not be a problem.

All of this means that membership of professional organisations is likely to remain optional for PR practitioners (or that, if attempts are made to make it compulsory, it will prove impractical and unworkable). In consequence PR's trade bodies, although styling themselves as professional bodies, have only limited powers to police standards in the industry: members are free to leave and carry on their business as before. This is one of the reasons the codes of ethics are rarely enforced: voluntary organisations which depend on their members' subscriptions are loath to expel members. On the rare occasions that they have taken sanctions against members they have usually been slight. Indeed the world's largest PR organisation, the Public Relations Society of America, states on its website that 'emphasis on enforcement of the code has been eliminated'. They admit they made this change because the code was unenforceable.

Why PR trade associations are important

Francis Ingham, Chief Executive,
Public Relations Consultants Association (PRCA)

PR trade associations might not always play the most glamorous role, but they do play a vital one.

Broadly speaking, they fulfil three functions.

First, they provide a collective voice for the industry. In an industry which is built as much on personal relationships as on anything else, there is a natural reluctance for one consultancy, individual or team, to put its head above the trenches on contentious issues, for fear of having it shot off. Associations are far more bullet-proof, and can say the things their members would love to but can't.

Second, they raise the professionalism of an industry which is still relatively young. PR isn't like accountancy or law – it's a much younger industry with much greater flux. Associations can work with the industry to raise standards both amongst their own members in particular, and amongst the industry as a whole.

Third, they allow the quality practitioners to stand out from the rest – they provide a means of differentiation. This is particularly important in an industry which lacks any statutory license-to-practise restrictions, and where the only barriers to entry are the possession of an email address, a desk and a mobile.

It's easy for member bodies to lose their way – to turn inwards and to forget that they exist to advance the interests of their members rather than themselves.

It's also easy for them to become far too pretentious. In my view, PR isn't a profession as such – it's an industry which is often very professional. The two are not synonymous. Professionalism isn't limited to professions alone and the people who drone on and on about PR being a profession are generally being irrelevant to the everyday challenges of the profession – and often just being self-servingly grandiose.

www.prca.org.uk

So how is PR controlled or regulated?

Formal systems for policing PR work may be doomed, but that does not mean that PR work is a free-for-all. The urgings of trade bodies may do some good, as may the attempts of PR educators to get students to consider ethical issues, but the use of controversial techniques is more effectively tempered by social pressure and the expectations of individual marketplaces in different countries. This recognises that PR people have to respond to a range of competing pressures – as our commentary on the Code of Venice indicates – and have to make swift decisions in difficult circumstances: their working environment is not that of an academic seminar. Those who overstep the boundaries of what is deemed acceptable in a particular society or working environment risk losing the standing they need to operate effectively. PR is a profoundly social activity, and lack of social acceptance – at least within the desired circles – renders the PR person useless. In this way the ethics of the PR business are placed ultimately in the hands of non-PR people – their employers.

PR people also face particular vigilance from the media, and from some other external sources. The fact that identifying and monitoring the subtleties of PR requires knowledge and effort means that it is not an obvious target in the way that advertising is, but this makes it particularly appealing to the critical cognoscenti and those who believe in conspiracy theories. The machinations of corporate and political PR – but seldom NGO PR – are the subject of specialist websites, such as www.prwatch.org, the extensive, professionally staffed PR monitoring service run by the Center for Media and Democracy in the United States; and www.spinwatch.org, a newer UK equivalent.

Case study: Kuwaiti babies, PR and the nature of modern journalism

One of the *causes celebres* most cited by critics of the PR industry dates back to the run-up to the first Gulf War, after Saddam Hussein's Iraqi army had occupied Kuwait in 1990. It was not certain how the outside world would respond. The Kuwaiti government-in-exile hired western PR people to make the case for America to become involved and use its military might to expel the Iraqi invaders. Money was no object – the campaign was to be one of the most expensive on record.

The most celebrated part of the resulting PR campaign was a heart-rending account of how,

following the invasion, Iraqi soldiers had entered the maternity wards in a hospital in Kuwait City and plucked newborn babies from incubators, leaving them on the floor to die. Eyewitness testimony confirming this was delivered by a teenage Kuwaiti girl in front of the Congressional Human Rights Caucus on Capitol Hill in Washington DC during an emotionally charged session. The allegations were widely reported in the media and quoted by politicians, including the then US President George Bush senior. They played a role in helping to persuade people that the ensuing war was justifiable.

However, following the conflict journalists and others who sought to investigate the story found no evidence to substantiate it. Amnesty

➡

International, which had endorsed the account, had to issue a retraction. It also emerged that the 'eyewitness' was in fact the daughter of the Kuwaiti ambassador to the United States and that Kuwait's western PR advisers had played a key role in preparing this tale of atrocities.

Whatever one thinks about the role of PR advisers in such circumstances, two things are often ignored when this case is discussed.

First, the PR people concerned were doing their best for their client in a situation which could scarcely be more critical – their country had been invaded and they needed help to liberate it. It is often said that truth is the first casualty of war and it is for a reason: no country would put truth before its vital national interests, particularly in times of war. As Winston Churchill famously put it, 'In wartime, truth is so precious that she should always be attended by a bodyguard of lies'.

Second, if the PR people serving Kuwaiti interests were doing what one might expect them to do, what can one say about Amnesty International – which itself deploys considerable PR muscle – and above all about the journalists who covered the story? It seems that in the heat of the moment, swept by herd instinct and the desire not to be left behind on a powerful story, they were too willing to report whatever they were told, without cross-checking the information, seeking out alternative witnesses or even establishing the true identity of the witness from whom they heard. In their haste basic journalistic principles were abandoned. One can argue that this example casts as least as much light on contemporary journalism as it does on PR.[9]

The Australian journalist and writer Phillip Knightley has written elsewhere:

> The military has a manual called Managing the Media at Wartime and one of the exhortations in that is never tell a lie unless you're certain the lie won't be discovered until the war is over.[10]

Imagine you are working for a very large PR consultancy in similar circumstances. Your client wants you to develop a similar campaign for similar reasons. What would you do and why? What factors would you need to consider? What might the consequences of your actions be?

- This chapter has shown that concerns about PR ethics apply both to the causes PR people serve and the techniques they use when serving them.
- The PR industry attempts to address these concerns with professional codes, but such codes are often capable of broad interpretation and are hard to enforce. Regulation of the PR industry remains highly problematic and has never been effectively attempted.
- However PR practitioners remain subject to social pressure which acts as an informal control on behaviour – if only because those who do not heed the discipline's commonly accepted standards are likely to find themselves without work, or unable to deal with the media.

---

1 What is the purpose of professional codes in the field of public relations, and how effective are they? Discuss with reference to any set(s) of codes (such as those of the PRSA, CERP, IPRA, PRCA or CIPR.)

2 'The rise of PR represents the direct control by private or state interests of the flow of public information in the interest not of rational discourse, but of manipulation.' In the light of this remark, discuss whether PR activity should be regulated and, if it were to be, how this might be achieved.

3 Devise your own ethical code which you think would be effective in regulating PR activity.

Some reading suggestions

For a refreshingly open, if occasionally naïve, look at all aspects of PR, try Moloney, Kevin, *Rethinking Public Relations: PR, Propaganda and Democracy* (Routledge 2006).

The classic critical account of PR is Stauber, John and Rampton, Sheldon, *Toxic Sludge Is Good For You: Lies, Damn Lies and the Public Relations Industry* (Constable & Robinson 2004), although the same authors' other books are well worth a look – as is the website with which they were long associated: www.prwatch.org. Or try the UK alternative: www.spinwatch.org

If you can get hold of a copy, still the best – certainly the best written – book about the character of the PR industry and its timeless dilemmas is Ross, Irwin, *The Image Merchants: The Fabulous World of American Public Relations* (Weidenfeld & Nicolson 1960). Films, TV series and novels about PR offer plenty of food for thought – see the reading list at the end of the book for further details.

For more on this, including exercises relating to PR ethics, see this book's website: www.palgrave.com/business/prtoday

THE MAKE-UP OF THE PR INDUSTRY

INTRODUCTION

In this chapter we look at the structure of the PR industry and its specialisations (although some merit chapters in their own right). However readers need to bear in mind the following:

The PR industry's composition and activities are notoriously hard to quantify. The biggest barrier to producing accurate statistics is the fact that PR is not a proper profession with restricted entry. You do not need to register anywhere in order to be able to practise PR. Consequently trade associations and professional bodies only represent a minority of those who work in the industry. The number of people who work in PR but are not members of one of these bodies remains a matter of speculation.

Another factor which makes it difficult to measure the PR industry is the fact that many practitioners are anxious to free themselves from some of the negative perceptions of PR and want to describe what they do in ways likely to enhance their status and income. As a result they describe themselves as almost anything but PR people: they are corporate reputation managers, campaigners, communication strategists, employer brand consultants, creative directors or corporate social responsibility specialists. A quick look at any medium offering jobs in the sector will reveal a myriad of titles. Who should be counted in and who counted out?

There are also problems of defining PR and its overlaps with other marketing communication disciplines. Are events organisers, and newsletter and website copywriters, involved in aspects of PR? Often they are, but if one included all such people in the PR headcount the numbers would balloon out of recognition.

LEARNING OBJECTIVES

- To understand the overall structure of the PR industry
- To understand the difference between consultancy and in-house PR
- To understand the differences between commercial, public sector and not-for-profit (or third-sector) PR
- To understand the range of and rationale for PR specialisation

STRUCTURE OF THE INDUSTRY

As can be seen in Figure 3.1, the PR industry can be divided in a number of ways. At its most basic the industry can be divided into two categories:

1. *In-house* – where the PR person is employed directly by an organisation, be it a business, charity, NGO or public sector body (occasionally wealthy individuals also employ PR people) and
2. *Consultancy* – where the PR person works for a consultancy or agency, an independent business, which is hired by organisations – or sometimes rich individuals and celebrities – to do some, or all, of their PR.

The PR industry can also be divided by the sort of work PR people do. This ranges from work focused on a particular industry sector (such as food, music, healthcare or celebrity and entertainment) through to work focused on particular PR skills (such as consumer, corporate, lobbying or public affairs, city and financial and internal communications). In reality most people working in PR are generalists, albeit with a bias towards some kinds of activity or sector. Whether working in-house or for a consultancy, they will undertake a wide variety of PR activities – although most commonly this involves supporting the marketing effort of the organisation they are working for or representing (see Chapter 4). They may, depending on whom they work for, specialise in a particular industry, but they will seldom undertake the work of the skills specialist. See final section of this chapter for more details on PR specialisms.

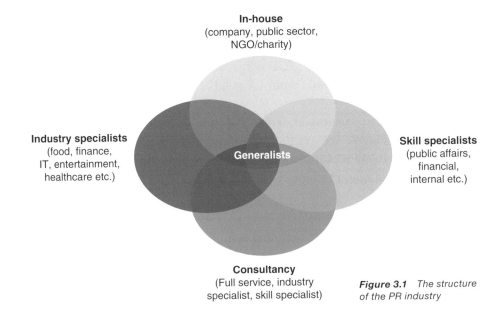

In-house
(company, public sector,
NGO/charity)

Industry specialists
(food, finance,
IT, entertainment,
healthcare etc.)

Generalists

Skill specialists
(public affairs,
financial,
internal etc.)

Consultancy
(Full service, industry
specialist, skill specialist)

Figure 3.1 *The structure
of the PR industry*

PR's split identity – both in-house PR and consultancy PR – is in contrast to other marketing services. Advertising has always been, and remains, essentially an external agency function, reflecting the fact that even the biggest advertisers have seldom been able or willing to recruit and retain high-quality advertising talent to work in-house. Marketing on the other hand is traditionally a core 'in-house' function for business and is seen as an indispensable part of a business's day-to-day functioning. Unusually PR involves both in-house and agency/consultancy services. Organisations generally like to have an in-house PR function which knows the organisation well, can get answers to media questions quickly and is completely trustworthy.

THE CONSULTANCY SECTOR

As we have seen, when PR consultancy was born in the United States about one hundred years ago (see pp. 10–17), specialists in dealing with the rapidly emerging mass media quickly emerged. Some of these specialists such as Ivy Lee, Edward Bernays and, later, John W. Hill of what became Hill & Knowlton realised there was more money to be made, and perhaps more interest to be had, through advising several organisations rather than just one.

Many of the early PR consultancies were essentially cottage industries, built around individual personalities (they often bore the names of their founders, and some of these linger on). They were akin in size to the multitude of small PR firms which still make up much of the PR consultancy sector, as at this stage the owner (usually a man) employed only a handful of staff, and had a direct hand in most important client business. In the mid-twentieth century some of these small businesses grew into big companies, at least by the standards of the PR industry, such as Hill & Knowlton (see pp. 38–39) and Burson-Marsteller. They began to expand overseas, particularly in the UK where PR was slowly taking off.

Developments in the 1980s, for the reasons we have described (see pp. 14–16), led to unprecedented growth in the consultancy sector, particularly in the UK. This pattern has more recently been repeated across formerly communist-controlled Eastern and Central Europe and elsewhere. The 1980s also saw a consumer boom and the emergence of the IT industry and Silicon Valley (which manifested itself in the emergence of a number of specialist IT consultancies). PR consultancies both made possible and responded to the growth in the media which occurred at the same time. They played an important part in the associated rise of celebrity culture but also benefited from it as journalists came to rely on them for their celebrity stories, a trend amusingly captured in the UK documentary film *Starsuckers*.[1]

This boom allowed the PR consultancy sector – or at least its more success-ful constituents – to mature from cottage industries to boutiques, and in some instances from boutiques to fully fledged international businesses. High-profile individual personalities continued to play an important role but were now backed by teams of more senior and higher calibre staff – PR was increasingly becoming a graduate occupation, belatedly catching up with advertising, although at this stage few entrants would have studied PR. Consultancies adopted a more formal structure and were now capable of dealing with substantial client business with-out reference to the founder and owner. Senior staff continued to have a range of backgrounds, many having started their careers outside PR.

By the late 1990s the PR consultancy sector was starting to take its current shape. The once dominant, high-profile personalities had for the most part left the firms they founded, having sold them to a series of large, international mar-keting services conglomerates. The remaining senior and experienced staff found themselves increasingly divorced from client work and instead forced to manage what were now large businesses. This change of emphasis led to many senior consultants, disillusioned with managerialism, quitting the new leviathans and establishing small consultancies offering both execution and strategic advice.

Despite the emergence of large international marketing groups the majority of consultancies are still very small. Indeed, even the big consultancies seldom have more than 200 staff in a single country. In the UK, according to the PR Week Top 150 Consultancies only 6 have over 200 staff. Most in the top 150 have staff numbers well below 30 – the average for consultancies ranked between 50 and 150 is around 23 staff.[2] Similarly, the vast majority of the thousands of PR firms in the US probably have fewer than ten staff; plenty will have just one. Many of these small firms – or individuals who may be operating freelance – come and go, expand and contract, merge with other firms, or change their names with great speed. So producing a precise map of the industry remains problematic.

THE EMERGENCE OF PR CONGLOMERATES

Today nearly all the biggest and best-known PR consultancies are owned by a small group of international marketing services or communications groups. These holding companies – which include direct marketing, digital and market research businesses – used to be dominated by advertising agencies. Although they still own most of the biggest names in advertising, the leading role of adver-tising has been blunted by the increasing fragmentation of marketing methods, itself influenced by the fragmentation of the media.

Initially these marketing services groups were almost all American. The 1980s saw the emergence of UK-based groups, led by WPP's Sir Martin Sorrell, followed more recently by the emergence of the Australian-based Photon group. French groups are also represented, a legacy of the historic strength of the French advertising industry. How long will it be before Chinese or Indian groups become major players?

Many of the subsidiary companies listed in Table 3.1 were major players in their own country – or in some cases even internationally – even before they were bought.

There are a number of business justifications given for the acquisition of a PR firm:

- The opportunity to cross-sell across marketing-related disciplines (both advertising and PR, for example);
- Reduced new business costs (at least in theory) as clients are able to buy a collection of services in one go;
- Group companies can benefit from economies of scale, with scope for sharing offices and services;
- From a client standpoint it is argued that major conglomerates can help major clients reach international audiences while deploying a full range of marketing skills; and
- From the acquired companies' point of view they receive a large amount of money and the opportunity to play on a larger stage and/or they are rescued from slow decline or even imminent disaster.

Table 3.1 The major listed marketing services groups and some of their subsidiary companies, ranked by market capitalisation

Marketing Group (in bold) and some PR Subsidiaries
WPP (UK): AxiCom, Burson-Marsteller, Cohn and Wolf, Finsbury, GCI, Hill & Knowlton, Ogilvy, Dewey Square (They also have a holding in UK quoted Chime plc.)
Omnicom(US): Fishburn Hedges, Fleishman-Hillard, Gavin Anderson, Ketchum Pleon, Brodeur Worldwide, Porter Novelli, Clark and Weinstock, Blue Current, GPlus Europe, Staniforth Communications, Cone, Mercury Public Affairs
Publicis (France): MS&L, Freud Communications, Agence Pietri, Publicis Consultants
Interpublic (US): Golin Harris, Weber Shandwick, MWW Group, Rogers & Cowan
Havas (France): Euro RSCG, Maitland, Cake Group
Chime (UK): Bell Pottinger Companies, Good Relations, Ozone, Resonate, Harvard, Insight Marketing, De facto and Baxter Hulme
Huntsworth (UK): Citigate, Grayling, Red, Huntsworth Health
Photon (Australia): Frank, Hotwire, Skywrite Communications, CPR
Creston (UK): Nelson Bostock, Red Door Communications
Next Fifteen (UK): Text 100, Bite Communications, Lexis PR, Inferno

Source: PR Week Top 150 Consultancies, 23rd April 2010

The regular purchase of PR firms is testimony to the indispensable role of PR within marketing services, while the retention by most conglomerates of a range of PR brand names – instead of attempting any major rationalisation – points to the perceived value of these well-established names. However it also indicates the ongoing problem which the groups have with what clients perceive as conflicts of interest. By maintaining several PR brand names it is easier to serve several competing clients under one roof.

In reality the amount of work shared by different companies within the conglomerates is limited. Clients often prefer to pick specialist services from different conglomerates, or from smaller suppliers outside the big groups. Internal rivalries within the big corporate purchasers of marketing services mean that people controlling different fiefdoms may want independent advice. Nor is the volume of international business as great as might have been hoped, although it is undoubtedly growing as markets become more global: advertising may lend itself more readily to cross-border campaigns, but the subtleties of PR cannot be exported so readily. International PR campaigns seem to be one of those glamorous aspects of the business which the industry likes to dwell upon longingly, notwithstanding the patchiness of the business. Every year a spokesperson for one of the groups is sure to say; '*This year* integration and cross border briefs are really taking off.' But while there is growth the truth is less dramatic. None the less, some companies such as Ketchum offer their staff the opportunity to apply for an overseas posting once they have been with the company for a certain time.

As we have seen, statistics and anecdotal evidence suggest that the great majority of the myriad of PR agencies employ at most a handful of people, operating within informal networks where extra assistance can be hired as required. They in turn service a handful of clients. The fortunate few among these firms may scale the heights of the industry, sometimes very quickly, perhaps undertaking some acquisitions or undergoing some mergers along the way (see the boxed case histories of Hill & Knowlton in Chapter 1 and GCI in this chapter). Overall the centre of gravity of the PR consultancy sector as defined by staff numbers is a level or two higher than a cottage industry – consultancies with more than a handful of staff but not many more.

When someone in PR talks about the consultancy industry they are usually talking about their small bit of it. This has an impact on discussions about the PR industry, particularly as some prominent spokespeople for the industry represent their own small firms rather than the major international players. In the absence of solid research, PR people – however distinguished or well-connected – offer views and information based on their experience and what they can glean from friends and colleagues. As a result they can usually examine only one or two square centimetres of the PR painting. Even the consultancy trade bodies represent only a minority of businesses operating in the industry. Writers for the trade press, such as PR Week, are among the few who have a clearer overview of the industry.

GCI UK to Europe

Adrian Wheeler, former Chairman of GCI Europe

Sterling PR, which became GCI in 1990, was typical of a dozen or so public relations companies which started up in the UK in the seventies and were lucky enough to be in the right place, doing the right thing, at the right time. In 1970, the UK PR consultancy business was embryonic, earning £20 million a year. It grew rapidly during the eighties and nineties – pausing for recessions – and is now estimated to be worth over £1 billion.

Sterling was set up in 1976 by two partners who shared three clients, two employees and two rooms in a central London mansion block. It was born on a damp November day when the owner of the consultancy where both John Brill and I worked called us into his office and announced his intention of retiring. To our astonishment, he meant there and then. We decided to call it 'Sterling' because we wanted our future employees to feel it was their company as much as ours; this principle did not, however, apply to the equity.

Our first step was to buy two tickets to New York on our American Express cards. We had the idea that US companies would want professional PR help when they were expanding into Europe via London. We thought this was an original insight. The trip paid off. We returned with our fourth client – The Federation of American-Controlled Shipping – and frequent visits to see them gave us the chance to build a substantial book of US business over the next five years.

I would like to say that we had a grand plan for the company, but we didn't. We just loved the PR business; there were no rules, everyone was making it up as they went along, and we were having much more fun than anyone else except The Rolling Stones. The best thing was that PR was producing terrific results. Clients were excited and told their friends. To us, it didn't seem like work; we often carried on right through the night. That seemed like fun, too.

On our tenth birthday in 1986 we took stock. Sterling had 30 staff, £3m in revenue and a top-flight client list: Philips – who paid us a million a year; the Jamaica Tourist Board; Food & Wine From France; Richard Ellis; Stewart Wrightson, at that time the largest insurance-broker in the UK; chemical giants ICI and Ciba-Geigy; and fourteen others. Our competitors – Shandwick, Paragon, Countrywide, QBO and the US agencies – were well-financed, while Sterling was still run with an overdraft secured on my house and John's house. We considered acquiring, merging and selling. During the year, we held meetings with 60 potential acquirees, merger-partners and acquirers.

We chose Grey Communications Group for three reasons: they knew nothing about PR, so we would remain autonomous. They believed in 'singularity of brand', so we would be the only Grey Group PR firm. They also offered us the best price for our shares.

With Grey's backing we were able to grow twice as quickly. During the nineties, we continued putting on 10–15 per cent a year organically, but we could now make acquisitions. Our first was MacAvoy Bailey, a City and public affairs consultancy. My partner, John, left the firm shortly after our earn-out finished in 1990, as did Claire Walker – to found Firefly.

In 1995, we started GCI Healthcare as a parallel brand, and in the same year began negotiating with Rupert Ashe, the owner of Focus Communications – our City affiliate – to acquire his company. Before 2000 we had acquired Lay & Partners, sports sponsorship specialists; Jane Howard Public Relations, a retail and FMCG (fast moving consumer goods) boutique; Maureen Cropper Communications, who specialised in OTC (over the counter) healthcare; and Delaney Communications, who concentrated on retail financial services. In 2001, GCI UK was the seventh-largest PR firm in the UK.

In 1994, Grey decided to extend the GCI brand in Europe, and GCI UK was closely ➡

involved in making acquisitions and opening offices as fast as we could go.

In 2004, Grey was bought by Sir Martin Sorrell's WPP group, a move which saw GCI join the WPP stable of major international PR groups. Today GCI have offices or affiliates in most parts of the world.

Public relations has no barriers to entry. Anyone with the wit, a bit of experience and the nerve can set up their own consultancy. Every year, many do just this; one in three stays the course and one in five does well enough to mount a serious challenge to the larger firms, like GCI. There are few other business service sectors where clients can choose between so many suppliers, large and small, or where the competitive landscape changes so continuously. This is good for clients, and good for PR.

In many ways, GCI's story exemplifies the history of the PR consultancy business.

PR consultancies continue to flourish because they can bring a freshness of perspective which an in-house team cannot, caught up as it is in the web of office politics and corporate culture which characterise any organisation. Consultancies can be more objective and, it is claimed, be better able to understand the world as the client's intended target audiences see it. It is no accident that PR consultancies are increasingly brought in to create and run high-profile one-off campaigns, leaving more run-of-the-mill reactive media relations work to in-house teams. Freshness of approach does not mean absence of knowledge: by definition an external consultancy can have a range of up-to-the-minute experience derived from working for related business areas, and even competitors, in a way that an in-house team cannot.

A consultancy can also leverage its client base: if it is working for two or more organisations which are not in competition and yet have some cross-over points in the popular imagination it is ideally placed to undertake mutually advantageous PR activity. Big players in the PR consultancy field can also acquire contacts and influence over the media which it would be hard for any in-house team to rival. This is true of some of the biggest financial firms. At the other end of the scale it is true of celebrity and entertainment PR firms. The media know, even if they do not like to admit it, that to please some top ranking financial consultancies such as Brunswick opens the door to more tip-offs and exclusives, whereas to offend them is potentially to be starved of the same. If you only represent one firm you only have one card to play.

Finally, consultancies can contribute expertise which it may not be possible or cost-effective to retain in-house: this may be the opportunity to meet and consult a particular PR guru; to enable an overseas company to acquire a local media handling capability; to use specific specialist skills; or simply provide extra pairs of hands to meet occasional needs.

IN-HOUSE PR

Despite its high profile the CIPR's research[3] estimates that in the UK the consultancy sector only accounts for around 18% of all PR people. The remaining 82%

work in-house, directly employed by the organisations they serve. In-house PR departments – often operating under the guise of 'corporate communications' or 'communications' or other titles – are now ubiquitous in all but the smallest organisations, throughout the private, public and voluntary sectors. Even in the US, birthplace of modern PR, senior figures in the consultancy sector can recall working with sizeable companies which lacked any PR capability of their own, and relied on PR consultancies for all aspects of their public relations. This is now rare. Organisations which once outsourced all their PR realise that routine work can be achieved more cost-effectively in-house: a consultancy after all aims to recover much more than its consultants' salaries when it hires them out, as it seeks to cover overheads (the cost of office space, equipment, insurance and non-fee earning staff such as receptionists), *and* achieve a profit margin for its shareholders. As in-house PR has grown it has also achieved the critical mass required to undertake more complex PR tasks on its own, and organisations using in-house PR enjoy the advantage of readier physical access: non-PR and PR staff can work together.

Just as the job titles of in-house PR practitioners vary, so do the size and role of their departments. It is harder to generalise about the in-house sector than the world of PR consultancy because the former is even more atomised – few organisations employ as many communications or PR professionals directly as the big PR consultancies. Thus, despite more PR people working in-house than in the consultancy sector, they are in even less of a position to have an overview of in-house PR, let alone public relations in general.

In-house PR is afflicted by a paradox – a paradox which also affects consultancies. While most business leaders concede that PR is important, no-one has been able to quantify its importance convincingly – and certainly not to demonstrate its financial value (although attempts have been, and continue to be, made – see pp. 224–233). As a result there is no real business rationale for determining the size of in-house PR departments or their budgets. Instead these tend to be the product of informal processes which are to a large extent dependent on the ambition and personal influence of senior PR people. Past experience may be taken into account, alongside the size of rival organisations' PR departments – or the PR budget may be based on a percentage of the organisation's overall spending on marketing communications.

The inability of in-house PR departments to justify their existence with robust financial figures does not necessarily mean that they, or the people who run them, lack power. Typically a large in-house PR team will include a communications or corporate affairs director. They play the role of courtiers: seldom on the main board of the company, they do however usually enjoy extensive access to their chief executives – to whom they typically report – as well as exclusive control of media relations. Their real influence hinges on their relationship with the CEO – and other key figures in the organisation – and the extent to which their advice is respected.[4] Their duties consist of communicating and trying to manage the overall reputation of the company and its standing in the outside world. This is something that matters enormously to all CEOs, who know that their careers may be only one damaging news story away from oblivion, and that even the most powerful organisations can see their fortunes change suddenly and are surprisingly vulnerable to hostile comment or the emergence of harmful information. CEOs seldom have the skills, experience or confidence – or indeed the time – to deal with such difficulties on their own. Other senior figures in the company may run large departments, control massive budgets, and have their own power bases, but senior in-house PR people are essentially creatures of the CEO, with whom they often stand or fall. Unlike other members of the senior management team they are unlikely to become CEOs themselves, and so do not pose a direct threat to the status quo. They can be compared to the palace eunuchs of history: well-placed, well-informed confidants who play a vital role behind the scenes without personally challenging the organisation's succession strategy.

It is arguable that as CEOs confront an ever more complex business environment – particularly the real or potential challenges of regulation – the role of adept in-house PR chiefs will grow in importance. Overall the balance of power has shifted in favour of in-house PR: both the numbers and the quality of the personnel have improved. Indeed, a move in-house can be seen as a good career move for senior consultancy staff who are put off by the managerialism of big consultancies and are not in the fortunate position of having their own businesses to sell.

Nonetheless turf wars between corporate affairs directors and marketing directors are common. Their relative power will depend on the nature of the business, their personalities and their degree of access to the rest of the senior management team. In the past much of a marketing director's power derived from the fact that they 'owned' the advertising budget (a sum that did – and still does for some organisations – run into many millions of dollars/pounds). In budgetary terms the corporate affairs director was the poor relation. However the fragmentation of media spend and the rise in the importance of public relations has led to a gradual shift in the centre of gravity towards PR, though tensions between the two persist. Some – though not many – businesses have overcome this problem by combining the two roles.

In the past corporate PR practitioners – be they in-house or consultancy – would nearly always answer to the head of corporate communications whilst their consumer PR counterparts would answer to the vice president or director of marketing. While this practice still persists there has been a recent trend to take a more holistic or 'joined-up' view of communications, reflecting the need to

integrate lobbying and corporate social responsibility into mainstream marketing programmes.

One problem with the merger of marketing and corporate roles is that the
pursuit of profit does not always sit comfortably with the pursuit of an excellent
reputation. The marketing department may want to increase sales of an alcoholic drink which is particularly popular with young people, while the corporate
PR people want to convince regulators and lobbyists that their organisation has
a social conscience and fosters responsible drinking. It can be difficult to satisfy
the media's – and consumers' – contradictory demands for easy availability and
low prices and 'responsible' social behaviour. Not surprisingly PR people sometimes tie themselves in knots and can appear disingenuous as they try to explain
themselves.

Other areas of conflict include internal or employee communications,
which human resources departments like to hold on to; and financial PR, which
some financial directors think they need to control. This is a circular argument.
Communication is so important you need a specialist to do it, but financial relations and employee relations are so important that you need a specialist to do
them too. Ultimately where the specialist sits is an issue only of interest to those
playing corporate musical chairs!

One of the major advantages of working in-house rather than in a consultancy is that although you only have one client – the organisation which
employs you – you are more likely to be involved in all aspects of its PR activity. If there is a political or regulatory issue, a crisis, a new product launch,

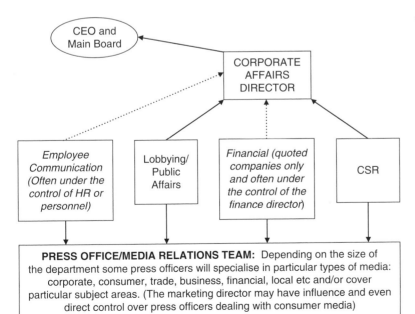

Figure 3.2 *A simplified
diagram of a large in-house
'public relations'
department*

an internal communication need or a financial drama such as a takeover, the in-house PR department will be involved. Working in-house also gives you the opportunity to get to know an organisation and an industry in depth and take pride in its successes. The PR consultant misses out on many of these things, though they may take pride and pleasure in the success of the consultancy they work for.

The downsides of working in-house include the following:

- Lack of variety, in terms of working only for one instead of several organisations;
- In-house teams are often small, so you have fewer people to learn from than in a consultancy (and consultancy work – by definition – involves rubbing shoulders more with the outside world);
- Consultancies are often hired to do the exciting or 'sexy' work leaving the in-house people to field dull or difficult calls from the media and massage the egos of the management team;
- In the consultancy sector there is a real possibility of a PR person becoming their own boss, and creating and ultimately selling a valuable business – something to which in-house PR people cannot aspire; and
- A perception that in-house jobs can lack the glamour of consultancies, whose offices are usually in fashionable (and expensive) city centres rather than out of town or in suburban business parks. It is no accident that PR consultancies tend to feature more than in-house PR in glamorous dramas!

The reality is there are good and bad consultancy and in-house jobs. Some love the variety and fast pace of consultancy work. Others prefer the more rooted and often more rounded work that is offered by in-house positions.

Having looked at the two main employment categories of PR – consultancy and in-house – we will now examine the three main sectors: commercial, public and not-for-profit (sometimes called the third sector).

COMMERCIAL PR

Commercial PR can be defined as PR undertaken for a profit-making organisation. It can be conducted in-house or by a consultancy. As the quest for profitability lies at the heart of such organisations, supporting the marketing and sales function often forms the lion's share of their PR activity.

Commercial organisations range from suppliers of fashion-driven consumer goods through to financial services such as pensions and savings, and on to major chemical and engineering companies. Almost every type of modern business will have some kind of PR function.

In addition to targeting customers and consumers (and remember, many organisations' customers are in fact other businesses or even government and public bodies) commercial PR will usually involve targeting trade media in order to impress suppliers and attract quality staff – as well as sometimes helping senior individuals build their industry profile with a view to improving their future job prospects!

As we will see in more detail in Chapter 6, in reality commercial organisations have a whole range of other audiences with which their PR teams are involved in communicating, ranging from suppliers and staff to investors, local communities and government and regulatory bodies.

If the commercial organisation is a public company (i.e. its shares are traded on the stock market) the need to deal with the financial media and other specialist financial audiences such as analysts and bankers is high on the list of PR priorities. However this area of PR is commonly undertaken by specialist financial PR consultancies as few organisations are large enough to employ a skilled team of financial PRs full-time (see pp. 82–83).

PUBLIC SECTOR PR

The public sector includes all publicly owned and funded bodies such as government departments, hospitals, educational institutions and regulators. Public sector PR used to be regarded as something of a Cinderella within the PR industry – poorly paid and dull. Both accusations are no longer true.

Today the public sector is fairly competitive with the commercial sector. When benefits such as pensions, training and holiday entitlement are taken into account, it is often as good if not better.

One way of looking at the difference between the commercial and public sector – albeit slightly simplistic – is shown below.

Table 3.2 Commercial and public sector PR objectives

Commercial sector	Public sector
Influencing consumer behaviour – BUY THIS	Influencing social behaviour – TRY (DO) THIS
Campaigns ultimately judged on contribution to sales profit.	Campaigns ultimately judged on contribution to behaviour change (Stop smoking, pay car tax).

Note: With thanks to Kindred Communications

Sometimes, unencumbered by the need to sell a product or service, public sector PR can be more acceptable to the media, hence allowing greater scope for creativity and making it, at least in theory, more interesting. For examples, please refer to Table 3.3.

   In reality, clever commercial organisations often use the same sort of 'social good' messages as the public sector to engage the media and their customers, but nonetheless public sector PR is generally focused on social benefits rather than business benefits. For some this is an attractive aspect of working in the sector. However, PR people who have left the public sector complain of political interference, a lack of focus on tangible outcomes, and moribund management systems – so the picture is not all rosy.

   As with commercial PR there are in fact a variety of other audiences that public sector PR may need to focus on as is shown in Figure 3.3.

Table 3.3   Commercial and public sector PR messages

Sector	Commercial message	Public sector message
Sport	Buy our shoes	Exercise helps you lose weight
Health	Buy our headache cure	Use your pharmacy for minor ailments
Transport	Buy our car	Drive safely
Finance	Buy our pension	Pay your tax on time

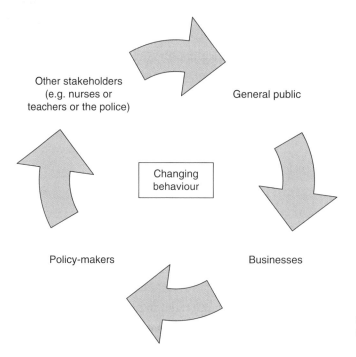

Other stakeholders
(e.g. nurses or
teachers or the police)

General public

Changing
behaviour

Policy-makers

Businesses

Figure 3.3   *Public sector campaign audiences*

Adapting Marcoms to the public sector

Chris MacLeod, Director of Group Marketing,
Transport for London

It is tempting to say that the principles of Marketing and PR in the public sector should be no different to those in any other sector. They are the requirement to have clear, ideally quantified objectives; a well-defined target audience; an insight-based strategy; and established ways of measuring success.

The reality, as in the private sector, is often somewhat different. The issues to be understood are frequently complex and difficult to reduce to simple messages. People don't like being told what to do and there is a challenge to overcome apathy. So the principles don't change: they just need to be worked at harder.

The stakeholder context is also particularly complex and many tasks fall into the so-called wicked issue category; that is social problems made almost impossible to resolve because of contradictory but inter-related features (think of alcohol misuse or recycling). And small incidents can quickly spiral onto the front page, accelerated by the developments in digital media.

Finally it is important to demonstrate value in your communications; again no real difference to the private sector but with longer term, more complex outcomes, you may need to work hard to demonstrate returns.

So in summary, public sector communicators need to build on the basic principals of good communication, recognise the complex stakeholder environment and aim to demonstrate value for money and 'payback'.

NOT-FOR-PROFIT/THIRD-SECTOR PR

Most people associate PR with the world of business, and are also familiar with its use in politics. However, they are less familiar with its – massive – use by the third-sector – not-for-profit organisations, non-governmental organisations (NGOs), charities, campaigning organisations, think tanks and religious bodies. This is partly because the third sector is another realm which carefully avoids the term 'PR' to describe what it does. It means that many outsiders who criticise PR completely overlook the activities of such organisations. The sector includes all charities and NGOs – everything from the local church, or dogs' home, through to Greenpeace and Oxfam.

Although there have always been charities, and examples of campaigning organisations can be found throughout history, the number of such organisations has grown phenomenally in recent decades. According to one estimate, fewer than a thousand such organisations were operating internationally in the late 1950s, but today there are more than 48,000 of them. According to another estimate they employ nearly 20 million people globally (quite apart from huge amounts of volunteer time) and enjoy an annual income of well over $1,000 billion.[5] Although many such organisation are small and obscure, they increasingly follow the pattern of the corporate sector, with a range of powerful, well-known global superbrands such as Greenpeace, Friends of the Earth, the World Wildlife Fund (WWF) and Amnesty International.

Despite their growing importance, such organisations are seldom identified with PR, but in reality they deploy an enormous amount of PR muscle power – even if they call it campaigning or something else – and are heavily engaged in media relations and lobbying. Unlike commercial organisations which have to produce goods or deliver services, campaigning NGOs can concentrate all their energies on PR, including high-profile publicity stunts – some of which break the law – of a kind of which commercial PR people can only dream. This means that NGOs offer good career opportunities for PR people. There is even a niche career path for seasoned NGO campaigners who go on to sell their skills and experience to private sector organisations which are being troubled by NGO activism. It also means that commercial and governmental PR people need to be well aware of the PR work of NGOs as they are usually at the receiving end of their criticisms and are likely to spend increasing proportions of their working lives dealing with them. Indeed, as the media's resources become increasingly stretched, NGO research and activism often pose a greater threat to business and politics than that endangered species, investigative journalism.

Some NGOs focus on offering real services, such as kennelling for aban-doned dogs, and largely avoid political campaigning. Some, such as Oxfam, not only provide services on the ground – such as help to victims of famine – but also campaign for political and social change. And some, such as Greenpeace, offer no services – other than, some would say, a good conscience to their donors and supporters – but spend all their energies trying to get other organisations such as governments to behave differently.

Not-for-profit PR has many of the characteristics of both public sector and commercial PR. On the one hand there is a need to attract members, donations and grants to finance and support their activities. On the other hand there is a need to achieve the objectives of the organisation. These usually include a desire to influence behaviour, be it to get a government to ban whaling, or to get people to show respect for those with mental disabilities.

NGO public relations starts with an in-built advantage: trust. Although the position can vary in different countries, this means that whatever they say is more likely to be believed and respected. Trust and sympathy – arising from their perceived altruism, in contrast to the profit-seeking nature of business – help NGOs secure large amounts of positive media coverage, and undertake the kind of publicity stunts which would be unthinkable for business. They are much less likely to suffer from negative media coverage.

The disadvantage of working in the not-for-profit sector is that it is usually not very well paid – though the NGO sector is now so large that there is a whole career structure and some serious competition to hire the best communicators. The main advantage, according to many in the sector, is that you can work on something you are passionate about, even if compromises on matters of detail are inevitable. (Although, as we have seen, there is an argument that people

Whom do you trust?

The weight people attach to the information and opinion they read and hear varies enormously according to its source. Depending on which country you are from you will attach different levels of credibility to different sources – this is dependent on a whole raft of factors which are specific to the culture concerned – and your view will also alter as circumstances change (for example the election of new government, or in response to business scandals or the financial crisis). Perceived levels of trust have huge implications for PR practitioners: some start with an inbuilt advantage (which they must not take for granted), while for others there is a challenge to surmount.

Edelman, a large international PR firm, conducts an annual survey of trust among opinion leaders in different countries.

NGOs regularly feature as the most trusted category of institution in many countries, including the USA, UK, Germany and France.

Interestingly, trust in NGOs has surged ahead in China, which Edelman speculates may be due to growing affluence and demands for environmental responsibility and public health (and possibly, one might add, to growing scepticism about government in the wake of its patchy role in recent crises).

Edelman's most recent survey shows some recovery in trust in business but, for example, CEOs still rank in the bottom two in the list of trusted spokespeople in the US and Germany. Within the business world there are significant differences, with technology the most trusted sector, and banks – unsurprisingly at present – in a much weaker position. Trust in government is generally stable, but has improved in the USA and deteriorated in Russia.

Edelman's survey also shows a waning of trust in traditional print and broadcast media, although reports from industry analysts and press articles remain the most credible sources of information about a company.

www.edelman.com/trust/2010/

who are passionate about a subject sometimes lack the empathy necessary to understand, and therefore persuade, those who are neutral or uninterested. As a result they end up 'preaching to the converted'.)

Another advantage of working in the not-for-profit sector is that you can take bigger risks – even break the law. As we have mentioned, the media and indeed much of the public tend to be tolerant of the behaviour of NGOs even when they do not entirely share their views. This is not really surprising. Business organisations are about making money. Public sector organisations are about exercising power or telling us what to do. The not-for-profit sector seems – uniquely – to be about idealism and doing good. Consequently, when Greenpeace illegally climb on a building to protest against climate change, or trespass on a private farm to oppose genetically modified food trials, they achieve considerable, largely uncritical, media coverage and often only a gentle ticking-off from the authorities. A commercial or public sector organisation breaking the law to secure publicity would not only provoke massive negative media coverage but face the full weight of the law.

NGOs such as Greenpeace and PETA are highly effective PR operations which know how to grab the attention of the media. Even a spell of work experience with such an organisation could make an impressive mark on an otherwise dull or undifferentiated CV.

The commercial sector has had to develop a response to NGO campaigning. One tactic has been to set up and fund organisations which can research and debate contentious issues, such as those relating to the consumption of alcohol or the environment. If these organisations are at arms length from the companies concerned they can be seen as more independent and therefore more authoritative – and sometimes their views are reported in this way by the media. However opponents often deride such organisations as mere 'front groups' for their corporate paymasters (see pp. 55–56). Another common technique has been to engage in dialogue with NGOs and to make – or appear to make – limited concessions, thereby appeasing the NGO concerned. This helps pull the debate on to more moderate ground and away from extreme positions. Those opponents who remain hostile can be depicted as an unrealistic, extremist minority and contrasted with moderate opponents. This need to placate campaigning NGOs is one of the driving forces behind corporate social responsibility (CSR) – see Chapter 8. Moreover campaigning NGOs can put governments, regulatory authorities and international bodies under considerable pressure to act to curb the activities of business. Pre-emptive action on the part of business can be used by government to demonstrate that the required remedial steps have been or are being taken, thereby reducing the pressure upon government to take action itself (which it is often reluctant to do).

But a final word of warning. The fact that people want to do good, or believe they are doing good, does not mean they are good, or that their sometimes dubious means are justified by the ends they seek. There are egos, self-delusion, politics, envy and greed in all walks of life including the not-for-profit sector.

The three ways NGOs succeed at PR

Robert Blood, founder and CEO of SIGWatch,
the global NGO tracking and issues analysis consultancy

- NGOs have totally integrated PR into the operation of their 'businesses'. For them, PR is not an add-on, it's fundamental to how they achieve their goals. NGOs are in the business of persuading the public and decision makers to buy into their ideas and beliefs. All they have is communications and everything they do, from media briefings to direct actions to stunts, are acts of communication. NGOs' medium and the message really are the same.
- NGOs understand that communications is not a process, it is a tool for generating change. Effective NGOs plan campaigns from the end – 'What has to happen to show that we have been effective?' and work back to 'What do we have to say and do to make this happen'. And because their campaigning is totally goal-oriented, the measures of PR effectiveness are built-in and transparent – if it works, it works.
- NGOs think politically. NGOs are intrinsically weak – unlike businesses or politicians or trade unions, they have no levers of power of their own, they must rely on influence and persuasion to make those with power act for them. Consequently NGOs are adept at working out who has the power and what they need to do to persuade – or force – them to use it to their ends: making a politician twist the arm of an industry regulator, or embarrassing a multinational into changing its purchasing policy to stop a foreign supplier harming the environment.

www.sigwatch.com

1 Discuss and write down the positives and negatives there might be in working in-house and in consultancy. Relate them to real-life examples, using either personal knowledge or research.

2 Use the chart below to record what the skills, knowledge and attributes are that might be needed for working in the 3 different sectors we have looked at? (Don't worry if there is some duplication.)

Table 3.4 Sectoral talent mix

	Skills	Knowledge	Personal attributes
Commercial sector			
Public sector			
Not-for-profit sector			

PR SPECIALISMS

As PR has spread itself across all areas of economic, political and social life a large number of different PR specialisms have emerged, above and beyond the three broad sectors outlined above. Indeed one of the characteristics of PR is the way in which it tends to specialise, both in terms of the careers of in-house staff and the consultancy sector. First there are *sector specialists* who tackle specific areas of largely commercial PR work – from food, fashion and travel through to healthcare and technology. Even large generalist PR agencies often have specialist divisions covering many of these sectors, and not infrequently give such divisions separate corporate names and identities as subsidiaries to highlight the special expertise they offer. In contrast to PR, large advertising agencies tend to cover most if not all business sectors under one roof.

Second there are *PR skill specialists* who do not service business sectors as such, but seek to meet generic industry needs. They include lobbyists, financial PR experts and media evaluation companies.

While some career movement within the PR industry is possible, these specialisms require different skills, interests and temperaments. The people who work in them are often very different from people in other specialist fields. Although neighbouring specialisms can overlap, it would, for example, be unusual – to put it mildly – for people who are settled in their careers to move between celebrity and financial PR, or between travel PR and lobbying (and it is also rather unlikely that many people would want to do so).

Corporate PR

The most basic division in commercial PR work is one we have already come across – between corporate and consumer PR (see p. 72). The former, sometimes called corporate communications or corporate affairs (the term 'PR' is normally dropped), concerns itself with a company or organisation's reputation and its relationship with its stakeholders, while the latter (see below) is about support- ing marketing objectives – with the focus on one stakeholder, the existing or potential customer.

Most big PR consultancies subdivide themselves along these lines. In-house, corporate PR is normally undertaken by a senior person who can have various titles – Director of Communications or Corporate Affairs for example – and is backed up by a small group of helpers. The nature of Corporate PR means that it often involves working closely with financial PR specialists and lobbyists (see below).

Corporate howlers and PR headaches

In a speech to Britain's Institute of Directors Gerald Ratner, then head of the leading UK high street jewellers Ratner's, joked that his shops 'sold a pair of earrings for under a pound, which is cheaper than a prawn sandwich from Marks & Spencer, but probably wouldn't last as long' while explaining that the reason one of the store's popular products was so cheap was because it was 'total crap'. Predictably this attracted instant media coverage and wiped an estimated £500 million off the value of the business. He later left the company which was subsequently rebranded.

EMI's chief executive caused offence in Finland when he explained that he was cutting the artist roster from 49 because he did not think that there were that many people in the country 'who could sing'.

Menswear retailer Topman's brand chief did something similar when in an interview he described the company's target customers as 'Hooligans or whatever'. He continued 'Very few of our customers have to wear suits to work...They'll be for his first interview or first court case.'[6]

Financial PR

Financial PR (sometimes called City PR in the UK because of its association with the City of London, Britain's financial centre) employs the most highly paid con- sultants in the business and can be hugely important, contributing to the making and breaking of companies. It is also one of the most secretive and least known PR specialisms.

Financial PR derives its importance from the decisive role a company's reputation plays in determining its share price. Media reports can quickly push the price up or down, with all-important consequences for the careers of senior executives. Typically the target audiences for financial PR are limited: they are the small number of financial analysts and others in the fund management field who determine whether large volumes of a company's shares are to be bought or sold.

PR always needs careful consideration when a company announces its finan- cial results, but really comes to the fore at times of change or crisis: mergers, acquisitions, and corporate difficulties. Undertaking PR in such circumstances can be likened to serving in an army in war time. Long periods of calm or even boredom are interspersed with sudden bursts of frenetic and high risk activity.

At such moments financial PR firms often receive massive fees for the extensive, round-the-clock work that is required. Hostile takeovers of companies are one area of commercial PR which can become personal and negative, as companies and their leaders seek to disparage each other. More generally, and to a much greater extent than most other forms of PR, financial PR is about playing down, within legal limits, news which companies do not wish to emerge. One way of achieving this is to employ large and powerful financial PR consultancies that have some bargaining power with the financial media.

The most relevant media for financial PR are specialist business publications such as *The Financial Times* and *The Wall Street Journal*, the business sections of the mainstream media and electronic business news services such as those offered by Bloomberg and Reuters. Significantly, specialist business media are much more international in reach than most other media – something with which financial PR has to keep pace. As in other areas of PR, journalistic expertise – in this case, that of financial journalists – is bought in, but in general a good understanding of finance and how the financial markets operate is fundamental to successful financial PR.

Financial PR work is concentrated in the big financial marketplaces, such as New York, London and Frankfurt, although increasingly such work has spread to other centres. Although in the first instance routine financial PR work can be undertaken in-house, the sheer volumes of PR work involved in major corporate battles and crises, together with the need to bring in additional expertise and PR bargaining power, mean the financial PR consultancies tend to play a big part in many critical situations. In view of the vital role of news and comment in the operation of the financial markets, financial PR has come to be more closely regulated than most other forms of PR work.

Brunswick

Brunswick is the biggest player in the UK financial PR market – and a substantial force elsewhere in the world – with its fee income estimated by PR Week to be around £50 million. Many of the biggest companies on the London stock exchange have at one time or another employed its services. Brunswick currently employs 470 people in 16 offices in 11 countries.

The founder of Brunswick, Alan Parker, is extremely well connected within the worlds of business and politics – he is said to be close to prime ministers, party leaders and chief executives – and yet ironically Brunswick, which remains a privately owned partnership, keeps a low media profile.

When the American conglomerate Kraft sought to take over the British confectioner Cadbury's it retained Brunswick to assist with the takeover (while planning to hire Edelman for other PR services after the merger). The battle made headlines which spread well beyond the business press, not least because in the UK Cadbury's was regarded as a cherished national institution. Finsbury PR, another big financial PR firm, helped Cadbury's to resist, although ultimately a takeover was agreed (see p. 120 for more on the PR implications of this takeover).

www.brunswickgroup.com
www.prweek.com

Consumer PR

As we shall see, consumer PR is about helping to sell consumer goods and is very much a branch of marketing (see Chapter 4). It is also known as business-to-consumer communications, or B2C. Typically consumer PR campaigns (and their budgets) are controlled by companies' marketing directors, and consumer PR is used alongside other marketing techniques, such as advertising and sales promotions. It can be undertaken in-house, but often consultancies are brought in to run specific campaigns. Although successful marketing is clearly fundamental to company's well-being, it is an ongoing activity to which PR normally only contributes one element, and it is therefore normally less central to the thinking of CEOs than corporate PR.

The first challenge for consumer PR people is – normally – to achieve any kind of media coverage at all for their client's product. Given the huge number of products in circulation in any modern economy, getting a particular product into the media represents a challenge which is compounded by the fact that most products are not inherently interesting from a news editor's point of view. Creativity and ingenuity is required to make the product newsworthy, while ensuring that it gets the right kind of coverage and that the message is not overshadowed or undermined by the PR. Typically this involves a combination of ingredients such as celebrity endorsement, a publicity stunt, a photo opportunity, a competition, or interesting facts and figures on consumer lifestyles.

Three key skills of a fashion PR

Julian Vogel, Director Modus Publicity / Modus Dowal Walker (Top Fashion PR firm)

LISTEN & UNDERSTAND – Ask questions – What are your client's key messages? What do they want to achieve? What do they stand for? Who is the consumer for your client's product or service – how do you reach them? What are they interested in? Where do they get their information? What do they read, watch, and listen too? Whom are they influenced by?

CULTURE VULTURE – A thirst for culture that surrounds you – fashion, beauty, film, dance, sport, art, architecture. Be interested in all things that could be associated with your client and end consumer. Create compelling and newsworthy content to help tell your clients story. Know your media and understand what your journalists want.

GATEKEEPER /PEOPLE PERSON – You are the centre of the information flow between client, press and consumer – ever professional, efficient, diplomatic. Ensure the message is delivered effectively. An ability to see the opportunity of how people or organisations could work together and create the connections.

PLAN, PLAN, PLAN & ADAPT – Ensure that everything has been planned and checked with every campaign and then be prepared to adapt and react when things change at the last minute. Keep calm under pressure.

www.moduspublicity.com

In addition to conventional consumer goods, in mature PR markets there are PR people using similar techniques for every kind of product and service.

Healthcare PR is an important specialism which can embrace everything from the use of highly specialised techniques to promote pharmaceutical products to doctors to marketing support for widely available products offering health and hygiene benefits. *Travel PR* helps to sell holidays and personal transport and accommodation for business trips. It typically does so by inviting journalists or well-known people to enjoy travel free of charge in the expectation that they will give the travel facilities favourable coverage. Other firms specialise in PR for hotels or restaurants. *Fashion PR* is an important specialism in its own right: it would be impossible to sustain the amount of international media coverage fashion receives without the availability of fashion PR people to supply content. *Music, entertainment – even celebrity – PR* are further examples of such specialisms. In all cases PR may be undertaken in-house or by consultancies. Indeed many of the bigger PR consultancies have set up specialist subsidiaries to capitalise on such opportunities. This recognises that the image and approach they offer their traditional corporate clients may not seem right for markets such as these.

Why PR sector specialists exist

There are several reasons why specialist PR firms focusing on particular sectors exist – and why other sectors, although economically very significant, are served by generalist PR consultancies.

- *Regulation.* In some sectors – healthcare PR being a prime example – regulation is a major issue and specialist knowledge is vital. Healthcare PR people, often working for pharmaceutical companies, have to abide by important restrictions when they communicate. For example, in the United Kingdom, prescription drugs cannot be directly promoted to the public. A generalist PR person could not be expected to be familiar with such regulations and hence would run the risk of infringing them, with embarrassing or even costly consequences.
- *Technical complexity.* Sometimes specialist knowledge of the product area is required. A generalist PR person might be uncomfortable talking about the properties of new pharmaceutical treatments with doctors, while in the early days of the IT revolution specialist knowledge was required to understand and then interpret the technical information and jargon, and specialist IT firms blossomed. The position can change. Now most mainstream PR people can do high tech PR.
- *Dedicated sector media.* In some cases the existence of specialist PR firms is a response to dedicated sector media. Some sectors are covered by specialist

magazines, newspaper supplements, or programmes on the national and regional media (often funded by related advertising), and dedicated journalists. For example, IT public relations was partly a response to the growth of the computer press – although this has now shrunk. Fashion and travel PR exist as separate specialisms in part because there are high volumes of dedicated media coverage. The relationship between PRs and journalists in such areas means that there is a high level of movement within the sector, usually from journalism to PR, due to higher PR salaries.

- *The dominance of individual personalities.* In several of the sectors serviced by PR sectoral specialists individual personalities play a major role – fashion designers, chefs, musicians, artists and cultural and social figures of all kinds. Such people are often celebrities, or wish to be. They lend themselves to smaller scale, more personal PR, often carried out by PR's own personalities.
- *Size of business.* Small businesses tend naturally to hire small PR consultancies, and indeed large consultancies might be disdainful about the fees on offer. Many of the sectors associated with specialist PR – fashion, restaurants, entertainment – are characterised by a large range of small or medium-sized businesses which can neither afford to maintain strong in-house PR departments nor to hire large mainstream consultancies.

The existence of sector specialists in PR is normally underpinned by one or more of the above factors. Part of the success of the PR industry can be attributed to its flexibility and its ability to adjust to changing needs. The start-up costs for PR firms are low, and PR's dependence on personal qualities rather than formal qualifications means that clients can easily follow a favourite PR person on the move from a mega-consultancy to a start-up firm. They can even help favoured journalists launch PR careers. It is also noteworthy that some of these specialisations involve the kind of 'glamorous' work which attracts people in PR in the first place, and that, for example, people who work in fashion or music PR are very different – and have very different interests – from those who work in financial or political PR: there is little if any cross-over.

This argument can be tested by considering some other areas of PR activity. Personal financial services PR covers products such as mortgages, insurance and pensions (as opposed to financial PR which is related to mergers and acquisitions and share prices). Although it operates in a highly regulated market, can be seen as technically quite complicated and enjoys dedicated media coverage, it has not spawned many specialist firms. As with high tech PR this is partly because personal financial services have become more mainstream and familiar. Another factor is that most financial services firms are large enough to employ in-house PR people, only using consultancies for brand building or to cope with peaks in their workload. Finally, such firms are not closely associated with dominant personalities. For similar reasons the automotive industry, despite its size and importance, has generated few specialist PR 'shops' or firms. Indeed major industries such as the utilities, transport, and communications, despite their size and wealth, have little in the way of dedicated media and consequently few specialist PR firms serve them.

BUSINESS-TO-BUSINESS PR

Business-to-business (B2B) PR may be lower profile than consumer PR but is very important. It is about businesses communicating with each other – for example, raw material and component suppliers communicating with manufacturers, and manufacturers communicating with wholesalers and retailers (and vice versa). Much of this communication takes place through the specialist business press – such as trade magazines – although the business and specialist sections and programmes of the media, as well as online media, can also be used.

DIGITAL PR

Digital PR is about the use of new media, especially the internet, to further PR objectives. In this sense it is distinct from other PR specialisms: it is not about a particular sector – digital PR can be used in all arenas; and although in its focus on one sector of the media it involves a particular skill set it is unlike other forms of public relations. (PR work has traditionally spanned all available media. Although the balance might shift according to circumstances, PR has exploited every outlet and no-one really thinks of TV- or newspaper-specific public relations work.)

PR's response to the rapid rise and general availability of new media from the 1990s onwards has been different to the way it reacted to earlier changes in the media, such as the rise of broadcasting. This time it has created a new specialism. Now most PR consultancies of any size have specialist digital PR divisions; there are specialist agencies which focus on digital media; and in-house PR teams have often expanded to accommodate online specialists. For more on Digital PR, see Chapter 7.

What it takes to be a publicist

Mark Borkowski, Head of Borkowski.do and author of *The Fame Formula*

To be a publicist requires three core necessities, if one is to survive the game. First up, one needs passion. Being a publicist is a vocation. I firmly believe some people are born with the 'stuff' and that it can be hard to impose, through rigorous training, the skills necessary to create a true publicist. With passion comes belief, in one's self, in one's client and in the stories one creates and seeds for the client.

Second, one needs an intense curiosity. Without passion and belief, a nascent publicist is not likely to find any curiosity at all, but if they ➡

do have the curiosity they may be able to manufacture the passion to a certain extent. An intense curiosity is essential to allow one to dig for stories and to understand the conversations that are happening around the client. With great curiosity come great ways of fitting one's clients' conversations into the rich media mix and, eventually, an understanding of both the media and the web's agendas.

Finally, and most importantly, one needs a thick skin and an ability to learn to love the word 'No!' Bear in mind that it can be hard to work one's way into a position where your clients understand you and you can make them understand the process they have to go through for you to be able to help them. With a thick skin comes the need for a sense of distance, a recognition that success can lead to addiction, and the absolute necessity that you are never bitter about clients leaving you.

Clients come and go, but passion, curiosity and a thick, thick skin will see you through – probably beyond the end of a long career.

www.borkowski.do

CELEBRITY PR

Celebrity PR has acquired a high profile and has become a popular starting point for those thinking about PR careers. Celebrities now play a central role in contemporary culture and a large and seemingly growing proportion of media content is devoted to their activities. The lion's share of this is supplied by the PR industry. Celebrity PR crosses over into other areas of PR partly because the original reason for a celebrity's fame often involves a sector covered by specialist PR – for example, music, entertainment, sport, fashion or food. In addition one of the most typical ways by which PR people seek to secure publicity for products (or indeed NGOs or even political parties) is to win celebrity endorsement together with celebrity involvement in associated PR activity. Too often this is a knee-jerk response to a PR problem: celebrities have to be carefully chosen and do not guarantee success.

As with other specialisms, celebrities can employ in-house PR people and/ or employ PR agencies – often smaller firms which specialise in such work and perhaps related areas of specialist PR. Indeed when the footballer David Beckham faced allegations (which he denied) of an extra-marital affair in 2004 it emerged that no fewer than three PR firms were responsible for his and his wife Victoria's image, while the allegations concerned a 'PR girl' who worked for another company which they had allegedly ceased to use. Much of the discussion of the case concerned the implications for the Beckhams' large range of product endorsements.[7]

However many large PR agencies are reluctant to work for celebrities. There are two main reasons. First, even if the individual celebrity is able to pay the substantial fees which such firms demand, they are often reluctant to do so: it involves parting with money from their personal earnings which feels more painful than it does for a large company which is accustomed to paying large amounts for marketing services. Second, large PR firms are accustomed to dealing with clients which are, in the main, structured, disciplined organisations which attempt to behave in logical and fairly predictable ways. Celebrities are individuals who have often achieved fame or even notoriety precisely because of their idiosyncratic behaviour and turbulent lives. If a new product causes problems it can be altered or dropped, but the scope for repackaging an individual personality is much more limited (there are parallels here with political PR – see Chapter 6). If an employee of a corporate client steps out of line they can be disciplined or sacked; if a member of a celebrity's family causes problems they cannot readily be dealt with in the same way. All of this means that celebrity PR and the handling of personalities it entails often requires a different approach and temperament.

A niche area of PR – although its exact status is disputed – has emerged in response to the growing numbers of 'wannabe' celebrities. Such people are seldom in a position to pay up-front for PR, but often their initial claim to fame is an association with one or more existing celebrities – most typically a sexual liaison. Whereas once upon a time they might have approached the media directly, increasingly they can choose to do so via PR people who are experienced in media handling and can negotiate a fee for the story and take a percentage for themselves. Although relatively few PR people make their living in this way it is a high-profile activity and is undoubtedly responsible for a significant proportion of media content. Many other PR people seek to distance themselves from such work, seeing it as distasteful. Its practitioners are often described as publicists, although that term has a wider meaning. While the rights and wrongs remain a matter of personal judgement, what is true is that the *modus operandi* of such people is significantly different from conventional PR. Normally PR people are paid by their clients or employers for media handling. In this case the 'PR' people are more akin to an entertainment industry agent in that they receive a percentage of their clients' fee, although they may also offer advice on other matters.

Max Clifford

Max Clifford is probably the most famous PR practitioner in the UK, although many PR people seek to disown him, seeing him as a publicist, not a true PR person. Clifford, unusually for the PR industry, cheerfully admits to lying on behalf of his clients:

> I stand up and say that an important part of public relations is lies and deceit. We all know that but they won't ever admit it.

An ex-journalist, Clifford set up what remains a relatively small agency in 1970. Since then he has been seen as the man behind countless newspaper headlines, particularly many in the British tabloid press which involve scandals in the private lives of UK celebrities and politicians. Such newspapers have described him as a 'PR mastermind' and the 'eminence grise of the kiss and tell market.' He specialises in celebrity clients – his most famous, internationally, include Shilpa Shetty and Simon Cowell – as well as people who want to be celebrities or just have a story to sell. When allegations of sexual scandal threatened the British footballer David Beckham in 2004 Clifford commented: 'They should have had the power to keep it out of the papers...that is half the job of a good PR.'

www.maxclifford.com

Case study: Chime plc: How the UK's largest public relations group is structured

Chime, headed by its Chairman, Lord Tim Bell, is a communications group which, at the time of writing, comprises around 50 companies. Its services span advertising, media buying, market research, design, brand development and sponsorship as well as public relations.

Chime includes numerous separate PR companies, of varying sizes, designed to address particular needs. Many bear the name Bell Pottinger, but others have distinct titles which reflect their origins and have their own brand value within the marketplace for communication services. For example Stuart Higgins Communications bears the name of its founder, a former editor of the UK's best-selling daily newspaper *The Sun*, and specialises in PR for high-profile individuals and related corporate work.

Chime's PR work exemplifies the nature of the consultancy world. There are companies with a geographical focus – covering the USA and the Middle East, for example, as well as regions of the UK. There are sectoral specialists covering health, technology, financial services, sport, and governmental or political work. There are also subsidiaries covering skills specialisms such as public affairs; corporate citizenship; change and internal communications; financial PR; issues and crisis; and even search relations designed to enhance clients' online profiles.

Big PR firms normally subdivide their offer in this kind of way which, apart from having organisational advantages and allowing their staff to specialise, enables them to offer a clear menu to clients. As with any group, some of their offerings may be more highly regarded than others. Chime is also typical in that subsidiaries are often a combination of organic growth and acquisitions of existing, independent PR firms – a process which seldom stands still for long. As new opportunities and needs emerge, new companies are created or bought. While Chime's companies can provide a full range of PR services, increasingly it works alongside its many clients' in-house PR teams, focusing on specific projects.

www.chime.plc.uk/

- Although today most PR people work in-house, that is to say they are direct employed by the organisations they serve, a significant minority work for independent PR consultancies or agencies which work for a variety of clients. In this PR is distinct from other marketing communications disciplines.
- PR people, in both the consultancy sector and employed in-house, work for every kind of organisation – for all sorts of commercial organisations, for governmental organisations of all types, and for non-governmental organisations such as charities and campaigning groups. Many such people prefer to avoid calling what they do PR, which can create confusion.
- PR firms often specialise in the needs of particular sectors, and the industry also includes skill specialists who offer particular skills, such as financial PR or lobbying, to anyone who needs them. Large PR consultancies are often structured to meet these different needs.

Think about the area of PR you would most like to work in – not just the sector, but maybe the specialism too, and whether you want to work in-house or for an agency. Now imagine you have got an interview for a dream job, one that exactly matches your wishes. The interviewer asks you to explain exactly why you are interested in the kind of PR work they are offering as opposed to all the alternatives. Explain!

Some suggestions for reading

Details of the make-up of the industry are constantly changing, so websites and the trade press are often a better bet than books. However Jackall, Robert and Hirota, Janice M., *Image Makers: Advertising, Public Relations, and the Ethos of Advocacy* (University of Chicago Press 2000) is a rather clever account of the industry and its advertising cousin, based on close observation.

PR, MARKETING AND ADVERTISING

INTRODUCTION

Marketing or consumer PR is probably the area of PR most visible to the outside world, perhaps only rivalled by the high-profile work of the much smaller tribes of political and celebrity PR people. It is estimated that 70% of people in PR are primarily concerned with marketing PR or helping sell goods and services.[1] Corporate reputation, lobbying, internal communications and corporate social responsibility may be the areas of PR on which some industry bodies – and some academics – like to focus, but the chances are that, particularly early on in your career, much of your PR work will be in support of marketing.

Typically marketing PR activity, which may be undertaken in-house and/or by consultants, is controlled not by the corporate affairs director but by the marketing director of an organisation, and is usually undertaken in conjunction with other persuasive disciplines, such as advertising and sales promotions, often under the banner of 'marcoms' (marketing communications).[2] As we have already seen, one of the problems with PR is that there is little agreement about what precisely it is, where it ends, and where other communication disciplines such as advertising, sales promotion and sponsorship begin. This is particularly true in the field of 'marketing PR'. But first let us examine what 'marketing' is.

LEARNING OBJECTIVES

- To understand what marketing is
- To examine the relationship between advertising and PR
- To examine the relationship between other marketing communications disciplines, or 'marcoms', and PR
- To understand what integrated marketing communications is
- To understand what brands are

WHAT IS MARKETING?

According to the British Chartered Institute of Marketing (CIM) marketing is 'the process responsible for identifying, anticipating and satisfying customer requirements profitably.'[3] (Although it should be noted that not-for-profit organisations also engage in what they term marketing.) This of course involves much more than PR, or indeed any other form of communication.

At the heart of marketing are the Four P's.[4] These are:

- **PRICE** – how does the price of your product compare with that of the competition? Is the market you are in price sensitive?
- **PLACE** – is your product readily available through the distribution channels preferred by your customers?
- **PRODUCT** – what does your product do? Can it be differentiated from the competition in terms of performance?
- **PROMOTION** – the 'marcoms' (marketing communication) tools, including PR, that you use to communicate the other P's, create a positive sales environment, drive sales and build brands.

 Research and analyse the four Ps for Apple Computer and for Dell computers. Compare and contrast the two. (If you like, split up into syndicates to explore this subject.)

WHAT ARE THE MARCOMS TOOLS?

Each tool has different strengths. A useful analogy is to think of them as akin to instruments in an orchestra. The job of the head of marketing is similar to that of a conductor. They need to bring in the most appropriate instruments for the marketing communications music they are seeking to play. Sometimes one instrument will predominate but usually, particularly in today's market with so much media choice and competition for consumer attention, the different marcoms instruments will all have a role to play at some point.

This list of ten tools and their main activity/benefit over and beyond sales is by no means exhaustive – for example it does not include corporate hospitality, or point of purchase – but it does cover the main areas.

In reality the instigation and management of these activities is seldom as neat as the chart implies. Despite the need, and often genuine desire, to work together there are sometimes 'turf wars' within the marketing communications industry.

But notwithstanding these differences and occasional difficulties all marketing communication has to start a campaign with a similar position analysis (this process will be described in more detail in Chapter 10):

Table 4.1 Marketing communications tools and activities

Marketing tool	Activity/benefit
Public relations	Build third-party endorsement and credibility
Advertising	Create awareness, interest and loyalty
Sales Promotion	Encourage trial and usage
Personal Selling	Persuade and negotiate
Exhibitions and Events	Develop face-to-face relationships and demonstrate products and services
Sponsorship	Build awareness aligned with complementary brands
E-Marketing (digital)	Build two-way relationships, advertise, sell
Design and packaging	Create a memorable and attractive visual identity
Product placement	Secure implied third-party endorsement by putting brands into the hands of actors and celebrities, for example in television programmes and films
Direct marketing/mail	Provide an immediate call to action – for example 'buy now and get money off'

- Whom are we targeting? What are they like?
- What are we trying to get them to think, feel or do?
- What is the market like? Is it new, mature or in decline?
- What is the competition like? What are they doing?
- What external factors might impact on us? Is the economy strong or weak? Is an election imminent?

A good marketing head will ensure that all the marketing communication instruments in their orchestra have this information and contribute to the current position analysis.

So now let us look in a bit more detail at the other communication disciplines with which PR works when supporting marketing and building brands, starting with advertising.

Advertising

According to the UK's Advertising Association[5] 'Advertisements are messages, paid for by those who send them, intended to inform or influence people who receive them.'

Advertising involves using paid-for space in the media and elsewhere (including everything from the area above urinals in men's lavatories through to the back of bus tickets), and traditionally such space is clearly distinguished from editorial space which is where PR aims to gain coverage. Thus PR might be seeking a favourable mention within a TV news programme, while advertising appears in the commercial breaks before, during or after the programme.

Advertising can be categorised in a wide variety of ways. We are going to focus on just four – the *type of media* it appears in, the *audiences* it targets, its *purpose* (the effect it is trying to achieve) and *the style of content*. To take each in turn:

By *media*

- **Broadcast** (TV, Radio)
- **Print** (Newspapers, magazines)
- **Online** (Banners, pop ups, paid for links)
- **Outdoor** (Posters)

Sometimes the images and messages used in advertising may be carried through and also used on packaging and at point of sale or in sales promotion – of which more later.

By *audience*

- **Consumers/Customers**: these are not always one and the same thing. For example a young child is often a consumer but is seldom a customer. The customer is the person who buys and pays and usually, but not always, uses the product or service. Interestingly, while it is often hard to prove what effect advertising has on consumer behaviour, there is good evidence that consumer advertising motivates retailers to stock a product (see below) and motivates the sales force to sell it with more confidence. Good consumer PR can have a similar affect on retailers and sales-staff. In the past most advertising focused on fast moving consumer goods (often called fmcg) such as groceries, toiletries and cleaning products. Today, in our more affluent society, advertisers are increasingly called upon to promote things such as financial services (including pensions), holidays, telecommunication products and health and fitness products.
- **Business-to-business**: Businesses buy things too! They are often very big and expensive things, or large consignments, so the purchaser likes to know the company they are buying from is reputable (advertising does not prove that a company is trustworthy, but it is often seen as a good sign – if they are advertising they have nothing to hide and are here to stay, or so the thinking goes).
- **Trade/Retailers**: Many products or services are sold through intermediaries. For example most grocery products are not sold by the manufacturer direct to the consumer but via retailers. Similarly many financial services products are bought from independent financial advisers rather than directly from a

financial institution. In both cases the makers of the product or service will want to advertise to the intermediary to encourage them to stock and promote their range.

By *purpose*

All communication is about making people feel, think or do something. Advertising, like PR, is a purposeful form of communication and generally seeks to influence behaviour. The most commonly used – albeit widely criticised – behavioural model used by advertisers is *AIDA:*

A = Awareness
I = Interest
D = Desire
A = Action

The ideal is that advertising over time, working with other forms of communication, moves people through these stages.

Analysed in this way there are four main purposes for advertising:

- *Building a positive image/brand/reputation* (beware: these terms are used interchangeably): This may simply be to increase consumers' propensity to select your product or brand over the competition. It can also be used to help attract good staff, offset pressure group criticism and impress trade customers such as major retailers.
- *Product and price information*: The sort of ads that say 'this is what it does', 'this how much it costs' and, in markets where there is little product differentiation, 'this is why it is right for you'. This may also include charity advertising, except that instead of asking you to buy a product they ask you to give money in exchange for a good conscience and a hope that the world will be a better place as a result.
- *Education, and affecting behavioural change:* In most countries one of the biggest advertisers is the government, constant exhorting citizens to drive safely, drink less, exercise more, recycle waste and so forth. Less frequently charities, NGOs, industry groups and even individual companies embark on such campaigns. For example in the UK the drinks industry has been spending a lot of advertising money encouraging people to drink 'responsibly' – though of course the sum is a drop in the ocean in comparison to what they spend to get us to drink their products!
- *Directional Advertising*: This is the sort of advertising that calls on you to 'ring now' or 'visit our website today' and often includes long lists of stockists or telephone numbers. The digital world and search engines have dramatically changed this area of advertising. Now many marketing departments are

focussed on SEO, which stands for Search Engine Optimisation. This involves trying to ensure that, if someone is searching online for something that you offer, your website or details appear near the top of the list that the search engine provides.

Try to find at least two examples of each of the four types of advertising above, starting with brand/image advertising. Now analyse each ad by the audience you think it is targeting and the media in which it appeared. Finally, try to think of a way in which PR could be used to 'amplify' the effectiveness of each of the ads you have selected.

Another way that advertising can be categorised is as *'display'* versus *'classified'*. This division usually relates to print media such as newspapers or magazines. Display advertising is generally paid for by a company or organisation and is strong on images and short on words; it is about selling a brand or a range of products and often takes up a page or more. Classified advertising is for specific one-off products such houses, cars or indeed jobs. It is paid for by a private individual or specialist retailer or company such as a recruitment agent, property agent or motor dealer.

With the advent of the web and digital media, classified advertising has fled from print to online – where you can see a car or flat in 3D, making print seem literally very two dimensional. This has led to a dramatic decline in advertising income for print titles, many of which earned 30% or more of their revenue from this source. As a result famous newspaper titles, particularly in the US, have been closing at an alarming rate. Strangely critics of advertising, and some naive PR practitioners, fail to understand that without advertising the vast majority of broadcast, online and print media would collapse or become totally dependent on unedited, PR-generated content. This would clearly do little for democracy or indeed PR. If there are fewer media and less demanding media you need not only fewer skilled PR people but fewer PR people in total. Public relations needs advertising to finance the media which remain, despite occasional claims to the contrary, essential if PR people are to carry out much of the work that is expected of them.

By *style*

Sean Brierley, in his excellent *Advertising Handbook*, categorises three basic styles of advertising.[6] These are:

- Presenter – a voice-over or actual presenter (usually an 'expert' or a trusted celebrity) testifying to the quality of the product and how it is used
- Demonstration – this shows how a product works: for example a new type of razor, or a tablet to ease indigestion.
- Slice of life – shows the product being used, supposedly in real situations

An alternative, and more informal, take on the styles of advertising sometimes quoted by advertising practitioners is:

- Courtier – giving advice
- Comedian – entertaining with humour
- Courtesan – luring with sex

 Get together in groups and think of advertisements in these styles. Why do you think the agency might have chosen the style it did?

Strengths and weaknesses of advertising

The big advantage of advertising over PR is that the appearance of your message in precisely the place you want, at the time you want and in the way you want is guaranteed (provided it passes legal and regulatory tests or does not come up against the occasional refusal of the media to carry particular ads). Moreover, advertising is very good at carrying a clear and simple message. However advertising is costly. The advertiser has to pay not only for the creation of the ad, which for a TV ad can exceed $1m, but also for the space in the media – a single page in a national newspaper in the UK can for example cost around £45,000 and a single 30 second TV ad spot during the American Super Bowl can cost $3m.

Advertising also has a credibility problem. Everyone knows that an ad is something the organisation is saying about itself, but, as we have seen (see p. 7) undoubtedly one of the great strengths of PR is that at it appears to carry the endorsement of credible third parties, be they the traditional media, bloggers or key opinion formers. Advertising attempts to bridge this gap by featuring celebrities and experts in ads, but there remains a sense that they may be 'hired guns'.

A problem arising from advertising's high visibility is that it tends to be in the front line when critics of 'excessive consumption' and anti-capitalists want to go on the attack. PR is less obvious and so tends to attract less of this sort of criticism. In consequence it is sometimes preferred by organisations who are worried about being attacked by pressure groups and NGOs. It is also true that advertising's visibility and transparent *modus operandi* make it easier to regulate either directly by the government or via the industry's self-regulation. In some cases advertising can be banned altogether – as, for example, tobacco ads are in many societies. The way PR works is more opaque and much harder to regulate. (We discuss some of the issues arising from this in Chapter 2.)

Historically, advertising was the dominant discipline in marketing, and large advertising agencies were in existence before the modern PR industry came into being. Big budgets and, in the post-war era, high-profile TV campaigns – often seen by tens of millions of people – ensured that the advertising agent rather than the PR advisor or sales promotion expert had the ear of the marketing director and even the CEO. However, while talk of the death of advertising is mistaken and foolish, it is not as powerful as it once was. There are a variety of reasons for this:

- *Fragmentation of the media.* With so many TV programmes, online sites and magazines it is hard for a single advertising campaign to cut through the enormous amount of communication noise and really stand out: the days when half the population might watch a TV show – and its associated advertising – have past. It has also made advertising more expensive as more media space has to be bought to reach sizeable audiences.
- *Growth of digital and 'new' media.* Advertising is good at talking *to* people but not at talking *with* them. Digital media allow for more targeted two-way communication. At the time of writing most of the marcoms disciplines are wrestling for mastery of communication in the digital space. Advertising agencies, like PR consultancies, are desperate to get a share of what they see as a very lucrative cake.
- *Growth of PR and other marketing disciplines.* Public relations, direct marketing and sales promotion have all become more sophisticated and can now target and evaluate their impact as well as, if sometimes not better than, advertising. Lord Leverhulme (founder of Lever Brothers, now Unilever) is alleged to have said: 'Half of my advertising works. The trouble is I don't know which half'.

DISCUSSION

Why is it so hard for advertisers to measure the effectiveness of their advertising?

Today the best companies brief their PR firm and advertising agency together. If a new product or service is being launched usually the PR kicks off first to ensure there is some credible third-party support for the forthcoming advertising messages. If the advertising itself is particularly outstanding or unusual there may be an attempt by the PR team at what is called *advertising amplification*. For example a targeted media title may be given the inside track on how the ad was made or given exclusive shots of any celebrity used in it. Once the campaign is underway the PR and advertising teams need to work together to ensure that their messages are in line and that their timings do not clash.

Some years ago one of the authors was involved in the launch of a new piece of electronic equipment. He was very pleased to secure front-page editorial coverage, including a photograph of it, in a key magazine. The advertising agency was less delighted that inside the magazine were two pages of advertising showing the machine draped in black with the dramatic caption 'To Be Revealed'.

Where advertising may come into conflict with PR, albeit usually on a small scale, is over activities such as advertorials (advertisements written or produced in the editorial style of the host medium). PR practitioners argue that as they are experts in editorial it should be their province. Advertising agencies counter-argue that they are experts in media targeting and can negotiate better deals for the space. However, now that fewer advertising agencies buy media space for advertisements – it is largely in the hands of specialist media buying organisations – this has become less of an issue, although advertising agencies may become agitated if the costs for advertorials are taken from their budgets.

Not surprisingly both sides tend to believe that their discipline offers better value for money. The truth is that which discipline is most important depends on the task in hand.

Below the line

'Below the line' is a term sometimes used by people in the world of advertising to describe all other forms of marketing communications activity. It has its roots in a time when there were few, if any, specialist sales promotion, direct mail or PR firms and this work was undertaken by advertising agencies. These agencies described the fees they were paid for such work as *below the line* – '*above the line*' represented the money they were paid in commission by media owners when they placed advertisements for their clients. (Today most advertising agencies are no longer paid by commission on the media spend but are paid, like PR firms, by fee, based on the time spent and the quality of the work undertaken.)

DIRECT MAIL

Direct mail is sometimes also called *direct marketing*, although the latter involves more than sending letters or posting leaflets. Direct mail is perhaps more commonly known by the pejorative term 'junk mail'. PR usually only comes into contact with direct mail when the mailing agency wants to include some positive coverage secured by PR in one of its mailshots.

Well targeted direct mail can be very cost-effective, particularly when it follows on from a high-profile advertising campaign. For example a letter sent to a potential purchaser of a new car which is in their price range may cost very little to produce, but it can result in a sale worth thousands of pounds. The problem is ensuring that the mail is sent to the right people – people who are likely to be interested. A major part of effective direct mail is ensuring that relevant and accurate mailing lists are used. These lists are either based on people who have had some prior contact with the organisation or are bought from specialist

list brokers. Not surprisingly, the internet has had a major impact on traditional postal mail with direct email (in some circumstances pejoratively called *SPAM*) taking an increasing share of the market.

Badly targeted direct mail can actually damage the image and reputation of a brand. Used wisely, direct mail can help to close the sale.

Sales promotion

Sales promotions represent incentives to buy or trial particular products – such as 'buy one, get one free' (also know as BOGOFs), money off coupons, free gifts, prizes and competitions.

The benefits of a sales promotion are that it can usually be organised quite quickly, can be targeted to particular customer groups or outlets and its effectiveness is often readily measurable in a way that advertising sometimes is not. Indeed sales promotions can be a useful way of collecting customer information and data, provided data protection laws are observed.

However, sales promotion carries a number of dangers. 'Money off' type offers may encourage regular customers to buy more now at the lower price, but may not in the long run lead to more sales, just less profit for the manufacturer or retailer. Similarly, if sales promotions become too regular customers start to jump from product to product according to who has the best offer. Consequently brand loyalty may actually be undermined rather than strengthened. Sales promotion can also cheapen the image of quality and luxury brands. Strong brands tend to focus on 'value' rather than price or short-term incentives.

Sales promotion comes into contact with PR in two main ways. The first is positive and is about the PR team communicating to the trade (if relevant) and the target audience that there is a promotion about to start – though in reality few sales promotions, rather like advertising campaigns, are in fact very newsworthy. The other area is more controversial. PR teams working in the marcoms area often organise competitions in the media, or reader offers. The PR argument is that they understand the media in a way that sales promotion teams do not. The sales promotion people counter that PR people do not fully understand all the legal ramifications of such activity, nor do they have the knowledge or systems to analyse the data that can sometimes be collected. These sorts of arguments seldom come fully to the surface but simmer away and can lead to resentment.

As with the disputes between advertising and PR, the best way to resolve them is for the head of marketing to decide who would do the job best in the particular circumstance.

Free flights fiasco

An extreme example of a sales promotion which backfired involved Hoover, the vacuum cleaner manufacturer. The company offered two free flights to anyone purchasing one of their products which cost over £100. In an age before cheap air fares over 200,000 consumers leapt at the opportunity. Hoover was overwhelmed and received thousands of complaints, huge volumes of damaging press coverage and a bill for £48 million.[7]

Sponsorship

Sponsorship is a process whereby an organisation pays money to another organisation, team or person in return for 'co-branding' (the inclusion of their name on all promotional material). There are many types of sponsorship, ranging from sport to culture, charities and conservation.

Sport generally attracts the biggest TV audiences so is popular with big brands targeting large groups of people. Everyone is familiar with seeing sponsors' names on footballers' shirts or on Formula 1 cars. Through association with a particular event or team the sponsor hopes that some of the popularity will rub off and perhaps secure interest in, and loyalty to, their brand that conventional advertising could not achieve. A secondary benefit of this sort of sponsorship is 'corporate hospitality'. This gives the sponsor the opportunity to entertain key customers and other people they may want to influence, such as journalists or politicians, at a prestigious event. Finally there is the opportunity to show commitment to the area or community in which the organisation is based. This can be awkward. The former UK insurance giant Norwich Union (now called *Aviva*) was reluctant to sponsor the local football team Norwich City as it feared being associated with failure!

Up-market consumer brands and business-to-business brands which want to reach their customers and opinion formers tend to focus more on the arts and cultural activities, while big corporations keen to demonstrate their green or caring credentials will often choose to sponsor environmental groups and charities.

Sponsorship can be highly effective in raising a brand's profile and generating positive associations. It can also be very expensive. Manchester United's latest sponsor, the American insurance giant AON, is said to be paying the club £20 million a season in return for which it hopes it will reach a massive global audience.[8] However the evidence suggests that it takes at least two to three years for the public to establish the association between a sponsor and the recipient team or event. And sometimes the link with the sponsor is forgotten or misunderstood. Some years ago Gillette – the male grooming brand – sponsored a major cricket event in the UK called the *Gillette Cup*. The idea was to appeal to cricket loving men, and in particular young men just starting to shave and making choices about which brand of razor to use. The problem was that it emerged over time that many in the target audience, when asked what Gillette did, answered cricket! The link to shaving had been lost.

The other big problem with sponsorship is that it is even harder to measure its impact than is the case for PR or advertising. There is also an uncomfortable truth that some sponsorship choices – including, notoriously, some sponsorship of golf – say more about the interests of the CEO or marketing director than they do about the marketing objectives of the organisation.

PR tends to make an important contribution to sponsorship, though it seldom manages or controls the big sponsorships agreements which now involve the negotiation of complex multi-million pound deals. However most sponsorship deals draw much of their value from wider media coverage, over and beyond straightforward TV or press coverage of a team or event, and therefore look to PR to help maximise and exploit potential media opportunities. PR will also be involved in inviting key journalists to hospitality events. Finally they will be involved in crisis management if the sponsorship becomes problematic – for example when players disgrace themselves or a team performs badly. This latter point highlights one further weakness of sponsorship...the difficulty of picking long-term winners.

E/digital communications

The most problematic marcoms discipline is digital communications. It is also the newest. One of the greatest difficulties is separating out where digital marketing ends and digital communication begins.

Clearly designing an ecommerce site such as Amazon or eBay or even an interactive information site such as the UK's NHS Direct (health advice) is a specialist activity requiring a vast array of commercial as well as specialist web design skills. Few, if any, PR firms or advertising agencies have those skills. What they do have is the skills to create communication that drives people to those sites.

Below are some of the main emarketing communication techniques with an indication of the types of marcoms specialist that in our view are most likely to possess the necessary skills:

- Communication with social networks (PR, Digital Specialists and Advertising)
- Monitoring and talking to, and via, blogs and other influential online user and customer groups (PR)
- Advertising on relevant sites (banners, pop ups etc) (Advertising or Digital Specialists)
- Joint promotions, links and partnerships with complementary sites (Sales Promotion or Digital Specialists)
- Securing editorial coverage on online sites (PR)
- Search Engine Optimisation (Digital Specialists)

Generally it is seen as the role of PR to monitor and interact with blogs – effectively a form of third-party media – as well as secure online coverage in the same way as PR secures print or broadcast coverage. However, when it comes to communicating with social networks or organising links and partnerships, specialist 'digital' agencies as well as sales promotion and even advertising outfits also claim expertise. (Almost all major marcoms players now claim to have some kind of digital facility.) Even search engine optimisation, which was seen as a rather technical specialist digital area, is now being claimed by some PR teams. The reality is that there is money in digital and so all the disciplines want to stake their claim.

In Chapter 10 we will look at PR in the digital world in more detail, but now let us look briefly at what PR brings to the marcoms party.

How PR aids marketing

Hugh Burkitt, CEO, The Marketing Society

My three ways are advocacy, transparency and cost.

Six-year olds understand the purpose of advertising, and by the time most consumers are ten they have developed a healthy level of scepticism about paid-for messages. So though advertising can charm an audience, and heighten awareness of a brand, it rarely persuades.

By contrast, messages about brands in editorial have an air of impartial authority. So PR can be a very effective way to increase advocates of your brand.

An active PR strategy will encourage you to be transparent and honest in all your dealings. The internet gives everyone the opportunity to complain if they don't get a good deal, and you don't want the key measure of advocacy – your net promoter score – to go negative. So learn from Innocent drinks – invite the customer into your business and don't have anything to hide.

Finally cost: good PR practitioners cost money, but they will cost less than most media budgets, and they can help you create more involving and cost-effective advertising campaigns in traditional media. The Dove Campaign for Real Beauty is a great PR idea that also makes a truly engaging advertising campaign.

PR IN THE MARCOMS MIX

PR's marketing communications responsibilities are mainly about media coverage, be it launching a new product, sustaining interest in an existing one or trying to build a positive brand reputation. In Chapter 6 we go into more details about how PR teams go about this, but broadly there are 5 main types of activity, the first three of which are designed to secure media coverage and thereby third-party endorsement:

Table 4.2 Methods and tactics matrix

Method (How we are going to get there?)	Tactics (What we are going to do?)
HARD NEWS (when the product or service is newsworthy in itself)	Press conference Press briefing, interviews Press release Journalist/key opinion former trials

Continued

Table 4.2 Continued

Method (How we are going to get there?)	Tactics (What we are going to do?)
CREATED 'SOFT' NEWS (when the product or service is not exciting enough to generate 'hard news' or has already been covered and so needs a new angle)	Survey Psychologists' predictions Report Index Study Guidebook Sponsorship (These sort of tactics are actually delivered using a combination of news releases, articles, briefings, interviews and features)
NEWS EVENTS	An unusual event (oldest, newest, biggest, fastest, oddest etc) Celebrity presence A major party Fashion show (These sort of events usually have a strong visual element and are popular with TV and picture editors)
PROMOTIONAL CONTENT (It is in this area of activity, and that of Direct News below, that PR most commonly comes into conflict with other marcoms disciplines)	Editorial competition Product giveaways Product placement Spo nsored pages or columns Advertorial (an advertisement produced in editorial style)
DIRECT NEWS (Media coverage is a secondary objective)	Exhibitions/ Seminars Conferences/Briefings Hospitality/Entertainment Special Reports Special Newsletter, video, DVD, web link

The activities described above will be the mainstay of most marketing PR teams' work. However, other areas of PR can help create a business and political environment in which it is easier to sell products successfully. For example lobbying or public affairs can help facilitate favourable legislation, good employee communication can ensure productivity remains high and strong financial PR can aid investment for growth. In these sorts of areas PR is clearly distinct from other marketing disciplines, which is perhaps why some in the industry are keen to play down the marcoms aspect of PR and play up the other, albeit smaller, areas of PR practice.

> With its emphasis on profitability of goods or services for sale, marketing is a narrower concept than public relations.
>
> Shirley Harrison, PR academic[9]

 Do a SWOT (Strengths, Weaknesses, Opportunities and Threats) analysis, highlighting each element in SWOT for each of the following marketing communication disciplines: PR, Advertising, Sales Promotion, Direct mail, Sponsorship.

Consider some purchases you have made recently – preferably not regular ones. What role did the different marcoms disciplines play in helping you to reach your decision (try to be frank with yourself!)? What lessons can you draw from this? You can also discuss this as a group exercise.

Integrated Marketing Communications (IMC)

Heads of marketing are understandably keen to integrate the various elements of marketing communications in pursuit of common marketing objectives and the greater good of the organisation. Properly done this constitutes 'integrated marketing communications' (IMC). The simple thought behind it is that the marketing communication whole should be greater than the sum of its parts and thereby reduce costs and duplication and increase effectiveness.

In practice reality can stop short of the ideal, not least because of human nature. As we have seen, because these different disciplines have grown up separately, there are professional rivalries and perhaps inhibitions about admitting the importance of other aspects of IMC. Nor is it just vanity – budgets and career advancement can be at stake. If, from a given budget, more is spent on one of these disciplines then less must be spent on the others, a fact of life which can lead to friction.

Indeed, given the importance to organisations of integrated marketing communications one might expect that there would be a myriad of top-flight IMC agencies. There are not. Client organisations still seem to prefer agencies that specialise in one field of communication rather than agencies that claim to have broad expertise.

According to Chris Fill, author of several major books on marketing communications:

> there seems to be a trade off between levels of integration and the expertise provided by different agencies. Clients who want to retain control over their brands and to find an integrated agency where all the required services are of the exact level and quality demanded may be expecting too much.[10]

The new marketing services groups such as WPP and Interpublic (see Chapter 2) are designed to offer, through a range of specialist companies, all these different services in a co-ordinated way. Despite the offer it is noticeable that few client organisations are willing to put all their marketing communication needs in the hands of one group.

What are brands?

Brands or branding have been much discussed in this chapter. They are also terms we hear a lot in the outside world. 'Designer Brands', 'Ethical Brands', 'Consumer Brands', 'Celebrity Brands'. Being a brand would seem to be a good thing. So what are brands?

Brands can be goods (iPods), manufacturers (Microsoft), services (British Airways), retailers (Harrods or Walmart), celebrities (David Beckham) or a combination of these things, such as Coca-Cola, Virgin and Shell, all of which are corporate brands but also product brands. Beyond the commercial world charities and NGOs such as Greenpeace and Amnesty International are also brands, and so are some political and government organisations and services.

According to the Chartered Institute of Marketing:

> A successful brand is one that creates and sustains a positive image in the mind of the buyer over time. The elements of a brand are both direct, as in the logo or trademark, and indirect, relating to the culture of the organisation and their values towards their customers.[11]

Another way of looking at brands is shown in the Brand Pie diagram below:

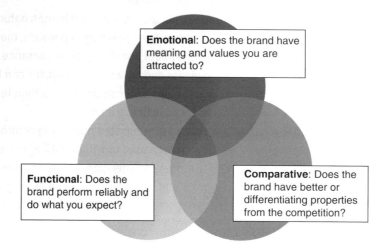

Emotional: Does the brand have meaning and values you are attracted to?

Functional: Does the brand perform reliably and do what you expect?

Comparative: Does the brand have better or differentiating properties from the competition?

Figure 4.1 *The Brand Pie*

The diagram shows the three segments with equal size. For most brands it is the emotional segment that is the most important. How else do you explain why people will spend thousands of dollars on a handbag that is no more efficient than a $5 bag, or why people have been murdered for their trainers? Many products and services today offer similar features at a similar price – think about mobile phone networks, family cars or bank accounts. Even when a real competitive advantage is gained it is often easily and quickly copied.

Other ways of describing a brand include a 'recognised name, look and set of values that are relevant to and resonate with the target audience' or 'a collection of psychosocial meanings'. It is notable that people refer to 'brand personality' as many brands are chosen because the consumer feels they are a reflection of their own personality – or at least what they would like their personality to be.

 Prepare contrasting Brand Pies for Microsoft and Apple; Pepsi and Coca-Cola; BMW and Lexus; and D&G and Chanel. Which brands have the strongest or biggest emotional segment? What is the emotional appeal of each? How could PR support this appeal?

PR has a large role to play in the creation of a brand's 'emotional difference', but so too does advertising. According to a quote attributed to the great advertising man David Ogilvy:

A company with a price advantage can be undercut. A company with a performance advantage can be outflanked. But a company with an emotional difference can potentially demand a premium forever.

Write down two brands that you like and two brands that you do not. For each brand pretend they are a person and write down what newspaper they would read, which online media they would use, what kind of house they would live in, what car they would drive and where they would go on holiday. Now compare your thoughts with someone else. (It should prove that some brands can have different appeals for different people!)

Consumers like brands for a variety of reasons. A trusted brand provides:

- Rewards in terms of ego and status
- Quality assurance
- Reduced risk of disappointment
- Quick and easy identification when buying/shopping

Organisations like brands because they:

- Permit premium pricing
- Enhance cross product promotion
- Reduce costs through integration
- Can provide enhanced legal protection

Famously, the CEO of Coca-Cola is alleged to have once asked a group of staff: 'What is worth more: the Coca-Cola brand or the $billion of production plant we have around the world?' The correct answer was of course the brand!

'The best job in the world'

In 2009 – in the midst of the northern winter – Tourism Queensland, responsible for holiday promotion for the Australian state of that name, advertised for a caretaker for an idyllic tropical island off Queensland's coast. The duties were to be light and the pay and conditions excellent. Details appeared on online job sites and in small display advertisements, both of which referred people to the website.

The campaign sought to secure favourable publicity for Queensland and its coast, positioning it as a tourist destination at a time of global economic crises when there were fears that numbers of holidaymakers would drop away.

The unusual and appealing job offer aroused enormous media interest. TV coverage included CNN and the BBC, with extensive newspaper and magazine reporting. According to those working on the campaign media coverage reached an audience of nearly 3 billion, there were almost 8.5 million unique visitors to the website, and almost 39,000 people from just about every country in the world applied for the job. During the application process jobseekers prepared videos and made extensive use of social media, adding to the publicity. Once the successful applicant was appointed he continued to be involved in publicity and had a high profile.[12]

How did this campaign make use of the disciplines of advertising and public relations? What evidence can you find of the success or otherwise of this campaign in achieving its objectives and – above all – influencing behaviour? (Material on this contest and its aftermath is readily available online.)

- Marketing is 'the process responsible for identifying, anticipating and satisfying customer requirements profitably'. This involves pricing, distribution and issues concerning the product and not just promotion.
- PR and advertising, along with sales promotion, are marcoms or marketing communications tools. Advertising's essential difference from PR is that it involves the use of *paid-for* space to put across its messages.
- Marcoms should be co-ordinated, like a well-conducted orchestra, in pursuit of the organisation's agreed objectives. In practice there may be rivalries and disputes between the different marcoms disciplines.

Explain what marketing is. In what ways does it overlap with, and in what ways is it distinct from, PR?

Some reading suggestions

Advertising: Brierley, Sean, *The Advertising Handbook* (Routledge 2005) is a good, wide-ranging overview of the advertising industry.

Branding: Pringle, Hamish and Field, Peter, *Brand Immortality. How Brands Can Live Long and Prosper* (Kogan Page 2008).

Marketing: Fill, Chris, *Marketing Communication: Interactivity, Communities and Content* (*Financial Times*/Prentice Hall 2009) has everything you are likely to need to know about marcoms.

Portal for much of the international trade press: www.brandrepublic.com/magazines/marketing/index.cfm

www.adassoc.org.uk Website of the UK Advertising Association, which is a federation of 25 trade bodies.

www.ipa.co.uk/ Institute of Practitioners in Advertising. The industry's main trade body in the UK.

www.cim.co.uk The Chartered Institute of Marketing

www.warc.com World Advertising Research Centre

WHAT IS INTERNAL COMMUNICATION

INTERNAL COMMUNICATIONS

INTRODUCTION

You may not have given it much thought, but if you have worked in a modern organisation of any scale or have studied in sizeable educational institutions, you will have encountered internal communications. It may be as simple as a staff newsletter, an intranet site, or internal emails. It may involve direct personal contact or even what one finds around oneself in one's working environment. A growing number of PR people are engaged in such work, although sometimes their role is disputed. This chapter looks at how to practise internal communications and raises some controversial issues about its function in contemporary working life.

LEARNING OBJECTIVES

- To examine what internal communications comprises
- To explore the case for making internal communications more professional, and for employing PR people to do it
- Top tips for effective internal communications, including selecting the right media
- To review why internal communications raises controversial issues for PR practitioners

WHAT IS INTERNAL COMMUNICATIONS AND WHY IS IT IMPORTANT?

All organisations, of whatever kind, have always had their own forms of communication – between management and staff (vertical communication) and among colleagues (horizontal communication). Internal communications does not seek to supplant these. Instead the term refers to planned, deliberate communication within an organisation which supplements existing communication channels and is increasingly undertaken by specialist staff. Thus, rather like PR, internal communications is not entirely novel, but the notion of employing people to go about it in a dedicated way is relatively new.

There are powerful arguments for maintaining a strong internal communications department within any sizeable organisation:

- In a media-saturated world internal communications is your organisation's chance to comment on or correct messages which employees will be picking up from the mass media. Such messages might mention your organisation, or they might involve issues with which your organisation is concerned. For example, many types of business want to reassure their employees that they are actively responding to environmental concerns, or inform their staff about business prospects in troubled economic times. It is also worth telling staff about favourable media coverage. Everyone likes to work for a successful organisation – and if there is favourable coverage it may be a chance to blow the PR team's trumpet a bit!
- Modern businesses need more and more highly qualified staff – and yet such staff can easily leave. This can become costly and disruptive. Good, motivational internal communications which inculcates new staff in organisational values and approaches can help to reduce staff turnover.
- Internal communications helps employees cope with change. Restructuring and other changes are a recurring feature of modern working life, and yet people are less and less likely to work together over long periods at a single location. Internal communications keeps workers up to date with what is happening and acts as a form of glue in increasingly scattered, fast-evolving organisations.
- With traditional branded manufactured goods customers never got to see the people who made them. But in the case of service industries the person you deal with *is* the brand. Making sure that, for example, call centre staff properly represent the organisation and its values is vital. Your competitors will probably be investing in internal communications and if you do not you risk being left behind.

> In order to get an effective service brand, people have to be taught to live the brand they work with. For the customer, the person who represents the brand is the brand.
>
> Wally Olins, Brand Guru[1]

There are also strong arguments for internal communications work being undertaken by PR people (the usual rival contenders are in Human Resources):

- PR people have a unique set of skills which are as relevant to internal communications as they are to external communications: they are – or should be – experts in the art of communicating different messages to different audiences, and selecting the right media for the task.
- PR practitioners are the closest thing organisations have to in-house journalists. They can prepare material for newsletters, websites and in-house broadcasts.
- What employees hear about their organisations via the media and other external sources will always compete with what they are told through internal communications channels. Any gap between the two has the potential to damage the credibility of internal communications. PR people are best qualified to take into account what is being said in the outside world. Employees are naturally very interested in what is said about them in the media: it can affect staff morale and productivity.
- Good, two-way internal communications will unearth positive, newsworthy stories from different parts of the organisation and bring them to the attention of the PR team. They can then be passed on to the media, boosting staff morale (everyone likes to be part of a good news story) and generating helpful coverage for the organisation.

TOP TIPS FOR SUCCESSFUL INTERNAL COMMUNICATIONS

Internal communications involves many of the same skills as other forms of PR work, but there are important differences. Internal communications is not about third-party endorsement: *you* decide what appears in your own managed media, with the downside that whatever is said does not bear the imprint of an independent journalist.

Modern organisations often have at their disposal a full array of media aimed at their staff – print media, internal TV, radio stations, intranet sites and even Facebook pages and Twitter feeds. And it does not stop there. Internal communications can include posters, 'direct mail', emails and text messages, speeches, meetings, and other group activities, but can also extend to the physical environments within which people work: such things as buildings, art, furniture and interior decoration can be used to underline how an organisation sees itself and wants to be seen by its employees as well as others.

So in designing an internal communications programme it is likely that you will use a combination of media to put across messages. You will need to consider the following:

- What kind of message are you trying to deliver? Is it precise information about your organisation and its activities, or more a matter of 'mood music,' designed to raise morale and give staff a flavour of what the organisation stands for?
- To whom are you trying to deliver the message? All employees or particular categories of employees? If it is to all employees then, in a large organisation which employs a great variety of people, it is likely that you will need to consider addressing different people in different ways. At times internal communications can morph with external communications: internal audiences are not hermetically sealed off from the outside world, and – as mentioned – are usually intensely aware of media coverage which concerns their employers. At the same time employers cannot ignore the blurring that occurs between employees and local communities and organisations – or indeed between employees and professional bodies, unions or other groups.
- What means are available to deliver the message? As we shall see, each medium has its strengths and weaknesses. Some may be completely inappropriate to your organisation or a portion of its workforce.
- Where are you starting from? Organisations have their own cultures, and the sectors or industries to which they belong have their own characteristics. Employees are also part of local and national communities with their own traditions and ways of doing things. People's views cannot be changed overnight, and in some cases it is difficult to change them at all.
- As with all forms of communication, internal communication costs money. You will have to balance your ideal solution against your budget.

Choosing media for internal communications

- *Traditional print media*, such as newsletters and staff magazines, can be relatively cheap to produce (although this will depend on their quality). They are a good means of conveying large amounts of detailed information, including facts and figures. They can also be relatively quick to produce, although the time taken for production and distribution means they can lag behind fast-moving events, particularly in a crisis. However it is hard to ensure that staff read them properly and digest the information they contain. Typically people will read material that they feel is immediately relevant to them – for instance, if it affects their pay and working conditions. For really important communications personalised letters are often used as they offer a way of guaranteeing that individuals have actually been sent the information. It is much harder to get people to read about what the organisation feels is important. To try to achieve this many large organisations produce softer focus magazines or similar materials which use journalistic skills similar to those found in the mainstream independent media in an attempt to make news and views about the organisation more interesting and palatable. Key new managers can be introduced through interviews and profiles, questions from staff can be answered, staff letters can be published and competitions run.

- *Internal TV and radio networks* are relatively expensive and are suitable only for particular kinds of workforces – people who can be made to watch or listen alongside, or in intervals from, their work. They therefore tend to be used in particular large, well-funded organisations where the workforce is in a position to watch and listen. Both TV and radio can be excellent communication tools, and can be a good second best to personal contact, although compared with print media they are handicapped in terms of the amount of detail they can convey: a half-hour TV programme typically contains fewer words than a large newspaper page. Moreover, although broadcast material can be recorded and repeated, it essentially belongs to the moment of time when it appears: people cannot so readily refer back to it, whenever they want and wherever they are, as they can to the printed word. This weakness is particularly important in the case of detailed information. It is also the case that some senior managers are not natural broadcasters – their promotion is normally based on other qualities – and their comments are better read than seen or heard.

- *Intranet sites and other forms of new media* can offer words, sound and images, and have the added advantage of immediate interactivity: people can discuss issues, respond to questions, or indicate areas of particular interest to them. However, websites are expensive to set up and maintain (they have to be kept constantly up-to-date), but once in place they can be used by large numbers of people without incurring significant additional costs. This makes them suitable for large organisations where staff are well equipped with computer facilities. Similarly *staff emails* can play an important communications role, and *mobile phones* can be used to send short text messages to employees on the road.

- *Talks, speeches and events* can play an inspirational role. Although they are not a good way of communicating large amounts of information (think about how much you recall from the last speech you heard), they enable key staff to tackle issues in a personal way which makes it hard for people to ignore or forget. For this reason direct contact of this kind will always play an important part in the 'internal communications mix,' and is expected particularly at times of change or organisational trauma when the personal touch is needed, and exclusive reliance on impersonal, remote and bureaucratic methods of communication would seem wrong. Speeches and talks can of course be interactive, with questions and debate, although if the organisation wants to discuss – or at least appear to discuss – the issues at stake then seminars or other forms of discussion can be used. This kind of communication can merge with staff training.

- *Other, 'ambient' media* can also play a crucial role, and, like speeches, are hard to ignore. Posters and signs can convey and reiterate simple key messages. More subtly uniforms, art, furniture, interior design, architecture and even the use of music can be used to reaffirm an organisation's values and how it wants its employees to see themselves. Are they modernists embracing change, or traditionalists who place great value on past achievement? In practice most organisations are a combination of both, but the balance is different in terms of how they present themselves. One problem with such features of an organisation is that they are often not only expensive but take a long time to put in place: a company cannot simply find a new headquarters building that suits a new image. Such things are also so fundamental to an organisation and its senior management that PR input is bound to be limited.

In producing an organisation's own media PR people need to display journalistic flair: they have to make their copy as attractive as possible. However there are several stumbling blocks they have to look out for:

- *Overreliance on one method.* Usually a medley of methods is employed, with different approaches reinforcing each other. As we have seen, each has its drawbacks, and varying the medium can help to freshen up the message.
- *Being boring.* The essence of good, lively journalism is usually conflict and controversy, but the scope for this in internal communications is extremely limited. Internal communications material would seldom if ever merit a place in any anthology of journalism! Management pressure only exacerbates this, and, as in all areas of PR, there is a tension between making material interesting and the bureaucratic and legal constraints on what organisations can say. It would be easy to write a widely read article speculating about forthcoming redundancies for example, but in practice organisations are greatly inhibited about what they can divulge about such matters. Varying the approach and using different journalistic tricks is essential.
- *Overdoing it.* Because you have a captive audience there is a danger of swamping employees with internal communications material. If you do they will ignore and/or resent it and so it will become counterproductive.
- *Contradicting or usurping normal channels of communication* within the organisation, which will arouse resentment. Remember that internal communications should supplement and not undermine management's role. Thus close collaboration with management is essential.

Imagine an important message with far-reaching implications, such as the raising of the retirement age, which has to be conveyed to all staff within an organisation you know well.

1) On the basis of your knowledge consider how the message might be disseminated (see table below).
2) Imagine that, following on from the above, you have to write a short article for your organisation's regular newsletter. Try drafting something appropriate, keeping your target audience in mind.

Table 5.1 Internal message matrix

Message	Internal audience you would need to address, broken down according to the nature of the message	Appropriate media and communications tools

WHY INTERNAL COMMUNICATIONS RAISES ITS OWN ETHICAL ISSUES

Internal communications plays an important and often healthy and proper part in organisational life, but like all forms of communication it is in itself morally neutral. In so far as people give it any attention (it seldom receives much scrutiny!) our views on it will vary, depending on what we think of the organisation concerned, the issues at stake, the methods used and the validity of any concerns of the employees. However internal communications also raises a special set of concerns of its own. As we have seen elsewhere (Chapter 1), PR people sometimes agonise about the relationship between public relations and propaganda and seek to put as much distance as they can between what they do and the work of propagandists. However, of all the main branches of the contemporary public relations industry, internal communications is the one that best realises the propagandists' dream. Unlike media relations work, where the PR practitioner seeks to influence – but never fully controls – media coverage, here PR people exercise full control over their own, managed media. There is no filter. Their messages can be promoted at will, while those seeking to put across alternative messages find internal media closed to them. Thus internal communicators enjoy a monopoly of communication, the ideal of propagandists. Employees can only escape the monopoly by leaving their employment.

Censorship

This monopoly also depends on an organisation's ability to censor rival forms of communication. Unlike other PR people, internal communicators enjoy the ability to apply real, formal sanctions. It is accepted – so much so that it usually passes without comment or consideration – that we relinquish many of our rights of free speech when we take up employment. The organisations which employ us are, with few exceptions, not worker-democracies but autocracies or oligarchies run by people who are usually accountable to others – shareholders, voters, or members and funders in the case of not-for-profit entities. Employees are obliged to receive the ideas and information communicated by their employers, and at the same time they forfeit the right to speak out. Bringing one's employer into disrepute is a commonly accepted basis for dismissal, while breaching confidences and speaking to the media without permission often constitute disciplinary offences. The employer's monopoly of formal internal media channels leaves only informal options fully open to employees. Typically these comprise emails and text messages, word-of-mouth exchanges – for example conversations around the water cooler or photocopier – or alternative forms of written media, such as graffiti. (Organisations can and do monitor online comments by members of staff, so the advent of social media has not really changed the principles outlined above – indeed it has in some ways made it easier to police staff behaviour through email alerts, careful searches and follow-up action. Social media leave a trail. People have been fired for criticising their employer on what they thought were private Facebook pages or Twitter messages.)

This degree of control has been sharpened not just by the growth of increasingly professionalised internal communications regimes, but also by the teetering and collapse of alternative channels of communication, most notably those provided by trade unions, coupled in some cases by increased job insecurity. Of course astute internal communication experts realise that making their control too obvious is counterproductive. Sometimes limited dissent is allowed – staff comments are sought – but this process is usually tokenistic and carefully circumscribed.

The resemblance between internal communication and propaganda does not stop there. Internal communication has the potential to deploy all the methods which have been used by propagandists down the ages – and indeed, as we have seen, is usually well-advised to use a combination of overlapping approaches. Organisations do not have to rely on their own print or electronic media to put across their messages. They can augment them with a range of techniques which barely feature in conventional PR but have always been familiar to religious and political organisations.

According to the head of human resources at the mobile telephone company Orange:

'I don't hold myself up to be a saint, but I try to incorporate the brand values into everything I do.' Then he laughed. 'It's beginning to sound like a cult.'

Or as a Microsoft employee puts it:

'People do say it's like the Moonies at Microsoft.'[2]

One reason for this is that organisations control the physical environments in which people work and can use them to supplement their messaging. Even office layout – glass walls, open-plan, hot-desking – conveys its own messages: these include openness, the importance of team playing, and a sense of urgency. Portraits and other works of art have always been used to illustrate the founding myths of institutions and their presence in the inner sanctums of power – corporate boardrooms for example – underlines their quasi-religious significance. Gradations of office furniture and decoration, as well as office size, can operate as incentive schemes, but the nature of design can be used to send subtle messages.

Internal communications techniques can be even more wide-ranging, in ways which can be quite insidious. Even if an employer had no dress regulations, there may be informal but powerful pressures affecting what staff may wear and their outward appearance (indeed, it is noticeable that those who enjoy a notional freedom to choose their own clothing – for example in the 'creative industries' – are often highly regimented in appearance.) Induction processes and work-related training can blur imperceptibly into internal communication. Organisations can and do set up their own rituals and ceremonies both inside and outside formal working hours, including activities which may involve families and local communities.

However internal communications is a relatively new discipline. While all these techniques and more are employed, their use is seldom thoroughly planned and co-ordinated. One reason is that many of the instruments of internal communication within any organisation have emerged haphazardly over time. PR people seldom control all the levers of power – despite occasional wishful thinking! Human resources or personnel management still controls the internal communications function in some organisations (and there will always be some overlap). But, more importantly, even if PR is in formal charge of all communications, this does not mean full control of internal communications. Given the range of techniques at the internal communicators disposal, full control would make PR people the most powerful people in the organisation, and – as is the case with propaganda, where leaders carefully parcel out responsibility – no chief executive or leader is likely to let that happen.

The employer brand

Internal communications is often seen as an extension of branding – it is sometimes called *employer branding* – and as a means of enabling employees to act as ambassadors. One reason it has come to the fore is because of the rise of service industries in modern western economies. In such cases the employee is often in direct contact with the customer and needs appropriate training and briefing to serve as a brand ambassador.

One of the prevailing characteristics of internal communications is the desire to appear benign. Although the discipline is sometimes known as 'change management', emphasising the role it plays when organisations transform themselves, the way in which internal communications often comes to the fore when tough or unpalatable messages have to be delivered tends to be played down. The gap between employer concerns – maximum production at minimum cost – and employee concerns (typically job prospects and remuneration) is fudged, and the underlying message of 'change management', namely 'change or leave', stays out of focus. Thus talk about internal communications is often imprecise and awash with euphemisms, and harsh truths tend to be tinted in rosy hues. In cultures which value democracy and openness the iron hand of authority at the heart of corporate life has to be carefully wrapped in velvet, and many secretly made decisions are portrayed as being the fruit of dialogue and consultation.

Most articles about internal communications in Europe's leading PR trade magazine, PR Week, concern organisations which have to sack or redeploy large numbers of staff. Despite this the tone is usually comforting and unchallenging. There is one exception. A new managing director describes his first day:

'I arrived at 10am and at 11am I sacked the manufacturing director. At 12 noon I sacked the technical director, so by lunchtime everyone knew I had arrived.'

The article draws the following conclusion:

'What makes this account so unsettling is that it explodes the warm and woolly thinking that can easily bedevil discussion of internal communication.
'To read half the articles on these topics you'd think that all a company had to do to be effective was empower people; have managers who give plenty of praise; create a listening culture and lo! the bottom line is magically transformed.'[3]

The comforting way in which internal communications is often described is helped along by a tendency to focus on sought-after workers with scarce skills in desirable jobs. But workers are not always difficult to recruit, or expensive to hire and train, and often internal communications regimes operate in much chillier environments, with internal communications used in lieu of higher wages.

Hidden persuaders

Internal communications has achieved one of the ultimate goals of the propagandist in one more way: it has crept up on contemporary employees in countless organisations unnoticed. In its ideal form propaganda seeks to achieve its goals unobserved and unremarked upon. It should be unobtrusive and its messages should pass into people's minds without their thinking that they may be victims of propaganda. To a large extent internal communications achieves this. Its rise has passed below the radar. Although there is a cacophony of criticism about modern marketing techniques, including advertising and PR, and their implications for society, internal communications is overlooked. Not only is it now so ubiquitous that people seem not to notice it, but critics of the PR industry and scholars have surprisingly little to say about it.

Those who have internal communications – or something similar – in their job titles may not sound sinister. Communication is, after all, seen as a positive thing. Nor, as we have seen, do they really control all the levers of internal communication. But, taken together, these levers are formidable. With increasingly professional planning and management, they are today in a position to exert more control than ever before. Internal communications are a necessary part of organisational life: they are not inevitably bad, but they are not necessarily good either. This is important because of the increasing importance they play in the modern world, where they form an important part of the backdrop to most people's working lives. Beyond paid work, they affect us elsewhere: in educational institutions at all levels for example, and within NGOs and charities: indeed NGOs have to place particular emphasis on internal communications among their volunteers because they offer no pay.

For most people in liberal democracies these internal communications regimes are the closest they ever come to experiencing the powerful, closed propaganda systems associated with communism, fascism or novels such as *1984*. But internal communications carries on and grows, largely unchallenged, unexamined, and taken for granted. People can always leave and get another job if they do not like it – or so the argument goes. But perhaps people who are truly interested in the role of PR in contemporary societies should pay it more attention.

 Examine the ways in which internal communications is used in any organisation you know well. What media do they use and in what circumstances? What ethical issues, if any, does it raise?

Case study: Kraft and Cadbury's: A corporate takeover and job fears

In early 2010 the US food giant Kraft took over the well-known UK confectioner and chocolate manufacturer, Cadbury's. At the time Cadbury's employed just under 7,000 people in the UK and Ireland. The firm's management had initially opposed the takeover, as had the trade unions, with considerable public backing: Cadbury's produces iconic British brands and its principal manufacturing site, Bournville, with its generous housing provision and social facilities, is often seen as an early expression of corporate social responsibility. Critics noted Kraft had earlier taken over the UK chocolate firm Terry's and shifted production to eastern Europe.

Shortly after the takeover Kraft announced the closure of one of Cadbury's factories which it had previously pledged to keep open. Kraft Executive Vice President Marc Firestone told a UK parliamentary hearing that he was personally 'very sorry'. Kraft gave a commitment to keep Cadbury's remaining manufacturing plants open for two years, although there were some job losses at Cadbury's corporate HQ, with more expected with the closure of Kraft's separate UK headquarters.

Kraft Chairman and Chief Executive Irene Rosenfeld attracted some criticism for not visiting any of Cadbury's UK factories until autumn 2010, when she said that 'I actually wanted to wait until we were able to look ahead'. However plans were confirmed for a Centre for Chocolate Excellence at Bournville, with Kraft workers moving from Germany. The unions have continued to express concerns despite most workers admitting that – for the time being – it has been business as usual at Cadbury's.[4]

If you were taking over responsibility for internal communications for Cadbury's, as part of Kraft's UK operations, how would you go about devising a suitable internal communications strategy (you might want to use some of the techniques described in Chapter 10)? What problems do you think you would encounter and how would you deal with them? (Remember, this story continues to unfold, so you can find out more details and update yourself online.)

- Internal communications is the specialised and planned activity concerned with conveying messages within an organisation. It is often – but not always – handled by PR practitioners.
- Unusually PR people in this field directly control the media through which they communicate. These can range from internal electronic and print media through to speeches, meetings and ambient media. This presents internal communicators with plenty of opportunities but also with a challenge: they have to produce content which conveys the organisation's messages and at the same time resonates with the intended audience.
- Since internal communicators have an unusual degree of control over their messages – unlike in conventional media relations work there is no external check on what they say and organisations can also take steps to silence dissenting voices – they can be likened to internal propagandists. This means that internal communications, although often overlooked, faces its own ethical challenges.

CHAPTER 6

LOBBYING, POLITICAL AND GOVERNMENT PR

INTRODUCTION

Some of the most-discussed and controversial areas of PR work involve politics. Confusingly the term public relations is seldom used by practitioners in this field, but, whatever name is given to it, the world of politics makes extensive use of PR. This includes the growing lobbying industry (although again many shy away from the term lobbying) which seeks to influence the actions of government; political PR which is used by politicians as they compete for political power and seek to win elections; and – overlapping with this – government PR which aims to provide citizens with the information they need in an even-handed way.

LEARNING OBJECTIVES

- What lobbying – or public affairs – is, and its relationship to PR
- Why lobbying is controversial and what can – and cannot – be done about it
- 'Spin', Political and government PR: how they are different and how they are intertwined
- Why political PR is different from commercial PR

LOBBYING

Lobbyists are important creatures of our age. Their activities are seldom out of the news in the United States and the United Kingdom, and scandals involving lobbying rock most democracies from time to time. The word is often used in the same breath as PR, and as with PR there has been some awkwardness about what name to give it. Lobbying may be the term in general use by laypeople, and the one, crucially, that is used in the media, but in the UK practitioners seldom call themselves lobbyists. Many opt for 'public affairs' (although this has a different meaning in the USA), which is often the name used by the big international PR consultancies. Terms such as 'political consultancy' (the UK trade body for lobbying firms is called the Association of Professional Political Consultants), 'political communications', 'government affairs' and 'government relations' are also used. Still more confusingly these titles can mean slightly different things to different people. Those working in the not-for-profit sector often dodge all these terms (just as they avoid calling what they do PR) and lump their activities together as 'campaigning'.

Lobbying – or public affairs – includes any activity designed to influence the actions of those who exercise the powers of government and those who make laws – the legislature. This includes not just national governments, but all places where political power is located, and wherever decisions are made about laws and regulations and their implementation. Thus lobbying embraces not just national legislatures but also central government ministries, agencies, and a growing army of regulatory bodies. It includes regional and even local tiers of government, but also covers an ever-spreading array of international organisations, operating either globally – for example the United

Nations, the International Monetary Fund, the World Trade Organisation – or in different parts of the world – for example ASEAN (the Association of Southeast Asian Nations), NAFTA (the North American Free Trade Area), the European Union, and the African Union.

Rather like PR itself, lobbying activity is timeless. It has been attempted in all societies throughout history, even if the techniques have evolved. Businesses and others have always had an interest in influencing government decisions: what is new is that they now do so in a planned and deliberate way, using specialist staff. However the origins of the word 'lobbying' itself are telling. It derives from the lobby of the Willard Hotel in Washington DC where business men and others sought to waylay and gain the ear of the US President Grant (President 1869–1877). Since then it has become a large, specialised discipline in its own right, employing tens of thousands of people in Washington alone. The biggest centre outside North America is in Brussels, the hub of the European Union's administration.

Lobbying v. 'The lobby'

Readers familiar with the UK should not confuse the practice of 'lobbying' with 'the lobby' or the 'parliamentary lobby', a group of specialist political journalists who enjoy special privileges at Westminster. Although both operate at the heart of government they are quite distinct.

In the United States and Europe lobbying gradually assumed its modern form as the role of governments in society and economic life grew. However the market liberalisation which began in the 1980s and which continues to sweep the world has given lobbying an enormous boost. Large sections of the economy which were in state hands are now privately owned and administered: direct government control may have ended, but government legislation and regulation have an enormous impact on how businesses are run, and hence businesspeople want to influence such decisions. Increasingly governments respond to popular anxieties about issues – be they to do with security, food, medical treatment, health and safety, environmental or other matters – through legislation and regulation. Often these feelings are articulated by NGOs which lobby on their own behalf. Governments also have to grapple with the consequences of increasingly rapid change. New phenomena such as the world wide web can sweep the world at an unprecedented speed, and as governments take urgent measures to seek to control of regulate such developments, those outside government resort to lobbying to protect their interests.

Lord Tim Bell

So charming that dogs cross the road to be stroked by him.[1]

For many years Lord Bell has been the biggest figure in the worlds of lobbying and public relations in the UK. The company he chairs, Chime plc, the UK's largest PR and advertising group, also undertakes considerable amounts of international business, including work in post-war Iraq, for Saudi Arabia, in Russia and Ukraine and for Belarus.

Tim Bell started his career in the advertising industry. Working with the Saatchi brothers (of Saatchi & Saatchi advertising agency fame) he was closely involved in Margaret Thatcher's political campaigns. The unrivalled contacts he has acquired in the political world are key to his lobbying successes. Although his firms employ more people than any competitor in the UK, Bell is still personally and directly involved in lobbying and media relations work.

Lord Bell on Spin:

It's a very hard thing to explain but half of me dislikes being called a top spin doctor and half of me quite likes it. The half that likes it I suppose is the ego bit – it makes me into something. It's no different than saying top footballer or successful surgeon. The half that dislikes it is because the image of the spin doctor is a negative image and it's a code word for deceiver and I've always known that what works in this business is the truth.[2]

Lord Bell is an active member of the House of Lords, the upper house of the UK's legislature (where he joined a number of people with lobbying or PR backgrounds). A controversial figure, particularly for those on the political left, and a staunch supporter of the Conservative Party, he and his firms nonetheless carried out considerable amounts of work for the Labour Government in the UK when it was in power. Indeed Tony Blair's former Press Advisor David Hill worked with Lord Bell before and after his time in government. In addition to its political and governmental work Chime also undertakes large amounts of commercial business: individual companies within the group undertake a full range of PR and communication specialisms.

www.chime.plc.uk

The work of lobbyists can be broken down as follows:

- First, and most basically, to provide information and advance warning. In the modern world it is hard for any organisation to keep up with the increasingly large volumes of legislation and regulation which might affect it (and which may have serious cost implications). Even if it is impossible to influence the final decision, the earlier organisations receive notice the better able they are to prepare themselves. Thus many organisations find it worthwhile to pay lobbyists to monitor the work of obscure arms of government, legislatures (or committees thereof), regulatory bodies and international organisations. Indeed, even some government organisations pay for such services in order to keep abreast with what the rest of government is up to – so big and so complex has the work of government become.
- Once alerted to possible changes, to seek to amend proposed government or legislative measures, to stop them in their tracks or, if all else fails, to over-turn them. This attempt to exert influence is the classic focus of lobbying. Lobbyists always stress the need to get involved at the earliest stage in the

policy-making process, before policy is settled. The earlier they are involved, the easier it is to change policy. However lobbying can continue up to and beyond the passage of legislation and the taking of formal decisions (there is, for example, often considerable leeway about how new laws and regulations are implemented).

- Lobbying can also be used to advocate government action – a classic focus of NGO activity.

Anyone can 'lobby'. Beyond the business world and the large campaigning NGOs such as Greenpeace and Amnesty International are many lesser charities and community groups: if a group of people in your neighbourhood is seeking to put pressure on the local council about improving a park they are lobbying. Even governments lobby: one of the principal functions of embassies in foreign capitals is to lobby their host governments.

Like other forms of PR, lobbying can be undertaken 'in-house', by lobbyists who are directly employed by the organisation concerned, or by an external firm – or by a combination of the two. Only relatively large organisations or ones which are particularly concerned about government action will normally deem it worthwhile to employ full-time lobbyists, but many businesses are members of trade organisations and one of the main functions of such bodies is to lobby on behalf of their members. Some organisations will retain the services of lobbying firms to keep a watching brief and then use them for specific campaigns when the need arises.

In common with other PR people, lobbyists can come from a range of backgrounds: no specific qualifications are required. However, just as journalistic expertise is valued in mainstream PR, political and governmental experience is often an entry ticket to the world of lobbying. A strong interest in political life is vital, and in order to influence government a proper understanding of the way it works is essential. Direct personal knowledge of key personalities is seen as distinctly advantageous (see below).

Shortly before the 2010 General Election in the UK, several former UK government ministers were secretly filmed by TV investigators agreeing in principle to work for a (fictitious) lobbying firm. The footage was aired in a TV documentary. It appeared to suggest that they would use their experience and contacts to promote the lobbying firm's interests in return for substantial payments – some also boasted about past work of this kind. The story provoked outrage and the former ministers were suspended from the then governing Labour Party.

Although no real lobbyists were involved in this particular expose, for many it seemed to underline how outside interests could get a hearing – and perhaps influence decisions – if they paid money to the right politicians. It was only part of a long litany of lobbying-related scandals which appear to show the scope for abuse of this kind, and the way in which the private world of lobbying can be rather different from the way it likes to be seen.[3]

Lobbying's links to PR

Some lobbyists like to distance themselves from the PR industry. They see media relations work as a blunt instrument compared with their ability to target the real decision-makers in government. This reflects the fact that effective lobbying often involves contact with only a handful of carefully chosen people, rather than the larger audiences PR typically seeks to influence. Such lobbyists are likely to be employed by independent, specialist lobbying firms which do not undertake general PR work. However almost all large PR consultancies offer lobbying as part of their menu of services and therefore employ specialist staff: it is now part of what clients expect. While lobbying can be carried on discreetly and effectively, lobbying campaigns may be combined with other forms of PR activity in pursuit of common objectives. This reflects the fact that politicians pay great heed to media coverage and public opinion, and so media relations can be used to apply additional pressure. The connection between PR and lobbying is underlined by the way in which many companies want the lobbying and PR services they buy to come under the same roof – whereas they have historically almost always bought their PR and advertising from different suppliers.

Any business sector may need to lobby. The world of fashion might seem as far from the world of lobbying as one might get, but even it has its own issues with which to contend. Concerns about super-skinny models and eating disorders have already raised their head politically, while the use of cheap labour by some big brand names has also aroused controversy. Fashion houses need to be concerned about all the government-related factors which might impact on their prosperity – from work permits through to taxation arrangements and concerns about fair trade.

Lobbying's own issues

Two major, interlinked issues haunt any discussion of lobbying and are the reason it remains so controversial. The first is that the ability of the rich and powerful to hire the skills of lobbyists is unfair and gives such people and organisations a stronger voice in society's decision-making processes. The second is a lack of transparency and the associated potential for corruption. From time immemorial lobbying has been connected to many political fund-raising scandals and sometimes the personal enrichment of politicians and officials. The resulting stigma is one of the main reasons so many 'lobbyists' shun the name.

The benefits of public affairs

Lionel Zetter, a Public Affairs consultant, author of *Lobbying* and *The Political Campaigning Handbook* (both published by Harriman House) and one of the biggest names in the lobbying industry as well as a former president of the CIPR (Chartered Institute of Public Relations)

In any mature democracy lobbying is undoubtedly a force for good. Despite the bad press which it sometimes attracts, lobbying is an integral part of the democratic process.

First and foremost, lobbying produces better legislation. There are at least two sides to every argument, and lobbyists ensure that legislation is scrutinised properly from every point of view. Lobbyists – and their clients – alert governments to the unintended consequences of badly drafted legislation.

The second reason why lobbying is good for democracy is that it helps to level the playing field. Governments have a huge advantage, in that they have the civil service machine at their disposal. Opposition parties, in comparison, lack resources. Lobbyists provide backbenchers and opposition parties with the ammunition they need to take on governments, and help to ensure that governments with large majorities do not simply ram legislation through.

Finally, the right to lobby is enshrined in the Magna Carta in the UK and the First Amendment to the Constitution in the USA. Both refer to the right to petition government for the redress of grievances, and that is ultimately what lobbying is all about. Any restriction to transparent and regulated lobbying is a restriction on democracy itself.

Lobbying adds to the power of the already powerful

The first concern – the notion that lobbying tips the balance even further in favour of the wealthy and powerful – is superficially attractive but requires a little more examination. It is understandable that critics of lobbying highlight the role played by wealthy businesses, and it is certainly true that the majority of clients of the big lobbying firms are large companies seeking to further their interests. However non-governmental organisations or NGOs are themselves skilful users of lobbying techniques, however hard they try to avoid using the term. As we show in Chapter 3, campaigning is a core business for the large and expanding NGO sector. NGO leaders gain experience of PR and lobbying throughout their careers, and indeed are often promoted on the basis of their talents as communicators. In contrast the rise of business leaders tends to depend on their mastery of a narrower range of technical and financial skills. They usually lack the PR aptitude and experience of the NGO leadership (the exceptional business leaders we have all heard of, people with charisma and high profiles, are just that: the exceptions).

Hostility to corporate interests can also blind critics to the fact that the business world is itself far from monolithic. Big businesses are in competition with each other, and there is also strong rivalry between business sectors. Smaller businesses which are unable to afford to conduct their own lobbying activities are frequently represented by trade associations. So governments tend to hear from a range of commercial interests, alongside not-for-profit organisations, before they make decisions. The true extent to which governments are influenced by these competing voices is all but impossible to assess. Governments may be happy to be seen as listening to different points of view as that is viewed positively, but are reluctant to admit that they are acting under pressure: hence they are not wholly reliable when it comes to admitting the extent to which lobbyists shape their decisions. On the other hand, like PR (and advertising) people, when talking about their influence lobbyists tend to both over-claim and under-claim. When they are seeking business they understandably talk up – in private – what they claim as their successes, but when they or their industry face criticism it is in their interests to play down their role: lobbyists do not seek a high public profile.

The defence of lobbying is that it is not only an inevitable part of life but also a necessary and positive one. It is simply a modern professionalised embodiment of the ancient right of people to petition their rulers, and, by extension, to seek the advice and support of others to help them do so. Modern governments are responsible for a vast range of policy areas which involves drafting and implementing detailed and intricate laws and regulations. On their own they cannot hope to keep abreast of all the information and opinions they need to take into account. Lobbying is a means of providing them with the raw material they need to make informed decisions which reflect the different interests in their societies. The ultimate check, in democracies, is that those decisions are subject to the final verdict of the electorate. It would be a rash government which simply listened to lobbyists and ignored public opinion.

The potential for corruption

The second issue which dogs lobbying is the potential for corruption. Clearly governmental and regulatory decisions can be of enormous importance to business leaders and have huge financial implications. This means that there is always a temptation to use any method if it achieves the desired goal, and one such method is the payment of bribes, which can take many forms. Inevitably some politicians and decision-makers will always be dishonest and greedy – no system of regulation or policing can wholly rule this out – and it follows that some lobbyists will always be tempted to exploit this weakness (on the basis that both parties believe it will remain a secret). In the UK the new and stringent Bribery Act 2010, which has been described as a mirror image of the US Foreign Corrupt Practices Act, will have implications for the lobbying industry.[4]

However bribery and corruption is not always blatant and can be hard to pin down (and prove). There is a fine line between legitimate hospitality and offering people luxurious meals, travel and accommodation. Skilful operators can perhaps influence politicians and others as much by the prospect of gifts or favours, including future employment for themselves or family members, as by gifts and favours themselves.

Asked about a glamorous Republican Party funding event held by President Bush senior, his spokesman, Marlin Fitzwater, replied:

'It's buying access to the system, yes. That's what the political parties and the political operation is all about.'... Asked how other, less wealthy citizens could buy into the system, Mr Fitzwater said, 'They have to demand access in other ways.'[5]

Another systemic problem in contemporary democracies arises from political parties' need to attract funding from wealthy individuals and companies in order to finance their activities – and especially to meet the costs of running their election campaigns. Few democracies provide all the money politicians need from public funds, so they are forced to look to private sources. However closely the system is regulated, there will always be suspicions about donations from people whose businesses are affected by government decisions. As the saying has it, there is no such thing as a free lunch. Providing large-scale funds to political parties all but guarantees access to senior politicians – dinners, receptions, and so on are the staples of fund-raising. And proving cause and effect between donation and decision is usually impossible, as the process is normally veiled and subtle, often involving many tiers of intermediaries. Politicians would not be human if, as they banked current donations, they did not consider how their behaviour might affect future largesse. The perception that favours are being promised or given, however hotly denied, will forever risk dragging lobbyists and politicians into disrepute.

Campaign for Lobbying Transparency

In the UK the Campaign for Lobbying Transparency, which campaigns about these issues, has proposed the following changes to improve transparency:

- A mandatory register of lobbyists.
- Recording of all meetings and correspondence between lobbyists and elected members, officials and ministers.
- Enforceable ethics rules for all lobbyists.

www.lobbyingtransparency.org

Regulating lobbying

The importance of lobbying and the scope for its abuse have led to many attempts to regulate it. Lobbying's own spokespeople, rather like those of the PR world, often see their trade heading towards the sunny uplands of moral probity, leaving any dubious associations far behind. Of course there is no reason why lobbyists should be more or less ethical than anyone else. Like PR, much lobbying is routine, mundane, and rather inconsequential. However lobbying scandals keep resurfacing around the world, and each time a scandal surfaces it leads to calls for action to curb particular forms of activity. But no sooner has one set of rules been imposed than another breach occurs. There will always be those who bend or break the rules. Lobbyists are fond of asserting in public that it is their understanding of the processes of government that matters, not personal connections, but there is no shortage of evidence that when they feel it is to their advantage, especially when seeking new business, many boast about the people they know and the way they can secure access to decision makers.

The European Union has recently been consulting on rules for interest representatives (lobbyists) who are in contact with EU organisations. They propose the following rules.
   Lobbyists should:

- Identify themselves by names and organisation
- Declare their clients and interests
- Ensure any information they supply is fully accurate and up-to-date
- Not seek information by dishonest means
- Not induce EU officials to contravene their standards of behaviour
- If employing former EU officials, respect the rules which apply to them.[6]

***

Taking a strong public stance against the abuse of lobbying has become a popular move on the part of politicians, although whether it amounts to more than gesture politics is more in doubt. As part of just such a crack down on lobbying, President Barack Obama banned former lobbyists who joined his administration from working for government agencies which they had recently lobbied, but almost immediately had to issue a waiver.[7]

Effective regulation of lobbying has proved very difficult to achieve. There are many reasons for this. Critics of lobbying normally call for transparency, including such things as details of meetings and registers of lobbyists' clients. This is much more easily said than done. Some lobbyists work for other professional service providers such as law firms, and many lobbyists work in-house with a great range of confusing job titles. The problem is akin to that of regulating PR – how could they all be covered?

Moreover many other people who would never think of themselves as lobbyists may from time to time be involved in lobbying: at what point do they become lobbyists? Lobbyists themselves often argue that it is better for them to take a back seat when it comes to meetings and direct contact with government. Indeed the only watertight way to ensure there was no contact between lobbyists and government would be to prohibit any contact between government and external organisations. Even if this were possible the preventive measure would surely be worse than the disease. Not only would government be denied vital outside opinion and information, but the fundamental right to petition government would be fatally undermined.

Partly to get round this problem, the emphasis is often on registering lobbying firms, or PR consultancies which offer lobbying services. However even here there are definitional problems, and such firms use a variety of names to describe what they do. PR and lobbying can blur together. Indeed, defining exactly what is, and is not, a lobbying firm could exercise many a legal mind. (For example, when the wife of the UK health minister was criticised for her involvement in lobbying she denied it, saying that she offered 'strategic policy' advice to clients.[8]) The basic problem is that what we call lobbying is so timeless and fundamental an activity that its clumsy regulation or proscription risks simply displacing it or causing it to adopt a new name or disguise.

Another problem arises from a characteristic which lobbying shares with PR. So many of its activities, including the most controversial aspects of it, takes place in private, in the course of small meetings and one-to-one conversations. And such discussions may well be subtle and nuanced – there are often no formal minutes or records. This means that the recollection of what takes place becomes one person's word against another's. It is no coincidence that lobbying scandals often surface only when hidden cameras and recording devices are used by investigative reporters. Although attempts can be made to register meetings with lobbyists, as we have seen, lobbyists may deliberately choose to remain in the background, simply helping to prepare for and arrange such meetings. The business of government involves an infinite number of meetings with outside groups: would listing them all be feasible? Often formal meetings are far from being the most important ones – is it practical for every politician and official to report every conversation he or she has at social occasions, even though such exchanges could be much more important than what happens at a proper, minuted meeting? Does too much formality simply mean that people will find other ways of holding confidential discussions?

The focus of those who wish to see lobbying regulated is corporate lobbying. There is seldom any call for scrutiny of the activities of NGOs and campaigning organisations. These normally conduct their lobbying in-house and are customarily more focused on lobbying than commercial organisations can allow themselves to be. They use all kinds of lobbying techniques, and their proposals and objectives are not necessarily sensible. However a fundamental sympathy for not-for-profit organisations, and for many of the campaigning groups' objectives, means that little thought is given to the regulation of non-commercial lobbying.

 Can lobbying be successfully regulated? If not, why not? If so, how could it be done? | You may wish to consider attempts to regulate lobbying in your society.

POLITICAL PR AND THE ROLE OF SPIN DOCTORS

The majority of business leaders may be uncomfortable communicators, but the politicians who govern us have always embraced the arts of communication. PR skills loom large in a politician's armoury. Even dictatorships care about public opinion, but in democracies it is the lifeblood of politics, just as financial realities and the iron laws of supply and demand constitute the foundation for business activity.

Political PR is yet another area which dodges using the term 'public relations' to describe itself. Politicians' sensitivity to public opinion has meant that in many countries they seek to distance themselves from the term as it has acquired negative overtones, often preferring words such as 'information' or the hard-to-disapprove-of 'communication'. This has not stopped outsiders and the media continuing to use the PR label, often in a negative way, to describe political communication.

Today, in the Anglo-Saxon world, the most common term used to describe political PR is *spin* – its exponents are called *spin doctors*.

Spin and spin doctors

The use of the word *spin* in the PR context can be traced back to the USA in the 1970s. Its origins seem to lie in baseball, and derive from the way in which the pitcher can manipulate the ball as he throws it towards the catcher, thereby tricking the batter (this is similar to the use of spin in cricket, making the term readily understood in many other English-speaking countries).

As a pejorative term for political communication spin came into vogue in the United Kingdom in the 1990s. It was firmly associated with New Labour under its then leader Tony Blair. Blair and his team placed particular emphasis on improving media management as they sought to make their party – which had languished in opposition for many years – electable again. The widespread use of the term indicates that it seemed to capture an important reality about contemporary political communication.

'Spin' conveys, more powerfully than the term PR itself, a sense of manipulation and even sinister menace. It is firmly associated with the exercise of power – when the word is used outside the world of politics it tends to refer to high-level corporate manoeuvring, not day-to-day marketing PR. Governments may prefer to talk about 'communication' and 'information': spin implies that the information communicated is carefully selected and delivered in such a way that it is to the advantage of the sender of the message. Since so much is at stake, the methods used can be ruthless: telling the truth may not be a priority.

Spin is the antithesis of what, traditionally, was seen as proper governmental (as opposed to party political) communication. Such communication work, at least in the UK, was firmly in the hands of permanent civil servants who served governments of any complexion and operated according to strict, non-partisan guidelines. Such, at least, was the theory. As we see below, government communication has always been subject to party political pressure.

Why political PR is different

Spin may not be unique to politics, but it exemplifies the way in which media relations is central to politics. It is a two-way street. Politics has always been central to the media in a way that individual companies are not. Only a company going through a major crisis begins to receive the kind of sustained media coverage that governments routinely receive in good times as well as bad. All over the world presidents and prime ministers feature on the front pages, or at the head of the news bulletins, in ways which would make most corporate chief executives tremble – and rightly so, because such coverage might well indicate that their jobs were on the line. Moreover there are long established traditions, particularly in the realm of print journalism, of the media adopting strong editorial positions on political questions. The media relations aspects of PR work is also important for another reason. The commercial world has always used paid-for advertising as a primary means of communication, but in many societies – including the UK and much of Europe – political advertising is sharply curtailed, forcing politicians to rely on editorial content to promote themselves and their policies (and to attack their opponents).

While political marketing borrows from commercial marketing (and *vice versa*), it takes place in a very different context, which means that simplistic comparisons should be avoided. The language of the commercial world often fails to ring true in the political sphere. The principle behind commercial PR is that its practitioners are informing people who exercise individual choices (and, then, usually enjoy rights to seek redress if they have legitimate grounds for dissatisfaction with their choice). In the political world the options are much more limited. The choice normally arises once every few years, and involves a decision which forces people to choose one 'supplier' for all their political needs, without any rights of redress or money-back guarantees. Above all it is a collective 'choice': the government has full powers to govern everyone within its jurisdiction: those who oppose it are subject to its authority as it compels its citizens to act in various ways. To put it simply, if an individual and a company choose to have nothing to do with each other that is normally – unless special conditions apply – the end of the matter. Not so with government: you may abhor the government but you still have to pay your taxes, and on the other hand you are entitled to the state's protection and whatever services it provides.

Romeo and Juliet

Political campaigning can be particularly demanding and has a much higher aggression quotient than ordinary PR. One of the great maestros of modern times is James Carville, who master-minded Bill Clinton's successful campaign for the US Presidency in 1992, and has since assisted with campaigns in other countries.

During the 1992 campaign he was having a relationship with Mary Matalin, a senior figure on George Bush senior's unsuccessful campaign for re-election. The two went on to marry and have children. They also co-authored (with Peter Knobler) a fascinating book, *All's Fair: Love, War and Running for the President*.[9] The two did not drop or change their political allegiances: Matalin later worked for George W Bush's administration.

These and other factors give rise to a range of differences between political, governmental and commercial PR:

- Companies, however large and complex, are simpler organisms than modern democratic governments. Within the law, their obligation is to do whatever best serves the interests of the people who own them – their shareholders. Democratic governments have a split agenda. On the one hand they have responsibilities to all citizens (and beyond that to the international community), but on the other hand they are controlled by political parties which never forget that they are campaigning for re-election. This difference has considerable implications for communication. Commercial organisations can afford to ignore audiences: for example, if you are unlikely either to be a potential customer or to influence one, then communicating with you about products is a waste of resources. Political parties are similarly in the market for votes, and know that some parts of the electorate will never vote for them. However when they control governments they have to suppress any instinct to ignore such people. Die-hard political opponents have to be told about state services and communicated with on the same basis as existing and potential supporters. This tension between government responsibility (providing essential advice and information to all who need it) and political marketing (showing how good you are in the hope of being re-elected) is at the heart of much of the controversy about government communication.

- Government (as opposed to political) communication may be about rights and entitlements, duties and behaviour, matters which affect all citizens regardless of their political allegiances, but messages about such issues are often sensitive and it is tempting for politicians to make the most of their achievements, and to talk up good news and play down the bad. Increasingly PR consultancies are used to help government put across its messages, another powerful weapon in government's hands. In theory politically neutral public officials should ensure that the system is not abused, but it is striking that the UK expenditure on (politically neutral) government advertising always rises just before elections!

- As mentioned above, the targets of companies' PR activities are ultimately a matter for commercial judgement. This means that the wealthier and more powerful you are, the more likely it is that commercial PR people will try to influence you: you are, for example, more likely to buy more of the goods and services their paymasters produce, or to own or buy shares. Poor, powerless people are – frankly – of less interest. Here government and political PR march to two different tunes. Government PR turns the commercial model inside out by being (or seeking to be) more interested in the weak and poor: government benefits and services are often designed with such people in mind. Whereas the wealthy and powerful are frequently seen as being able to take care of many of their own interests, their counterparts are the intended audiences for advice on such matters as financial benefits, health, education, training, employment and housing. The political – as opposed to the governmental – position is different again. The brutal realities of political campaigning mean that the only target audiences which matter comprise those people who: (1) are likely to vote (so increasingly the elderly matter more than younger people because they are more likely to bother to vote); (2) might vote for the party concerned, but have not yet finally decided (committed voters are unlikely to be swayed); and (3) vote where their votes count (this will depend on the electoral system, but piling up surplus majorities in particular areas achieves nothing). Indeed if people are likely to vote for a rival party, the (usually unmentioned) logic is that is better to discourage them from voting at all.

- In commercial marketing market share matters, but market size is all-important. There is little point in a company increasing its market share if its sales are plunging as the market contracts. In politics, market share is king: there is no point winning a record vote if your opponent does even better, and a victory on a low turn-out is still a victory.

- Access to taxpayer funding means that governments have potentially unlimited resources for communication at their disposal. They can not only employ thousands of their own PR staff, but hire PR consultancies and engage in associated activity such as advertising. No company can match this scale of activity. Large-scale and sophisticated communication is necessary if governments are to inform their citizenry about what they are doing, but given the conflicting interests outlined above there will always be a temptation to exploit this advantage in the hope of being re-elected – rather than helping citizens. To some extent this advantage is tacitly accepted as one of the legitimate spoils of electoral victory: opposition parties and politicians look forward to using it themselves when the political wheel of fortune turns in their favour.

- However not everything favours governments. Whereas businesses face competition from other companies which are engaged in similar day-to-day activities, in democratic politics the position is different. Opposition parties are not responsible for anything (apart from the limited but important matter of running their own campaign machines). Instead they are campaigning organisations which enjoy considerable freedom to choose what they wish to speak about and propose. In contrast governments are responsible for an enormous range of functions. Their PR people have to defend a long border. Not only may the opposition attack at any point, but governments are constantly at the mercy of events: at any time the government may be put on the defensive about an unexpected problem, at home or abroad – one has only to think of the difficulties caused to European air passengers by volcanic ash from Iceland, or the effects of the oil leak at BP's facility in the Gulf of Mexico.

- Political PR is much more likely to be negative than its commercial equivalent. Commercial PR realises that negative campaigns raise awareness of rival companies, making potential customers more likely to consider alternative options. It is significant that the best-known negative commercial campaigns involve competition between well-known rival brands, where the danger of raising awareness can be largely set to one side. Such campaigns, which can degenerate into mudslinging, can seem undignified and distasteful, reflecting badly on those who conduct them. They risk putting off those they seek to influence and threaten to drag the relevant business sector into disrepute. Companies may seek to improve their position but know that in the end they have to co-exist with competitors. In politics the stakes are different, for the winner often takes all (or at least hopes to do so). As a result negative campaigning is carried on with few holds barred. Moreover in many democratic elections there are only two realistic contenders for the top job. Since both are high-profile, the danger of publicising a rival can be largely set to one side. And in their anxiety to win power through the ballot box, the other pitfalls of negative campaigning are overlooked. It is worth considering the effect of this on the public image of politicians and political life as a whole. How would we change our view of a business sector if its leaders publicly tore into each other in the way we have come to expect of politicians?

- The reliance on negative campaigning is inseparable from the way in which political marketing is personality-based – to a much greater extent than its commercial equivalent. While a few corporate chief executives have become well known, most people do not associate the individual names and faces of corporate managers with most of the products they buy. Instead companies rely on the public choosing brands which they promote heavily through PR, advertising and other forms of marketing: indeed some of the largest multinationals such as Unilever and Procter & Gamble are mainly known to the general public for their brands, which have many different names, rather than as companies in their own right. In politics the position is reversed. Politicians may try to create brands (and the public sector certainly spends a great deal on branding) – but in most cases the branding is weak. Relatively few political brands survive the test of time, and even those which continue to resonate – such as the New Deal or the National Health Service – struggle to compete with the prominence of political leaders from those times, such as President Roosevelt or Winston Churchill. Individual politicians, their lives and even the lives of their families, are the focus of media coverage in a way which is rarely equalled in the world of business, not least because the media like to tell stories based on individual personalities rather than abstract policies. This different focus is reflected in political PR.

- The use of modern marketing techniques in politics is one of the factors behind the reliance on personality. In mature markets there is seldom much difference between competing products – the drive for competitive advantage means that most distinguishing features of successful products are ironed out quickly as competitors emulate them. Blind tasting may reveal that most people cannot tell the difference between the best-selling lagers, or actually prefer Pepsi to its better-selling rival, but a massive investment in marketing ensures that people are not only aware of the separate brands but express and act upon strong brand preferences. A similar process has occurred in politics. A political party such as the UK Labour Party, which was once driven by ideology and advocated policies determined by party activists, found that its traditional approach did not provide an effective platform for winning elections. Now increasingly sophisticated market research techniques are used to find out what people want, and then politicians seek to sell themselves as the people who can deliver it. The logical consequence of this – since all parties use similar market research techniques – is that they offer similar policies (although because they are in competition this is something they fiercely deny). If particular policies prove unpopular, they are quickly modified or dropped – and popular policies proposed by rival parties are adopted. What then distinguishes political parties and candidates? There is a lingering afterglow from the ideological past, although in the political world this is perhaps more often expressed negatively, in terms of a refusal to vote for a party because of how its brand is perceived. But beyond that, the main differences between parties, and the one that cannot be so readily changed, are the personalities of their leaders. While PR and other techniques can have some influence on how a personality is regarded, an individual's unique personality (including their appearance, mannerisms, life story and family associations) is not something that can be readily transformed. It is tempting to see personality playing an ever-greater role in contemporary elections – a trend which is compounded by the media's natural interest in personality-based stories.

Compare and contrast a big political PR campaign with a major commercial campaign of which you are aware. (Consider similarities and differences in terms of the nature of the objectives, audiences, messages, strategy, tactics, media and outcomes.)

Government, politics and the global financial crisis

The global financial crisis which marked the closing years of the first decade of twenty-first century included many dramatic episodes – of which perhaps the collapse of Lehmann Brothers bank in 2008 was the most striking.

It posed many communications challenges for politicians and governments. First of all, they had a duty to all their citizens – and the wider world – to maintain confidence in the system, while putting across with urgency their messages about what they were doing to put matters right. It was generally agreed that if they failed to do so the consequences could have been catastrophic. However politics is also a blame game, and the same politicians who had been eager to take credit for the previous economic boom were anxious to escape responsibility for the financial crash. The events aroused considerable public anxiety and it was clear that they were likely to have huge electoral significance and would impact on the careers of individual politicians around the world.

Governments had been responsible for the system of regulation to which financial institutions were subject before the crash, and regulators and central banks also wanted to defend their records. The banks and their managers were also under attack as they sought to continue their work, sometimes under new or public ownership. As new ideas for financial regulation were developed after the crash, the European Union's Internal Market Commissioner Michel Barnier announced that he would be tackling the dominance of the bank lobby in the expert groups that advise the European Commission on financial regulation, and seeking greater representation for consumer groups, unions, small businesses and NGOs.[10]

As a group, review the key events of the financial crisis in your country – you can research them online. Then divide yourselves up and, individually, imagine yourselves to be responsible for PR for one of the following: the governing party or head of government in your country; their main political opponent or opposing political party; the main financial regulatory authority; a major bank; and an bank customers' consumer group. Draw up a list of your likely communications tasks and outline how you might seek to tackle them. Then discuss them with the other members of your group: what conflicts emerge?

- Political PR and lobbying are important industries, but operate under many aliases, a fact which reflects sensitivities and controversy about their role.
- Lobbying, or public affairs, is concerned with attempts to influence laws and regulations and the decisions and actions of government bodies – at all levels. It is closely linked to PR but faces its own controversies, leading to attempts at regulation.

- Political PR is often referred to as 'spin' and is about competing for political advantage. It can, at least in theory, be distinguished from Government PR, which is concerned with communicating with citizens without seeking political advantage.
- Political PR has its own characteristics. It is usually much more negative and personal than commercial PR.

What is lobbying? Identify and research a lobbying campaign. What did it achieve?
What – if any – are the special characteristics of political PR? Research and discuss examples.

Some suggestions for reading

McNair, Brian, *An Introduction to Political Communication* (Routledge 2003) offers a good readable introduction. O'Shaughnessy, Nicholas Jackson, *Politics and Propaganda: Weapons of Mass Seduction* (Manchester University Press 2004) is stimulating. Machiavelli, Niccolo, *The Prince* (Penguin 1999), offers a practitioner's insights and is still immensely influential 500 years after it was written.

On lobbying, try a lobbyist's account: John, Steven, *The Persuaders: When Lobbyists Matter* (Palgrave Macmillan 2002); but also Palast, Greg, *The Best Democracy Money Can Buy: An Investigative Reporter Exposes the Truth about Globalization, Corporate Cons and High Finance Fraudsters* (Pluto 2002) – a strongly critical account by an American, but including an account of an lobbying affair which rocked the UK government.

In addition to the PR trade bodies listed at the back of the book, UK lobbyists have their own: www.appc.org.uk – the Association of Professional Political Consultants.

CHAPTER 7

PR IN THE ONLINE WORLD

> The things that keep me awake at night are the internet and China.
>
> Sir Martin Sorrell, Chief Executive, WPP Group[1]

INTRODUCTION

Wispa was a chocolate bar that Cadbury's had ceased to make. Then following a 'bring back Wispa' campaign on Facebook (20,000 people signed up) the product was resurrected in a fanfare of publicity with national newspaper headlines such as 'An outcry on the web brings back the Wispa'. In fact the whole campaign was carefully orchestrated by the London-based PR firm Borkowski which won a major PR Week award for their efforts.[2]

On the other hand you only have to Google 'Wal-Mart Edelman' to find evidence of an online campaign that went wrong and resulted in the derogatory term 'flog' – as opposed to blog – being coined.

Not surprisingly, given these sort of examples, there has been much debate as to whether the advent of the online world has changed the sort of skills required to do PR, has just added to the list of skills needed, or has made little real difference other than speeding up the pace at which things happen and messages are communicated.

LEARNING OBJECTIVES

- Understanding the digital PR model and the opportunities and risks it presents
- What makes a good online press office
- How to create an effective online press release
- How to drive traffic to your website
- How to achieve direct audience engagement

DIGITAL PR

One of the original reasons for the emergence of digital PR as a separate specialism was that the digital world, its techniques and the language it used were unfamiliar to PR people who had grown up in an environment dominated by traditional media. The emergence of new media and their growth were particularly sudden and rapid. PR consultancies not only felt they needed to be able to exploit the new opportunities, but by highlighting the availability of their new specialist teams they were able to jostle for competitive advantage. PR firms always have difficulty singling themselves out, but one of their tried-and-tested marketing techniques is to claim that they are surfing the latest trend. And not only are digital media new, but they continue to evolve with exceptional speed, with the focus having shifted from largely static websites to interactive online opportunities such as blogs, Twitter and different forms of social media – for example Facebook and LinkedIn. (This more interactive form of online media is often called *Web 2.0* – it is not so much the technology that is important as the behaviour that it facilitates.) The evidence so far is that new media trends wax and wane much more rapidly than has been the case with traditional media, where many television and radio channels have thrived for decades with relatively few changes – and some newspapers for much longer.

New media have undoubtedly created fresh opportunities for PR, although they do not always match up to the sales talk of digital PR's enthusiasts. Use of digital media fits comfortably with the profile of commercial PR's traditional targets – affluent people and opinion formers in the developed world: such people are avid consumers of online media. But at the time of writing only a minority of the world's population is online, and that it likely to remain the case for years to come. The poor, the elderly, the badly educated and – especially – the majority of people in developing countries are much less likely to enjoy the same level of access to digital media (if they have any access whatsoever). Well-equipped PR people in modern offices need to remember that only 24% of the world's population are connected to the internet (and in many cases that connection might only be a poor quality one via an outmoded computer shared with many others).[3] All of this makes such media much less useful for many public sector campaigns concerned with, for example, health, education or social benefits, and all but useless in many societies around the world.

Online media – and in particular interactive web 2.0 social media – are good for what is called *narrowcasting*. Given enough time and resources, individuals and groups of people can be targeted far more precisely than with most traditional media. We all use digital media in our own highly distinctive way, looking at, and interacting with, different sites at different times: it is not comparable to millions of people watching the same television programme simultaneously, or buying the same newspaper on the same day. This means it is far harder to communicate with a truly mass audience and create a large-scale shared experience via online media alone. Significantly, many of the most viewed websites are those belonging to established 'old' media organisations such as the BBC, and many digital media stories only really achieve an impact once they surface in traditional mass media.

Increasingly the trend is for conventional, online and social media to become more and more interlinked. Not only do most conventional media now have online versions, but they also have a Twitter feed and Facebook links. Similarly conventional news journalists use social media to monitor news and find news stories.

The initial momentum behind some of the public demonstrations for political change in the Middle East in 2011 undoubtedly built up in social media, but were given real traction when conventional media such as TV and the press picked up the story. Use of social media remains a two-way street however: following the earlier abortive demonstrations for political change in Iran the authorities were able to trace those who had posted critical messages or instigated anti-regime activity.[4]

A quick glance at web statistics from around the world will reveal that the greatest number of visits is to social media sites, such as Facebook, and search engines, such as Google, both of which are used in highly individual ways.[5]

However volume of traffic is not a clear indicator of influence. One of the most significant of the UK's political blogs, that of 'Guido Fawkes', www.order-order.com, is viewed by a relatively small portion of the population, but the top readership sources are the Houses of Parliament and the universities of Oxford and Cambridge, followed by many media and financial institutions. Even so, Guido passes some of his biggest stories on to the mainstream media rather than attempting to handle them himself.

Much of what appears online fails to reach a wider audience. Rumours of Tiger Woods' extra-marital affairs had appeared online well before the scandals surrounding the celebrity golfer generated a media storm in 2009 – but it took a car crash and huge volumes of traditional media coverage to bring Woods' adultery into the open. And of course there have been notorious example of online hoaxes, so reliability is often an issue. Traditional news may not be perfect but at least the organisations which provide it endeavour to maintain some editorial standards, if only for reasons of self-interest as they seek to protect their brands; in contrast anyone can say anything they like online.

One of the principal challenges for traditional PR is that it is like trying to force information and comment through a funnel. Countless organisations want to get their messages out to the world, and the potential audiences they want to reach are infinite. However that information had to pass through the narrow funnel of the media – traditionally a handful of print and broadcast national media outlets, plus specialist and regional ones – which have to reject most of what is offered to them. Moreover, even when a story does run it bears the imprint of the journalist: the positive information supplied by the PR people may be cast in a partly or wholly critical light. At first glance digital PR in its role as a content creator seems to sidestep this problem. Anyone can, quite economically, set up a website or blog, or tweet, or use a range of social media. Once they have done so their communication is available worldwide. And in the process they enjoy the benefits of 'disintermediation': the information they wish to put across is conveyed exactly as they wish it to be – though social media such as Facebook and Twitter make it hard to control the resulting comments, which can just as easily be negative as positive.

These advantages are the same as those which apply to advertising (see Chapter 4), but they suffer from the same drawbacks. When it creates its own media, digital PR loses PR's unique selling proposition: third-party endorsement, usually and hopefully from an authoritative media source. And the ease with which new media can be created also means that they are seldom 'mass media' in the sense of having readerships or audiences of millions. In fact most of the many millions of websites, blogs and other forms of new media content in existence are seldom if ever visited or viewed. It is perhaps more realistic to see them as similar to books in a vast library – a handful are in frequent demand but most simply gather dust on the shelves, even if they remain available to readers who want to track them down. For anyone using their new media platforms to get across their messages, the first challenge is to get anyone to see it.

New media offer another advantage: ready interactivity. Two-way communication has always been a prized goal of PR and the internet makes this practical in an immediate and economic way. It is possible to mobilise support for causes and interact with publics in quick and convenient ways which were hitherto unthinkable. Paradoxically however the ease with which people can respond online brings its own problems. Popular causes may quickly attract broad support but it can be shallow and short-lived. Getting someone to join a Facebook campaign while sitting at their keyboard is not the same as getting them to donate money or take concrete action to further a cause. Similarly, the vast majority of tweets go largely ignored.

Nonetheless, for this and other reasons, the digital world presents a threat which PR seeks to counter. Lone complainants about a company's services can suddenly band together with other aggrieved individuals whom they would never have known about in the past. Sometimes campaigns of this kind develop momentum and create serious issues for the organisations concerned. Material that is posted online is available worldwide and is hard to eradicate: it is likely to be permanently available to those searching for relevant information and comment. The real problems that such adverse comment and information can cause is the scary stuff of many a PR presentation – it is one of the principal sales pitches for digital PR. Such issues have to be taken seriously and online comment monitored carefully, but it also has to be said that most isolated voices on the world wide web remain just that, and any organisation of any size faces and survives online hostility. For example it is easy to find criticism of big PR companies online, but this does not usually cause their senior management to lose much sleep (indeed they might feel aggrieved if critics were listing firms known to be effective in dealing with their client's opponents and their's was not included!). To be significant criticism has to include new, important and believable information; contain comments that strike a chord with an audience which matters to the organisation concerned – not people who are already die-hard opponents; and/or come from an unexpected quarter – not the 'usual suspects'. One of the harder judgement calls of online PR is knowing when to ignore the postings of others, and when and how to act.

The online world also presents its own ethical and legal challenges. Traditionally PR people's stories were filtered by journalists, and the onus was on the media to assess the sources that they used and weigh up the truth. Digital PR creates the opportunity of reaching audiences directly, which means that PR people have to think carefully about the implications. If they participate in online discussions of any kind they have to consider how they present themselves: do they introduce themselves as PR people paid by a relevant organisation, or pretend they are ordinary members of the public. Not only would many users of online media consider the use of subterfuge outrageous – it could provoke a strong public reaction – but in the UK, for example, it is now illegal for PR people to post comments in this way without declaring their interest. In the US anyone posting a tweet for which they have been paid – common practice when celebrities are paid to endorse products – has to indicate clearly that this is the case.

At its best digital PR can help organisations negotiate their way through this new environment, seizing the opportunities and overcoming the challenges. But a little scepticism is in order. For every much-trumpeted digital media PR success story there are many more pieces of new media content languishing unseen. PR people are seldom in the lead when it comes to setting up and using new media platforms – others, often with more advanced technical skills, usually get there first. There is a quiet turf war between the PR and advertising industries over the use of digital media. Big advertising agencies are often deploying more resources on digital work than PR firms, and are more familiar with the skills needed to prepare lively online content. On the other hand advertising agencies are less used to the notion of interactivity, which runs counter to their tradition of sending out messages. In the UK the recent extension of advertising regulation to include online content with a marketing intent[6] will help make online promotion more familiar territory for experienced advertising people – whereas PR people are at greater risk of getting it wrong, though the PR trade associations, at the time of writing, are trying to get to grips with the issue.

PR people have to address these realities, not simply dream of online mastery. Many PR people will continue to be outgunned in the digital world, and generating one's own online content runs counter to PR's mainstay of seeking third-party endorsement. The most distinctive contribution PR can make to the use of digital media is to realise and exploit the connection between different media forms – to recognise that traditional media, which remain hugely important, now often depend upon new media for their stories and that new media in all its forms must be taken into account in almost every campaign.

The future of digital PR

Paul Borge, Head of Digital, Consolidated PR
(Top UK PR consultancy)

Three predictions for the next five years:

1) *Social media will stop being a specialism and become more of an integral part of PR and marcoms.* At the moment the disruptive effect it is having means that agencies need specialist teams with different skill sets to stay on top of a continually and rapidly changing media and web environment. As time goes on this skill base will broaden out and we'll see a new generation of communicators emerge that naturally count expertise in search, social media and digital marketing as a part of their roles. 'Social media gurus' will, I hope, become a thing of the past!

2) *The media landscape will complete the seismic shift it is currently going through.* The printing press was invented in 1440 and has been the mainstay of media for hundreds of years, along with TV over the last sixty years. In a fraction of that time the internet has come along and dramatically shaken up every part of the news and media chain, and continues to do so. Driven by innovation and changing consumer behaviour media types have evolved and converged, the news cycle has shortened and media power has been devolved and dispersed across a whole range of new channels and influencers. At some point this will all settle down, as commercial requirements kick in.

3) *Location-based services and augmented reality will permeate social media.* Social networking finally went mobile after years of promise – the ubiquity of GPS enabled smart phones has made location-based services viable. Now there's a critical mass of users. Standalone services such as Foursquare and Gowalla will fall by the wayside, as existing giants such as Facebook and Google adopt and deploy sophisticated GPS-based services to their significant userbases. Likewise, augmented reality technology will break out of the desktop PC and onto smart phones as mobile hardware becomes more capable. Technology like facial recognition and photographic 3D mapping will make social media on mobile phones very compelling indeed.

www.consolidatedpr.com

THE DIGITAL PR MODEL

There has been much debate as to whether the problems that the online world poses PR practitioners outweigh the benefits. These debates are now largely academic – digital is here to stay and PR people have to deal with it.

The benefits of the online world are obvious and many:

- Faster, cheaper contact with the media. You can get your message and your pictures to the media in seconds without having to rely on the post or couriers.
- The opportunity to reach niche target audiences quickly and effectively. While there is a plethora of specialist print magazines there are even more specialist online communities and websites which can unite audiences across geographic boundaries and time zones – something that few forms of conventional media are able to do. (For example, pharmaceutical giant GSK, working with Echo Research, mapped the most important and influential patient groups in Asia Pacific, many of which exist primarily online. They were able to target the most influential with a view to building beneficial long-term relationships.[7])
- Social media are particularly good at reaching people in review driven markets, such as music, games and film, where the opinions of fellow users and fans is highly valued. Good reports of your product in social media are the ultimate form of third-party endorsement and may outweigh negative reports by professional reviewers in conventional media – for example there are many movies that have done well despite poor reviews by conventional film critics.
- Many more media in need of your PR content. There is an infinity of online titles, communities and blogs in desperate need of ideas and content.
- More, and better, two-way internal communications. (Intel, a global business with 80,000 employees operating in 100 countries, has been able to build better internal communications across borders by encouraging staff to blog and communicate online.[8]).
- The opportunity for real two-way communications with customers as well as journalists. Sometimes what customers and journalists say might make uncomfortable reading, but there is usually something to be learned from it.
- By setting up an effective website you can quickly, and cost-effectively, inform, and even sell, to customers without having to go through the intermediation of a conventional journalist.
- Rapid research providing consumer insights and trend tracking based on regular monitoring of relevant websites, online communities and blogs.
- Twitter can be highly effective in giving service updates – for example during travel disruption – and answering questions that the media or users have raised and which need a rapid response.

However, there are problems with the online world as well as opportunities. To help assess these we have divided the online and digital PR universe into three inter-related sections as shown in Figure 7.1.

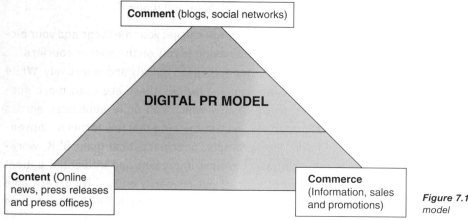

Figure 7.1 *Digital PR model*

> If bloggers are saying nasty things about you, you can indulge yourself in a campaign to try to improve what they are talking about. PR has become more important structurally as a result.
>
> Sir Martin Sorrell, Chief Executive WPP Group[9]

Probably the biggest problem that the online world poses to PR is the ability of critics and dissatisfied customers to attack quickly, at any time and from anywhere. Before the advent of the online world, PR: a) knew the enemy; b) had some control over how their voice was heard; and, c) had time to organise and plan a response to any criticism. Today the critics can strike wherever and whenever they like. Moreover, this potential for speedy surprise attacks on an organisation has been coupled, in most societies, with a decline in deference to authority and trust in experts. People are now more prepared to argue with authority, be it government or business, and will use the power and speed of the internet to find out the views of people they trust and then push their point home.

BLOGS AND BLOGGING

Some of the biggest threats to organisations arise from blogs. These are in effect online diaries or articles. The vast majority – and there are now an estimated 126 million blogs according to BlogPulse[10] – are little more than gossip and chat amongst friends or like-minded people and pose no threat, other than extreme boredom, to those who chance upon them. However, there are a relatively small but influential group of blogs written by people who see themselves as *'citizen journalists'* and either wish their views to be widely known or want to punish an organisation. Many writers of blogs care passionately about particular issues such as the environment or animal rights and raise points and publicise activity that mainstream media have yet to pick up on, or have chosen not to cover.

Overnight, and without warning, an organisation can find itself discussed all over cyberspace and, with only a short delay, the subject of scrutiny by more conventional print and broadcast media.

Some blogs are set up specifically to attack particular organisations. Dell, the direct-selling American computer company, was attacked for its poor service under the title 'Dell Hell'. Within no time at all awareness of the phrase mushroomed until 'Dell Hell' started ranking higher in search engines than 'Dell' alone. Dell had to launch its own corporate blog to counter the criticisms.

MacDonald's, the fast food eatery, continues to be the victim of blogs attacking it for everything from its environmental record to its treatment of animals and its working conditions.

However, it is important to keep a sense of perspective. As we have mentioned, almost all organisations of any size face online criticism, and most survive and thrive: individual postings online do not always resonate as effectively at the examples above – which does not mean that one should not be vigilant, only that one should not overreact and perhaps even draw attention to what might be a very small problem.

According to TNS Media Intelligence only 3.5% of news actually breaks in the blogosphere.[11] Instead blog news content is still overwhelmingly drawn from mainstream media. But it would be foolish to dismiss blogs altogether. A recent piece of research in America showed that 59% of journalists regularly use blogs for story ideas.[12]

What blogs can do is to keep an issue going long after conventional media have moved on. In essence, what the online world has meant is that it is easier than ever to complain, and once it is on the internet a complaint or an attack can linger, be found quickly by search engines and hence come up again and again. It is easy for others to research an issue, add fresh comments or to refer to, or link to, an old complaint. Moreover a social media comment, email or blog post is not only faster and less trouble to execute than a letter or phone call but also, once posted online, can be viewed globally.

Organisations have three options when it comes to deciding how to respond to online complaints and criticism.

1 Listen in
2 Take Part
3 Take Cover

To *listen in* an organisation needs to monitor what is being said. Fortunately online resources make this is easier than one might expect. Not only are there devices such as Google blog search and Technorati[13], Blogpulse[14] and Feedburner[15] but, for bigger volumes, there is also specialist software. Media evaluation companies will also monitor online comment about an organisation and its competitors – and the issues that concern them – in chat-rooms, and examine those blogs with the most links, comments, ratings and bookmarks. Finally there are specialist consultancies such as SIGWatch[16] who will monitor pressure groups that may impact on the organisation.

Having listened in and found things it does not like on a blog or critic's website, an organisation needs to decide whether to take part or take cover. As a general rule it is probably better not to respond: there is a danger of fanning the flames and making the story bigger than it might otherwise have been. Many bloggers are naturally anti anything they see as 'the establishment', such as business and government, and will take a response as an admission of guilt and weakness and step up their criticism.

However, if the criticisms are valid the best response is first to correct the shortcomings, and second to apologise. A greater difficulty is when a complete untruth is published in a blog or on a critical website. Uncorrected the untruth may gain popular currency – there have, for example, been allegations of products being carcinogenic when they are not. But trying to correct the untruth may just amplify the rumour and increase the damage caused by what might otherwise have been a story of limited interest. There can be no hard and fast advice in situations like these: you just have to weigh up the risks and make a judgement.

One way of handling persistent detractors is try to get them onside. This can be done by a mixture of flattery and dialogue. For example an organisation can offer to meet with a critic which will make them feel important. Detractors can be consulted about new products or future plans and even offered new products to review. The difficulty is that some bloggers love such approaches while others feel insulted and believe that you are trying to corrupt them. Microsoft came under fire in 2006 when its PR agency in America, Edelman, sent laptop computers with the Windows Vista operating system to influential bloggers. Some protested at what they saw as an attempt at bribery. This sort of problem may lessen as the whole blogging culture becomes better established and more similar to traditional media. Indeed, some successful blogs are already turning themselves into money-making enterprises, though this raises the question of whether blogs will lose their special impact when they start to behave and be seen like other mainstream media.

As an extension of trying to get blog critics onside some organisations have tried to join the blogosphere. This is usually done in one of two ways.

The first technique is to post a rebuttal or correction on the offending blog. At best you may correct serious errors and at least communicate your point of view. At worst the posting may stir further controversy and attacks. Some firms – or their PR consultants – have attempted 'disguised' postings whereby they try to hide their real identity. It is impossible to say how often this ethically dubious and potentially illegal approach works. What is certain is that those who have been discovered doing this have usually found themselves in a worse situation than the one from which they started.

The other technique is to create a corporate blog. One big advantage of a corporate blog is that it can greatly increase your search engine optimisation (SEO[17]). However the danger with corporate blogs is that they end up looking like a boring corporate website rather than a real, personalised blog. This is more likely to offend critics still further rather than win people over. The essence of the blogosphere is its informality, frankness and openness. Running an effective corporate blog takes time – frequent updates are usually necessary – and a willingness to show the skeletons in the company's cupboards. If you write a corporate blog you must be serious and honest about it.

As mentioned at the start of this chapter, the giant American retailer Wal-Mart ran into trouble when it emerged that a pro-Wal-Mart blog, purportedly created by a couple travelling across the United States, was in fact funded by 'Working Families for Wal-Mart'(WFWM), a front group or organisation set up to show Wal-Mart in a good light. Transparency is paramount for corporations trying to go head on with critics in cyberspace.

At their best corporate blogs can be an extension of customer service, provide consumer insights, and even open up new areas of business. At their worst they can do far more harm than good. So before creating a corporate blog make sure you have a first rate online press office (see below).

SOCIAL NETWORKING AND TWITTER

In addition to blogs there are now a wealth of social networks ranging from Facebook (with a claimed 500 million users), LinkedIn (a business network with 90 million members[18]), and Twitter which, at the time of writing, claimed to have 175 million users,[19] and is now seen by some as the glue binding together journalists, bloggers and public users of online media.

These social networks greatly excite marketing and PR people as they are made up of defined communities of people with some shared interests. The dilemma is how to reach and influence them without alienating them. The experience thus far seems to be that people do not mind being made offers that are directly linked to their interests. For example, if you say on your Facebook page that you like a particular sort of music it is possible for promoters of that music – for a cost similar to advertising – to post special offers (not generally seen as a PR role). Where it becomes more problematic is when organisations try to start, or stimulate, communities. The Cadbury's Wispa campaign is an example of one that worked, and there have been others. But there is a real danger that either such attempts never take off, or that they backfire and stimulate opposing grassroots 'anti' groups. Some of the initiatives on social networks that are most useful in PR terms have been started not by organisations, but by genuinely delighted or enthusiastic customers. This sort of unpaid for and spontaneous endorsement by third parties can be hugely valuable. For an organisation to try actively to intervene can undermine the independent credibility that is so precious. Any attempt to engage with enthusiastic customers or fans needs to ensure that it follows some basic principles:

- It should be open and transparent
- It should be in the language of the social media – not corporate speech
- It should, wherever possible, offer something special and exclusive – online communities are like clubs, they appreciate privileges and benefits
- It should offer interactivity – communities involve dialogues not monologues
- It should have 'social currency' or 'talkability'

There have been some notable 'viral' successes. These may occur when an organisation, in a planned way, stimulates people to talk about and forward some content they have produced. The most famous example comes from America where a maker of kitchen blenders posted online film of the CEO blending unusual items such as phones![20] The images were funny, surprising and sold the product very effectively. Similarly, in the UK the mobile network T Mobile secured a lot of online coverage – particularly on YouTube – for the filming and subsequent broadcast of its engaging 'flash dancing' advertisements at major London railway stations.

But for every success there are many more examples of failure. The content (often derived from advertisements) placed online has to be genuinely funny and original. Much of what companies are now trying to create a buzz about online is not. There is also a danger of companies being laughed *at*, rather than *with*, for their attempts to engage with the online community.

In reality viral marketing on social networks is something of an oxymoron. The more it is planned, controlled and contrived the less likely it is to be successful.

Twitter is the latest online fashion and has inevitably attracted businesses keen to take advantage of it. There are some concrete examples of success, in particular when it comes to customer service, but generally Twitter is used as part of a multi-media strategy rather than as a standalone device. When the UK furniture retailer Habitat tried to use Twitter as a sales tool it was subjected to a customer and media backlash.[21]

Not surprisingly there are many new services emerging around Twitter from Tweetdeck to Twitalyzer[22]. The latter seeks to measure Twitter influence, though most digital PR experts at the moment agree that the overall impact of Twitter is hard to assess.

The vast majority of successful consumer PR campaigns now contain some elements of social media activity. On the other hand most award-winning campaigns still include a large amount of conventional media coverage. It seems that for the most part social media is complementary to, rather than an alternative to, conventional media.

Someone has messed around with your organisation's current TV advertisement and posted it on YouTube. They have made it look as though your boss is high on drugs and is advocating drug taking... The reworked version is getting lots of hits. Some comments are rubbishing your firm. What do you do?

Content

There are several ways of getting content into online media. One of the most important is through the creation of an effective online press office.

Online press offices matter. Journalists (and bloggers) use them a lot. There are six main reasons why journalists use an organisation's website. These are:

1 To find a contact (name, telephone, email or Twitter address)
2 To check basic facts (turnover, number of staff etc), including past and present press releases
3 To see what angle or 'spin' the organisation puts on issues
4 To check financial information
5 To download photographs and other images
6 To access social media newsrooms

In fact an online press office can also be used as a direct means of providing media content by making available downloadable articles, features, photographs and even competitions.

It is also worth including in your online press office comment from external sources. For example, if you are selling medical products include quotes from, or links to, relevant reports, or institutions that have used and recommended your product. Similarly include examples of positive press coverage. A piece of positive coverage from one journalist is more likely to influence another journalist positively than all your persuasive PR words!

But while websites can be powerful communication tools, they all too often fail to realise their potential. One reason is that often the guiding force is that of the technician and the web-designer, rather than that of PR people. Websites – particularly those belonging to big organisations – quickly grow too large and unwieldy for PR practitioners to be able to exert full control. PR people, who are traditionally more familiar with print and broadcast media, also often lack the necessary expertise. Many parts of a huge website may be highly specialised and require little PR attention, but nonetheless your role is try to keep the focus on how the website can best communicate the messages that you want to send to your target audiences. You can help to establish clear guidelines, and can certainly maintain direct control of the electronic newsroom.

Major websites are usually designed using the latest technology available. Their designers view them on state-of-the-art equipment using the best connections – most of the actual users will not have all these advantages. Websites can be a place to display technical wizardry, but that is usually not quite the same as your objective (although it may overlap). Instead your concern is message delivery and interactivity with your selected audiences, who may not be so familiar with cutting-edge web design and may not be so well equipped to use it: will they, for example, like images which might take a while to load on their computers?

TOP TIPS ON WEB DESIGN

Study what works: First of all, have a look at a good range of websites which are trying to achieve something similar to what you are setting out to do. Imagine you belonged to their intended audiences. Then think what you can learn from their approach. What could you do better?

Keep it simple: Think carefully about what appears on your web pages. People do not normally like reading huge amounts of text on screen – indeed unless it is very interesting or important (and especially relevant to them) they are unlikely even to want to scroll down. Instead people typically like small amounts of information on a page – and then a clear way of clicking on to another page. This means that writing for the web involves thinking in three dimensions. Instead of people following the logical and familiar page sequence of a book or brochure, people will click on to whatever seems most interesting or relevant to them.

Make navigation easy: Clear navigation is essential: users will not usually be familiar with your site and need to be able to find their way around. A good home page, a search function and site map are all useful. Keep your focus on what will be meaningful to your target audiences. The way your organisation structures itself will usually be both unfamiliar and unimportant to outsiders: they will want to find the fastest route to the information and functionality *they* want, and navigation and contents lists should be designed with this in mind.

Avoid blandness and platitudes: All too often websites are impersonal, bland and dull. Organisations which pride themselves on their personal touch find it deserts them on the web. Senior people within the organisation seldom have the time or inclination to give websites a personal touch, and often much of the content is in the hands of technical or other specialist staff rather than PR people.

Understandable legal and regulatory concerns can make the content very boring. The site can appear to be producer-led, rather than reflecting the interests of its intended users. Blogs are often seen as a way round this, but as mentioned above these can also present problems. A website should be as interesting, and sometimes entertaining, as a newspaper or magazine – not as dull as a bad brochure.

Evaluation: one of the beauties of using a website or other forms of online media as communications tools is that they enable you to monitor user activity much more easily than is possible with traditional media. Make sure that your web-designers ensure that use of the site can be effectively monitored when you brief them. The crudest measure is the overall number of 'hits' on your site, but you can go much further than that. To start with, how do they come to your site – what do they search for? If there are links to it on other sites, for example, how often are they used? Once there, which pages do people visit and in which order? How long do they spend on each page? How, if at all, do they respond to or interact with the site? When are they visiting?

Interactivity: One of the truly unique features of the web is the scope it offers for fast and easy interactivity. Users can post comments, take part in live online discussions and many other activities readily and conveniently, including Facebook and Twitter. By requiring people to submit their email addresses (as well as other data) you can assemble a marketing database which can also be exploited easily and relatively cheaply. This means that the www comes close to realising a public relations ideal – two-way communication between an organisation and its publics.

Limitations: it is important not be bedazzled by new media, important though they are.

- First, remember that, while the means of delivery is new, the content is still material which could be, and often is, found on old media. It is also worth noting that according to Nieman Journalism Lab[23] more than 96 per cent of newspaper reading is still done in the print editions, and the online share of the newspaper audience attention is only just over three percent. Moreover, people reading online generally spend much less time reading than people reading conventional print media. So your copy needs to be short and to the point unless you are a major reference source.

- As we have seen, only a few websites could really be called mass media. Anyone can post material online, whereas gaining coverage in the more limited range of traditional mass media has always been more difficult to achieve. One important difference of the www is that you have in some way to seek out a site from among those millions, and one of the main items of expenditure for website promoters has been traditional advertising and PR to market and promote their sites. Moreover use of new media is much more varied and individual than is the case with traditional media. Even if a site is visited it may be only one small part of it – and perhaps then only briefly. The range of possibilities is infinite and the way in which people view websites and blogs, usually as lone individuals, is intensely personal. This is why it is much harder – although not impossible – to generate a shared experience which gets talked about via new media than is the case if something appears on the front page of a national newspaper or on a popular TV programme. Indeed new media breakthroughs into popular consciousness often depend on them being taken up by old mass media outlets.

- Use of new media is patchy and changes swiftly. Even in some wealthy societies large groups of people can find themselves on the wrong side of the digital divide, unable to access the internet. When they can access it, they frequently find themselves left behind: those still relying on dial-up access will find themselves in a very different position to those with broadband access (itself available at ever higher speeds), and technology has advanced – and continues to advance – so quickly that computers which are only a few years old will no longer give people optimum experience of the www. PR people have to be careful about excessive reliance on new media: much depends on the audience.

DIGITAL PRESS RELEASES

Another important aspect of online content is the digital press release.

Increasingly the press release is going online. The post, or snail mail as some call it, is on the way out. But does an online press release need to be different from its more traditional paper partner? The answer is, essentially, no. An online release must have a great story up-front, be well written and sent to the right people at the right time. Nothing new there. What does change is the ability to enhance the release with some or all of the following:

- click-throughs and links to relevant background sources and references
- photographic and video attachments or links
- links to MP3 files, podcasts and computer graphics
- the opportunity for the journalist to communicate online with you in their own time

All of this should make the life of the journalist who is interested in your press release much easier. However there are several dangers inherent in the online release. First, there is a danger that because it is easier and cheaper to send an online release PR practitioners will be inclined to send more. This will mean more journalists' time being eaten up scanning irrelevant press releases and more journalists becoming increasingly frustrated with all PR people as a result. Emails are easy to ignore, particularly if the subject line just says 'press release' rather than giving a punchy summary of what the release is about. Second, there is the danger that the story gets lost in the technology and the attachments: journalists can have the same problems as the rest of us. The paper release remains a useful tool, particularly at press events: after all, it is much harder to scribble in the margins of an electronic release.

Exercise for two or more teams

1 Your team work for CABLE – Consumers Against Bank Loan Exploitation. You believe that banks lend irresponsibly to people who cannot really afford to borrow. You want to shame the banks into being more careful about whom they lend to. In your team(s) devise an online PR campaign to achieve your goals.
2 Your team works for the banking industry trade association. You are coming under attack from a group called CABLE – as above, Consumers Against Bank Loan Exploitation – who want you to be much stricter about whom you lend to. What arguments can you make in your defence and how will you respond to their online campaign?

DIGITAL COMMERCE

The final part of the Digital PR triangle is 'commerce'.

Commerce is all about creating interactivity and sales with customers and other key audiences. This is clearly an area where PR crosses over with sales promotion, direct marketing and advertising, but PR practitioners who do not want to be left behind need at least to understand the basic principles. Here we will highlight three key issues:

- *Make your website a destination.* As we said earlier, a website is essentially passive. Unlike a letter, phone call, piece of editorial or advertisement it does not force its way into your life. People have to know your website is there and want to visit it. One way of achieving this is by making your site a source of useful information and advice. Think about what it is your audience would like to know – beyond how wonderful your product or organisation is – and provide it. Then try to forge links with as many relevant websites as possible. So, for example, if you work for a chain of hotels you might try to appeal to hikers by commissioning a range of downloadable walks that you make available not only via your website but through links to tourist authorities and hikers groups.
- *Offer discounts and benefits to affinity groups.* One of the huge benefits of the web is its interconnectivity. For example, if you represent a driving school think of what sort of organisations you might have 'affinity' with. This could lead you to link up with colleges and car manufacturers to offer their students and customers respectively special discounts. The colleges and car-makers gain from being able to offer their customers something extra and you gain by being able to direct traffic to your site.

- *Optimise your position on search engines:* This is called SEO or search engine optimisation. While generally the more visitors and links you have to other sites the higher you will be when people do a search, there are now a variety of specialist companies who can help you drive your site even further up the search engine tables (some also offer to de-optimise hostile or unflattering online references). For example, think of the words or terms that people might use when looking for your product or service and make sure they appear in all your online communications.

Top sites for PR students (and practitioners)

Richard Bailey, PR educator and trainer, and creator of prstudies.typepad.com, a PR education blog

PROpenMic (www.propenmic.org)

This is a social network that encourages PR students to discuss issues with PR practitioners and academics in the US and around the world. It goes beyond Facebook by showing that social networking is good for learning and good for business too.

PR Conversations (www.prconversations.com)

A group blog featuring some well-known practitioners and academics that takes a global perspective and doesn't hide from big ideas. Some of the debates and discussions are more valuable than much of what appears in the academic journals – and this suggests one future direction for specialist blogging.

Wadds' PR Blog (www.speedcommunications. com/blogs/wadds/)

Many PR consultants have realised the benefits blogging brings in terms of reputation, client referral and networking – and there are many thousands you can read. This one that stands out for me is by a consultancy director who has a lot to say to PR students and young practitioners.

Twitter (www.twitter.com)

If blogging seems slow and unrewarding and social networks seem limited, then Twitter is the place for public conversations and connections. Once you get beyond following celebrities and describing your last meal, Twitter is the place to introduce yourself to the world and build traffic to your blog, website or online portfolio. News, comments, job offers, interesting conversations are happening in real time.

Case study: Sexual health tests

Lloyds Pharmacy – a UK chain of pharmaceutical outlets – hired the PR firm Citigate Dewe Rogerson (CDR) to promote their sexual health tests.

The tests themselves were not new so a new idea was needed to promote them.

CDR spoke to 6,000 people about their sexual history to create a database. This was fed into a unique online calculator that enabled people to calculate how many indirect sexual partners they had had.

The campaign was called *Sex Degrees of Separation* – drawing on the idea that you can

be linked to everyone in the world through at most six individual personal connections. By entering the sex and age range of each of the people with whom they had had sex, people could work out how many people they had indirectly slept with and thereby their sexual health risk.

A mixture of conventional and online media was targeted. The resulting coverage led to 1.4 million page views of the calculator. Sales of the online sexual health tests increased by 21%.[24]

Why did CDR use conventional media to promote an online tool?

Why was important that the tool was available online?

- Know what is being said about you in the blogosphere and social networks.
- If you respond to comment do so as a human being rather than as a 'corporate', and be as transparent as possible if you decide to join in. You would not like someone who tried to join your club under false pretences.
- Use technology to its full extent. Offer online images, video and voices. Provide advice and information and special offers and discounts. But make sure it is easy to access and avoid hard selling, particularly on social networks. No-one likes someone they have just met who immediately asks to borrow money or tries to start selling them something.
- Do not forget how powerful traditional media are, particularly in places like Asia, and do not forget that traditional media still set most of the news agenda and that people who read print media spend at least twice as much time reading as those who read online versions.[25]
- Online is great for narrowcasting – reaching smallish groups with shared interests ranging from prostate cancer patient groups to Star Trek fanatics. It is not so good for broadcasting and reaching mass markets.
- Online penetration amongst the old, the poor and the socially excluded, and those living in underdeveloped regions is still low, and in some parts of the world negligible, and even when such people have access to the internet it is often very limited. Do not assume that because you and your circle enjoy broadband on the latest equipment your target audiences are in the same fortunate position.
- Try to speak the informal language of the online world, but if you are a serious organisation do not fall into the trap of acting like a middle aged man dancing at a disco with his baseball hat on the wrong way round. You will only be laughed at!

You are responsible for a new kind of sound. If you download it and then play it through your earphones it will keep you awake, thereby enabling people such as students, who want to study through the night, to avoid sleep without taking dangerous stimulants.

You only have a small budget. Devise an online campaign to promote the idea to students. (The sound itself is harmless played at a reasonable level, but doctors and teachers point out that students should not go without sleep.)

CHAPTER

CORPORATE SOCIAL RESPONSIBILITY

INTRODUCTION

Corporate social responsibility (CSR) refers to the increasingly popular idea in affluent democracies that businesses should not just make a profit but should exercise a range of social and environmental responsibilities – to their employees, suppliers, local communities and wider society – and must not only act on these concerns but be seen to act in an accountable way. PR people often claim to play a key role in CSR. In the US it is a core part of PR briefs and nearly all major PR consultancies now claim to offer CSR either as essential part of their activity or as a discrete service.

LEARNING OBJECTIVES

- Understanding what corporate social responsibility is
- Employing the seven CSR guidelines
- Understanding the three dilemmas of CSR

WHAT IS CORPORATE SOCIAL RESPONSIBILITY?

In reality, CSR is a new name – designed to attract more fees and help claim a place in the boardroom – for what is an old practice. Well-run businesses which are concerned about their reputation have always responded to public, government and NGO pressure to improve the quality of life both through their own business practices and by helping and supporting charities. The public and media's reaction to such initiatives have always been rather ambiguous. (Once again there is a sensitivity about names. Some proponents of CSR prefer to call it 'Corporate Responsibility', or use terms such as 'Corporate Citizenship' and 'Responsible Business'. It is also closely linked to the notion of *sustainability*, which focuses on the responsible use of natural resources.)

In the comic film *Four's a Crowd* (1938) Errol Flynn plays the Hollywood's first self-styled PR man. When challenged about what precisely his job entails he replies:

> It's simple. Most of my clients have more money than reputation. I sell them fine reputations through their donations to charity. So they'll die with easy consciences and the public hailing them as great benefactors. They like to die that way...

Or, as Jack Lemmon's PR man in the film, *Days of Wine and Roses* (1962), puts it as he seeks to impress his stern, sceptical father-in-law:

> I suppose you might say my job is sort of to help my client to create a public image... well, for example, let's say my client, corporation x, does some good, something that could be of benefit to the public ... well, my job is to see that the public knows it.

As is the case with other PR specialisms, CSR has now blossomed into a professionalised sub-discipline. Today some CSR practitioners claim – with, perhaps, a hint of self-interest – that a positive CSR programme is effectively a 'license to do business'. Without it, they argue, a business is unlikely to prosper in the long term.

Certainly, in many wealthy societies, where basic needs have been met, people now want and expect all kinds of businesses not just to be good but to do good. Sometimes they want this because it is much easier if someone can be good on their behalf rather than their having to make the effort themselves. It is certainly easier for NGOs to blame companies rather than the ordinary purchasers of their products, and for us as member of the public to blame businesses rather than consider our own behaviour as consumers, or to bear in mind that, through our pension funds, we often own the corporations. People also want businesses to assist because they have seen that charities supported by business can be more efficient than large public sector bodies. Sometimes they want it because the only way to achieve some kinds of change is through corporate action. The attempt of businesses in the developed world to respond to these sentiments has evolved into what is called *CSR*. Perceptions of an organisation's CSR can have an impact on all of its stakeholders. They can affect customers and potential customers, and shareholders and potential shareholders. A positive image can make it easier to recruit and retain good quality staff. And of course it can have an impact on public opinion and on how the media, pressure groups and indeed governments treat a business.

You must be the judge of how far the above is true for businesses operating in your society, but you need to bear the following three points in mind:

1 First, even if you feel that the circumstances outlined above are not yet fully applicable to your society, it is likely that things are heading that way: you need to be prepared.
2 Second, you need to be aware that many overseas investors will have CSR as an important agenda item when they start to talk about doing business, even in countries which do not themselves make it a priority.
3 Third, businesses operating and selling internationally – particularly in those markets where CSR is taken most seriously, by governments and regulatory authorities as well as other companies – need to think carefully about CSR issues: being seen to act responsibly can be a means of securing competitive advantage.

'Asian companies selling to overseas clients are finding they cannot win a contract without satisfying the other side that their treatment of the environment and their staff meets certain ethical standards.' In some cases, multinationals seeking deals in Asia are having them granted only on government conditions that they put 'X' amount 'back into the country' through community projects.

'Others are moving less out of necessity than fear; having seen the likes of Nike shamed in the international media for the working conditions of their Indonesian factory staff, they are devising policies and programmes that can be used to give them a more friendly public face.'[1]

In such situations the job of the PR professional must be to help and guide the organisation on, first, how to be good and, second, how to be seen to be good.

There are 7 guidelines that should be followed:

1. *Do more than the minimum.* When devising your CSR plan you should ensure as a minimum that your organisation meets all the basic legal requirements. However, this is often not enough. Ask yourself – and then the board – whether they would be comfortable defending such a position on television. The answer is probably not. How can your organisation go beyond the minimum and show

itself to be a responsible and forward thinking company? The answer is to do more than is generally expected in your industry or sector. Try to have the best safety record, the most flexible working arrangements, the fairest recruitment strategies, the cleanest and greenest manufacturing systems, the most socially responsible and forward thinking suppliers.

Chinese Lenovo beats America's Apple on green credentials

In a recent 'green ranking' of the world's biggest electronics companies, Greenpeace, the international environmental organisation placed China's Lenovo Group Ltd. at the top of the list, which is based on the recycling and toxic content policies of companies and is designed to get them to reduce waste.

Previously Lenovo had come bottom of the list.

'It's a surprise that a Chinese firm which was bottom place in the first edition has climbed slowly to the top,' said Zeina Alhajj, a toxics campaigner at Greenpeace.

Apple criticised the rating system and criteria used by Greenpeace, but that didn't change the fact that Lenovo got the positive coverage whilst Apple was forced on to the back foot.[2]

---

2. *Make staff aware*. Make sure that all your staff are aware of any CSR or charitable initiatives that the organisation is involved in and try to create opportunities for them to be involved. Employees are, or at least should be, ambassadors for the business. They cannot be if they are unaware of what is being done and why. And do not just stop at the staff. Most organisations have an array of media at their disposal that they control such as websites, newsletters and direct mail. Use them to tell customers, shareholders and other stakeholders what you are up to and what contribution you think you can make.

3. *Make it relevant*. Any CSR initiative or charitable involvement should be as relevant as possible to your business or, more importantly, your customers. That way it is more likely to have an impact and be remembered. For example the focus for energy and mining companies is likely to be on how green and environmentally friendly their processes can be. Similarly, for a company that sources most of its products from the developing world much of the emphasis is likely to be on the treatment of suppliers' staff – do they use child labour, are staff paid a living wage, are working conditions safe?

4. *Be consistent*. Some companies change their charity arrangements annually. This makes it difficult to achieve any real communications impact. The British retailer Tesco, which now operates internationally, operates a renowned Computers in Schools scheme which is famous in part because it has been around so long – over 13 years – and also because of the large sums raised – over £84 million. Similarly, Travelex have earned brand recognition – at least amongst theatre goers – by sponsoring low cost seats at London's National Theatre.

5. *Be popular and topical*. The chairman may love golf but most people do not. Children, animals, the environment, other forms of sport and culture are all popular and topical issues and will generate far more coverage. This may seem cynical (is it about corporate social responsibility or corporate social popularity?) as there are many deserving causes that are neither popular nor particularly topical. If your organisation is prepared to be brave and different that is fine, but you and your colleagues will have to be prepared for the extra effort and money required to gain a profile for such activity.

6. *Be proactive and professional*: Doing good gives you no automatic right to media coverage. Almost all organisations now claim to have some sort of commitment to CSR. And there are literally tens of thousands of charities and businesses working together at any given time. You will need to apply as much effort to the PR for these as you apply to the PR for your core business.

7. *Do not over-claim*: The media and NGOs are quick to jump on over-claims by companies trying to be seen to be good. In particular they are cynical about some businesses' assertions that they are green, which have resulted in the emergence of the term 'green-washing' – the attempt to make what is viewed as a bad practice look good. Oil companies seem to be particularly vulnerable to this sort of criticism. So while it is important to make people aware of your attempts to achieve good practice and improve society, you need to be careful, and not sound unrealistic, complacent or as though you are boastful or exaggerating. At the heart of businesses' attempts to be socially responsible are some dilemmas and contradictions. It is better to be honest about these than to claim everything is perfect when it is not. Claiming to be virtuous – or even just over-claiming – can do more harm to an organisation's reputation than making no claims at all.

Better Coffee, Better Life: a Hill & Knowlton campaign in Thailand

Working for their client, the global coffee giant Starbucks, the international PR consultancy Hill & Knowlton were charged with three tasks:

- Launching Starbuck's locally grown Muan Jai coffee blend in Thailand.
- Positioning Starbucks as socially responsible.
- Educating people about Starbuck's 'Commitment to Origin' programme which is designed to improve the lives of the coffee farmers.

Five per cent of the proceeds of Starbucks' Muan Jai blend were allocated to the development of water systems and the provision of school materials for the Northern Thailand tribal community where the coffee is produced. Sales of the coffee – and production – soared.

www.hillandknowlton.com

THE THREE DILEMMAS OF CSR

CSR in some form has been with us a long time and is likely to remain with us for many years to come – but the same is true of criticism of CSR.

There are three main dilemmas.

1. *How to balance businesses' financial duties with their social and environmental responsibilities:* Publicly owned companies – generally the biggest and most influential businesses – have a fiduciary or legal duty to shareholders (which, it should be stressed, include pension funds and millions of ordinary people through their savings) to not waste money and to make a profit. It is claimed that companies with good CSR tend to perform above the average. However, there are also plenty of examples of large companies which are – rightly or wrongly – seen as not caring much about CSR but which still do very well. For example it is unlikely that Ryanair, Walmart or Primark would come top of a poll measuring CSR activity. It is often relatively small companies which major on their ethical approach to business. Big companies with a broader range of stakeholders tend to be more cautious about their claims. So can the benefits to shareholders of CSR be measured? The answer is that it is difficult. At the heart of this dilemma is how you balance what can be competing business and social imperatives. For example, the need to sell a lot of beer, set against the need to be seen to be encouraging responsible drinking. The need to compete with low prices and the need to pay workers well – if you increase pay too much jobs may be lost. The need to be green versus the need to build a new power plant – and should that power plant be nuclear- or wind-powered? These are tricky and complicated moral issues to which, whatever they may claim, PR practitioners cannot offer the 'right' answers (see Chapter 2 for more on these debates).

2. *Doing good vs. looking good.* PR is seen as glamorous and, sometimes, powerful by the outside world – but not wholly trustworthy. Unsurprisingly, PR practitioners, particularly those involved in the PR trade bodies, are generally keen to emphasise PR's involvement with CSR. Knowing that PR does not always have a positive reputation, they like to use CSR to try to give their industry a veneer of morality and social responsibility. But in so doing they may generate public cynicism about CSR – 'if PR people control CSR it must all just be PR spin and window dressing', or so it might be thought. Sadly, this can undermine the credibility of some genuinely positive moves by businesses. And what PR's most active proponents of CSR never explain is why PR is specially qualified to wield a moral compass or why PR practitioners are particularly well-placed to

advise on what is responsible (as opposed to popular, or how things will play with the media, arenas where they have some expertise). Can PR people really claim to be experts in rival methods of power generation or be able to resolve arguments about carbon offsetting, arenas where many technical experts disagree? Finally, they fail to explain properly how PR can reconcile some of the dilemmas and contradictions inherent in a business trying both to make money and do good.

> ❰❰ To gain widespread acceptance over a period of time, a corporation's policies must seem to be in the public interest. Whether they are or not is often a matter of considerable debate.
>
> Irwin Ross[3]

3. *PR professionalism versus personal politics:* Is a PR person's first duty to serve the client, assuming that what they are asked to do is legal, rather than to promote their personal view of what is responsible? Many PR people involved in CSR use terms such as a 'softer form of capitalism' and 'reinvigorating ethics'. Both statements are loaded with value judgements. What are their qualifications to judge what is 'responsible' or say what is ethical? Some stakeholders might oppose supporting a gay charity while others want to combat AIDS; some would like to support a church or mosque. Some abhor alcohol, others do not.

Thus the focus some PR people put on CSR raises awkward questions which they often seek to dodge. Are CSR people really more moral or ethical than others? Or are they just more opinionated? If they really are more moral, should they be in politics, religion or the public sector rather than in PR? Is there a danger that their passion could undermine their objectivity and duty to give best advice?

In reality, CSR people seldom advise their paymasters to do something they think is 'responsible' or 'ethical' but which is unfashionable and unpopular – and which will lose money. They would not be long in a job if they did. Instead they have to walk the tightrope of dilemmas and contradictions at the heart of doing business in a pluralistic society.

In summary, as society continues to progress along broadly liberal lines, business, as ever, will play a key if controversial role. PR will be at the forefront of communicating what are at times contradictory goals.

As an interesting final point for discussion, it is noteworthy that the main academic centre for the study of CSR in the UK was founded with money from BAT (British American Tobacco) at Nottingham University.[4]

Case study: Should companies volunteer to pay more tax?

Corporate social responsibility is not confined to issues of employment rights or the environment. New issues can surface. As people in the UK came to terms with the implications of the crisis in government finance in 2010, a new pressure group called UK Uncut emerged. Apparently originating in a discussion in a London pub, it quickly acquired more than 11,000 Facebook members and 11,000 followers on Twitter. It saw itself as a citizen army of volunteers determined to make wealthy tax avoiders, who use legal means to minimise their tax bills, pay more tax.

Several large companies were targeted by UK Uncut, including Boots, Vodafone and Arcadia, the clothing retail empire of Sir Philip Green, which includes Topshop, Dorothy Perkins and Burton. Direct action by UK Uncut has forced Green's stores in London and Manchester to close for brief periods, and has attracted considerable amounts of media coverage.

While Green has acted in accordance with the law, UK Uncut and others believe that, in avoiding UK taxation as far as possible, he is evading his moral responsibility to the country where he makes most of his money. On the other hand it could be pointed out that he seems to have plenty of satisfied customers, employs 44,000 people and still pays considerable amounts in corporation tax.[5]

Imagine you are working for Arcadia (or, if you prefer, another company in a similar predicament) when this issue rises up the agenda. Your company has gone to great lengths to minimise its tax bill by legal means, and is saving considerable amounts as a result. However demonstrations are occurring and your tax arrangements are receiving considerable amounts of negative publicity. As a corporate social responsibility expert, what advice could you offer your company?

1   How can PR resolve the 'three CSR dilemmas'?
2   Is a business's first duty to make a profit?
3   Is CSR just liberal cultural imperialism?
4   To what extent can a manufacturer of fattening carbonated drinks or a tobacco company claim to be socially responsible?

- Corporate social responsibility (CSR) is a new name for the idea that companies need to take social and environmental concerns into account in their business practices.
- There are seven guidelines for successful CSR work:
  - Do more than the minimum
  - Make staff aware
  - Make your CSR relevant
  - Be consistent
- Be popular and topical
- Be proactive and professional: coverage does not come on a plate
- Do not over-claim
- CSR practitioners face three dilemmas:
  - How to balance financial against social and environmental responsibilities
  - Doing good versus looking good
  - PR professionalism versus pursuing personal political agendas.

PR AND THE LAW

INTRODUCTION

If ethics is about what you *should* do, the law is about what you *must* do. Many people are attracted to PR because it seems less hidebound and subject to legal interference than many other occupations. As we shall see, to some extent that is true. On the other hand PR is sometimes likened to legal work because it involves representing people in a kind of court – the court of public opinion – but it is a court with few of the formal rules or sanctions which apply in real courts of law. What is true is that PR people remain very much subject to the law and cannot afford to be complacent. Although legal systems vary and keep evolving, and no-one expects PR practitioners to offer expert opinions on the law, they must still be aware of how the law can impact on their work and know when to seek professional advice. Nor is it just about facing legal action. As a PR person you must also point out the PR ramifications of taking legal action to those you serve (there is little point in winning a small court case if you lose a big battle for public opinion), and keep an eye on future legal developments which might affect your work.

> **A legal disclaimer!**
>
> The authors are not lawyers. This chapter cannot provide definitive advice – that should be sought from lawyers – nor can it seek to cover the implications of different countries' legal systems, and indeed different approaches to enforcement.

LEARNING OBJECTIVES

- How to develop a critical awareness of those aspects of the law which are most relevant to PR practice, and hence know when to seek professional advice
- How to contribute PR advice when legal action is being contemplated and why you need to remain vigilant about the possible impact on PR of future developments in the law

WHY THE LAW MATTERS

The law may not be at the forefront of most PR people's minds, in contrast with journalists, who often work with lawyers looking over their shoulders. Whereas the media offer rapidly put-together information and comment about countless people and organisations, all of whom may be upset at what is reported, the mainstay of PR work is putting across positive information about, and with the full authority, of the organisations for which the PR people work – an inherently less risky (but not risk-free) activity.

Nor is PR quite like other forms of business activity. Legally enforceable contracts lie at the heart of conventional business life, as people seek to buy and sell goods and services, and of course they play their part in PR. But, although the media relations work which is central to PR has many of the characteristics of a marketplace (see Chapter 1), the relationships between PR practitioners and journalists are much more informal and are seldom viewed in legal terms: you cannot normally have recourse to the law if the favourable story you hoped to appear fails to do so. Moreover, in one important area of PR work, that of campaigning NGOs, PR people often set out deliberately to break the law – for example committing acts of trespass or obstruction – knowing that by so doing they can achieve maximum publicity at little cost (see p. 50).

This does not mean that you can afford to be complacent or ignorant of the law. PR practitioner's day-to-day work involves making highly public statements on behalf of the organisations they serve, and saying things which can have serious implications – a company cannot readily walk away from something that it has said in a press release or at a press conference. And PR practitioners from time to time also comment on other organisations, particularly those which compete with, or are hostile to, their own paymasters. So PR people remain at the mercy of the law and can fall foul of it. This could have potentially embarrassing and costly consequences for you and those who employ you.

PR people have to adhere to the law of the land where they work, and increasingly need to consider legal systems in other countries and international law as well (for example, it will not be enough for those seeking to export brands to worldwide markets to satisfy themselves that they are complying with domestic law). You also need to bear in mind that the law and its interpretation are constantly changing: keep an eye on developments which might affect you.

Some aspects of the law impinging on PR are ones that concern everyone working in business. For example, those running PR consultancies are also businesspeople in their own right and need to be conversant with the key principles of commercial law and employment legislation. Both they and in-house PR practitioners may find themselves putting in place many legally binding contracts as they set up PR campaigns. In addition, particular branches of PR have their own legal preoccupations. Financial PR people have to be particularly careful about what they say because of the growing body of law governing the operation of the financial markets. Similar concerns affect healthcare PR in some countries, while lobbyists (and others) increasingly find themselves subject to laws designed to stamp out corruption.

As a PR person you may not be a lawyer, but you need to know when to stop what you are doing and get expert advice before you proceed. Remember you are also likely to be your employer's first port of call if they feel their legal rights are being threatened in the media. – the law is there for you as well, and there may be times when you need to take legal action (or at least threaten to do so).

How legal and PR advice can diverge

Even the best-run organisations can have problems which cause serious inconvenience or worse to customers, employees, local communities and others. In such situations crisis management techniques come to the fore (see Chapter 14). One tried-and-tested approach which may often be of use is to apologise for what has gone wrong and any harm caused (even if you do not admit that your organisation is responsible), thereby defusing at least some of the public hostility. However traditionally lawyers advising organisations have been reluctant to allow this, seeing it as a potentially dangerous admission of liability. This concern may be exaggerated. PR people tend to give more weight to the need to staunch the torrent of bad news and make the organisation appear to have a human face as a failure to do so can have serious implications. In such situations PR people need to be able to make their case intelligently and robustly.

INTELLECTUAL PROPERTY AND BRANDS

Every PR person needs at least a basic awareness of intellectual property law as it is fundamental to branding and corporate identity and hence touches on much of what they do. Intellectual property law operates both nationally and, increasingly, internationally. It is a double-edged sword: you may be at risk of infringing someone else's rights, but similarly you may need to act to protect your own. Intellectual property rights extend to the online world, even if this an arena where they are often abused. A useful source of information is the World Intellectual Property Organisation – www.wipo.int. The two main forms of intellectual property are *copyright* and *industrial property*.

Copyright, often referred to as author's rights, gives protection to many common forms of expression such as books, articles, speeches, music, paintings, photos, films, and computer programs and databases. This means you have to be careful about using the work of other people in your PR campaigns and other activities, as you may well need prior permission and have to pay the copyright holder (the author, or whomever ownership has passed to). Although there are some exemptions – for example, allowing brief quotations in certain contexts – there is a risk otherwise that you could be sued for infringing the owner's rights.

In most countries copyright is conferred automatically: there may be no particular sign to indicate that material you find in the media or online, for example, is copyright, but it remains protected (although people often seek to emphasis copyright with a formal claim, for example at the end of an article). Nor can you assume that the work you commission for a PR campaign belongs to you: unless the contract states otherwise, copyright remains with the author. Thus, for example, if you commission a photographer to take photographs for a particular brochure and then decide to make further use of them you must ensure that this is covered in your original contract or reach a separate agreement. By the same token your own organisation's work is also protected by copyright and you can take steps to defend it.

It is important to note that copyright protection only extends to the actual form of expression – the words, images, sounds and so on – not the ideas which are conveyed. However using other people's ideas may create other legal problems and, even if not illegal, the practice may cause embarrassment if it is exposed.

Industrial property includes, among other things, trademarks; commercial names and designations; inventions or patents – new solutions to technical problems; and industrial designs.

Trade marks – the logos, or words, symbols and images which are now inseparable from many familiar products – together with commercial names and designations are fundamental to brand management and are fiercely protected by companies. Any attempt to use someone else's trade mark or commercial name could leave you facing legal action, and even using something similar to an existing trade mark or name could be deemed to be 'passing off', in itself an infringement. Once again, the rule is that if you are in any doubt you should seek expert advice.

Reasons to be careful

One of the authors' PR consultancy ran an advertisement to promote itself in the PR and marketing trade press. The centre of the advertisement featured a tin in the shape of, and with a design similar to, a famous brand of baked beans. The words on the tin read 'Not all brands are equal'. Despite the advertisement being an implied compliment to the brand of beans, the consultancy received a legal letter from the manufacturer telling them to pull the ad. They did!

While the other forms of industrial property seem less immediately relevant to PR, there have been attempts to patent ways of doing business, thereby securing legal protection for them, and the position varies internationally. If these apply – or, in the future, come to apply – they could have important implications for PR, not least because many consultancies claim to have developed distinctive ways of running PR programmes. The position on the protection of computer programs also varies, and so PR people need to think carefully about the implications of using these.

A Lager Saga

Following the collapse of communism, the American brewer Anheuser-Busch (now Belgian-owned) found itself in a renewed dispute with the Czech brewer Budvar as the later was now well placed to re-enter the international marketplace. Both companies produce lagers called Budweiser, which Anheuser-Busch long ago registered as a trademark. While the legal issues are both complex and important, the smaller Czech company thinks it can also reap some PR dividends from the problem. As their UK CEO puts it: 'It does give us an interesting angle on the brand. It keeps us fresh in people's minds, it keeps us fresh in the consumer and business press and it gives people interesting stories to talk about in the pub.'[1]

 You are preparing materials for a PR campaign and one of your team points out that the design you intend to use looks similar to that used by a well-known company (one with which you have no connection). What do you do and why?

DEFAMATION

Most PR may be about promoting organisations and their products, but sometimes PR work involves attacking competitors and rivals. In such circumstances you need to remember that you are just as much subject to the laws of defamation – libel and slander – as anyone else, whatever form of expression is used (be it a press release, a brochure, a phone conversation, or something posted online). Defamation cases can be long-drawn-out, high-profile, potentially extremely embarrassing and very costly – and always involve an element of uncertainty. Although the position of defamation varies greatly between different countries' jurisdictions, in general any criticisms must either be seen as fair comment – a reasonable opinion that anyone might form – and/or based on hard evidence.

Defamation cases involving PR firms are rare. One example involved the Australian actress Nicole Kidman who was in dispute with both a British newspaper, *The Daily Telegraph*, and a PR firm, Exposure, over claims she used a scent other than Chanel. It is understood that both the PR firm and the newspaper ended up out of pocket.[2]

Another example involved one of the spin doctors employed by the former British Labour Prime Minister, Gordon Brown, who invented several potentially damaging stories about the private lives of Brown's Conservative opponents and their families with a view to circulating them online. One of the Conservative MPs has been paid damages and costs by the spin doctor concerned, who left his job after the reports of his activities emerged. At the time the MP concerned said that she was contemplating legal action against the then Prime Minister's office and another party activist.[3]

Threatening legal action can be one way of deterring the media from publishing a damaging story, as the media are wary of the risks and costs inherent in defamation cases.

(A second possibility – of growing importance in many jurisdictions – is that the media are fearful of regulation and are under pressure not to infringe people's privacy. Threatening recourse to some legal or regulatory sanction – for example invoking the emerging body of privacy law or appealing to regulatory bodies - can worry the management within media organisations and cause them – and indeed their rivals – not to use the story.)

The law as a weapon in PR's armoury

During his time as a government press officer, one of the authors dealt with a number of potentially damaging allegations about the sex lives of government ministers. When journalists rang up with enquiries, the agreed response was often that the allegations were completely untrue and that if anyone published them they faced the risk of legal action. (This response had to be confirmed with the minister concerned and legal advice taken into account.) The rationale for this approach was that it would make the journalists involved – and their editors – think twice. If they ran the story in the face of a full denial *and* had been warned of possible legal action the damages in any court case might well be higher. In most cases this tactic seemed to work, and some well-known politicians were able to continue their careers untroubled by the publication of salacious stories. Media organisations are reluctant to publish serious allegations for which they lack incontrovertible evidence.

However if an organisation for which you work considers actually suing for defamation, you will obviously need to consider carefully the PR implications of such a move. Even if legal victory seems to be guaranteed, is a long drawn out court case in which lots of embarrassing evidence emerges really going to be in your organisation's best interests? Remember that senior company officials who are not used to answering difficult questions under the spotlight of publicity will face cross-examination in open court. What about the cost in terms of management time and resources? If you taking on a small media outlet or a group of activists will your organisation be seen as acting like a heavy-handed bully?

The organisation for which you work has been libelled by a local newspaper. Legal advice has been sought and your lawyers are 100% confident that in a court case your employers will win substantial damages. In their view the newspaper may well offer to apologise and publish a retraction.

Your chief executive has asked for your PR advice on how to handle this. What information would you need to provide such advice, and what factors would influence the advice you offer?

OTHER ASPECTS OF THE LAW

PR people have been affected by international moves towards, on the one hand, freedom of information legislation and, on the other, enhanced data protection and privacy laws. The former can mean that they are forced to reveal stored information: in the United Kingdom, for example, the government faced some embarrassment when it was obliged to reveal comments media relations staff had made about well-known journalists. On the other hand data protection laws mean that you have to be evermore careful about what you say publicly about customers and others associated with your organisation. The enhanced privacy rights which are developing in many jurisdictions and which seek to protect individuals' private lives from media intrusion can have similar implications, but more usually it is something that PR people increasingly consider using to protect the individuals, such as celebrities, for whom they work from unwanted media attention.

Potential legal issues which can arise when corporations make public statements

In the USA Nike, the world's largest maker of sports shoes, was accused of making false statements about its use of labour in Asia to manufacture sportswear. Activists claimed that the workforce was forced to work in sweatshop conditions and that American consumers were being deceived.

Nike sought to 'fight to preserve the right to free and open debate … Companies should be free to voice their opinions through PR or advertising on major issues that impact their business.'

Nike claimed that the US Constitution's protection of free speech guarantees the right to make their statements when they are about a social issue, rather than the product itself. Claims about the product are regarded as commercial speech which is regulated.

In the end Nike agreed to pay $1.5 million to the Fair Labor Association to settle the case.

The case was closely watched and widely seen as a test of corporate free speech. Aside from the legal issues it clearly had considerable PR implications for Nike and indeed its critics in the Fair Labor Association.[4]

Case Study: the McLibel Case: a legal own goal?

In the 1990s the global fast food giant McDonald's took legal action against two hostile activists who had been leafleting outside its branches in London. They won a victory in the courts but were generally seen to have suffered a major PR reverse. Nor did they receive damages as the leafletters lacked funds – which meant that there had never been any likelihood of McDonald's recouping its considerable legal costs either (putting to one side the vast amounts of corporate time and energy that must have been devoted to the case).

The original court case lasted from 1994 to 1997 (there were subsequent appeals), making it the longest libel case in UK history and a *cause celebre*. In contrast, before McDonald's

launched its legal action few had heard of the leafleters' low-key campaign.

Large amounts of embarrassing evidence was pored over in open court, and hence widely reported in the media over a long period of time. Company executives who were unused to speaking in public were summoned for cross-examination as witnesses (while defendants in a libel case face a difficult task in establishing that they told the truth, there is considerable scope for washing dirty linen in public along the way, and the media are free to report it). The company was widely seen to be exploiting its corporate power and taking a sledgehammer to crack a nut.[5]

Discuss what this tells us about the roles of legal and PR advice in such situations. What can PR people contribute?

- As a PR person you need to remember that you are not exempt from the law and that there are times when you need to seek legal advice. Otherwise you could cost your employer money and appear incompetent - or worse..
- Although the law varies around the world, and keeps evolving, two areas of law are particularly important for PR people:

intellectual property, which has a particular relevance to branding; and defamation, which is about protecting reputations.
- You also need to be able to contribute to discussions about when to take legal action, and to be able to balance expert legal advice with your own PR advice: there is no point in your employer winning a small legal victory if it suffers a devastating PR defeat.

Explain the impact of the legal system on the practice of public relations, and discuss how this might change in the future, relating it to examples in any country.

PART

PLANNING AND STRATEGY

POSTAR: POSITIONING, OBJECTIVES, STRATEGY, TACTICS, ADMINISTRATION, RESULTS

INTRODUCTION[1]

One of the biggest differences between PR and journalism is that generally journalism is a very short-term business. At the end of the working day or week the journalist clears their desk and starts on a new story. The exception to this rule is the specialist or investigative journalist. They may take months or even years to build up their knowledge about a particular area of activity, but both are relatively rare creatures. Broadly journalists work to short planning cycles. Not the PR practitioner.

PR practitioners must plan a long way in advance, but how do you devise a PR plan? What is the difference between a business objective and a PR objective? How is strategy different from objectives? What tactics are most appropriate? How can you persuade the people who hold the purse strings to support your plan? How do you know if your plan worked?

LEARNING OBJECTIVES

- How to plan and structure a public relations campaign
- How to analyse internal and external factors that may impact on a campaign
- How to differentiate between business, communication and PR objectives
- How to devise a strategy
- How to analyse an audience and the issues that relate to them
- How to model messages
- How to select and employ the main PR tactics
- How to budget and manage a campaign
- How to evaluate a campaign

In this section we explain the POSTAR planning model. Not all of POSTAR will be relevant to all people all of the time, but it provides a clear and practical framework for formulating a PR plan. It is not meant to be a straightjacket but an aid. Think of it as scaffolding. Depending on the size and shape of the 'building' you will need to focus more or less on the different elements of the POSTAR plan. But it is your experience, judgement and initiative that will add value to your use of POSTAR: creating a successful PR plan is not about being mechanistic!

A major international organisation may have an overall communications or PR plan made up of a number of POSTARs, with one each for consumer, financial, political, internal and even local community audiences. A small local firm may just have a basic consumer plan, and a public sector body may have separate plans for a range of campaigns designed to change behaviour or inform people of their entitlements. But all organisations need a plan because relations with your publics are something you have whether you like it or not, in the same way that no business can exist without some sort of financial plan. As we have seen, organisations from time immemorial have practised PR, albeit often unconsciously. The challenge for the modern PR practitioner is to go about it in a planned and deliberate way, in order to secure maximum advantage.

So what does *POSTAR* stand for?

*P*OSITIONING
Where are we starting from? (Situational analysis)

*O*BJECTIVES
Where do we want to be? (What we want to achieve)

*S*TRATEGY
How are we going to get there? (Overall plan)

*T*ACTICS
How are we going to get there in detail? (The action elements of the overall plan)

*A*DMINISTRATION
What time and resources do we need/have to get there? (Budget and management)

RESULTS

How will we know when we are there? (Evaluation)

So in essence POSTAR determines where we are, where we want to be, how we are going to get there, what we need to get there and how we will know when we are there. What could be simpler? Unfortunately the devil is in the detail.

Let's look at each of the stages more closely.

POSITIONING

A BACKGROUND OR SITUATION ANALYSIS can be broken down into two distinct parts. The first part looks at the organisation itself and may be described as the INTERNAL ANALYSIS, although it includes an analysis of the market in which the organisation operates, its customers or audience and the competition. The second part looks at all the outside influences on the organisation and can be described as the EXTERNAL ANALYSIS. It includes political, legal and even environmental factors that may influence the success of your organisation and your PR plan. Let's look first at the INTERNAL ANALYSIS.

Internal analysis

The internal analysis examines three separate groups:

- The organisation
- The market (this can be a market for ideas and behaviour as well as for products and services)
- The audience

The first thing to look at is *the organisation* you are working for. It's amazing and a little depressing how many PR people forget this basic need.

What sort of organisation is it? Who owns or controls it? Is it big or small? Is it conservative or radical? Is it well funded or comparatively impoverished (lofty ideals always have to be tempered with reality)? And, most importantly, what are the overall objectives of the organisation? If you don't know what the *organisational objectives* are you cannot devise a relevant PR plan. Remember too that there is often a gap between how the organisation likes to see itself and how others see it – this is highly relevant to PR.

The next area to look at is *the market*. Most of this data should be available from your marketing or commercial department. Market data is particularly important if you are involved in marketing public relations but is also relevant to organisations involved in activity not usually described as marketing. For example, a public sector body may wish to use PR to reduce binge drinking. In this case the examination of the market will include current alcohol sales patterns and the other pro- and anti-drinking messages that are out there.

The sorts of questions that need to be asked in a market analysis are:

- What is the size of the market? Is it growing or declining and, if so, why?
- What are the trends in the market? For example is there a move away from conventional retail and towards online sales? Are prices rising or falling?
- How is the economy performing and what is predicted for the future?
- What is the competition like and what are they doing? Are they aggressive or defensive? What sort of PR space do they occupy?

Inextricably linked with your analysis of the market is an analysis of *your audience*. If your customers are consumers, as opposed to other businesses or organisations, you need to ask questions such as:

- What age ranges do they cover? (Clearly targeting young people as opposed to older people will involve different media and tactics.)
- What social class are they drawn from? For example there would be little point in devising a strategy involving heavy use of electronic media if they have little access to such media.
- What attitudes and cultural values do they share? An approach that might be right for a sophisticated and liberal urban audience could backfire badly with more conservative rural communities.
- Where do they live, and what are their leisure/shopping/buying traditions and patterns?

It is all too easy for well-educated and comparatively affluent PR people living and working in major urban centres to become out of touch with less privileged groups in society and to assume, for example, that they have access to the same online media or have cutting-edge tastes. By the same token it can be hard for PR people fully to understand some of the needs and preoccupations of the super rich. As with so much in business, the answer is putting planning and analysis ahead of preconceptions. As a military leader once said: 'Fail to plan and you should plan to fail'.

If your customers are other organisations – for example B2B PR – you need to be asking questions such as:

- Who owns and controls them?
- What are their traditional buying patterns and are these likely to change? Who are the actual buyers, who are the recommenders and who are the 'rubber stampers'?
- Are these organisations tending to get larger and consolidate or are there a lot of new dynamic young players emerging?
- What are the issues affecting these organisations? (See the SLEPT analysis below)

So having analysed the organisation, market and customers you now need to think of the other groups who may impact on the success or failure of your organisation.

External analysis

There are three stages to external analysis. The first is the *stakeholder analysis* which looks at those who need to be directly influenced and those who influence the organisation and therefore may also need to be communicated with. This is sometimes called examining the COURT OF PUBLIC OPINION.

The second stage is what is called a *reputation driver analysis* and looks at the areas of reputation that most concern the different stakeholders.

Finally there is the *SLEPT analysis*. This involves examining the external factors and issues not covered in the earlier analysis that may impact on the organisation and its stakeholders. First we need to look at the stakeholders, or the 'court of public opinion'.

Stakeholder analysis

Figure 10.1 is an example of a *stakeholder map*. Different stakeholders will be relevant to different organisations, but what is certain is that no organisation can function effectively in PR terms unless it has drawn up a stakeholder map. It is also worth noting that 'staff' are included in this external planning phase when they are really an internal audience. The justification for this is that staff are not only an organisational asset but also an audience. They need to be communicated with not just in commercial terms but also in broader terms as a group which

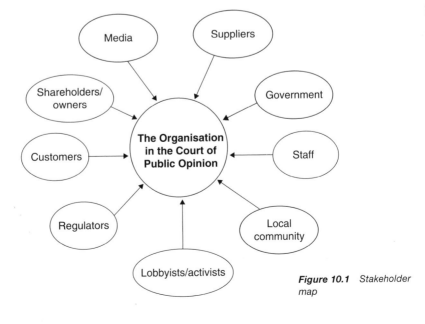

Figure 10.1 *Stakeholder map*

will have strong opinions on what the organisation says and does. For example, if your organisation is a food producer it has to be sensitive to different attitudes towards animals such as cows and pigs in different societies. These religious and cultural views will affect staff and their families as private individuals. How can this best be handled?

Having drawn up the map the stakeholder groups need to be prioritised. Which group is most vital to your interests and which, at least at the moment, can be left alone or be the subject of only minor effort? Some of these questions can best be answered by looking at the reputation drivers.

There is a tendency for people to talk about reputation as though it is a solid and consistent thing. In reality it is nuanced and multi-faceted. Things can be seen in different ways by different people at different times. What for one person is a safe and respectable business is for another predictable and dull. Views can vary for other reasons: one might not want a long-term relationship, say as an investor, with a risky venture, but might regard its products as exciting and want to purchase them. One might even publicly decry an organisation and yet use it in private. Many business sectors – for example pornography and gambling – which are seen by many as rather disreputable manage to thrive. This is why we need to look at *reputation drivers*, the issues which concern stakeholders, and match them to the relevant groups.

The next diagram shows a standard list of reputation drivers.

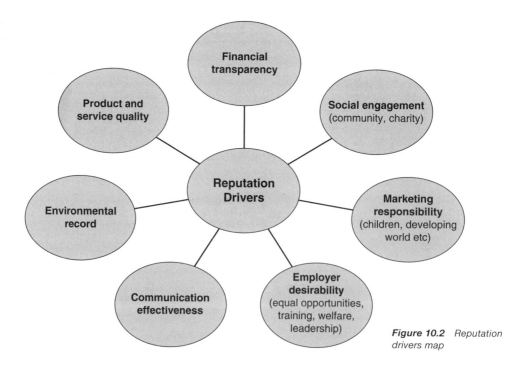

Figure 10.2 *Reputation drivers map*

Any major organisation, be it public or commercial, will have an analysis of stakeholders – usually by importance or ranking – and an understanding of the reputation drivers that most concern each stakeholder group. Even when constructing a POSTAR plan designed for a clearly and narrowly defined audience such as customers it is worth knowing who the other stakeholders are and what reputational issues drive them. For example, you may work for a drinks company that wants to attract 18–24 year olds to its brands. Before devising a plan you would want to know what the government, regulators and lobbyists/activists are likely to think. They may not buy your product but they can certainly affect your ability to do business now and in the future.

Table 10.1   Stakeholder and reputation driver matrix

Stakeholder	Ranking	Driver
Shareholders		
Suppliers		
Customers		
Consumers		
Government		
Activists		
Media		
Employees		
Regulators		

 Do a basic Stakeholder and Reputation Driver Matrix for the institution/organisation you are in now, or an organisation you know well. For example, if you think 'Employees' are the most important stakeholder write a 1 by them and then write which of the reputation drivers you think most concerns them.

SLEPT analysis

The final stage in analysing the POSITION is the *SLEPT Analysis*.

SLEPT is a simple acronym. It stands for *Social, Legal, Environmental, Political* and *Technological* – all issues likely to impact on your organisation. Many of the areas overlap not only with each other but with the reputation drivers we have just looked at. However it is worth looking at each separately so as to ensure that all bases are covered.

a) *SOCIAL*: What are the social trends that you need to be aware of? In much of the world the move from the country to the town is a major issue. This affects not only employment patterns but traditional family structures, transportation and even voting patterns. A good plan looks to the future rather than bases its actions on data drawn from the past, so it is important that future trends are examined.

b) *LEGAL*: Are you threatened by legislation or is there legislation that you would like to see changed? Should you be considering self-regulation to avoid more formal and potentially heavy-handed legislation being imposed by central government? Is the regulatory environment likely to change?

c) *ENVIRONMENTAL*: The environment is one of the biggest social, political and economic issues of the twenty-first century. How green are you? Do you need to do more and, if so, how much and how fast? Do you have a crisis plan for environmental disasters? What is your strategy if you are attacked by environmental groups?

d) *POLITICAL*: What are the issues that are exciting the politicians? Are you likely to be in the firing line? Do your labour relations match political expectations? Is the government protectionist or laissez-faire? Is the political leadership likely to change and if so in what way? Do you have friends among future as well as current leaders? Is power being devolved from the centre or centralised? And if you are a government or public body, what is the mood of the electorate and the public? What are the issues that are vexing them?

e) *TECHNOLOGICAL*: Are there developments that are likely to change the way you do business or the way people do business with you? How will you deal with blogs that criticise you? Will you be able to employ sufficient people with the right technological skills to run a sophisticated online service?

By analysing each of these factors and overlaying it on your stakeholder and reputation driver matrix you will build up a thorough view of the organisation you represent. This will help you secure the ear of senior people and will in turn help you have more influence on the direction of your organisation.

 Do a SLEPT analysis for the organisation/institution you are in now, or another you know well. Does it include factors not covered in your earlier stakeholder and reputation driver analysis?

All too often PR people are left to communicate the ill-conceived plans of their bosses. These are plans that they could have shaped and influenced had they been asked and had the ear of the senior players. A thorough *position analysis* helps PR secure a place at the top table.

But even if you are not at the top table and do not have the resources or time to do a full position analysis, any PR task you are asked or choose to undertake needs a clear set of OBJECTIVES and that is the stage we move on to next.

OBJECTIVES

PR objectives are subsidiary to an organisation's overall or business objectives. There is, in effect, an hierarchy of objectives.

One analogy to explain this hierarchy of objectives might be a country at war.

For example, the president of a country may determine that they need to go to war to achieve the objective of removing the threat of attack from a hostile neighbour. The president's generals then have the objective of defeating the enemy with minimum casualties. Meanwhile a senior officer on the ground has the objective of capturing a particular town, and a more junior officer is tasked with seizing an important building in the town.

In other words the generals and officers are all working to the same overall objective set by the president – removing the threat of attack – but are also working towards slightly lower level objectives against which their performance can be measured

In effect responsibility and objectives cascade down. The same happens in civilian life. The CEO sets the overall business objectives, the Communication Director then sets the PR objectives and finally the PR manager or consultant sets their own objectives.

Take another example. This time imagine a football club (or any professional sports team). Table 10.2 shows in a simple form how the objectives, strategy and tactics hierarchy might work in such a club.

Table 10.2 Football club strategy matrix

	Owner	Manager	Team captain
Objectives	To be the most successful and profitable team in 3 years	To buy the best up and coming players	Get the new players playing as a team
Strategy	To borrow money from the bank to buy the best up and coming players	Make the most experienced player the captain to ensure the new players play as a team and not as individual stars	Organise training sessions followed by activities for all the players' families
Tactics	To increase seat prices as the team's performance improves and thereby pay off the debt	Start a club academy to develop young local players for the future	Get each of the new players to mentor one of the young local academy players

Now try to apply it to your own organisation using Table 10.3.

Table 10.3   Organisational strategy matrix

	Chief executive	Communication director	Public relations manager
Objectives			
Strategy			
Tactics			

Once you clearly understand your organisation's objectives and where you sit in the organisational hierarchy you can start to analyse the other aspects of your positional plan. To continue the earlier military analogy, you can now look at the disposition of the enemy forces, how big or small they are in comparison to your own, and how the layout of the battlefield may affect your plans.

As we have heard, PR objectives are subsidiary to the overall organisational objectives. *If PR alone cannot achieve the objectives specified then they are not PR objectives but marketing or organisational objectives.* PR objectives must be achievable by using PR. There should also not be too many objectives. Too many objectives are a sign of a lack of clarity and make it hard to prioritise activity.

PR objectives – like business and organisational objectives – need to be measurable. If they are not measurable how will you know if the changes in behaviour, sales, attitude or media coverage your PR campaign set out to achieve were actually achieved? (See Evaluation pp. 224–233.)

Some typical measurable objectives might be:

- To increase sales of Shiney Shampoo by 10% in the next 12 months
- To increase awareness by 15% over the next 12 months of the need for single women under 40 to test themselves for unusual lumps in their breasts or armpits
- To get politicians to drop the current proposed legislation affecting your organisation
- To increase membership of your organisation by 25% over the next two years
- To increase donations to your charity by $2m by 2014
- To increase by 5% over the next 12 months the number of children under 5 given the xxx vaccination
- To get government to eliminate the illegal trade in counterfeit xxx products
- To increase the favourabilty ratings of your organisation by x% over the next 12 months
- To increase by 50% over the next twelve months the volume of positive media coverage about the Chief Executive
- To secure 12 pieces of national media coverage for your organisation by the end of the financial year

Of course the list is potentially as endless as the types of organisations there are – although they all fall into three broad categories: OUTPUT – media coverage; OUTTAKE – increases in awareness or improvements in attitude; and OUTCOME – changes in behaviour such as sales or votes.. What unites them all is that they are, to a greater or lesser extent, *SMART*[2]:

SMART objectives

S....Specific
M....Measurable
A....Achievable
R....Realistic
T....Timed

Specific: Vague objectives such as, 'to launch the new Zoom car successfully' are meaningless. How will you know if you have succeeded? Will it be when media coverage of the Zoom car has been achieved, or when the Zoom car is the best-selling and most profitable car ever? Similarly objectives such as 'to raise awareness of the need for the xxx vaccination' are little better. How much awareness, and among which publics? And why awareness? Awareness is no good if people take no action as a result of it. Objectives are generally no good if they are not measurable.

Measurable: Whether you are talking about media coverage, sales, awareness, or the actions of politicians your objectives should be measurable. However, there are three major problems with measurability. These problems can seem so great that PR people are deterred from specifying measurable objectives which in turn leads to accusations that PR is not a proper management discipline in the way that sales or finance are. The issue of evaluating PR has preoccupied many people and deserves separate attention: we have explored it in more depth at the end of this chapter.

Achievable/Realistic: PR can be a powerful tool but is badly served by false claims, so make sure that what you intend is achievable, particularly if you are not in control of all the levers that may affect the outcome – such as the vital matters of price and distribution. If you are being pushed to specify objectives that you feel are unrealistic, try breaking them down into long-term and short-term objectives, or into business and PR objectives. So, for example, you might say the overall business objective is to make the Zoom the best-selling car in the market, and to help achieve that your PR objectives are to get all key motoring journalists to write a review with the aim of achieving 30,000 test drives in the first 6 months and 100,000 sales in the first 12 months.

Timed: Timing is an obvious but often neglected aspect of objective setting. A good campaign is reviewed as it goes along so that the lessons can be learned and changes made, but it is also necessary to have a firm date when a full evalu-ation of the results can be undertaken. Again the message is be realistic. Too tight a time frame and your campaign is unlikely to have had a chance to achieve its full effect, too long a time frame and your campaign is likely to lose direction and energy, if not have been forgotten about altogether.

In summary PR objectives should:

- Be about media coverage (Output), changes in awareness or attitude (Outtake) or measurable changes in behaviour such as sales, web hits, votes (Outcome)
- Support the overall organisational objectives. (It is usually a good idea to record the relevant organisational objectives before listing the PR objectives).
- Describe *where you want to get to* not *how you are going to get there* (The latter is strategy.)
- Be as SMART as possible. As a minimum they should say WHAT is going to be achieved (measurable) and by WHEN (timed)
- Be used to check that all tactics are 'on strategy' and aren't simply being undertaken because they will get coverage. It is not being famous that is important but what you are famous for.
- Be clearly linked to the RESULTS section

Objectives are like a thread of steel that runs through any PR proposal from its beginning to its end.

STRATEGY

Having chosen the objectives we know where we are going (or so we hope!). We now need to know how we are going to get there.

There are some key questions that you need to ask yourself before you devise your strategy. How many of these questions, and in how much detail, will depend in part on the complexity of the task and in part on how thorough and effective your position analysis was. The better your position analysis is the easier it will be to devise the strategy.

The questions are:

- Who is my target *audience*?
- What *message* do I want them to hear and respond to?
- What *media* are best for reaching them?
- What *methods* are best for reaching the target media?

The Science of Sexy

PR consultancy Edelman/JCPR combined the use of celebrity, events and original digital content to secure extensive offline and online coverage for Wonderbra's new range designed by burlesque star Dita von Teese under the banner – 'The Science of Sexy'.

The results included over 600 pieces of conventional coverage, 3,200 blogposts, as well as a huge number of YouTube hits. They also claim sales were well ahead of expectations.

A combination of lingerie and a 'sexy' celebrity might seem an obvious and easy PR task, but the consultancy still had to get a lot of detail right, including media targeting, events planning and budgeting.[3]

Audience

Try to be as specific as possible about your audience. Be wary of saying you want to target everyone, or all adults. This is seldom the case and, even when it is, there are normally some groups that are more important to you in terms of their influence on others, their spending power or how receptive they are likely to be to your message. So ask yourself, given a limited amount of money and time, who are the people you *most* want to reach?

Even saying all shoppers or all housewives is usually too vague. Are they well-off or poor? Are they rural or urban? Are they young or old? By answering these questions you can be more precise with your messaging and media selection. You would not, for example, expect to target your mother in the same way as you would an 18-year-old student.

There are a number of ways in which an audience can be broken down and profiled for analysis:

Audience profiling

- Age. Try to break down the ages into life stages that affect behaviour. For example, teenagers living at home, students away from home, young singles, young couples, young families, families with teenage children, empty nesters – that is adults whose children have left home, early retireds, older retireds and so forth.
- Marital status (e.g. single, co-habiting, married, divorced)
- Income
- Sex
- Social class
- Education
- Occupation
- Hobbies or interests (e.g. sport, culture, travel)
- Social values (e.g. liberal and modern, or conservative and traditional)

- Political allegiances
- Religious beliefs
- Geographic location
- Nationality/ethnicity

More often than not, you will need several descriptors to define your target audience. For example, you might be trying to promote a new, sweet-tasting premium-priced alcoholic drink. The fact that it is premium-priced will restrict its appeal to people with high disposable incomes. The fact that it is sweet is likely to make it attractive to the young, and in particular young women. The fact that it is alcoholic means that it may not appeal to people of some religious persuasions and the socially conservative. Your audience is therefore likely to be between 18 and 30, with high disposable incomes, predominantly but not exclusively female, socially liberal and, perhaps, living in major towns or cities.

If you are launching a new product or trying to promote a new idea or concept you will need to think about who the key opinion formers are. For example who are the people who always buy the latest gadgets? Who are the people who influence the uptake of new ideas and influence social behaviour?

According to marketing and communication theorists the consumers or users in most markets can be broken down into distinct groups. These can be called:

a) Innovators
b) Early adopters
c) Followers
d) Resisters

If you are entering a new market then clearly the 'innovators' and 'early adopters' will be key. If however you are entering a mature market the greatest potential may lie with the followers. The audience profile for each group is likely to be different.

Along with defining your objectives, clearly defining your audience leads to better results, more efficient use of resources and more accurate evaluation.

Analysing and defining the audience is usually not too difficult for those working in marketing PR as the sales and marketing departments often have extensive customer data. If this sort of data is not available you will need to do some market research among your target audience, using some or all of the categories above, to find out what they are like and, from that, determine the best media with which to reach them (see pp. 193–197).

Targeting a financial or political audience can be more problematic than targeting a consumer audience. For example, imagine you want to change a piece of government legislation which is currently under consideration. To whom do you need to talk? Is it all politicians or just the ones who have shown an interest in the issue, or have taken a particular stance on it? Who is drafting the legislation? Should you be talking to civil servants and other interested third parties? Is there a local audience that needs to be addressed?

This sort of information is generally much harder to collate and often involves extensive desk research using directories, online sources, personal contacts, journals, minutes and records. But despite the difficulties, the information can usually be found. Politicians and leaders of charities and NGOs are generally not shy about expressing their views and love to see them in print or on air which means the media themselves can be powerful market research tools.

One way of categorising what we can call political audiences is as shown in Table 10.4.

Table 10.4 Categorising political audiences

Allies	Neutrals	Opponents

Allies are those who support, or are likely to support, your goals. Usually – unless they are for some reason embarrassing to be associated with – it is advisable to work closely with them as the more groups and people you have on your side the more credible and stronger your case will seem to the neutrals.

Neutrals are generally the most important group. It is hard to convert your 'enemies' but easier to win over neutrals. As any politician will tell you, the most important voter is a floating voter – the one yet to make up their mind. These are the people who decide elections.

Opponents are those who oppose what you are trying to achieve. You may seek to win them over, ignore or even undermine them.

So in summary, you need to research, analyse and then categorise your audiences before you can select the most appropriate media through which to target them.

Media

Once the target audience has been defined and analysed you can start drawing up a media plan. Twenty years ago this was a comparatively straightforward task. Few countries had more than a handful of TV stations and a dozen or so radio stations. Today most developed nations have literally hundreds of television stations and thousands of radio stations, with magazines and newspapers appealing to every taste and interest. Over and above that there is the internet. In addition to millions of websites there are millions of blogs, plus social networks such as Facebook, Twitter and YouTube with which to contend. Media targeting has got more complicated.

There are two ways of categorising media – by type or by content.

In most countries media can be broken down into three familiar types. The broadest definition of these types is:

- Broadcast (television and radio: international, national and local)
- Print (newspapers and magazines: international, national and local)
- Online (websites, blogs and other online social media)

Beyond the media there is face-to-face communication (such as parties, seminars, conferences, exhibitions).

However, categorising by media type is only of limited value as audiences do not just 'watch television', they watch particular television programmes and read particular newspaper articles and magazines. The nature of media consumption is something that PR practitioners have to think about. It varies in different countries, and even within the same society it evolves over time. In developed countries, for example, newspapers have changed from being relatively expensive products which were shared by many people into relatively cheap – even free – and easily discardable items. More recently increased television ownership, with multiple sets in individual households, has meant that viewing is less of a shared experience, which typically brought together the family. And now television faces the rival attraction of the world wide web which, despite the scope to interact, remains in essence an individual experience and one where exact patterns of viewing are not shared by groups in society (millions of people may still watch the same major TV shows simultaneously, but the same is seldom true for online experiences). Online media are also in many ways at odds with traditional ideas of the mass media: while some major websites and blogs enjoy heavy traffic (albeit often to only a few of what may be many millions of pages), most are seldom visited – they remain largely unused but available to those who ask for them.

People's media preferences are in large part determined by content – and media content generation is at the heart of public relations. With more and more media outlets and more and more broadcasting available 24 hours a day, seven days a week, the media are desperate for content. This hunger is further fuelled by the economics of the modern media which dictate that the minimum number of journalists is employed. In the USA and the UK there are now estimated to be more PR people than there are journalists.[4] Without PR-created content there would be much less media. Indeed, estimates of the proportion of PR-generated news in the United States go as high as 80%.[5] In some cases this proportion will be lower but in many cases - such as fashion and celebrity magazines - it will be higher.

The proliferation and fragmentation of media offers PR practitioners a fantastic opportunity to get their messages across. After all media organisations want to fill their pages or airtime with the best possible material at the lowest cost, and PR can supply such material at no charge to the media. But in order to take advantage of the opportunity they need to understand the media they are targeting.

Later we will look at how to devise media-friendly content, but first of all we need to examine the media in a bit more detail.

The first stage is to examine the audience, or readership profiles of different media to see how well they match your target audience. With sophisticated media which are funded in part by advertising this is easily done: the advertising departments of the broadcasting stations and print titles will have detailed audience profiles which they use to attract advertisers. In many countries this information will also be available from independently produced online or print directories produced specifically to help PR practitioners, advertisers and marketers. Alternatively, a direct approach to the targeted title will secure you the information. What is certain is that the broader your target audience is the greater the range of potential media. This is both a problem and an opportunity. An opportunity because it means there is plenty of potential for coverage of your messages, but a problem because prioritising your media targeting may be a much more time-consuming process – unless your funds are so endless that you can afford to target all potential titles equally. This is not a situation that often occurs.

Having profiled the media that best fit your target audience you now need to look at the media's content to see what titles and programmes are most likely to cover your story and reach the target audience. Really big stories will be carried on general news pages and programmes and carry enormous influence as the news tends to attract vast audiences and have great impact. However, only a miniscule percentage of PR stories will ever make it onto general news so the effective PR practitioner needs to look for richer pastures.

Some media can be described as VERTICAL. Media of this sort are dedicated to a particular interest such as sport, fashion or business. Other media can be described as HORIZONTAL meaning that they cover a wide range of interests from general news to sport, personal finance and home decoration. Newspapers are usually horizontal whilst most magazines are vertical. Television now offers both horizontal content in terms of general channels and vertical coverage in terms of special interest channels for sport, music and so on. Online media have tended to mimic the television model with a mixture of horizontal and vertical websites. You need to identify and get to know the opportunities in each of your target media, be they horizontal or vertical.

Finally, there are 'face-to-face' opportunities. These cover events owned by others or created by yourself at which the target audience can be reached. These are not really media in the conventional sense of the word, but are nonetheless vital channels – sometimes the only channels – of communication for your messages.

Like conventional media, face-to-face 'media' are created to inform, entertain or educate an audience. The numbers of people who can be reached at such events are far fewer than can be reached by conventional media but they are often very significant because they bring together or can reach the key opinion formers and innovators and early adopters of new products and ideas. Fashion shows are a classic example of face-to-face events – the number of people who actually attend is quite small but they are people who exert enormous influence and whose presence often attracts media coverage.

In the process of drawing up your target audience profile certain events, or exhibitions or shows may have come to your attention. You now need to consider them in the same way that you have examined the other forms of media. For example in the music arena there are normally a limited number of venues or clubs that are setting the trends. How can you achieve face-to-face opportunities at these with young opinion formers? At the other extreme most societies have a formal establishment – for example the government and royal family – and a less formal but nonetheless powerful informal establishment consisting of business people, artists and cultural figures, influential thinkers and writers, academics and certain politicians. Where do these people meet? Is there a dining club, conference or party circuit that you can access?

If there are no appropriate events that you can successfully access could you create one? People with similar interests, be it pop music or political power, like to meet each other. Can you help facilitate that meeting and in so doing get your message across?

Imagine a target audience you might want to reach. Sit down with some friends and colleagues and imagine what media your target audience consumes and why, and then fill in the chart below ... you will probably need at least a page per media type. Once you have filled the chart you can use publicly available data to check that your assumptions are correct. In the process you may also find some media of which you had not previously thought.

Table 10.5 Target media plan

Type of media	Name/title of medium	Section, programme, feature, page
Newspaper • International • National • Local		
Magazine • Consumer • Business • Specialist • Trade (industry specific)		
Television • International • National • Local		
Radio • International • National • Local		
Online • Website • Blog • Social network		
Face-to-face • Exhibitions • Seminars • Conferences • Parties		

In summary, you need to draw up a target media list and then cross reference that with the particular sections, programmes or writers through which you want to communicate. It is also worth bearing in mind that, exceptionally, PR people sometimes have to step beyond the conventional mass media and help people who are producing books or films.

 Imagine you are trying to target well-off retired people. What media might they consume and where might they, or the people they look up to, meet?

Message

A message is basically a communication sent by one organisation or person to another. In PR terms it is what you want the audience to read, see or hear as a result of your activity. The successful receipt of a message makes it more likely that the audience thinks, feels or does whatever it is that you intended by your activity.

A clear definition of your messages is important for three main reasons:

1 It will give focus to your PR activity ... if it is not 'on message' don't do it

2 It will ensure that you have a checklist to use in all communication – including those executed by salespeople or call centre staff

3 It will help make your evaluation more precise

Determining what messages you want to communicate should naturally follow on from your objectives and target audience selection. The clearer your objectives and audience selection the easier it will be to define your messages. But do not just think you can define your message and the rest will take care of itself.

Imagine that you see someone you find attractive at a social event and decide that you would like to speak to them. First, you must speak in a language they understand. Second, you must measure your approach: if you are too forward you may repel them, too timid and they may not understand your interest. Their response will also be determined by how they perceive you. What is your reputation? How do you look and dress? Is your tone of voice appropriate to the occasion? And finally their response will be determined by their own values and level of social confidence. As with all social communication there is much that can go wrong and plenty of room for mistakes and misunderstandings. Now imagine that it is not you doing the talking but a third-party on your behalf! That is what generally happens with public relations. You, the sender of the message, relay it to the media who in turn relay it on to the intended recipients (see Table 10.3) along with a range of other messages that may be more or less interesting to the recipient. Other messages are often called *noise*, because, to extend the analogy of the social event, a lot of background noise can make the message hard or even impossible to hear.

Choosing your messages

So when devising your messages there are at least four things you need to think about:

- *How your organisation is perceived.* The language you use and the messages you convey must be interesting and relevant to the audience, but they must also be in keeping with the image and reputation of your own organisation. A conservative bank trying to use the language of the street will never sound right. Similarly an organisation recently exposed for pollution will not be listened to if they suddenly try to proclaim how green they are.
- *The language and style of the media to be used.* Technical and management language is fine for media that write in that way. In fact few media titles are

technical. Most media, for obvious economic reasons, try to appeal to the broadest possible audience. Use their language and their style. Can the message be expressed in an image or diagram? Not all messages have to be in words.

- *The values, views and language of the recipient.* Media are generally sensitive to the values, views and language of their readers, viewers and listeners, so if you have got the previous stage right you are well on the way to getting this one right. The key thing is to think what will appeal to them. How would they want to hear about this?

- *What are the other messages being communicated at the same time?* The surrounding communications noise can make a big difference to how your message is heard. This can work in two ways. First there is *competing communication.* Is there a lot going on that might drown out your message? For example at election time or in times of national crisis the media are often full of hard news that could squeeze out or diminish your news. Similarly you need to be aware of *contradictory communication.* The key messages you use to communicate a new savings scheme will – following the collapse of a major financial institution that has robbed thousands of their savings – be very different from what you might have otherwise have planned.

This information should be readily to hand if you have conducted an effective position analysis, profiled and defined your target audience and drawn up your target media list.

 Think of an organisation which you know well. On the basis of its current PR work, try to complete the following table. While you may lack all the information that their PR people have, it is nonetheless helpful to start thinking in these terms.

Table 10.6 Planning a message

How the organisation is perceived	
The language and style of the media to be used	
The values, views and language of the recipients	
What are the other messages which are being communicated at the same time	

So having considered these factors you now need to write down your messages.

How to express your message

There are two ways of expressing your messages. The first is to express them in the words that you would like the media to use. This is the best route if your evaluation is primarily based on media coverage. *Be realistic* about what the media might say. Most media are not going to publish or broadcast everything you say without criticism. Nor will they normally publish it word-for-word. Indeed, as a general rule the better and more credible the media – and therefore the more effective when they do carry your message – the less likely they are slavishly to do your bidding. Remember that journalists like to see themselves as independent, as people who choose their own angles on stories and their own words, and trampling on this can be counterproductive. You also need to *avoid jargon*, unless you are targeting a technical audience.

So 'Whizzo has a new sub molecular structure that erases enzymes' should become 'Whizzo is designed to clean more, faster'. Similarly, 'The symbiosis between Whizzcar's technical and sales strategy is predicted to enhance forward growth' becomes 'The new Whizzcar is being priced to compete with Ford and independent industry experts say it should sell well'.

At best technical and management jargon is useful shorthand for those in the know, at worst it is a barrier to understanding and a smokescreen for sloppy thinking and uninteresting news and ideas. One of your main tasks as a PR person is to try to make your organisation understandable to the outside world. The people working there will be all-too familiar with it, and use jargon accordingly. Not only can this be boring or incomprehensible to outsiders, but in some situations it could sound insensitive: imagine an organisation talking bureaucratically about a situation which has led to deaths or injuries. You have – diplomatically – to decode and rephrase the words of senior managers before they reach the media and the public.

The other way of framing your messages is in the language the target audience would use. This is most appropriate when your evaluation includes some tracking studies and benchmark research to see how and if the target audience's attitudes have changed. Sometimes this may correlate directly to the language used by the media but more commonly should be expressed as a 'Take-Out'. A take-out is what the recipients of a message say to themselves having received the message. So using our two examples above they might say 'Whizzo sounds better than what I'm using, perhaps I should give it a try' or 'Next time I change the car I will give the Whizzcar a test drive'.

In reality the messages you are likely to need to communicate will be more numerous and more complicated than those used above. However, it is important to *have no more than three or four messages* (preferably with one clear overarching primary message) and *keep all messages clear and simple.*

So for example we might say:

Primary Message: Whizzo cleans more, faster
Secondary messages: Whizzo is based on the latest safe science; Whizzo is made by a firm you can trust; Whizzo is kind to the environment

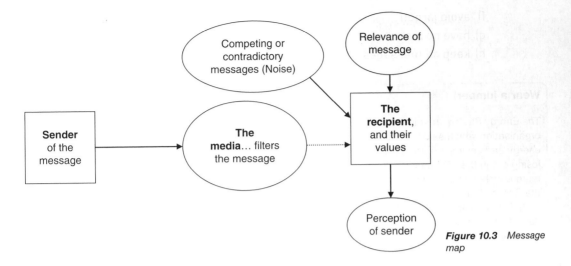

Figure 10.3 *Message map*

Another example might be:

Primary Message: The proposed tram system will move more people more quickly
Secondary Messages: The tram system will cost no more than the building of the pro-
posed ringroad; the tram system will reduce pollution by 35% in two years; and the
opposition to the tram system is financed by the main motor manufacturers.

Clearly for some audiences and some activities the secondary messages will become primary, but in both cases the overarching key message is clear and simple. The secondary messages are also simple and easy to remember. Bad PR proposals and plans tend to have many messages which are impossible to remember, are not relevant or interesting to the audience and sometimes even contradict other messages being communicated elsewhere by the organisation.

 For an organisation that you know well, try to imagine a PR campaign and think of a primary message and secondary message(s).

Summary

Think about:

a) how your organisation is perceived
b) the language and style of the media to be used
c) the values, views and language of the recipient
d) what other messages are being communicated at the same time

and:

e) be realistic

f) avoid jargon

g) have no more than three or four messages

h) keep all messages clear and simple.

Wear a jumper!

The Energy Saving Trust is a publicly funded UK organisation which seeks to raise recognition of energy and environmental issues. It found it was losing out in the PR battle for awareness with more aggressive environmental groups such as the Carbon Trust and Friends of the Earth.

Its PR consultancy, Weber Shandwick, decided to fight back with a creative news strategy. It produced three quarterly reports called *Green Barometers* which tracked consumer attitudes and developed from them a range of media news hooks. One of the most compelling was the threat to the environment from patio heaters – the simple message was don't use them, 'wear a jumper'. According to PR Week, who gave the campaign one of its coveted awards,[6] not only were there over 100 pieces of TV, print and online coverage, but top retailers Marks and Spencer and B&Q were prompted to turn their backs on the heaters.

Methods

So we know who our audience is. We have selected our target media and defined our messages. Now we need to think of what methods we are going to use to secure relevant coverage or content in the target media.

There are an enormous number of ways that PR can be delivered. Many years ago one of the authors wrote out a list of possible PR tactics – he gave up when he reached a hundred! Some of these tactics will be outlined in the next section, but what we want to focus on in this part is the categorisation of types of activity. We call this the 'methods'.

As we saw earlier, broadly all PR approaches can be categorised into five different types or methods which can carry our chosen messages. These are:

- Hard News
- Created or 'soft' news
- News Events
- Promotional Content
- Direct News

Each of these methods is in essence a form of media content. The choice of method or methods will depend on your message and media selection.

Before looking at each of these methods it is worth recalling what the media are looking for.

The media have three simple goals (over and above making money), namely to INFORM, ENTERTAIN and EDUCATE. It is what people read, watch or listen to the media for. The problem is that much of what an organisation wants to communicate is not essentially interesting or entertaining and, even when it is, what they want to say is far from being the only messages that the media and ultimately the target audience are asked to consider. Therefore the PR person's job is to take what is often dull or undistinguished and make it interesting and/or entertaining.

The 180 degree turn

To do this the PR person needs to do something called the *180 degree turn*. This involves thinking about what will interest the media and the target audience, rather than what interests the organisation, and creating content that will grab their interest while successfully carrying the agreed messages. For example, computers are not very interesting for most people, but the chance of working from home is. Saving money is not a riveting subject but luxury goods, holidays and a safe and secure old age are. This is the 180 degree turn, from talking about *me* to talking about *you*, from talking about the organisation to talking about the target audience. We can map this out on the diagram below (See figure 10.4).

The best place to be is in the top left hand quadrant. In theory an important *and* interesting story should guaranteed coverage – although the reality is that few stories are guaranteed coverage, particularly if they have been sent to the wrong media.

Clearly the worst place to be is in the bottom right hand quadrant…a place where sadly quite a few organisations find themselves. However, probably the most common place that organisations find themselves in is the bottom left hand quadrant – important but not interesting. The task of the PR is to make things interesting.

Finally, a word on the top right quadrant. What can be interesting but not important? Well, think of celebrities, gossip, fun and trivia. All these are excellent ways of getting essentially unimportant messages into the media.

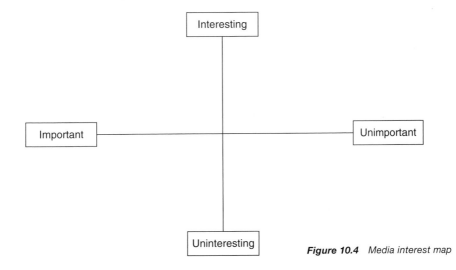

Figure 10.4 *Media interest map*

Think about the following types of organisation and activity. Which quadrant do they fit into and how could you move them into a better quadrant? Insurance, computer upgrades, socks, a celebrity marriage, the resignation of a senior government minister, global warming, beer.

Hard news

'Hard news' is a newspaper term. It means news that relates to real events of real importance. The outbreak of wars, the calling of elections, and the discovery of murders are all front page news for national newspapers and TV news programmes. Very occasionally a company will make the front pages with a 'good news' story, perhaps for a new invention, a dramatic rise in profits or for hiring large numbers of staff. More commonly they will make the front page because of financial or product failures – and often this amounts to a crisis which threatens the survival of the company (see Chapter 14).

Of course what is considered hard news is different when it comes to specialist media, or specialist sections in general titles. For example a healthy growth in profits for a national computer company is likely to be covered by the business pages of the national print media, the computer trade magazines, the specialist business and financial media – including online media – and local press around the company's main offices and factories. But it is unlikely to get any coverage on a news bulletin on a popular music channel.

Even if you have a news story you need to present it in a way that ensures that busy news desks spot it. 'Computer Firm publishes financial results,' is unlikely to grab the attention of a harassed journalist. On the other hand, 'Profits double for computer giant' might just do the trick provided it has been sent at the right time and to the right people. Similarly, a new product may be of interest in its own right but is even more likely to get coverage if it is supported with a great photograph, particularly if it is one featuring a celebrity.

When drawing up your plan you need to make a realistic appraisal of how much 'hard news' you are likely to have over the time period of your plan. As we have seen, what is considered no news at all by one medium may be considered very hard news by another – for example a local media outlet close to a company's main factory. The key is to be realistic in your assessment of what news is and who is likely to find it worth using.

Hard news which an organisation is likely to want to promote includes:

- New goods
- New services
- Expansion (more people, shops or factories)
- A new boss
- New discovery or new research that changes the way people think

And then of course there are plenty of more negative hard news stories, but to deal with them see Chapter 12.

Try to think of likely positive hard news stories for an organisation you know well. What stories would have to be covered by which media?

If the answer to your audit of hard news possibilities is 'not a lot' you will need to consider some or all of the methods outlined below.

Soft or 'created' news

Soft news is also sometimes called *news out of nothing*. Typical examples of created news are:

- Surveys, research, and interesting facts and figures
- Predictions of future trends
- Psychological profiles of different types of people relevant to your market
- Expert Guides and top tips designed to help people with relevant problems or activities

Created news is a popular method when an organisation is unlikely to have much hard news. Commonly this will apply to well-established companies or marketplaces when there is little new to say. Let us take the example of a mobile phone company.

In markets where there is genuine competition between companies the media and the consumer are subjected to a constant barrage of new services and offers. Most are instantly copied and many rarely get a media mention other than in paid-for advertising. So how does the clever company keep its name at the forefront of the media and consumer's mind? The answer often involves research. Sometimes this will be data that the company has gathered naturally in the course of its business, sometimes it will be data that it has specially collected – often using a specialist research firm – that tells us something new about the market and its consumers. This sort of activity can be called anything from a report, survey or index through to a study or even a strategic discussion paper. At its heart are research and data. The media love facts and figures because they give scale and credibility to a story.

For example the mobile phone company may have data that show what kind of people buy which kinds of phones. It might even employ a psychologist to say what your choice of phone says about you as a person. Alternatively it may commission research to find out what are the most common kinds of text messages and whether people have used texts to arrange a date or finish a relationship.

It is not just consumer product firms that use research to create news. Insurance companies can tell us what sorts of businesses are most likely to suffer fire or crime. NGOs can use research to show what people's attitudes are to particular social problems and accountancy firms can use research to talk about business trends. Often organisations are sitting on a gold mine of information if only they think of using it. In the UK insurance companies – operating in hardly the most interesting product area – have revealed everything from how star signs seem to influence the likelihood of having an accident or choice of car colour through to the most bizarre excuses for having had an accident and the most popular music played at funerals.

Another way of creating news is to predict future trends: the media adore speculation about what lies ahead. So food retailers can talk about future eating habits. Medical companies can discuss twenty-first century diseases and NGOs can predict the effects of global warming, declines in animal populations or increases in specific kinds of poverty.

As touched on above, psychology is another way of creating news out of nothing. Is your future mother-in-law a lion, a snake, a cat or mongoose? This could be used by a bridal ware company, but who could resist finding out? Or, from a firm of business advisers, 'are you a leader, innovator, manager or outcast?' None of this is really hard news but it is interesting – we all have egos – even if it is seldom truly important.

Then there are guides. As with the use of psychologists, these are often supported by some research data. For example our mobile telephone company could produce a guide on 'Long Distance Love...how to keep in touch when your loved one is far away'. A funeral company could produce a guide on how to handle bereavement; a car company could produce a guide to the ten best scenic drives in the country; and an anti-binge drinking public body could give tips – perhaps on a credit card-sized guide – on how to avoid getting drunk but still have a good time.

All these are examples of news created by PR people for the purpose of securing media coverage to convey key messages. All are also examples of things that are informative, entertaining and educational. Just what the media want.

News events

News events are created to make otherwise rather weak news stories stronger or to generate news in their own right. For example, a cosmetic company is launching a new perfume. In fact there is not much that the media can usually say about a new perfume: it is, after all, fantastically difficult to describe a smell. So to grab the media's attention the perfume company might hold a party to which top celebrities are invited. The release of a new record by a well-established star might be spiced up with an invitation to the media to see them perform in an unusual location such as a children's home or a prison. A firm launching a new motorcycle safety suit might simulate a dramatic crash in a densely populated city centre. Or a bottle making company might decide to create a large-scale model of a famous building out of glass bottles, thus ensuring plentiful exposure for its name and enhancing its reputation as a company with new ideas.

Care has always to be exercised as eye-catching ideas can attract the wrong kind of publicity. In 2007 the President of Cartoon Network had to resign following a publicity stunt which went seriously wrong and triggered a bomb alert in Boston.

Politicians seem particularly adept at using news events. An announcement of a small increase in funding for school sports that might otherwise have gone unnoticed is suddenly a news event when the minister launches it by playing five minutes of football with a school team. (This sort of approach is apt to backfire if the minister overrates his or her own footballing prowess and falls over.)

By knowing your media you will soon get to know what sort of events get coverage and in Chapter 12 we describe in more detail how to create an effective PR photograph or photo opportunity.

Travelodge

The British budget hotel chain Travelodge is a particularly adept user of proactive PR techniques. It has featured regularly in the UK media, using a range of soft news and news event techniques. For example:

- It publicised the case of a couple who had chosen to live in a Travelodge hotel for 22 years.
- Its 'annual sleepwalking audit' revealed a rise in the number of naked male sleepwalkers.
- It analysed which cities in Britain had the biggest snoring problem (the worst example was Coventry!).
- It published a study showing the benefits to tourism of London hosting the 2012 Olympics.
- It announced the creation of a £25 million bounty payable to members of the public who help Travelodge find new sites for their hotels.
- The establishment of Britain's only professional Santa School at a central London hotel was topically announced in mid-November.
- It publicised plans to recruit more long-term unemployed people as hotel staff.
- Announcing the opening of a new London hotel, Travelodge said it would feature the first 'kipshaw' service – rickshaws fitted with single beds on which guests could snooze as they travelled to central London.
- Numerous hotel openings around the country, typically involving celebrities and prominent local people, were publicised.

But Travelodge did not stop there. They also invented new services such as the cuddle pillow for guests who were missing their partners and a goldfish bowl hire service ... apparently looking at goldfish helps you go to sleep.

As all this illustrates, Travelodge demonstrate keen news-sense. They managed to raid their own larder for newsworthy material, such as the story of their long-term guests (something which involved efficient internal communications). They also succeeded in publicising research on a range of topics related to the hotel industry. Some were simply quirky and amusing and reported as such, others were more serious and worthy but potentially significant, such as the

➡

report on the benefits of the Olympics. The story about the £25 million bounty introduced the concept of a competition. Meanwhile industry-based stories and accounts of local hotel openings appealed to the hospitality trade press and local media respectively.

Given Travelodge's rather prosaic business, their PR team managed to generate an impressive range of stories and secure an enormous number of namechecks for the company, thereby demonstrating their awareness of the media's needs and likely interests.[7]

Things can also go horribly wrong!

Cadbury's controversial Indian ad for its Temptations chocolate bar suggested the disputed Kashmir region between India and Pakistan is – like the chocolate bar – 'too good to share.' It was made by a local ad agency and signed off by the marketing department of Cadbury's India – a department that Cadbury's admits contains no PR staff.

PR Week commented that the PR disaster inherent in selling chocolate through jokes about a conflict that has killed 50,000 people means it will not be long before Cadbury's forms a PR arm for its Indian operations.[8]

Promotional content

Promotional content includes activities such as:

- competitions
- giveaways
- sponsored pages, supplements and programmes.

Promotional content is different from standard media relations in that it involves the provision of goods or money to the host media. Some even argue that such activities are not proper PR and should be under the control of advertising agencies. The authors believe these sorts of turf wars are unhelpful. The owner of the activity should be the person best able and qualified to execute it. Promotions are different from advertising in that they are usually conducted in the editorial style of the host media. Properly trained PR people should be expert in the editorial style of the host media and have useful contacts among the relevant journalists.

Promotional content is unlikely to be used as the sole method of PR communication, but is an increasingly popular approach because, first, the media in their thirst for content welcomes it; and, second, because it guarantees the inclusion of your messages, usually in a way that you can control. So, for example, a driving school, working together with a media title with a good reach among young people who are old enough to start learning to drive, might run a competition in which readers or viewers have to recognise the profile of famous cars. The winners receive free driving lessons and the driving school benefits from branded coverage and positive mentions of their successful pass rates. If the competition is run over a number of weeks the medium attracts not only reader or viewer interest but also loyalty as the readers have to buy each issue or view each episode.

Similarly a public health body might sponsor – and help write – a column of health tips in a woman's magazine, while a perfume company might offer one hundred free bottles of scent to the first one hundred readers to write in. A tourist authority could sponsor a whole travel supplement featuring holidays in a particular country, or a national business organisation or government might sponsor a supplement containing articles about its country as a business destination and place to invest.

The benefits in all these cases are the implied endorsement and approval of your product by the media partner, positive descriptions of whatever it is you are 'selling' (if it is good enough to be a prize it must be good!) and in certain cases, and provided it does not breach data protection laws, the collection of names and addresses for future contact.

Direct news

Direct news is about delivering or sending your messages directly to your target audience. This can be as simple as handing a report or paper outlining your position on an issue to a select group of influential politicians, through to holding a massive celebrity-filled party or organising a major conference. This may sound like a repetition of what was described under News Events and in some ways it is. The difference is that with direct news any media coverage is a secondary objective. The primary objective is to reach the target audience directly, without the mediating influence of journalists, but usually with the some influential key opinion formers present.

This sort of activity is, as we observed when looking at face-to-face media, expensive. The cost per audience contact, when compared with a conventional media campaign that might reach millions for fractions of a penny per head, are high, but so too are the potential returns. Direct news can be cost-effective. The value of exposing the right group of celebrities to your product and their becoming ambassadors for it is almost incalculable. Similarly a major conference involving planners and political and business leaders on the future of urban transportation will ensure the organisers – say the foremost firm in the development of trams – make contact with the people most likely to influence their future success. Any media coverage that results is just a bonus.

Try to think of examples of how each of the above techniques could be used for your chosen organisation.

Having defined the methods to be used we can now look at how to bring the methods to life with creative tactical ideas.

Three ways PR in the USA is different from UK PR

Duncan Burns, Senior Vice President, Hill & Knowlton (US)

1 There's a much greater opportunity for invention, re-invention and failure in the US. It's much more accepted. In PR terms that provides rich material to work with in the US, whereas in the UK it can be more of an albatross to get over.

2 The US is a huge country with a diverse news environment, still heavily dominated by TV, whereas print is still the dominant agenda driver in the UK (for the time being). There are few US national outlets of any media, so local and vertical becomes a key part of most campaigns, although a local newspaper can still have 100,000s of readers – more than some 'nationals' in the UK. Running campaigns in the US tends to be expensive too. Combine these and it's a lot harder to have impact in the US than the UK.

3 I've found that PR in the UK can be more irreverent and humorous while the US tends to be a little more corporate, straight-laced and risk averse. Seems like a stereotype, but sometimes they're true – though social media is helping humour break through in the US. Part of this is also the fairly intense cynicism on the part of the UK media. It exists in the US, but nowhere near the same level!

www.hillandknowlton.com

TACTICS AND CREATIVE THINKING

Tactics are the delivery mechanisms of public relations. They carry the messages to the target audience. But they only succeed if they are the right tactics for the chosen media and have content that is attention-grabbing. A press release, a survey or a photo opportunity is no good in itself if it does not secure coverage. It is the idea behind it that is important.

In this section we are going to examine the variety of tactics available to the PR practitioner and how they can be turned into memorable and effective ideas.

The Methods and Tactics Matrix table on p. 103 is designed to indicate some of the tactics that can be used for each of the 'methods' discussed in the previous section. Inevitably this list cannot be exhaustive. It is also the case that some of the tactics can be used with some or all of the methods.

As you may have noticed some of the tactics overlap with other disciplines such as advertising and sales promotion. This is particularly true in the marketing public relations (MPR) sector. As we saw earlier, occasionally this leads to turf wars within organisations. It should not. Instead it should encourage close cooperation between teams and, where appropriate, cross skills working.

The thing to remember with all of these tactics is that they must be backed by great ideas. Content is king and content is where creative flair comes in. Indeed creativity is what makes PR so different from other management disciplines. PR people, in common with lawyers and accountants, undertake research and analysis and have planning systems, but, to a much greater extent than lawyers and accountants, PR people also need creative flair. They have to produce ideas that turn the mundane and ordinary into the exceptional and exciting. It is one of the things that makes PR such a popular and attractive occupation.

How to be creative

This section is divided into three main parts:

1 How to create a creative environment
2 How to run a successful brainstorm
3 How to turn great ideas into effective PR activity

How to create a creative environment

Isn't creativity all about inspiration? You just sit at your desk and creative ideas will come to you. The reality is very different. This may sound like a contradiction in terms, but creativity needs to be planned.

There was a famous golfer called Arnold Palmer. One day a sports journalist told him that he thought Palmer was very lucky. He replied; 'And the more I practise the luckier I get'. Sometimes people describe footballers who score a lot of goals as lucky. But how lucky are they? To score a goal you have to be in the right place at the right time and finish with enough skill to beat the goal-keeper. Great PR people are the same. They have to combine experience, a positive attitude and skill to achieve success. Creativity in PR is 90 per cent perspiration and 10 per cent inspiration.

How to have a creative attitude

To be creative you need a creative attitude, but what is a creative attitude? There are certain attributes and habits which are essential:

- Be open minded
- Be interested in other people's lifestyles and ideas
- Be familiar with the media and consume a wide variety of them. Read newspapers and magazines, watch TV, go to the cinema, surf the world wide web, experience the blogosphere, join social networks. As you do so, take yourself out of your comfort zone – simply reading one newspaper regularly and viewing a handful of favourite programmes or sites is not enough.
- Get out and do things!
- Realise that your life, and perspective on the world, are untypical of many groups in society

SO

- Think about how to turn information into media stories
- Watch out for, and make a note of, new trends and ideas

- Look for things that touch peoples hearts *and* minds
- Watch and learn from what the competition are doing
- Challenge conventional thinking

If you work in a team, or have colleagues you think would be interested, have a half-hour meeting once a fortnight (first thing on a Monday morning is a good time) and ask them all to bring along an article, news story or video clip that has made them think differently about something.

Try to make your office a creative space. Stick up articles and images that encourage and inspire people to have ideas.

Rules of brainstorming

A brainstorm should be like a meeting, only much more fun!

The purpose of a brainstorm is to get together a group of people to generate new ideas. At the end of the brainstorm you should have a range of ideas you can develop into full blown PR tactics. Like any sort of meeting, if a brainstorm is to be effective it needs to be planned in advance. There are some basic rules that need to be followed.

People

A maximum of about seven people is best. Too many people and it becomes hard to control and hard to include a contribution from everyone (and there is nothing worse and more energy-sapping than people sitting in silence throughout a brainstorm).

All the attendees should be looking forward to being there. It is hard to be creative if you are in a bad mood. So make sure when you invite people you make it sound fun, and a bit of a compliment that they have been invited. And once they are there praise them.

Don't just use people from the PR or marketing team. Bring in people from elsewhere in the organisation, or even outsiders if possible. They may bring a fresh perspective, particularly if they are drawn from the target audience at which you are looking. You would not expect a 70-year-old to be good at coming up with ideas to target 20-year-olds, and yet all too often a group of people in their twenties try to come up with ideas for targeting 70-year-olds!

Try not always to use the same people in brainstorms because if you do you will tend to end up getting the same sort of ideas.

Finally, appoint someone to keep notes of all the ideas. You will be too busy encouraging and stimulating ideas to record them properly.

Location/atmosphere

Offices are not great places for brainstorms. People are easily distracted by telephone calls or someone wanting 'a quick word'. Offices also induce a 'work' frame of mind which is goal orientated. If you are asked a question in the office, you give an answer. But brainstorms are not about answers but ideas. So if you can have your brainstorm offsite it will make people more relaxed and better prepared to think freely.

If you have to have the brainstorm in the office bear in mind that it does not have to take place around a table. If there is an area with some comfortable chairs use that. And think about providing some refreshments. It is hard to think when you are thirsty or hungry. Also remember to bring along samples of any product being discussed as well as copies of the media you are targeting. This will help the participants get in the right mood.

Finally, provide people with a notepad and pen each and encourage scribbling and doodling. It also helps people get in the right frame of mind.

Structure

How you structure your brainstorm is critical. The best structure has three phases:

SCOPE ------------------------ GENERATE----------------------- EVALUATE

Scope

At the start of the brainstorm, having welcomed everyone, you need to scope the subject. This means describing the background to the topic under discussion and what you want to achieve from the brainstorm. It is important in the scoping stage not to give too much detail as this tends to confine people's thinking. It is also important, for the same reason, not to burden participants with previous problems, or your own preconceived ideas about what is needed or what will or will not work.

Generate

Once you have scoped the topic you can move on to generating ideas. At this stage it is vital that no idea is criticised, however impractical or daft it may seem. Even ideas which seem bad can stimulate good ideas. Moreover, as soon as an idea has been criticised the less confident people in the group will tend to clam up, fearing that if they come up with an idea it will be criticised.

When people do come up with an idea thank them and make a note of it, even if you think you are never going to use it. This will stimulate others to contribute. In the unlikely event that the ideas really are going off track gently nudge people back on track without appearing to denigrate their ideas. This apparent acceptance of ideas that are off target goes against most business instincts. In business the emphasis is usually on precision – the right answer as soon as possible. But in the generating phase of a brainstorm you are not looking for the right answer. Instead you are looking for a range of answers so you can choose the best. Psychologists will confirm that the creative part of the brain is different from the critical part. We find it difficult to be creative and critical at the same time. Hence in brainstorming the critical phase is left to last and is kept distinct from the generating phase.

To help you with the generating phase you may wish to consider a number of different types or styles of brainstorm. These are described later in this chapter.

Evaluate

The third and final phase of a brainstorm is the evaluation phase. Some people prefer to keep this entirely separate. They simply thank everyone for all their ideas and then take the ideas away and in the privacy of their own office decide which to develop. This might be sensible if most of the participants are not PR or communication people, but not if most of the participants are communication-literate.

A good way of evaluating the ideas is to write them up on large sheets of paper and stick them up around the room. Then ask the participants to put dot stickers or a big tick on the ideas they like the most. Having done that, ask the participants to sit down again and discuss with them the ideas that have come out on top and why. By the end of the session you should have recorded a range of workable outline ideas.

How to turn these ideas into effective PR activity is covered in the last section of this chapter.

Types of brainstorming

There is a variety of types of brainstorm. We have decided to focus on three that we have found particularly useful.

Future-thinking

This is a simple but highly effective technique. The first stage is to think of at least five trends or issues that could affect your organisation's market or consumers in the future. Most research is about the past but what people really want to know is what will happen in the future. For example if you were in the motor industry you might predict that: a) more women are going to learn to drive and have their own cars; b) there may be legislation to outlaw big or polluting engines; c) that traffic congestion will encourage a return to two wheels; d) more families will share cars; and e) there will be increased demand for pedestrianised shopping areas.

Having made your predictions you can now try to generate some PR ideas. For example you might produce a report on women drivers, how many there are, how many there will be and how they are different from male drivers, perhaps with a comment from a psychologist. Alternatively you could ask a group of women to design the perfect car and have a model made up to show to the media. To show you care about pollution and congestion why not create and sponsor an award for the best pedestrianised shopping centre? Or link up with a foldaway bike company and devise a special promotion in print media read by commuters?

Random association

This technique is particularly good when you have been working for a long time on something and the ideas seem to have dried up.

Just think of two words. Ideally one should be an object and the other a living thing. So for example you might choose a suitcase and an orange. You then simply ask people to call out any words that come to mind related to your two key words. This might give you a list as shown below in Table 10.7.

Table 10.7   Random association

Suitcase	Orange
• Clothes • Travel • Protection • Aeroplanes • Money in the suitcase • Smuggling • Holidays	• Florida • Dutch football team • Bad sun tan • Mobile phones • Juice • Zest • Vitamin C

At first glance an entirely random selection of words. But imagine you are a firm of solicitors (lawyers) and look again. Look first at the words under 'suitcase'.

You could suggest an article on how the law is trying to keep up with money laundering and online smuggling. You could carry out a survey of how many people's holidays or travel plans are ruined by rogue operators and give hints and tips on how to get your money back. Or looking at 'orange' you could compare legal practice in your own country with that in Florida in the USA. You could look at the legality of the football transfer market, or offer a mobile-phone-based rapid response legal service. Almost every word seems to have the potential to generate ideas for an organisation that a few moments before seemed dull and uninspiring.

Talking walls

Scope the problem or issue first (remember not to provide too much information) then give the group five minutes in silence to come up with one individual idea and ask each of them to write it on the top of a large piece of paper. Stick the sheets of paper up around the room and then get everyone to walk around and add a comment or new idea to each piece of paper. It is amazing how the original idea can stimulate further ideas. This technique is also particularly good for getting normally shy but creative people to contribute.

You can also mix and match techniques. For example, you could use the first part of random association to generate some words then write those words on sheets and stick them up around the room for people to add their ideas. Similarly you could take the future trends generated through future thinking and write them on the sheets as a starting point.

And here are a few other techniques you can try.

- Bite-sized brainstorms (just two or 3 people for 15 or 20 minutes)
- Brainstorms on the move (get out of the office and go for a walk with two or three other brainstormers)
- Use TV soap operas as the springboard for ideas. What would the characters think about your product or service?
- Think up advertising ideas and then turn them into PR ideas

 Using a chosen organisation as a springboard, get together with some colleagues or friends and try brainstorming ideas for an imaginary PR campaign. Try to use as many of the methods described above as you can.

Turning ideas into activity

The first thing to do is have another look at the five main methods described on pp. 103–104.

- Hard news
- Soft news
- News Events
- Promotional Content
- Direct News

Now think about the core story behind your idea. What is the target audience problem or issue you are addressing? What is the solution or assistance that you are offering? What is in it for the media?

Does the idea have some of the key elements of a great media story?

- *Conflict, controversy, drama, surprise*: money, power, health, sex, crime, glamour
- Facts, figures or trends
- Expert views, advice or predictions

- Celebrities
- A great photograph or visual
- Case histories/human interest

Imagine you are doing the PR for a new kind of handbag that can only be opened by scanning the owner's fingerprint. You have had an excellent brainstorm that has focused on the fear of crime and now you are drafting out your ideal story. Would it read something like this?

Women are now more frequent victims of street robbery than men, according to new research

One in ten women will have their handbag stolen this year according to a report published today by Securebag, who have launched a handbag that can only be opened by scanning the owner's fingerprint.

Mr Green, Securebag's security consultant, said: 'Street robbery is reaching near epidemic proportions in some areas and looks set to increase by a further 25 per cent over the next two years unless people start taking action to protect themselves.'

Last week in London Miss Megastar was robbed outside her Chelsea home. Mr Green commented: 'Her security guard was no help. The bag snatcher had gone before the guard could react.'

Lorna Li of Los Angles (see picture) was robbed last year and now always uses a Securebag. She said: 'With street crime on the increase I think it makes sense to do everything you can to deter robbers. Fortunately the bags are very stylish too.'

In under 200 words this story has all the key elements – drama, facts, experts, celebrities (who haven't had to be paid), and a human interest case history. It also conveys a strongly positive message for Securebags. However there may be more that can be done with the story.

The final stage is to check if you have covered all the media opportunities. Is it tailored for different audiences? Think about how you can:

- *Sectorise your story*. For example if you have a computer-based story you can tailor it for every industry sector that uses computers – which nowadays is just about every industry. Everything from pharmaceuticals to sewage.
- *Regionalise your story*: The more local you can make a story the better. If you are using research, for example, try to break down the figures by region or district and lead your story with the figure that makes that area look the best or worst.
- *Do business and consumer versions*: All consumer focused stories have a business angle of some sort. Is what you are doing to target consumers of interest to other businesses?

- *Visualise your story*: What could you do to make this a story that would appeal to television.
- *Asset strip your story*: Could you turn this into two or even three separate stories.

The Securebags story could certainly be tailored for regional media, business press and fashion media. Some film of a thief trying to open a Securebag might also win the story some TV or YouTube coverage.

 Think up an imaginary story about a new product available from your chosen organisation. Can you give it all the characteristics of a successful news story?

So, having decided on your methods and tactics you can finally start to draw up a detailed tactical plan.

Table 10.8   Detailed tactical plans

Tactical objective			
Audience(s)			
Message(s)			
Method/Tactic			
Budget/timings			
Measurement (results)			

ADMINISTRATION

In this section we look at what we need to achieve – our objectives in terms of the three Ms, *Manpower*, *Minutes* and *Money*.

In the last section we eulogised the creative element of PR, but creativity is nothing without rigorous systems and, in particular, tight budgeting. Sadly, too many PR practitioners forget this and in so doing undermine their standing with senior and financial managers. Much of this can be overcome by understanding a simple business formula called the TIME, COST, QUALITY EQUATION. This equation is particularly important for PR consultants who are selling their time, but it is also useful for in-house PR people who need to justify their own salaries and those of their teams, and to manage their workload and priorities.

The time, cost, quality equation (see Figure 10.5) dictates that the buyer of any service can only determine two of the three factors. So if they want high quality they must accept that either it will be at a premium price or it will take longer to execute. Similarly, if they want low cost they must accept that either timing or quality will be affected. Service providers who promise to do the best job at the lowest price in the quickest time will end up disappointing the buyer and will quite probably end up out of pocket themselves. It cannot be done.

In fact the first thing a PR person trying to cost a PR programme needs to do is to decide if they have the right people for the job.

Manpower

There are four broad skill areas that are needed in PR:

- *Strategic skills* (the ability to liaise with senior management, understand and analyse business objectives and translate this into an effective PR strategy)
- *Management/Administrative skills* (the ability to plan, manage, cost and follow up people and activities)
- *Technical skills* (for example writing, designing and selling stories to journalists)
- *Creative skills* (the ability to come up with new content ideas)

In small organisations you may be called upon to play all roles. In larger organisations there is a greater opportunity to specialise. In reality most people are only really good at two, or at most three, of these skills. (How many people do you know who are both highly creative and really well organised and efficient? These attributes require different parts of the brain and are seldom equally balanced in one individual.) If you, or your team, are lacking in some of these skills you will need to think about where you can get them from. Can someone with the right skills be seconded, or do you need to hire a specialist?

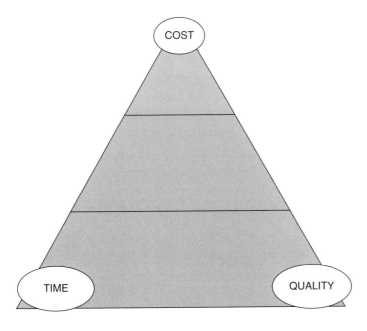

Figure 10.5 *Time, Cost, Quality Equation*
Note: Any buyer of services can only seek to control two of the three factors.

> ❝ ...those of us who have reached the top through our abilities to advise clients are generally lousy commercial managers and are to blame for the poor performance of the industry – the low margins, the huge over-servicing issue and the high staff turnover.
>
> Neil Backwith, author of *Managing Professional Communications Agencies*[9] and former European CEO of Porter Novelli, berating PR consultancy chiefs for their lack of business skills at a PRCA conference.

Manpower measurement

Having got the right mix, you now need to assess how much time will be required of each of the team. To do this you need some form of measurement of time. This is best done via timesheets. Without them you can only guess at how many hours any particular activity will take. By using timesheets from previous activities you will be able to predict much more accurately, for example, how long it takes to devise, commission and analyse a piece of research, then write it up, get it approved and send it to the media.

Time is often the biggest cost in any PR campaign. If you cannot realistically estimate the time that a project is going to take, you cannot realistically cost that project. Time sheets are an essential management tool.

Table 10.9   A sample timesheet

	Planning	Writing	Meetings	Administration	Total hours
News event					
Media Promotion					
Research-based created news					
TOTAL					

The choice of headings should be based on the kind of work you do, but it is well worth including a 'meetings' heading. Whilst meetings have their role, they can also use up an enormous amount of time. Only when you use timesheets can you be certain just how much time, and therefore cost, is required.

Timesheets should be collected each day. It is even better if they are loaded on to people's computers so that they cannot log off until the timesheet is completed. Timesheets should then be analysed and discussed on a monthly basis. Gradually a clear picture will emerge of how much time, on average, different PR activities take.

Minutes (Time!)

There are three aspects to devising a time plan. The first is to know how long particular tasks are going to take, covered in the section above on manpower measurement and timesheets. The second aspect of timing is much harder to gauge: namely how quickly, or slowly, your organisation can approve and implement a programme. (Generally the bigger the organisation the more slowly it moves.) The third aspect requires you to consider external time factors. For example, will your activity clash with some big event and therefore be squeezed out of the media? When is the optimum time to undertake your activity? New Year stories just after New Year do not work. Similarly there is little point doing a story on how to get a good suntan just after the summer. All these points need to be considered.

There are essentially three stages to drawing up a time plan.

Stage One: The first stage is to *identify the key tasks.* This involves breaking the programme down into its component parts. So, for example, you need to allow time for planning and creating the programme. You then need to allow time to present it internally to ensure you get funding and support from those who matter, and then finally there is the execution phase. How long will it actually take to complete each of the activities?

Stage Two: The second stage is to *draw up a critical path analysis.* This entails understanding which activities are time critical. For example if you are building a house you can't do anything until the foundations are in place and there is no point in plastering the walls until the wiring is installed. The same applies to PR. If the research is late the created news story will be late. If the celebrity is not booked by a certain date you may not be able to secure their services or have time to print a programme including their name.

Stage Three: The third stage is to check the plan against the calendar for known (or, where possible, likely events) such as elections, major sporting competitions, seasonal activities such as public holidays and of course your own organisation's and competitors' activities.

Figure 10.6 shows a critical path analysis for a simple guidebook that has to be ready for 30th April

You will now be able to draw up a proper calendarised timetable for your whole PR programme for the year. Table 10.10 shows a much simplified version:

Table 10.10 Basic PR timetable

	J	F	M	A	M	J	J	A	S	O	N	D
News event			News									
Media promotion						- - - - →		→	→			
Guidebook				→	- - - →							

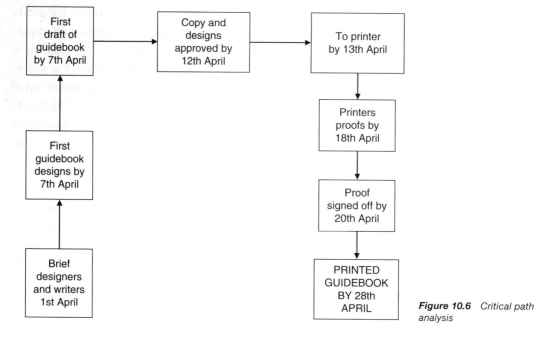

Figure 10.6 *Critical path analysis*

All that remains to be dealt with now is the money.

Money

In some cases you will have little say in the overall budget which will have been determined by the chief executive or finance director based on previous practice, or as a percentage of sales, or as a proportion of the overall marketing or communication budget. If this is the case you will have to tailor your programme to the money you are given. If you are luckier you will be allowed to work out what you think needs to be done, cost it and present it for approval. In reality many budgets are determined by some combination of these two approaches.

There are three elements to the costs of any PR campaign. They are:

- People costs
- Physical costs (such as design, print, celebrity fees and research)
- Expenses (such as photocopying, phones and postage)

People costs

Whether you work for an in-house PR team or a PR consultancy, people are usually your biggest cost. There are two aspects to people costs. The first is of course salary, and many PR budgets are based simply on this cost, but there are also a range of secondary costs arising from anyone's employment. These secondary costs include holidays, training, employment taxes, pensions and the physical space consumed within the office plus the cost of accounts, reception-ists and other support staff. Broadly you can estimate that, in total, someone costs twice their salary.

However many consultancies aim for the *three thirds principle*. This princi-ple dictates that a third of costs is salary; a third is overheads, including all the factors mentioned above; and a third profits. In reality profits in excess of 30 per cent of income are very rare and around 13% is much more common, but this does not undermine the value of the three thirds principle as a goal. It also explains why consultancy costs can at first glance look so high.

Another way of working out the overhead cost per person is to take the total number of employees in your organisation and then divide the total overhead costs by that number. This will give you an overhead cost per employee. From this you can work out an average cost per hour per PR employee. You should now be able to estimate the approximate people cost for any PR programme.

Physical costs

These comprise the extra costs generated as a result of the campaign, ranging from research and printing through to celebrity fees and the hire of locations for events. PR consultancies will sometimes add a mark-up of between 10 and 15 per cent to these to cover the cost to them of administering the purchases and financing the cost until they are paid by the client.

It is important to negotiate the best prices for these physical costs while remembering the principles of the TIME, COST, and QUALITY EQUATION men-tioned on pp. 218–219. Good work is seldom the cheapest.

A well-organised PR person keeps a record of all supplier quotes so that they can build up a data bank of possible prices to help with the costing of future projects.

Finally, there are expenses.

Expenses

There are three ways to cover for expenses such as phones, photocopying and postage.

The first is to record them accurately and charge in arrears accordingly.

The second is to make an estimate based on past experience and quote that. (However, this can be a risky business as you cannot always precisely control these costs.)

The third is to base expenses on a percentage of the time cost. So, for exam-ple, if the time cost is to be ten per cent of the total time available over the year then ten per cent of the expenses incurred over that period should be charged to the project.

An outline PR budget may therefore look like this:

Table 10.11   Outline PR budget

Cost Item	Actual Cost
People Costs (100 hours at $100.00)	$10,000.00
Physical Costs: 1. Guidebook (writing, design and print) 2. Psychologist's fee 3. Research	$1,000.00 $1,000.00 $1,000.00
Expenses	$1,000.00
Total	**$14,000.00**

Imagine that you are organising a seminar for leading business figures. It will start at 9.30 am and finish at midday. What sort of staff need to be involved? How much of their time will be needed? How much will that cost? What costs will be incurred in organising the seminar (you may want to refer to Chapter 13 for help on this)? Now complete an outline PR budget.

The plan is now nearly complete. All that remains to complete our POSTAR is to show how we intend to tell if we have succeeded or not. In other words, how we will measure our results.

RESULTS

There are three main ways of measuring results. These are *output, outtake* and *outcome.*

Output

This is the most common way of measuring PR results, though also the least meaningful. Output means media coverage. That is the coverage that results from, or is the output of, the planned PR activity.

Output can be measured in a variety of ways. The most basic is *circulation* (or *reach*). This means the number of people who potentially saw or heard the planned messages. It is arrived at by adding together the published circulation, viewing or listening figures for all the media in which coverage is secured. With a very successful campaign that secures a large amount of coverage this can result in a total figure that is greater than the whole population. As a measurement it is rather crude because it does not take into account whether the coverage is good, bad or indifferent. Nor does it measure whether people actually took on board the messages or changed their behaviour. However, it does have some value as a crude measurement, particularly when compared with the results for similar sorts of activity by your own or competing organisations.

The circulation figure can be made to look even bigger when *readership* is taken into account. Readership is the figure that shows how many people are estimated to read each copy of a newspaper or magazine. For example an evening newspaper in your town may have a circulation of 200,000, including Mr Jones. However, Mr Jones, who reads the paper on the train, takes it home where it is read by three other members of the household giving a readership, for that particular copy, of 4 people. It is not unusual for some papers to claim to have a readership three or four times greater than their actual circulation. As with circulation figures, readership numbers prove nothing more than the number of people who potentially saw the message you wanted to communicate. It tells you nothing about the number of people belonging to your potential target audience who might have seen the message, and the impact – if any – of the message is not revealed. (Television and radio programmes produce their own ratings figures which estimate their audiences.)

A better use of circulation and readership figures is to link them to *target audience figures*. For example a newspaper may have a claimed readership of 750,000, but a reach of 250,000 among your target audience. Target audience reach gives a lower, but more meaningful, figure than circulation or readership.

A further level of sophistication can be added by measuring how much of the coverage includes some or all of your planned *key messages*. This can be refined still further by measuring the *size and prominence of each piece*. For example a piece of coverage that dominates the front page is likely to have far more impact than a small piece buried on p. 32. Finally, you can compare your coverage with that of the *competition*, though obviously this increases the time and cost involved in evaluating your work.

In one sense online readership should be easier to measure. Most reputable online services can tell you not only how many people visited a site and when, but also what parts of the site they visited and how for how long. (It is difficult to know with conventional print media what parts are actually read, though research does show that people tend to read print media more thoroughly and will read longer pieces than they will if they are using online media.[10])

The advantages of measuring by output – be it online or in conventional media – are that is it is relatively cheap, easy to do and readily understood. The disadvantages are that it does not tell you what the PR actually achieved in terms of attitudinal or behavioural changes. It only tells you what has appeared. To find out about attitudinal changes you need to look at 'outtake'.

Outtake

This is concerned with what people 'take out' from having heard, seen or read your messages. It measures changes in attitude. For example do people now believe, as you had planned, that you are a superior manufacturer? Have they changed their mind about the factory you are proposing to build? Are they willing to consider voting for you?

The only way of finding this out is through research. An expert researcher identifies a sample group of people who have been exposed to your PR messages. The researcher then asks them a series of questions to find out how far, if at all, they have been influenced by your PR. If, for example, 50 per cent of the sample say they have been positively influenced then it is not unreasonable to conclude that fifty per cent of all those exposed to your messages were influenced in the same way.

The advantage of this approach is that it gives a much clearer indication of whether the messages have got through. However, it is not cheap. Indeed a true measure of what a PR campaign has achieved normally requires a preliminary, benchmarking survey to find out what people thought before the campaign and then subsequent research to test the campaign's effectiveness. It is therefore often out of the reach of smaller organisations, and fails the cost-benefit test for all but large PR campaigns. Moreover, this sort of research can never be totally accurate, first, because it only looks at a sample not the whole target audience, and second, because people are not totally honest when answering researcher's questions. For example, questions relating to sex, money and morality are notoriously tricky. Even when answering a computer-based questionnaire people like to look good. Admitting you are mean, promiscuous or immoral does not generally enhance people's self-esteem, so they tend to be less honest than usual. Moreover by asking people questions you are obliging them to take an interest in something which may not much concern them: surveys of this kind have difficulty in establishing how strongly people feel about an issue.

> **❝❝** Perceptions are real. If you're playing to win they have to be favourable. Your ability to persuade people to listen to you, understand what you are saying, and support you will determine whether you win or lose.
>
> Lord Tim Bell, Chairman of Chime Communications plc, Britain's largest PR group[11]

Outcome

The most effective way of measuring a PR campaign is by looking at changes in behaviour. This is called the *outcome* as it describes the outcome of your activity. The measurement of outcome is comparatively easy when PR is the only communication discipline at work and there are no other factors involved. Any increase in sales, calls to the help centre, hits on the website, changes in voting intentions and so forth can be simply measured and put down to the PR campaign. Proof perfect that the PR has worked. You can even work out the cost per sale, enquiry or vote by dividing the cost of the PR campaign by the total response figure. However, this is more difficult when – as is usually the case – there are other communication disciplines or other circumstances at work at the same time.

In such cases there are a number of things that can be done to try to clarify PR's contribution. For example, the PR activity can be timed to occur in the gaps between the advertising. Alternatively, PR can, if practical, be allocated different helpline or sales numbers or PO boxes, and also a different web address. In this way PR's contribution can be differentiated from other communication activity.

Online is particularly good for measuring outcomes. Click-throughs from the coverage to a site where the viewer/reader can make a purchase, sign a petition or get more information – if such services are offered – can be measured.

Success has many mothers; failure is an orphan

Barack Obama's election as US President in 2008, the culmination of a huge campaign which combined traditional media and much-talked-about online activity, would seem to vindicate his PR strategy.

Maybe. The campaign has certainly become the stuff of modern legend. However the intelligent student of PR needs to think harder. Many experts – including Obama supporters – were pessimistic about his chances earlier in the campaign. Arguably the way the sudden escalation in the economic crisis was associated with the Republican administration dealt a deadlier blow to hopes of his Republican rival, John McCain, than the PR skills of Obama's team. People wanted a change, although even that should not be exaggerated – the result was not a landslide.

People are quick to hail PR when it seems successful (PR has its own mythology!), but the part it played in Obama's success is difficult to gauge, and his online strategy would not be studied so closely had he failed. (Indeed it is even possible for a party or candidate to win despite what is seen as a badly run campaign, although no-one would recommend that as a strategy!) What is true is that during the campaign PR and communication was the main variable under Obama's control (he could not control the economic situation), so he was right to give it maximum attention.

Measurement forces PR practitioners to be realistic about what they can achieve. Too often in the past the credibility and value of PR has been undermined by PR people making unrealistic claims about what is going to be achieved. What is certain is that while the evaluation of public relations campaigns is fraught with problems, without proper evaluation of the effectiveness of its campaigns PR cannot claim to be a measurable management discipline in the way that other management functions are. Moreover, without the endorsement provided by measurement – in a form that is accepted by outsiders, not just PR people themselves – PR will always have difficulty claiming a place at the top table of the organisations that use it, or indeed significantly increasing its budgets (PR people often compare their fee levels unfavourably with those of lawyers, who have similar difficulties with measuring effectiveness, but organisations have a long tradition of paying for legal advice and in many cases are compelled to seek it because vital interests are at stake). Despite all of this the proper evaluation of PR results remains something more talked about than practised at the highest level. Why?

There are at least *three barriers to the effective evaluation of PR*:

- Cost
- Confusion
- Containment

Cost

When PR is used as a part of the marketing mix its cost is usually the lowest of all the marketing communication disciplines. An advertising campaign for a national company may well cost millions of dollars in terms of buying media space. The cost of evaluating results when set against this may seem quite small. For example, if $5 million is spent on advertising the cost of evaluation might be $100,000, or two per cent of the total. Now let's imagine that $100,000 is spent on a PR campaign and that the cost of evaluation is $50,000. So the total cost of the evaluation is much less than for the advertising, but the cost as a percentage of the total is fifty per cent. Rightly or wrongly many organisations would rather trust their own judgement as to whether a campaign has worked rather than spend half as much again on evaluation. Ironically, PR's perceived cost-effectiveness militates against it being properly measured.

Consequently, and all too often, instead of measuring the actual effect of PR on the target audiences' attitudes, PR evaluation measures the effect of PR on the media – the 'output'. While research evidence indicates that generally media coverage helps change people's attitudes this falls a long way short of proof of the effectiveness of each and every PR campaign. And without firm proof of results PR continues to struggle to earn the respect and budgets it deserves.

Confusion

Another problem that PR confronts when used as part of a marketing communication mix is the confusion that arises over what part of the mix achieved what. For example, let us imagine that a company launching a new motorcycle carries out a marketing campaign that includes extensive public relations in specialist and general media. The PR secures some excellent reviews of the motorcycle in key media. The PR also achieves the endorsement of a couple of leading celebrities who appear in photographs in lifestyle magazines and on TV riding the new bike. Within just three months sales are well ahead of target and the factory is working round the clock to meet the demand. The PR has surely been a huge success? Well, yes, probably.

The problem is that at the same time as the PR was going on there was a nationwide poster advertising campaign costing five million dollars. Market research shows that 80 per cent of the target audience saw the advertising and liked it – only 20 per cent of the audience said they had seen the PR-generated media coverage. There was also an online email campaign which achieved a five per cent response rate (well above the average for conventional through-the-letter-box direct mail). Finally, there was a sales promotion campaign in key motorcycle retailers. It was noted that the retailers with the sales promotion material sold twice as many bikes as the retailers without it. You can probably see the problem. The other marketing disciplines have some hard data to prove their effectiveness. All the PR has is the coverage and a rather disappointing 20 per cent recall rate.

In fact most research asking people where they saw information on something underreports the effects of PR. Indeed is not unusual for consumers to say they found out about a product through advertising when there has been no advertising! This is not because people are liars, but because people give little thought to their answers, particularly when they are being asked about something – quite often as they are rushing along the street – that happened a little while ago. Answering with the word 'advertising' is much easier than saying 'media coverage' or 'editorial'.

So what role did PR play? Well the best way to find out would be to conduct the campaign without PR to see what happens. Of course this cannot be done – and ironically few would want to take the chance because most people involved in communication believe PR plays a very important role… they just find it hard to prove. (Some very big campaigns are trialled using a mix of different marketing techniques to see what works best, but first this is costly and second it is not entirely accurate as the trials are usually conducted in different areas and one area is seldom just like another and hence the process may give a distorted picture.)

The likelihood is that PR played an important role in our imaginary motorcycle company's fortunes. Without the positive media coverage would so many people have responded to the email campaign, thought positively about the advertising and bothered to go into a retailer to have a look at the new bike? The answer is almost definitely not.

Containment

As we will see in Chapter 14 on crisis management, containing bad news and keeping damaging stories out of the media, or at least reducing the volume and softening the tone of negative coverage, can be a vital and much valued PR role. Indeed moderating bad coverage in a crisis situation is usually harder to achieve than getting a little positive coverage in good times. But how do you measure that? How can you say how much bad coverage there would have been had you not been able to intervene, and how can you measure what the effect of the coverage, *if* it had appeared, would have been? The answer, of course, is that you can't do so with any accuracy at all. Instead you have to use judgement. A survey in the UK by PR Consultancy Bell Pottinger and Henley Management College of chief executives of top businesses found that the majority were convinced that PR was a valuable and important tool, but believed that it was not really possible to measure its true value.[12]

MEDIA ANALYSIS AND EVALUATION

Despite the barriers to effective evaluation of PR results, the measurement of PR is on the increase and is becoming more sophisticated – particularly where it is the only communication discipline involved or when its effects can be isolated and examined separately. It is not perhaps surprising that a lot of PR measurement tends to focus on what is often seen as the heart and soul of PR, namely media coverage (including new media). Positive media coverage in itself does not prove a change in behaviour or attitudes (nor is it necessarily the result of PR – not everything that appears in the media is the fruit of PR activity!) but it is likely to be a strong indicator of success. After all, if it has appeared in the media it means that journalists think it is interesting and journalists are usually considered shrewd judges of what their viewers and readers will find interesting. It is also simpler to measure media coverage than wider issues of PR's impact on outtake and outcomes.

Why evaluators cannot draw easy conclusions

Cut price airline Ryanair was the subject of a BBC TV documentary entitled *Why Hate Ryanair*. The purpose of the programme was to investigate the airline's alleged 'hidden charges'. Despite the seemingly negative tone of the programme – Ryanair had refused to cooperate with the BBC – the airline sold 800,000 extra tickets in the four days following the broadcast. Michael O'Leary, CEO of Ryanair, referring to the 30 minutes of prime time coverage the BBC gave his company said: 'You just can't buy that sort of publicity'.

Certainly in this instance media coverage, however bad, seemed to lead to higher sales![13]

As the sophistication of the PR industry and the budgets given to it have grown a new specialist media evaluation industry has emerged, with its own trade body, the Association of Media Evaluation Companies (AMEC: www.amecorg.com). In many countries there are now specialist firms that will not only monitor the media for you and send you copies of your coverage, be it in print, online or on air, but will also analyse it in terms of audience reach, inclusion of key messages and in comparison to the competition – even in terms of how individual journalists cover the topics that interest you. To do this they employ trained readers and a variety of sophisticated computer programs. Their reports can show changes over time, measure coverage in different media outlets, regions and countries, and even show how individual journalists report on a subject. Apart from the economies of scale and specialist expertise they offer, these sorts of firms have one big advantage: their view is seen as objective. PR people measuring their own success are always likely to be somewhat suspect.

Media and digital evaluation plan

- *Objectives?* What are your overall objectives and what are you trying to achieve in terms of coverage?
- *Key target audiences?* Whom are you talking to and trying to reach?
- *Issues:* What are the issues that need to be addressed?
- *Key messages to be tracked?* Try to ensure they are concise and realistic enough to be articulated in digital, print and broadcast media
- *Which media?* Volume of coverage and impact of coverage may not equate. For example is broadcast more important than regional print media? Are all blogs equally important?
- *What scale of coverage?* What media, countries and languages can you afford? The average cost of digital PR reporting alone is at the time of writing estimated to be £1500 per month
- *Benchmarking.* Do you need to benchmark against competitors?
- *Sourcing.* How will you source coverage, cuttings and transcripts?
- *Reporting.* How often do you require reports or presentations, and in what form?

- *Timing.* What time period do you want to cover?
- *Budgeting.* What can you afford? The UK's Central Office of Information, which employed PR firms on behalf of government departments, recommended that you should allow 5–10% of the total PR budget for evaluation.
- *Sharing the results.* Can other departments help share the budget?
- *Using the results.* Have a plan for how to use them. Don't let them sit on the shelf.[14]

In the UK the Central Office of Information, the Government body which was in charge of the rosters of PR firms deemed suitable for government contracts, mandated which databases should be used for evaluation in an attempt to introduce some standardisation. (These include NRS, BARB, JICREG and RAJAR for quantitative metrics – see at the time of writing the COI website: *www.coi.gov. uk*) There are currently no established or formally approved sources for digital PR evaluation.

The checklist is adapted from one available on the AMEC website

---

However, although media evaluation companies can analyse what has appeared in the media, they cannot measure PR's effectiveness in delivering the message to the intended audience (let alone its impact on behaviour), nor its financial value. Computer programs which analyse coverage have obvious limitations – machines cannot measure humour, sarcasm, irony or the impact of images! Even the professional readers and viewers employed by evaluation companies have to act as substitutes for the real intended audience which, however careful the training, always presents a problem: a middle aged male reader may not respond to something in the same way as a teenage girl, but ensuring an exact match between audience and professional readers would be prohibitively expensive. Another problem is that proper media evaluation takes time. If you are running a high-profile PR campaign those paying for it will be forming a far more instantaneous view of its success or failure based on glancing at TV or looking at the print and online media: the important role of what is called *gut-feeling* should not be overlooked.

PR consultancies and in-house departments continue to measure their own effectiveness (not least because of the cost of external evaluation). One technique which is often used in-house (media evaluation companies tend to disdain it) measures *Advertising Value Equivalence (AVE)*. This asks the question: if your advertising people had bought the same space as your PR-generated coverage how much would it have cost? This technique is much criticised for being unscientific and akin to comparing apples with pears – surely a glowing one-page editorial feature is worth a lot more than a one-page ad, while conversely a two-word namecheck in a piece covering a range of competitors is worth a lot less than a strong one-page advertisement? In an attempt to simulate the greater value of editorial coverage the advertising equivalence value is sometimes multiplied by a factor of three or more. However in practice editorial coverage, while offering the all-important advantage of third-party endorsement, is usually far more nuanced than advertisements (which contain only what the people paying for them want to appear): the same story can contain a mixture of criticism, praise and neutral or irrelevant information, making it hard to assess its overall value.

The advantages of AVE are that it is relatively easy to calculate – most media have what is called a *rate card* which tells you how much it costs to buy different size spaces or time slots for advertising – and advertising rates are figures that most marketing directors and chief executives are comfortable with. Indeed it represents the only quick, cheap and easy way of putting a concrete monetary value on PR work. This is the language which business understands and is particularly important when budgets are under pressure.

A further problem with media evaluation is that, while it may be the most used form of PR measurement, by definition it only applies to media relations work. This may be the heartland of PR, but excludes many other areas such as lobbying or public affairs, and internal communications. Proper evaluation here can be terribly difficult: in public affairs, for example, a whole host of factors may cause a change of government policy and it is very difficult to attribute it to the activities of an individual lobbyist – and next to impossible to prove it beyond doubt. Gauging the success of a lobbyist will probably forever remain a matter of judgement.

What is certain is that without an attempt at proper measurement PR will not secure a seat at an organisation's top table. However, by using the checklist above and the simple Results Evaluation Grid below you should be well on the way to having an effective evaluation policy.

Table 10.12 Results evaluation grid

Objective	Target	Actual results
OUTPUT: what PR has produced – coverage, readership, inclusion of key messages, equivalent advertising cost		
OUTTAKE: researched changes in attitude and awareness, acceptance/ agreement with key messages		
OUTCOME: Changes in behaviour – sales, enquiries, website hits, votes etc		

 Take a PR campaign you are familiar with – perhaps one you have planned and created in class – and try to devise a set of realistic evaluation targets for it using the Results Evaluation Grid.

CONCLUSION

Ironically, often the most common barrier to creating and executing a successful PR plan is or will be the people within your own organisation.

There is an old saying that 'The Golden Rule is that those who hold the gold make the rules.' Without money and the backing of those at the top of an organisation no PR plan can hope to succeed, and the most brilliant PR plan will be fruitless if you cannot persuade senior management of its wisdom. Moreover, even when the funding has been secured and the go-ahead given from the top there are still other internal groups who need to be persuaded.

Few PR plans exist in a vacuum: other parts of the organisation need to be on side and singing from the same song sheet. There is little point, for example, in securing excellent press coverage for a new initiative if the resultant stakeholder or customer interest is met with ignorance or even antipathy by employees or departments who have not been got onside at an early stage in the planning. In practice therefore a large amount of diplomacy, persuasion and compromise is an inescapable part of the planning process.

POSTAR

• POSTAR is a checklist designed to help you to construct your PR plan. In this chapter we have reviewed each element in the checklist while at the same time being realistic about some of the difficulties faced in devising and implementing such a plan in the real world.

POSTAR stands for:

• *Positioning* – where are you starting from?
• *Objectives* – where do you want to get to?
• *Strategy* – how are you going to get there (the masterplan)?
• *Tactics* – how are you going to get there (the details)?
• *Administration* – managing human resources, time and money
• *Results* – how do you know when you have got there?

1 What do the following acronyms stand for – POSTAR; SLEPT; SMART?
2 Devise a POSTAR plan for an imaginary new mobile phone service that will alert people when they are due to take medication. If possible do this as a group exercise: devise your plan individually and then compare it with those of others and discuss each plan's strengths and weaknesses.
3 Write a short essay (600 words) on the difficulties of evaluating PR and what might be done to improve the situation.
4 Debate the motion: *It is better to be a great PR person with good business skills than a great business person with good PR skills.*

PART

3

PRACTICE

CHAPTERS

PRESENTING, PITCHING AND PUBLIC SPEAKING

INTRODUCTION

Presenting, pitching and public speaking are an important element of PR work. We will start by looking at how to plan, write and then present a speech as most of the skills required are also fundamental to making a successful pitch.[1] Once we have laid the foundation stones for speaking to an audience we will explore some specific pitching strategies.

Making a pitch, presentation or speech can be a nerve racking experience for even the most experienced person, but is something almost all PR people will have to do at some point in their careers – be it to an external audience or a group of senior managers or colleagues.

LEARNING OBJECTIVES

- How to plan a presentation
- How to structure a presentation
- How to speak persuasively
- How to use visual aids
- How to answer questions
- How to manage nerves
- How to pitch effectively

MAKING AN EFFECTIVE PRESENTATION OR SPEECH

These are the key stages:

1 Planning
2 Structuring
3 Preparing
4 Speaking
5 Answering questions
6 Managing nerves

First let us look at planning.

Planning

There is an old military saying, 'if you fail to prepare, prepare to fail'. Even the most brilliant public speakers such as Barack Obama spend a lot of time planning and preparing their speeches. But what exactly does planning a speech involve? There are four key elements:

• Research the audience and the situation
• Define your purpose
• Focus your message
• Identify what you want the audience to gain and any action you want to follow from the speech

Research the audience and the situation

The audience is your consumer. As with any form of PR communication you need to understand them or you will not connect with them. This is as true for a large public audience of hundreds at a conference as it is for the sort of small audience which normally listens to a PR pitch.

What do they want?
What are they like?
What will turn them on?

Having considered the audience you need to examine the situation:

How long are you to speak for?
What audio visual equipment is there (and will it work)?
What are other speakers – if any – talking about?
How will you be introduced? (How you are introduced is important. It establishes your credibility.)

The answer to some of these questions may seem obvious, but think of some of the awful speeches you have heard delivered by politicians, fellow students and even lecturers! How many have you endured when the speaker hasn't even got the right equipment, let alone thought about their audience and what they want to know? Are you sure that what *you* want to talk about is what *they* want to hear?

Define your purpose

What are your objectives? What do you want the audience to feel, think or do having heard your speech? What change do you want to occur? Is your purpose to:

a) Inform (add to their knowledge)?
b) Persuade/convince (change their attitudes or actions)?
c) Inspire (enhance their motivation)?
d) Debate/discuss (consider change)?

The way you define your purpose will help define what action you want the audience to take following your presentation.

Focus your message

Your message is what people remember when they have forgotten all the details. It is what they take away with them to act on, or think and talk about.

The best speeches are built on the foundations of a simple message. Too many messages and people forget or misunderstand them. Let us imagine that you are presenting a proposal for an increase in PR budgets to your bosses. You can probably think of many reasons why the budget should be increased. But if you present too many reasons the chances are they will not remember any of them. Try to focus on what, for the audience, are the three most important benefits of what you propose. In this imaginary case this might be that:

- We will get more and better media coverage
- We will then sell more products
- If we don't we will be overtaken by the competition

These are not only simple and memorable points but also provide a natural structure for your speech. It is also worth noting that these benefits include a carrot and stick – good things that will happen if we do what you propose, and a bad thing that will happen if we do not. A mixture of the two is usually more effective than giving them just a carrot or a stick.

Identify what the audience will gain and any action you want to follow

Listening to a speaker involves time and concentration so audiences want to know from the outset what is in it for them. Tell them at the outset what they will gain from your speech, how you will help solve a problem, provide them with some benefit, or offer some insight.

Amuse the audience if you can, as this will help keep their attention, but do not let an attempt to be humorous get in the way of your main message. Entertaining the audience is just the icing on the cake.

If your purpose is to alter behaviour, be clear what it is you want them to do. The action should be 'do-able' and easy to achieve.

Structuring

Structure is important. The audience's minds are pattern-seeking devices. This means that audiences look for structure in what the speaker is saying.

People remember messages not words. Using bullet points will help keep a focus on messages rather than words.

And, importantly, establish an overall three-point structure:

- tell them what you are going to tell them
- tell them
- tell them what you told them

In other words, at the beginning tell them what the subject, structure and purpose of your speech is, then expand on each of those points, and finally sum up by repeating the main points of your presentation. Some repetition is a good thing. You may have heard and rehearsed your message a dozen times in your head: your audience only gets to hear it once.

In a pitch there is less need to 'tell them what you are going to tell them' as generally the audience will know, though you still may wish to give them headings of your POSTAR plan (see Chapter 10). But it is still vital to sum up and 'tell them what you told them'. You do not want to finish a pitch by talking about budgets or evaluation – badly done this can lose pitches, but, however good, will seldom win them. Finish instead with a clear summary of your proposal.

Beginning: sell the speech
- Why you are credible
- Value (what is in it for them)
- Purpose (what you want them to think, feel or do)
- Structure (what the elements of your presentation are going to be)

Middle: the talk itself
A maximum of five points. Something along the lines below usually works:
- Situation/background
- Problem/opportunity
- Solution
- Benefit

End: a reminder of the key points and your message

- Summary of your case
- Call to action – if appropriate

Preparing

Speak – do not read

It is easier, and usually more effective, to speak from notes than to read a prepared text.

If your notes follow a clear structure and you are confident of your purpose and message you will not lose your way. Even better, speak from bullet points or use visual aids.

You will be able to:

- look at and involve the audience
- monitor the audience reaction
- speak more naturally
- seem more spontaneous and informal
- spend less time preparing

Try to write your notes on thick card rather than paper as, if you are nervous, paper amplifies hand trembling – which, by the way, is perfectly normal.

Full text speeches are really justified only when you have to be incredibly careful about the words you use, for example in legally or politically sensitive situations. Full text speeches also tend to be boring.

Limit the information and technical detail

No one can remember a lot of facts – least of all the audience. Try to stick to the essential information needed to understand what you are saying. They can always ask questions at the end if they need more information.

Use signposts

Signposts prevent people getting lost, and also help slow you down if you are a fast talker.

Here are a few examples:

There are three arguments for this … .
Let us now look at why we took this decision…
Having outlined the problems I now want to look at the opportunities …
We are proposing a four-stage approach to the consumer called AIDA … Awareness,
    Interest, Desire, Action … First I'm going to talk about awareness …

Use visual aids

Used well they:

- add clarity
- add colour
- act as an *aide memoire* for you

But do not:

- look at them rather than the audience
- reveal what you are going to say before you have said it
- fail to differentiate key points from detail. Key points should be larger, or at least in a different colour
- have too many slides. We have all sat in presentations and seen on the screen, as the computer is loading, '1 of 49 slides'. The heart sinks and attention slips away even before the speaker has begun
- put too much information on the slide as if you do they will be reading it, not listening to you (As a guide, no more than 6 lines with 6 words a line on any one slide.)
- keep the slide on the screen when it is not needed. If you are using PowerPoint simply press the 'B' key on the keyboard and the screen will go black. Press it again and the slide returns (Pressing the 'W' key turns the screen white.).

Below is an example of how not to do a slide, followed by an example of how to do it.

1) *Necessary Conditions for Propaganda?*

Propaganda is a complicated subject and one on which many people over many centuries have commented. Some of these comments may lead us to believe there is no easy answer to defining propaganda. Perhaps propaganda is really just a persuasive message you don't like. However, there is a system that you may find useful that was devised by a leading academic and lecturer at Westminster University, Simon Goldsworthy. He says that there are three tests that can be used to examine if something is propaganda or not. He asks a) is it planned? b) does it involve mass communication? c) is censorship also involved? He argues that if all three are in play then it is almost definitely propaganda. But is 'almost definitely' good enough? Does a really useful definition have to be one that can be applied all the time without qualification?

2) *Necessary Conditions for Propaganda?*
- Planned
- Mass
- Censorship

Rehearse

Ideally rehearse with someone. If that cannot be done use a tape recorder.

Remember that the actual length will be at least 10–20% longer than the rehearsed length.

When you rehearse think positively and picture yourself succeeding.

Persuasive speaking

According to the Greek philosopher Aristotle there are three key elements to a great speech. These are ETHOS, LOGOS, and PATHOS.

ETHOS – This is social/professional appeal – the appeal of reputation and personal merit. If the person introducing you has not established your credibility you must.

LOGOS – The appeal to reason. This is the logical and factual part of your speech.

PATHOS – The appeal to the heart and emotions. This offers the audience one or more of the following feelings:

- Security/self-preservation
- Status/prestige
- Pride of membership/belonging
- Power and control
- Fulfilment of aspirations

LOGOS without ETHOS or PATHOS is not much of a speech. ETHOS and PATHOS without LOGOS is usually just a crowd pleaser....ask a successful politician! A really good speech will have all three.

Be graphic and enthusiastic

Use visual and oral examples and illustrations. Paint pictures in listeners' minds. Be enthusiastic. Low energy speakers engender low energy audiences.

Benefits, not features

Benefits are what people are interested in. The 'what it does', not the 'what it is'. For example:

A saucer is round and goes under a cup

versus

A saucer prevents hot tea spilling all over your lap when the cup jogs, prevents marks on the table, and gives you somewhere convenient to put your teaspoon.

Our computer has a 3mb memory

versus

Our computer will enable us to keep all our customer addresses so we can stay in touch with them

It is about what the audience will gain.

Carrot and stick

As mentioned earlier, it is often effective to express the negative consequences of rejection of your case as well as the positive benefits of acceptance. Some of your audience will be more frightened of failure than attracted by the possibility of success – particularly if the possibility of success entails more work for them.

Give evidence

Turn your opinions into facts and use stories and case studies to prove your point. Tell them how organisations or experts they respect have done something similar or support the idea.

Set up the counter-arguments and knock them down

Predict the barriers your audience will put up against your arguments and knock them down. For example, *'some will say this is going to be very expensive, but in fact by the end of year one we will have actually saved money.'*

Power pauses

Do not gabble. Speak slowly. People speak quickly because they are afraid that the audience will not want to listen, but no one can concentrate on someone who is speaking too fast. It is much better to say less more clearly. Remember silence is power. A pause gives emphasis. A well-structured speech with good signposting gives plenty of natural opportunities for a pause.

Action

If you want people to change their behaviour make clear what action should follow. Too often an audience is left feeling they ought to do something, but are not sure what or how.

Answering questions

- Look and sound pleased to receive them.
- Accentuate the positive even if the question is aggressive. If you are polite with aggressive questioners the audience will be with you and against them.

- Thank the person for asking the question.
- If you are not sure you have understood the question ask them to clarify or rephrase the question yourself in a way that you are happy to answer.
- If you do not know the answer say so, but say you will find out or refer them to someone who can answer better than you.
- If the question is 'dangerous' do not hesitate to say this is not the forum. Or ask the questioner what they think the answer is.

Managing nerves

Being nervous before making a speech is normal. In fact actors say that the time they are really worried is when they stop feeling nervous before a show because then they know they will not give a top performance because it will lack energy. Nervous energy gives you the extra element you need to project your personality and make your presence felt.

There are several ways you can limit your nervousness:

Take a little exercise: Fear produces adrenalin which is meant to help us fight or run. With no-one to fight and nowhere to run to the adrenalin dissipates itself through the trembling associated with nervousness. So burn up the adrenalin by pacing up and down or even run on the spot.

Relax your muscles: If your muscles feel tight, gently lift and roll the shoulders and tighten and relax your facial muscles.

Take deep slow breaths: When we are nervous we tend to breathe too quickly. Inhale deeply and then breathe out slowly. This will not only reduce tension but help your voice.

Visualise success: Think positively. Imagine yourself succeeding[2]

In short, use the nervous energy you feel to positive effect.

 Using the techniques above devise a three-minute presentation on any subject that interests you – it could for example be about a hobby or political or university issue. Having devised it present it to your colleagues.

STRATEGIES FOR PITCHING

The tips and guidelines above, if followed properly, should help you become a more effective and confident presenter. However, there are some further points to bear in mind if you are pitching.

Pitching as a consultant to a new company is a bit like a first date. You need to impress them – and yet if all you do is talk about yourself or show off you are sure to fail. It is the difference between being confident rather than pushy: you must be a good talker but also a good listener. A lot of PR firms pitching for business make the following classic first date mistakes:

- talking too much about themselves
- not listening to what is said
- not watching the body language
- going into too much detail
- showing-off
- lacking confidence
- not being themselves

As with dating, a few pitchers seem doomed to perpetual failure, but most people can become at least competent pitchers with time and effort.

Pitching within your organisation is a bit different – more like an anniversary than a first date. The date (usually the boss in the case of pitching!) still wants to be flattered and romanced, but while you want to talk about the good times you must not pretend everything has been perfect – unless it has. It is also important to promote new ideas and activities, but without implying that what went before was wrong or inferior in some way.

In both cases it is important to realise that people in business make choices based on their head and heart, their reason and their emotion. A great plan or proposal is not enough to win. They have also got to trust you and, ideally, like you. This is often what is referred to as 'chemistry' – which is really just a way of making an emotional decision sound scientific.

The irony is that although PR is not a science the chemistry – or relationship – between the consultant and the client is very important. You may have the best idea, but it will remain just an idea if you are not liked or trusted enough to be able to put it into action. This is no doubt one of the reasons why PR people tend to be gregarious and sociable.

Top tips for pitching

Meet and speak before the pitch: Many pitches are won even before the formal pitch has actually happened. Meet and speak as much as possible to the client audience before the pitch itself. Find out what turns them on and whether there are any hidden agendas. You can also use this time to float ideas and even question the brief. (It is much better to question the brief in advance – if you question the brief on the day itself you may, in front of their peers, embarrass and even humiliate the person who wrote it.) If you get this stage right you will on the pitch day walk into a room of people who are already onside.

The thread of steel: While chemistry is important, it is still important for your proposal to have intellectual coherence. There should be a 'thread of steel' running through it. Your positional analysis which says 'where you are' should naturally link to the objectives. The strategy, which describes 'how you are going to get there', should naturally follow on from the objectives, which say 'where you want to get to'. The tactics should all fit with the strategy and of course the results or evaluation section should link closely to the objectives – the results should show 'how far you got in getting where you wanted to go'. A great proposal should flow like a story, or a well told anecdote. For more on this, see this book's website: www.palgrave.com/business/prtoday

Don't talk about yourself too much: While it is legitimate to reiterate your credentials to do the job, do not devote too much time to it. The audience want to hear about themselves and what you can do for them. You would not be in the room pitching to them if they did not a) already know a bit about you; and b) think you were at least capable of doing the job.

We hear all too often from disgruntled clients about PR consultancies that have spent the first 20 minutes, and 20 slides, talking about themselves.

Keep it short, clear and simple: Forty to forty-five minutes is as long as most presentations should be – with fifteen to twenty minutes allowed for questions. Try to restrict the number of slides (12 to 20 max), and limit the amount of text on each slide to headlines. (The detail can be said, or included in an appendix.) Always try to finish with a summary of the main thrust of your proposal – a simple chart or diagram rather than lots of words. Budgets and evaluation are important but they do not win pitches whereas good strategy and creative ideas do, so reiterate both in your summary. This links to the next point.

What do you want to be remembered for? In a competitive pitch the audience will probably be seeing three or four presentations. Realistically only three or four points from each pitch are likely to stick in the audience's mind (consider just how much you can recall after presentations which you have attended). Decisions on pitches are often made days, if not weeks, later and long supporting proposal documents are seldom actually read. It is therefore important to think 'what are the three things we really want them to remember?' This will probably include:

1 Why you are right for the job (experience/enthusiasm/likeability)
2 Why your strategy is right (audience insight, media understanding)
3 Why your creative tactic(s) will be effective (the big idea!)

Cast it, do not staff it: Put forward the best team for the job, not just the people who are available or have the least work on at the moment.

Case study: Steve Jobs: Presenter *par excellence*

Steve Jobs is the co-founder and former CEO of Apple. Many business leaders shun the limelight, but he has played an unusual and conspicuous role as his company's salesman and presenter-in-chief, taking to the stage whenever Apple launch one of their new products at one of their high-profile promotional events. Jobs performs the task with consummate flair, although it is also fair to say that latterly he has done so with a following wind: he presents as someone whose immense real achievements are well known.

We suggest that you watch some of Jobs' widely broadcast presentations – which are available on YouTube and elsewhere. Do you consider him to be an effective presenter, and, if so, why? Consider all aspects of his presentational style – his use of language, his tone and delivery, how he utilises movement and body language, his use of visual aids, even his clothing and so on. You might also want to apply the following test – show one of his and, for contrast, another presentation to colleagues. Afterwards, without forewarning, get them to note the key points. Discuss what tells you about memorability.

A checklist for speech-making and presenting:

PLANNING
- Research the audience and the situation
- Define your purpose
- Focus your message
- Identify what the audience will gain (and what they should do)

STRUCTURING
- Beginning – sell the speech
- Middle – make your case
- End – sum up

PREPARING
- Speak, do not read (i.e. use notes not full text)
- Limit information and detail
- Use signposts
- Use visual aids
- Rehearse

SPEAKING
- ETHOS, LOGOS, PATHOS
- Be graphic and enthusiastic
- Sell benefits and features
- Use carrots and sticks
- Give evidence
- Set up skittles and knock them down
- Be clear on the action you want

QUESTIONS
- Look and sound pleased to receive them
- Accentuate the positive
- Thank the questioner

TOP TIPS FOR PITCHING:
- Meet and speak with the client before the pitch
- Your proposal should be intellectually coherent: it should have a thread of steel
- Don't talk about yourself too much
- Keep it short, clear and simple
- What do you want to be remembered for? (It will be at most three or four things)
- Cast it, do not staff it: make sure the right people are in your team.

In teams of three produce a pitch proposal for one of the following. You will have 15 minutes to present and may use no more than 9 slides (you may of course choose to use no slides at all).

A) It is 'The Barbie Doll's 60th Birthday.' The client wants some PR activity to rekindle awareness and boost sales.

B) The Government's Department of Health have developed a service that texts you when it is time to take your pill(s) for medical purposes. It is anticipated that the service will reduce death and illness and unwanted pregnancies resulting from the failure to take prescribed pills. The client wants people to sign up online to the service. It only costs a few pennies per text. The Department wants a PR campaign to promote the new service.

C) *Fabulous Fifties* is a new range of anti-ageing and grooming products for men aged over 50. The targets are up-market, affluent males. The range will be available through major department stores. The client wants to create awareness and desire through coverage in lifestyle pages and in sports interest magazines.

D) Gold Homes builds flats and apartments for single people over the age of 65. Every block has a warden. With house prices falling they are keen to maintain interest and sales in their properties and a positive view of the brand.

PR MEDIA SKILLS

INTRODUCTION

Notwithstanding what some in the PR industry like to say, media relations remains the core skill of public relations: if in doubt, try speaking to most of the people who spend good money on PR services. It is what differentiates it from all the other communications disciplines, many of which offer some similar services to PR, such as digital communications, events management, promotions and leaflet production. It is the PR person who is left to pitch the story to the sceptical journalist, or to take that difficult call when the media have uncovered a damaging story. It is a role that the people who run big organisations value. It is no accident that so many of PR's top figures – and highest earners – are known for their media handling abilities.

Take away media relations from the PR equation and what is left? Among the possible exceptions are lobbying or public affairs and CSR, but even these tend to boast of their media relations prowess – particularly public affairs practitioners when they are competing with lawyers who sometimes offer their own lobbying services. Another exception, internal communications, may well be in the hands of human resources, but anyone who has dealt with internal communications in an organisation which is in the media spotlight will know that whatever is in the media is central to the concerns of a successful internal communicator.

Moreover PR is vital to the media as we saw in Chapter 1. Without it journalists and reporters would struggle to find stories and fill their pages and airtime.

In this chapter we are going to look at what the media want and how PR people can give it to them while still achieving their persuasive objectives.

LEARNING OBJECTIVES
- Understanding what the media want
- How to tell a news story
- How to prepare a press release
- How to write good copy (news and articles)
- How to do a media interview
- How to use photography and images successfully
- How to sell a story
- How to deal with the media in good and bad times

UNDERSTANDING THE MEDIA

As we saw earlier (see Chapter 1), in the world's two biggest PR markets – the US and the UK – there are more PR people than journalists, although there is now much more media content than ever.

Three things seem to have happened. First, the explosion in the volume of media has meant that advertising, which is still the primary source of income for most media, has been spread more thinly. All the existing and new titles have been unable to make the money needed to increase their staff numbers even though the journalists now often have not only to write hard copy but also produce webcasts, podcasts, blogs and separate copy for online news editions.

This financial shortfall has been exacerbated by a second factor, the flight of advertising revenue from traditional media such as print and TV to online media. For example in the UK up to 30% of advertising used to be what is called classified – personal advertising to sell flats, houses, cars and even advertise job vacancies.[1] A huge proportion of this sort of advertising has now switched online. Why would you look in a newspaper for details about a flat when you can gather more information online and take a virtual tour of the property? As a consequence there has been a further fall in advertising revenue.

This decline in revenue might not matter so much if online media were highly profitable and able to employ thousands of journalists; but online media, just like their older relations traditional media, are struggling to make money in an incredibly competitive market. The media, with the exception of publicly owned corporations such as the UK's BBC, are businesses. They need to spend less than they earn to make a profit. One way of ensuring that is by using pre-cooked PR material, and PR sources, rather than trying to gather fresh ingredients and prepare all their content themselves!

But not just any oven-ready PR material will do. Journalists may be hungry for content but they still have standards and demand a good story which is well presented. The best PR people understand this. They know that they need to educate, entertain and inform (the original BBC mission). They also know they need a compelling narrative.

In his frank and readable account of his career in travel and leisure PR, the leading practitioner Jim Dunn describes how travel programmes came to rely more and more on PR companies although the relationship had to remain veiled:

We always had to be careful of course. With BBC film crews, we had to watch that they weren't seen to be in our pocket, although they certainly were during filming as we usually paid all the expenses. Flights, hotels, cars, drinks – you name it, it usually came out of our PR budget. We took full advantage.[2]

There are four key elements to PR news:

- STORY: Recognising or creating news and telling the story
- STRUCTURE: Structuring press releases so the story emerges in the most compelling way
- STYLE: Writing good, clear copy
- SELLING: Knowing when and how most effectively to call a journalist

Story

What constitutes news is hard to pin down, but to be a successful PR person you have to have an intuitive sense for newsworthiness – seeing things the way a journalist or editor sees them. Remember that most of what comes to their attention on any given day is not covered – it is not considered news*worthy*. One famous saying is that when a *dog* bites a man it is not news, but when a *man* bites a dog it is. This sums up the idea that news is what is surprising, unusual and interesting; something new that people want to read about, hear about and see on television.

What constitutes news will also depend on the media organisation concerned. Sometimes this is obvious. Local media will be interested in local angles – the implications of national events for the locality they serve, or the involvement of local people or organisations. Trade and specialist media will be concerned about what is relevant to their particular audience. But national media outlets will have their own characteristics and special interests. Popular newspapers, for example, will respond particularly well to human interest and celebrity-based stories, while business journalists, especially in the more serious media, are interested in anything with implications for the financial markets. This can be extended to individual journalists as – particularly in the case of those who are specialists – they have their own interests and prejudices.

Most journalists have short memories, and most are general reporters, covering a wide variety of news and hence often coming fresh to each story they cover. This means that usually they will not know much about the background to the story: you have to bear this in mind and help them. As a result, with care, good news can often be announced more than once, in slightly different forms, giving you extra opportunities to get your message across.

It is not an accident that we all use the expression 'news story'. Even important news can fail to break through if its story is not well told. So having identified 'news', how can we turn it into a story that people will want to read?

We said earlier (see p. 203) that a good PR people perform a 180 degree turn. They look at stories from the audience's point of view. This means not assuming that because your organisation has done something or is announcing something other people will be interested. Instead your task is to try to think why the audience would be interested. What is in it for them?

One way of approaching this is to use the PROBLEM/SOLUTION/BENEFIT approach. This involves identifying the problem or opportunity that your initiative is the solution or answer to and then outlining the benefits. For example:

Problem/Opportunity: People are dying unnecessarily because motorists are speeding in built-up areas.
Solution/Answer: The government is introducing 25mkh speed limits in all built-up areas.
Benefit: It is predicted that this will save 2000 lives a year.

The same story can also be approached using the VICTIM/VILLAIN/HERO approach. This is popular with NGOs and charities and follows the classic narrative of fairy stories.

Victim: Innocent people are dying needlessly on our roads because of speeding.
Villain: The government are too frightened of the motoring lobby to do anything about it.
Hero: Which is why we at 'Safer Roads' are holding a mass demonstration in the city centre on Friday lunchtime and are calling for a 25kph speed limit.

PRESS RELEASES

Having identified the narrative we can start focussing on the press release.

Press releases, media releases and press notices (they are just different words for the same thing) remain one of the cornerstones of media relations work. They are a well-established and recognised way by which organisations put across news and views to the media, and as such are usually expected by journalists when an important announcement is made. They have several advantages.

- They can be issued quickly – almost instantaneously – and easily, through well-established distribution networks, in a format familiar to journalists. They are probably the cheapest way of making basic news and information publicly available, and are an accepted way of putting information on the record.
- They can be readily stored – for example in online press rooms, making them available for journalists seeking background information. They can also include links to additional background information, including downloadable pictures and even sound.
- You can control the exact content word-for-word – as you cannot if, for example, you ring a journalist and start a conversation.
- You can also control the timing of when the press release is issued – to the minute.

- Press releases can be made available to all media organisations simultaneously, avoiding accusations of favouritism.
- They are one of the best-known PR tools, known well beyond PR circles, and the people paying you, and your non-PR colleagues, will often expect you to write and issue them. But most press releases remain unused by the media – they are all too often just an attempt to show that something was being done about an organisation's PR and to please paymasters and internal audiences!

While in some form press releases continue to play an important part in media relations work they also have drawbacks:

- They are used far too often and there are far too many of them: most are simply ignored, deleted or binned.
- By definition the information in a published press release is not exclusive – but exclusive material is what journalists prize above everything. Moreover hard news is often what an organisation *doesn't* want the media to find out. All in all, surprisingly few of the biggest news stories – most of which are about disasters, mistakes and wrongdoing – start off as press releases.
- By the time everyone in the organisation, including lawyers, has agreed to a press release the desire to be on the safe side means that the wording is often quite dull.
- If it is a big story the press release is only a starting point. Journalists will have additional questions as they try to develop their own angles and gather news and views from other sources. They will also want to interview people, and photographers will want their own pictures.

Today press releases may appear more in online press offices on organisations' websites than on the printed page. The latter remains useful at press conferences or PR events when journalists may be away from their screens. In such circumstances journalists still welcome pieces of paper. Whether the medium is electronic or paper the essence remains the same: press releases represent a way to try to get information and opinion reported – on *your* terms.

Most media releases, as we said above, never get used. This is often because there is no clear story or narrative, but it can also be because the release is badly structured and poorly written. So, having looked at what constitutes a story, we now want to look at how to structure a good release.

Structure

Use your organisation's headed news release paper – that way
the journalist will immediately know whom it is from

Up at the top, the date – and perhaps a serial number to assist filing

A SIMPLE, SHORT, CLEAR HEADLINE

The opening paragraph is the most important one. It should be short (no more than 18–30 words) and summarise the key elements of the story. Remember many journalists will receive hundreds of releases a day.

By the end of the second paragraph you should have covered most if not all of the key questions: *who* said or did something (and, often, to whom), *what* did they say or do, *why, where, when* and *how* did it happen (and, often, *how much* did it, or will it, cost).[3]

After reading this far a journalist will normally have decided whether the press release is of any interest. Journalists are busy people, working under pressure. Most press releases are discarded. So a strong headline and opening paragraph are VITAL.

The main text of the press release then follows, in descending order of importance: keep the main points to the fore, with background and explanation following up in the rear. In this press releases resemble news stories.

Journalists like to include direct quotes in their stories, and it is usually a good idea to include them – perhaps your Chief Executive or someone similar commenting on the announcement – as it is a good, personalised way of getting across your organisation's opinion about the events in the press release in a way which journalists appreciate. Quotes which constitute external, expert or celebrity endorsement can also be helpful. Put these quotes close to the beginning of the release, certainly on the first page. The quotes should use plain simple language – the sort of thing you would want to say to someone, *not* the sort of thing you would write in an official report.

Notes for editors (at the end of the release, after the main text)

Despite what they are called, these are really intended for journalists, news editors and sub-editors. The news belongs in the main part of the press release, but this is the place to include supplementary information which might be helpful for anyone writing up the story. This often includes basic facts about your organisation. Remember the journalist reading your release may know little about the subject and they have got to write a full story quickly – try to imagine yourself in their situation!

Don't forget to include contact details (including how to get in touch outside office hours) – journalists may have questions or want to arrange an interview at any time of day or night. Highlight additional sources of relevant information, such as your website.

Figure 12.1   *Press release template*

Top tips for writing press releases

- Always keep in mind the needs and wants of the immediate intended audience – busy journalists. What do they need to write the story?

- Shortness is a virtue: short words, short sentences, short paragraphs, short press releases.
- The headline and opening paragraph are most important: spend some time making them perfect! (Do not be tempted to write a clever or 'punny' headline – that is for the journalist to do once they have decided that your release is actually newsworthy.)
- Your writing should be clear, simple and forceful. Press releases are not great literature or examples of fine writing.
- Avoid clichés, generalisations, superlatives – journalists will probably be sceptical if you say something is 'unique' or 'wonderful' and will not report it. It is better to explain exactly *why* it is unique or wonderful.
- Use key facts, figures and examples to make your announcement come to life. And paint pictures with words – saying something is as long as the Great Wall of China or the Mississippi river is much more vivid than just giving its length in kilometres.
- Avoid in-house jargon (every organisation has it!) and acronyms – keep in mind that you're writing for a busy journalist who probably won't be familiar with either. As someone who is being paid by an organisation you may be under pressure to write things in a particular way, but remember, you're trying to communicate with people *beyond* the organisation.
- Using quotes from key people in the organisation or elsewhere (experts or celebrities who are endorsing the news in the press release) is often a good way of getting across opinions and making the press release usable. Try to make the quotes lively and as free from platitudes as possible.
- Always make sure that your press release has been cleared by everyone who needs to see it within your organisation: you are issuing a very public announcement on its behalf, one that could have serious implications, including legal ones, for you and those employing you.
- Finally, find time to get together with someone else to read it through carefully before you issue it. Mistakes – even typos – are easy to make, particularly when you are working under pressure, and can be highly embarrassing – they can even become a minor news story in their own right.

A good way of building the structure of a release is to follow *the 6 key elements of a great media story* as outlined in Chapter 10.

- Conflict, controversy, drama – violence, money, health, sex, crime, glamour
- Facts, figures or trends
- Expert views, advice or predictions (from inside or outside the organisation)
- Celebrities (these could include a character in a soap opera, a real-life celebrity or a very successful business person)

- A great image – photograph, graph, cartoon
- Case histories/human interest – to bring the subject alive and show it matters to real people

Following this guide our government story can now become:

An estimated 2,000 people die on our roads every year as a result of speeding in built-up areas, which is why the government is introducing 25kph speed limits from next year.

According to David Driver, Minister responsible for Traffic Management at the Ministry of Transport, research by London University has proved that slowing down by just 10kph slashes the number of pedestrian accidents: 'The carnage on our roads has to end. Road calming and advertising the dangers of speeding have helped reduce the death toll, but we can do and are doing more.'

Actress Tracey Sugden, whose daughter was tragically killed last year when she was run down by a speeding motorbike outside her house, is supporting the move. She said: 'One death is one too many. I welcome the government's move.'

ENDS

Note to Editors: ....

Attached is a graph showing the reduction in deaths for each 5kph by which the speed limit is reduced, and a picture of Tracey Sugden standing by one of the new 25kph road signs.

 Now write a release from our imaginary charity 'Safer Roads' announcing their new campaign.

Having looked at STORY and STUCTURE, we know need to look at STYLE and the writing of simple plain English.

Style

The following are tips used by newspapers and PR professionals. Remember that few things can let you down more quickly than bad written English.

- Think about your copy before you write: you will cut a lot of clutter.
- Study what you write. Make sure every word is working for its living. Use spell check (carefully!) and the thesaurus.
- Examine your 'simple' English to make sure you are using it correctly. For instance, to 'try and...' does not exist. 'Try to...' is invariably correct. You can compare 'with' or 'to'. Generally 'to' emphasises similarity, 'with' marks a difference.

- Be specific. Pick the right words to bring your copy alive.
- For example, say wet and foggy, rather than poor weather. Say red, gold and green, not colourful.
- Use simple words: begin, not commence; said, not stated. Avoid the sort of verbs that policemen use in old films: 'He was proceeding in a westerly direction...'.
- But do not use simple words where their meaning is not sufficient. Demonstrate means much more than 'show' or 'display'.

Quotes

- Quotes are reported speech. Always make them sound real, like someone speaking – not a dummy behind whom you are working. Your quotes should not say: 'Our mission is to re-frame the communication to develop understanding that invites public engagement.' They might say: 'We want people to respond to our ads'.
- Structure sentences with quotes in the way newspapers do.

Put the name of the person being quoted before the quote: the quote's value is defined by the person saying it. Use the person's name and then the job title: it's more human. Use 'said' after the name, not before it. Then use a full colon, a single space and a quote mark. Each paragraph of quotes should start with a quote mark. Only the last paragraph of reported speech should end with one.

Said or says? 'Said' is harder, newsier and a snapshot of something that has happened. 'Says' is descriptive, timeless and describes a state of affairs. You should tend to use 'said' for news, 'says' for features and magazines.

And, but

There is no reason why you cannot start sentences or paragraphs with 'and' or 'but'.

But do not overdo it.

What about writing for 'quality' media?

What is the difference? You can use some longer paragraphs and words. That is all.

Blobs

These are useful tools. They're one-liners used to sell a series of story hooks on your first page and work well with studies and statistics. A story with blobs works as follows:

THE knack of writing a complicated press release using 'blobs' was revealed today.

The 'blob' guide describes how a handful of punchy news hooks can be linked to increase their impact.

The guide says 'blobs' should be:

- kicked off with a colon and closed with a full stop,
- begun with a verb, noun or adjective – not a mixture,
- kept short and tight, and
- limited to four.

And the guide says: 'Then you can stick in a bright, simple quote summing up what's interesting about your story.'

Commas, colons and semi-colons

Punctuation in written English mimics the pauses you take – for breath or emphasis – in spoken English. Reading copy aloud helps you punctuate correctly.

Commas denote a pause. They often, like this, come in pairs around a clause. Do not miss out one of a pair.

Dashes – used like this – make clauses stand out more than commas. Use them when that is what you want. They can also tack an extra clause onto the end of a sentence – a little extra whammy.

Semi-colons are used for complex lists, or for longer pauses than commas. Generally, releases should not have complex lists or long pauses in them.

Colons are not 'nearly' full stops. They are used to structure a particular type of sequence in a sentence. They 'deliver the goods that have been invoiced in the previous words'.[4]

Think of a colon as meaning 'namely':

He wore Armani: a lilac linen shirt with a navy single-breasted suit.
They stole the best car: a 500cc Mercedes.

Do not use exclamation marks to prop up bad jokes or poor headlines. Only rarely use a string of dots...

Never be afraid to transplant a full stop into the heart of a dying sentence. It will, more often than not, save its life.

Plural and singular

If there is only one of something it is singular, however big or grand it is.

For example: The Metropolitan Police are the UK's biggest force. Are it?

The worst offence under this heading is mixing singular and plural, e.g.: The Metropolitan Police *is* the UK's largest force and they *are* still growing.

Apostrophes

These are never for denoting plurals. They are for denoting the possessive, or the absence of a letter. Its, the possessive, as opposed to *it's* – it is, is the exception.

Split infinitives

Watch these. Some people will refuse to boldly go where others might. You should aim not to split an infinitive, but there is nothing to stop you. If it is clumsy when written (and said) correctly, and you can't find another way of saying what you want, then split that infinitive.

Reversing into sentences

Never reverse into sentences. It leaves the best until last. Here is an example:

'Following extensive research into youth crime, carried out among 1,000 13-year-olds last year, Inspector Fred Bloggs today announced he was doubling the number of officers on duty in schools.'

instead of:

'The number of officers on duty in schools is today being doubled…'

Numbers

For one to nine, always use the word. Dates or titles – the M1 motorway – are exceptions.

For 10 and over, use the number – unless the word should be employed for impact: 'millions of'.

Never start a sentence with a number. If you have to describe a quantity at the start of a sentence, use a word.

Always use 'per cent' instead of '%'. (Financial writing, such as 'interest at 4.25%', is the exception.)

But before you use any numbers, work out what they represent.

Forty-one per cent might be better as 'two in five'. And 150 per cent might have more impact written as 'half as much again'.

Now we have a good story, a well-structured and well-written release, what do we do with it?

Targeting and timing

Many press releases are issued in a single format for all media – the cheapest and easiest option. However research backs up commonsense: if a release is tailored to the needs and interests of particular media outlets it is much more likely to be used than a standard, one-size-fits-all version. Thus, for example, if adapted versions of the press release featuring local examples are sent to local media it is much more probable they will meet their news criteria. Adapting and targeting press releases in this way is potentially expensive. PR people have to strike a balance in terms of cost/benefit, and judge how far to go down this route.

The best time to send a normal press release – something that is not exceptionally newsworthy but for which you want plenty of coverage – is as soon as possible after the appearance of the last edition or programme. For example, a weekly magazine or newspaper that comes out on a Thursday will start planning its content for the next edition on that Thursday or first thing on Friday morning. At that point they will almost literally have a clean sheet of paper and will be more receptive to your news release than they will be the following Wednesday morning when they have decided on most of their content.

The writing of feature articles and opinion pieces is less pressing in terms of timing.

Media handling in China: How Chinese officials treat Chinese journalists

Wang Hui, General Director, Information Office of Beijing and Chief Spokesperson for the 2008 Beijing Olympic Games

Chinese journalists made great progress as the Beijing Games were prepared and held. The Chinese Government assisted Chinese journalists in enhancing their influence on world opinion and provided lots of chances for them to get information.

1 From 2005 to 2007, Beijing sent 30 journalists to Britain each year on one year courses. The journalists improved their English and learned more about the working methods of foreign media. When the Beijing Olympics was prepared and held, the journalists attended news conferences and conducted interviews with foreign journalists, as well as interviewing officers from the International Olympic Committee (IOC) and athletes in English.

2 Chinese journalists were invited to attend news conferences and interviews were arranged with officials.

3 A range of channels for journalists was created, allowing them to communicate with officials, including the establishment of mechanisms making it easier for officials to engage with journalistic opinion-makers.

4 Journalists had a greater right to monitor and criticise the government's work.

FEATURE ARTICLES AND OPINION PIECES

If you leaf through newspapers and magazines you will often find articles 'written' by politicians, business leaders and heads of charities or NGOs. The articles have these people's names on them, and sometimes their photos, but who do you think actually writes them, and makes all the arrangements for them to appear? Yes, writing articles for the print media is another thing you may be called upon to do.

The opportunity to place articles in the print media can come from media themselves, or it may be a matter of you taking the initiative. Sometimes newspapers will want an authoritative figure to write on an issue which concerns their readers, and you may want to seize this opportunity to state your organisation's case. At other times, you may be the one making the call. As a PR person employed by an organisation, you are the nearest thing it has to a journalist. Your writing skills will therefore be in demand when it comes to putting together articles for the print media. You are also the person best placed to negotiate with the media.

Often such articles – particularly opinion pieces 'written' by senior people – are little read. This is largely because they are predictable and bland: senior people with heavy responsibilities are not free to be daring and use humour, gossip, speculative comment, controversy and colourful language in the way an ordinary newspaper columnist is. Your job is to make the article as lively and enticing as possible, but it will always be difficult: even if you are a better writer than your chief executive you are still bound by the same limitations. However even if the articles remain largely unread they often have an impact, not least because the newspaper can make a news story out of them, or use them to stimulate debate. Your boss may also like the attention. It can also be a way of enhancing media relations: as a rule of thumb, the less important a media outlet is relative to your organisation, the more flattered it will be to get an article from you. Like many good things it can be overdone. At one stage so many articles by former UK Prime Minister Tony Blair appeared in the British local newspapers that he was sarcastically given an award as columnist of the year (the articles were in fact the work of a special unit of ex-journalists which was set up to produce them).

Top tips

- Make yourself fully familiar with the newspaper or magazine the article is going to appear in. What is its tone and style? What assumptions does it make about its readership? You have to bear this in mind as you prepare your article. There is no point adopting an abstract, academic approach if you want to appeal to the readers of a popular newspaper. Instead you might want to think about a strong human interest story which would vividly illustrate your argument.
- But do not go overboard. The person for whom you are writing also has her or his style and her or his own reputation to consider. You have to strike a balance – between the need to find the right tone for the reader (and create a piece of writing which people will actually want to read) and the need not to

embarrass your boss and undermine your organisation: he or she simply cannot do all the things a newspaper might want them to do.

- Try to consider – as far as is possible – what context the article might appear in. Take into account other stories in the news.
- Be wary of agreeing editorial changes after you have submitted the article. This can skew its meaning. Also be careful about the headline the newspaper chooses – that can have the same effect.
- If preparing an article does not appeal to you, you can always offer other options – for example to answer readers' questions on an issue. These can be livelier than full length articles.

 Think of a large organisation which you know well. The local newspaper covering the area where the organisation has its headquarters asks for a 500-word article on the contribution the organisation is making to the local community and to the environment. It will appear under the name of the organisation's chief executive, but you have to write it.

PHOTOGRAPHY AND IMAGES

As we have already noted, pictures and images are a good way of increasing the impact of your story.

In the UK a picture editor on a national newspaper may well see over two thousand images a day and yet probably only use thirty or so. Your photograph has to be very good to get into a national newspaper. However, there are thousands of magazines and local newspapers as well as online media which are all desperate for content – particularly visual content. In line with the old saying 'a picture's worth a thousand words', it is well worth making the effort to create a great photograph, image or even a broadcast video clip for online titles.

Here are our top ten tips:

- *Study the media*. Look at the magazines and newspapers you are targeting. What type of pictures do they use? Do they like conventional shots of smiling people sitting at desks or shaking hands, or do they like unusual shots with people in unconventional poses – for example standing on a fire escape and photographed from below. Draw up a list of what works. You will find that national newspapers, magazines and online media not only often have different tastes but also different technical needs. (DPI is a useful term. It stands for dots per inch and tells you about the quality of the image. As a general rule 72 DPI is web standard, 150 DPI newspaper standard and 300 DPI glossy magazine standard.[5])
- *Make multiple images so the media can choose*. Given the different tastes of different media it makes sense to give them a choice of images. This will also

mean that each picture editor has a better chance of having an exclusive picture rather than one that all her or his competitors are using.

- *Do not use advertising photographs.* Advertising photography belongs in advertisements. Press shots are much more natural. They are not as strongly lit and the people featured are not usually wearing make-up. You can normally tell the difference between an advertising picture and a PR or press photograph by the fact that people in PR photographs look normal rather than perfect! Use a photographer who specialises in press and PR shots.

- *Do not over brand.* Much though your boss may want you to, do not stick your company logo or message all over the picture. Most picture editors do not mind one logo in shot but more than that and they think it is starting to look like an advertisement and will not use it.

- *Provide vertical and horizontal shots.* Not all page layouts are the same. Some need wide shots (often called landscape) and some need tall shots (often called portrait). Give the media a choice.

- *Write clear and concise captions.* Captions are important. They should clearly and simply say what is in the photograph so that picture editors, who may not even read your press release, know what they are looking at. If the photograph is funny you might want to write a funny caption, but make sure you put the hard facts about the story in first.

- *Keep a portfolio of people, product and creative shots available on your website.* Increasingly the media expect to be able to go to your organisation's site and find good photographs – with supporting information – quickly. Make sure you keep the site updated. Your Chief Executive will not like it if the press use a photograph of her or his predecessor.

- *When organising an event think about the photo opportunities at the planning stage.* Will there be enough space for photographers to move around and take shots from different angles? What is in the background...you do not want to see an advertisement for a competitor over the shoulder of the celebrity you have hired at great expense. If it is outdoors do you have a contingency plan if it rains?

- *Think about using graphs:* Not every story lends itself to photography but almost every story which is based on some kind of research lends itself to simple and easy-to-understand charts, graphs and diagrams. Have them available in camera-ready artwork form and downloadable.

- *Think about using cartoons.* A good cartoonist can be quite expensive for a small magazine or local newspaper and yet cartoons can enliven a page and add zest to a story. So if, for example, you have a story about lifestyles or families ask a cartoonist to draw something for you and then attach it to your story.

- *Think about creating video clips*. One of the great advantages of online media is that they can include moving images, sound and voices. For example, if you are launching a new product why not provide a short clip of it working? If you have held an event that some journalists were unable to attend send them a clip of it. But, and this is a big but, do not make your clips too long. Thirty seconds is good, one minute is probably the maximum. Any longer and the journalist will lose interest and probably judge that their readers/viewers will also lose interest – and so not use it.
- *Beware copyright laws*. Copyright is about who actually owns the image (see Chapter 9). You may think that because you have paid a photographer or photo library you can use the images in any way you like. This may not be the case. Copyright laws vary from country so it is not possible to give hard and fast guidance, but one clear rule is always to check the terms and conditions and copyright position when using an image.

Earlier in the book we talked about cultivating a creative atmosphere. A good way to get you thinking imaginatively about photographs is to make a collage of great press photographs and stick it up on the office wall. Hopefully, over time, some of these pictures will be replaced with ones you helped create.

A photo-opportunity

The British entrepreneur Sir Richard Branson is known for his readiness to participate in eye-catching publicity stunts. When he launched Virgin Airways' flights to India he flew to New Delhi, donned the costume of an Indian prince, danced, and then rode through the streets on an elephant. These colourful but appropriate images ensured massive amounts of coverage in the Indian media.[6]

HOW TO DO A MEDIA INTERVIEW

Sometimes the PR person is called upon to be interviewed either by a print journalist or on radio or television. This can be a nerve-wracking experience if they are not properly prepared. What follows are some top tips from the professionals on how to win with the media.

The most important thing to do is prepare. Write down in bullet form the points you want to get over. A good technique is to follow the PROBLEM/ SOLUTION/BENEFIT or VICTIM/VILLAIN/HERO approach we discussed on p. 254. Be absolutely clear about the two or three key points you want to get over. The interviewer may well not ask the questions you want – or even like – but this should not put you off. You need to be the boxer, not the punch bag. Almost regardless of the first question get your key point over at the outset.

For example, the interviewer may say: 'So you are going to reduce the speed limit. Why has it taken you so long?' The answer should be: 'Too many people have been dying on our roads. We have already introduced other measures such as road calming and believe that the public will fully support this next step in reducing road deaths by up to 2,000 a year'.

Whatever you do, *do:*

- make a few simple points phrased as simply and appealingly as possible. Don't be afraid to repeat key points,
- forget *your* problems. Readers and viewers do not want to hear about you. They are interested in themselves or other people. Even if the interviewer is rude do not get angry,
- use plain and simple language. It is important everyone understands you. Avoid using jargon.
- prepare and rehearse answers to potentially difficult questions but always be positive: never repeat the negative in a question.
- correct anything that the interviewer says or implies that is inaccurate or damaging. Interrupt – politely but firmly – if necessary.

Tips for radio/pod casts

- Do not move backwards and forwards, or your voice will come and go.
- Avoid rustling papers, clicking your pen or jingling the coins in your pocket. It sounds terrible on radio.
- Speak normally. It is up to the studio engineer to get the right level. Before you start you may be asked to say a few words 'for level'. Whatever you do, do not tell a joke. Just say something mundane.
- If the interview is being recorded and you want to change something leave a short pause and then begin your statement again.
- Talk to the interviewer. Do not talk as if you are addressing thousands. *Speaking into the microphone is like speaking into the listener's ear.*

- The audience cannot see you, so express your feelings with your voice. Vary the tone and pitch.

Tips for TV

Appearance: Avoid extreme colour contrasts, checks or stripes. Do not wear reactolite glasses, or they will turn into sunglasses under the lights and you will look like a gangster. Accept make-up if it is recommended. Check hair, tie, collar, shoulders for dandruff. (It may also be a good idea to take a change of tie and/or shirt/top in case of any spills.)

Women should avoid wearing short skirts and tops that reveal cleavage. What looks fine in the office can be distracting on TV.

Arrival: If it is a live broadcast from a studio, you will probably be asked to arrive well in advance and be taken to a waiting room for refreshments ('hospitality'). Avoid alcohol.

During the interview: Sit up straight, well back in your chair, arms resting on arm-rests or lap. Legs crossed. Always assume the camera is on you. Look at the interviewer, not at the camera. Ignore movement on the studio floor by lighting or sound staff.

Ending: Thank the interviewer and stay in your seat looking at them until directed to leave.

A) In a group, review some recent broadcast interviews with politicians or business people (there will be many examples online) and analyse their strengths and weaknesses.
B) Create a Problem/Solution/Benefit narrative for one of the examples below and then ask a fellow student to interview you on the topic. You can make up the detail – provided it is realistic!
   1. Your firm is launching a range of disposable digital thermometers designed to eliminate cross infection.
   2. A budget retailer you represent is launching a wedding dress for just £100.
   3. The trade association that represents newspaper owners is launching an advertising campaign to encourage students to buy newspapers.
   4. You represent a charity that is calling for drugs to be decriminalised.

SELLING TO THE MEDIA

Whether it is a news release or a feature article, for you as a PR person calling a journalist and selling in the idea often forms an important part of the process. In this section we are going to look at selling a story.

Journalists are busy people. They can also be rude, particularly to PR people who phone them up and ramble on about things that are of no interest to them. So why bother to phone them? Why not just send them the press release and hope? Well, first because many journalists do not like press releases – some receive literally hundreds a day. Second, stories are about people, not pieces of paper. You cannot develop a relationship with a journalist if you never speak to them. As you do so you can develop a better feeling for their interests – there may be future opportunities. Feature article ideas are particularly difficult to sell using the printed word alone. And sometimes there is insufficient time to write and send out a press release, or you may wish to offer an exclusive story. Even if you do send a release you may need to follow up with a phone call.

So how do you get the result you want and avoid annoying the journalist?

There are five steps to phone success. They are:

1 Prepare
2 Bridge
3 Taster
4 Offer
5 Close

Prepare

The first thing is to know the media you are contacting and know at least something about the journalist you are calling – what did they last write about, what are their main interests? Why is this relevant to them?

Also think carefully about timing. For example, contact weeklies and monthlies a day or two after publication when they have plenty of empty space to fill, not the day before they go to print. Contact morning papers only in the morning when they are starting on the next edition. By the afternoon they will be too busy. The only exception to this rule should be if you have an amazing story. For most PR people this may only happen once in their lifetimes.

For TV and radio news and magazine programmes it is generally best to contact the planning desk the day before the possible broadcast.

Finally plan what you are going to say.

Bridge

Establish a relationship between you and the journalist;

'I read your piece today on ... and thought...'
'You know the story you have been running on ...'
'You remember the coverage last week about car servicing rip offs...'

NOT

'Did you get my press release?' How should they know? Why should they care?

Taster

As quickly as possible give the journalist the story or news hook. It is the one reason they have for bothering to speak to you.

'There is evidence that people are being ripped off by...'

'Our CEO thinks the civil servants have got it all wrong and is saying so in a major speech tonight.'

'Our new safety suit could save two thousand lives a year...'

'One-third of women say they prefer chocolate to kissing according to...'

NOT

'We are launching a new product.'

Offer

Having given them the taster get straight down to what you are offering. Tell them it is survey findings, an interview or a photo opportunity or whatever. Then ask when and how they want it (for example by email, or courier) and make sure they get it.

Close

When you close you simply confirm what has been agreed:

'So I will email it over to you by five this evening'

'Lord Morris will meet you at his club at midday tomorrow'

'We will deliver the safety suit to your office on Monday'

Keep everything as brief and to the point as possible. Email is the place for large amounts of detail if that is required.

If they ask whether they can have the story as an exclusive – which means no other media can use it – you will have to use your judgement. Is it better to get one big bit of coverage or several smaller bits? Can you give them an exclusive angle without giving them the whole story? These are judgements that can only be made at the time.

So remember:

Prepare
Bridge
Taster
Offer
Close

Imagine you are approaching a journalist about the Safe Roads announcement (see pp. 254, 258). Prepare an outline of how you would approach a journalist with this story over the phone. Then ask a colleague to pretend to be a journalist. For extra realism, if you cannot go into a different room and use a phone, turn your chair to face away from your 'journalist' colleague so you cannot see each other's face and have to depend on listening to the tone of voice.

We have looked at how to create, structure and sell-in news stories, but what do you do when the media are pursuing bad news and want to know things that your organisation believes they do not have a right to know? And how do you increase the likelihood of your story being covered when there are other equally good stories around?

TRADING WITH THE MEDIA

PR people deal with journalists all the time. Success comes from knowing your 'enemy', which is the major reason why so many ex-journalists flourish in the public relations industry. Regardless of your background you need to understand how the media and journalists operate – and how to exploit that knowledge to your advantage.

As we have seen in Chapter 1, PR people are important players in what amounts to an information marketplace, and journalists are another group of players. They have to trade with each other – even if in most countries no money actually changes hands – and each wants something out of the bargain. PR people want the best possible coverage for their organisations and their messages, and journalists want a supply of the best quality news. These two desires are frequently in conflict. PR people often want coverage for things which the media do not deem newsworthy – if, for example, every new product received the kind of coverage in the media that PR people seek then we would read and hear about little else! On the other hand, what journalists reckon to be newsworthy is often exactly what PR people want to suppress or minimise: 'bad news', stories about arguments, problems and even disasters.

Sometimes the crisis is real and the media interest is legitimate – there are clear dangers, failures or wrongdoings (see Chapter 14) – but in other cases the public interest is less clear cut. It could be that the journalist wants to reveal commercial secrets relating to a new product or service development, or publish disclosures about the private life of a senior figure in the organisation. In such situations there is often a strong difference of opinion between the organisation and the media. The latter will claim that what they are doing is legitimate journalism and in the public interest, while the organisation will claim that they have some right to confidentiality for commercial reasons or even out of respect for personal privacy.

To drive the best possible bargain in the information marketplace you need a thorough knowledge of how it operates and to keep up to date on market conditions. The following tips are designed to help you trade to advantage:

How to deal with journalists

Paul Mylrea, Head of Press & Media Relations at the BBC, President of the CIPR and a former journalist

Contrary to popular opinion, journalists are human too. They face huge pressures getting their stories, pressures that are increasing sharply as the internet fractures the media landscape and eats into the income of traditional media organisations. So first and foremost, you have to understand these pressures. It's no use calling up with a comment five minutes after deadline or offering something that's half baked, badly written and has absolutely no news value whatsoever. So learn how journalists work. Learn the differences between broadcast, print and online, between writers, photographers and cameramen (and women).

Next, get to know the journalists in your area. You need to understand what they are looking for, what kind of stories excite them – and what turns them off completely. It's only by building up those relationships that you will be able to influence the coverage you get. It's also the only way that you can have those difficult conversations when you're really not happy with what they produce about your client or your organisation. Those moments are rare, but they do happen. When they do, it's better if you understand each other to start with. That way, there's some chance you'll keep talking afterwards.

Timing

- If you want maximum coverage for a story, 'sell' it when news is in short supply. For example, government and commercial activity tends to slow down at weekends, when offices are closed and fewer announcements are made; but on Mondays newspapers still have to fill their pages and radio and television news has to fill its airtime. This has given rise to PR people offering 'Sunday-for-Monday' stories, where they hope to benefit from the lack of competition for news space. Holiday periods can be similarly exploited, simply because there is less official and commercial news about.

- On the other hand, if you are obliged to announce something which does not reflect well on your organisation, wait until there is a glut of news – whether it is one event that is dominating the headlines or a series of big stories. Sometimes such stories can be anticipated, but at other times the opportunity arises on the spur of the moment, as an unforeseen event or disaster unfolds. If the media are preoccupied with such stories, and consider them more important than your announcement, then yours will receive less coverage than would otherwise be the case, or even none at all.

A good day to bury bad news

On September 11, 2001 – the day of 9/11 – as the twin towers were attacked in New York, Jo Moore was working as a 'spin doctor' for a British government department which was not involved in the events unfolding across the Atlantic. As she followed the story and saw its magnitude she spotted an opportunity. Her department needed to make an announcement about local politicians' expenses. The news was – mildly – controversial, and she wanted it to receive minimal attention. She emailed colleagues that it was a 'very good day to get out anything we want to bury'.

Moore's plan only become public because she had used email – rather than a deniable conversation – and her words were leaked to the media by colleagues. Her remark was deemed extremely insensitive and caused a media storm in the UK, forcing Moore to apologise. Moore was finally forced to resign from government in 2002 following further allegations that she had wanted to 'bury' more bad news by announcing it on the day of Princess Margaret's funeral.[8]

- All journalists are slaves to deadlines, the exact times when they have to submit their stories for publication or broadcast. It is hard to overestimate the importance of deadlines – after all, once a deadline is missed the news is useless to the journalist concerned – and so they have to be factored into a PR person's calculations. Obviously journalists would like to receive news well before their deadlines in order to give them time to prepare their stories. If the story you are selling is *not* major news then helping the journalist in this way is advisable: once they are close to their deadline they are less likely to bother with new material unless it is of the utmost importance. If the story is much bigger the calculation is more complex. Sometimes it may be advantageous to give the media plenty of time to prepare their stories. At other times it can be beneficial to make your announcement right up against the deadline. This reflects the fact that the news media have to cover really major developments as soon as they occur – even to the point of newspapers publishing extra editions and broadcasters breaking into programmes. If your story is big enough – and that means really big for the medium concerned – they will have to cover it in this way, and largely on your own terms, as they will have little time to seek alternative information or views.

Study your media target

To do all this effectively means being familiar with the media world, and being able to answer the following questions:

- What is being said about your organisation in the media?
- What is being said about its rivals and competitors?
- What kind of coverage are issues which concern, or might concern, your organisation getting (think back to the SLEPT analysis in Chapter 10)?

- What kinds of journalists are involved in writing these stories? Knowing what they have said in the past can give you a good idea what they will say next. What are their characteristics and what opportunities and threats do they present?

Remember the media are moving targets. Media content, notions of what constitutes newsworthiness, and the ways in which stories are covered all evolve. Personalities change, altering editorial styles and approaches. Television shows, online news websites and radio programmes come and go. New magazines appear (and often disappear). Newspapers sprout new sections to reflect new specialist interests. Fresh kinds of journalism emerge in new, online media. To have a chance of hitting the target you have to keep studying it.

Trading news

The effectiveness with which you can trade news depends on the balance of power between the PR person and the journalist. A small, little-known company will have little bargaining power with the mainstream media. Its aim is typically to secure any positive coverage it can for its products. Larger and more powerful organisations normally have more bargaining power because, as regular subjects of news stories, journalists are in constant need of their help. In the same way, 'famous' journalists who are big names in the media have more bargaining power than junior reporters: they are much less reliant on PR people and if they express negative views they can carry considerable authority.

Offering 'carrots' – the inducements PR people can offer journalists

- What journalists want from PR people is news, and what they want more than anything are 'exclusives' or 'scoops', news – as important as possible – which they can have first, before the rest of the media. Journalistic careers – and the fortunes of media outlets – can be built on exclusives, and so they are a valuable currency – indeed it is hard to overstate their importance. So exclusives, and even the hint of future exclusives, are both an inducement and a reward. They should be offered carefully to journalists who are likely to use them in a way which serves the purposes of the PR person's organisation.
- Journalists also like privileged access to organisations – for example, interviews with senior figures, briefings from experts, opportunities to film, or even simply a good relationship with PR people so that they remind them of forthcoming events or are particularly helpful when answering ordinary enquiries. Sometimes this assistance might involve an article written by a senior person

at the organisation – and almost invariably this is arranged and written by the PR person (see pp. 262–263). This kind of general helpfulness is again a valuable commodity – without it a journalist's life can become difficult – and it should be granted judiciously.

- Journalists are only human and also often appreciate other perks of the job which PR people can offer them – which might range from lunch or entertainment through to free samples of goods, or fully paid for overseas trips (a particular feature of travel PR).

Using 'sticks', or what to do with problem journalists

The measures below can usually be applied without any direct action or threat. Often only a hint is required. The position is well understood by most participants, and only in extreme cases is real action required.

- If, above all, journalists want exclusives, then denying them (or even threatening to deny them) exclusives can be an effective tactic. The same applies to other forms of help: even the implied threat of withholding assistance can be used to exert leverage.
- If the organisation itself is insufficiently powerful to have this kind of bargaining power it may seek to purchase additional leverage by hiring a leading PR consultancy to work on its media relations. Journalists will immediately be aware that, in dealing with a large PR consultancy with a range of important clients, they are dealing with a potential source of many important stories, now and in the future.

DEALING WITH HOSTILE STORIES

This is best undertaken as soon as possible, ideally before the story actually appears in the media. Usually a combination of the tactics below is used; judgement and experience are required to assess exactly what to do.

- Complain to the media. PR people can complain about a story – ideally before it even appears – to the journalist concerned, but can also go over the journalist's head and protest to editors and senior management, or even the proprietor of the media organisation. This can certainly place the journalist in an uncomfortable position, and many media organisations will hesitate if they face a barrage of high-level complaints.
- Such complaints can be backed up with threats. In addition to the 'sticks' outlined above, the threat of legal action, typically for defamation or breach of privacy, is often employed. Even if they think they might win, media organisations

fear the risk, costs and waste of time involved in long drawn-out legal proceedings. Rival media organisations may be deterred from running the story if they are told about the threat of legal action. Other threats can include appealing to any relevant media regulatory bodies and the possible withdrawal of advertising.

- If bad news is anticipated, expectations can be managed by off-the-record briefings and leaks which give the media advance notice of what is happening. If the bad news is already known it is no longer really news: the sting is removed. Everyone – including journalists – immediately puts a news story into the context of what they already know. Indeed PR people working for highly successful organisations have to be particularly careful because expectations are so high. If a company which was expected to make enormous profits made a very small profit it would be reported more negatively than an announcement by a company which was expected to make very large losses and in fact only made a small loss.

- If the PR person is in a powerful enough position they can create and offer alternative news – decoy stories which serve to distract the media from the 'bad news' story.

- If the story does appear, PR people should ensure that it is rebutted as quickly as possible. Challenging the facts in a story is made easier by the speed with which journalists work. News stories habitually contain inaccuracies or errors, or rely on sources which might change their stories. Even if the central thrust of the story is correct, by undermining elements of it the PR person can weaken its overall credibility.

- Other tried-and-tested ways of undermining problem stories include the following:
    - *Swiftly acknowledging and, where appropriate, apologising for faults or errors, and thereby achieving 'closure'.* Although this may seem a hard thing to do, once this is done the story often peters out, unless there are fresh ingredients, or the problem is too big for a simple apology to suffice. This technique can be combined with the following approaches.
    - *Attacking or discrediting the source of the story.* Personalities are key ingredients in any news story and if they lack credibility or appear ridiculous anything they say is undermined. Sometimes you can supply an alternative source with equal or greater credibility who can contradict or undermine the negative story.
    - *Making the problem historic.* If your organisation faces criticism, make it clear that the criticisms relate to the past (which by definition they must) and that things have now changed for the better.

- *Pushing the problem away.* Typically this involves setting up a review or inquiry, or commissioning a report. This is easily portrayed as a sensible and responsible course of action, but media coverage will normally die down while the review or report is undertaken. The delay can be used to prepare properly and you can of course legitimately refuse to comment further while the outcome of the review or report is pending. Governments tend to be keen on this tactic.
- *Accentuating the positive.* Even in the most critical reports there are often positive aspects. Part of your job is to find them and give them plenty of emphasis. Make sure that anyone from your organisation who is likely to speak to the media is fully briefed on whatever is positive. Even if they have to acknowledge or apologise for problems they can spend much longer talking about good news and what went right.
- *'Starving' the media.* To keep going news stories need fresh fuel. If the organisation at the centre of the storm refuses to be drawn further and refuses interview bids the news often dies down (provided of course there are no further revelations from elsewhere).
- *Exploiting journalistic and media rivalries.* Media outlets (and individual journalists) have a vested interest in undermining – where possible – their rivals' stories.

All these points carry two important health warnings. First, they depend on the amount of power you have and are seen to have – including your ability to control the news emerging from your organisation (not always something that be guaranteed when things go wrong). Adopting a tough stance with journalists and media organisations may be necessary but inevitably stores up resentments which can come back to haunt you when you and your organisation are vulnerable. Second, you will ultimately be judged on whether your approach was a legitimate one which was in the interests of the organisation and did not endanger or disadvantage the public; or whether your approach was simply designed to protect an organisation that was seriously at fault and had avoided taking proper remedial action and responsibility for the alleged crisis or problem.

Examine closely some 'bad news' stories in the media. What evidence can you find of PR being used to play down the stories, and how effective do you think it was.

Handling Chinese media stories

2008 was a busy year for China's media handlers. The Summer Olympics in Beijing had long been scheduled for August 2008, but unrest in Tibet during March, and its suppression by the Chinese authorities, generated enormous international media interest. Western reporters' access to the affected areas was curtailed. Concern at China's actions meant that when the Olympic torch was borne through cities such as London and Paris there were demonstrations and ugly scenes.

In May 2008 the serious earthquake in Sichuan seized the headlines. There was international sympathy and China's response, including prompt intervention by senior politicians, won praise.

As the Olympics came to an end, China was rocked by a baby milk contamination scandal: human lives seemed to have been put at risk by reckless or criminal behaviour on the part of a major Chinese company.

These stories have as their common denominator China, a country with very different traditions of media handling and a tradition of state control of what the media can report. However in each of these cases Chinese media handlers had to deal with overseas-based media whose content they could not control.

Research online coverage of these events – or other events if you prefer – and assess how the media handling operations were conducted and what lessons can be learned.

- The media rely on PR people for good quality content. You need to study the media in order to meet their needs in ways which serve your interests.
- This includes drafting high-quality press releases; using written English effectively; ghosting press articles for others; providing the media with the right kind of images; preparing for and conducting interviews; selling in stories to journalists on the phone; and using your knowledge of the media and a range of 'sticks and carrots' to minimise unfavourable coverage.

Assemble some up-to-date newspapers and search for other media materials online. Analyse what they tell you about the media handling of one good news, and one bad news, story (you may also wish to check the online presences of the organisations involved in the stories).

CHAPTER 13

EVENT MANAGEMENT

INTRODUCTION

Event planning and management is, for many people in PR, a significant part of their job. It is also what many in the outside world think PR is primarily about. Be it a launch party, press conference, fashion show or major business conference, events are a time consuming and costly, but also exciting, facet of PR.

Many students interested in PR say they are attracted by the need for social skills and the opportunity to meet people. But organising a great event takes a lot more than that. The skills needed range from a strong creative eye (for set designs and displays) through to good administrative skills – including budgeting – as well as strong social skills. An ability to keep calm in a crisis is essential. PR people tend to be naturally optimistic, but a little pessimism is helpful in event planning and management: if it can go wrong it often will, in ways you never expected, and just because you have booked or arranged something does not mean it will happen. Hope for the best, but plan for the worst.

LEARNING OBJECTIVES

- How to plan an event
- How to budget
- How to administer an event
- How to socialise successfully

EVENT PLANNING

We have already looked in Chapter 10 at deciding on objectives and how to create great ideas, but some of the key points are worth reiterating here.

The most important thing is to be clear about what you are trying to achieve – the objective(s).

Are you trying to meet new customers, secure media coverage, raise money, build staff loyalty, express gratitude to existing customers, or talk to key opinion formers? If you do not have clear objectives you cannot evaluate the results.

Given the cost of events and the time taken to organise and run them, you should always ask if this is the best way to achieve your objectives. For example, is a press conference necessary? Is your news story so strong that busy journalists will leave their desks and travel to it? If they do come, is what you have to show or demonstrate to them enough to justify their effort? Could the same result be achieved with a phone call and a press release?

If you are in the fashion or celebrity business, holding a party might seem like a great idea, but it could turn into an own goal if the party overshadows the message you are trying to communicate. (And in image conscious industries of this kind, if you cannot attract the right kind of guests you may actually damage your reputation.)

So having decided on your objectives, the second most important thing is to have a clear theme or idea that will give the event a purpose and engage the target audience in the desired way. This is, in effect, your event strategy.

What will the audience be interested in? What are good times/dates for them? (It is imperative that you check that the date you choose does not clash with something else that may lure your audience away ... and that clash could be a major football match, not just an obvious competitor event.) Generally the sorts of people you want at an event are busy people so make sure you have thought all these issues through. Will they expect something lavish and flamboyant, serious and prestigious, or modest and short? Is the event meant to be a treat for the guests or a useful business development opportunity? Is the event appropriate to the organisation and the context in which it is operating (for example, in straitened circumstances might holding an expensive event generate counterproductive publicity)?

Once you have a clear set of objectives and a strategy you can start to complete the event planner as shown in Table 13.1 below. This can be updated and added to as the project progresses.

Table 13.1   Event planner (overview)

WHY are we having the event? (Objectives)	
WHOM are we targeting	
WHAT sort of event? (Strategy)	
HOW are we going to make it special? (Tactics)	
WHEN is it going to happen?	
WHERE is it going to happen?	
HOW will we measure success?	

Once you have the answers to these questions you need to produce an estimated budget. This will not be too difficult if you have done events before, but if you have not then you will need to consider some of the factors outlined below before finalising it.

Organising an event can seem daunting, so it is worth breaking it down into manageable parts, each of which will need its own checklist and critical path analysis (see pp. 221–222).

Some suggested key parts are:

- *Invitations.* Be clear on timings, appropriate dress and so on. We recently attended a charity event with stated timings of 7.30–10 pm. We turned up at 8 pm thinking we did not want to be first and, along with many others, missed the important speeches at 7.45 pm.
- *The venue.* A great venue will not make up for a poor event, but people do like to go to new and interesting places.
- *Staging.* Staging, lighting, and sound all cost money.
- *Performers.* Remember to brief them. One of us once hired a famous comedian who was much more sexually explicit in real life than he was on television and shocked some of the audience. If someone is making a speech refer them to pp. 237–245.
- *The media.* Will they require internet connections and other special facilities?
- *Accommodation*
- *Transport*
- *Prizes/Awards*
- *Gifts/Goody bags.* Instead of giving them a carrier bag of brochures why not give them a branded memory stick loaded with the presentations?

> **A high-profile event**
>
> A UK PR company, working closely with a Russian PR agency, was involved in the launch of a new luxury railway service on the Trans-Siberian Express route in Russia. The activities involved a visit to a factory by journalists and dignitaries, a cocktail reception at the British Embassy attended by a member of the British royal family, a naming ceremony for the train, and an inaugural journey to the scene of the murder of the last Tsar of Russia in Yekaterinburg. The events were intended to publicise a successful Russo–British joint venture and received extensive press coverage.[1]

BUDGETS

There is a tendency to exceed budgets when running events. Some costs can change and/or are beyond your control. The important thing is to try to cost as much and as accurately as possible from the outset in order to avoid nasty surprises. The budget pro forma below should help, though each item will consist of many points. For example, the invitation needs to be designed, printed and possibly posted, all of which costs money.

Table 13.2   Budgets pro forma

Item	Description	Budget/quote	Actual Cost
Invitations			
Venue			
Event Staging			
Media			
Accommodation			
Transport			
Prizes/Awards			
Gifts/Goody bags			
Performers			
TOTAL			

ADMINISTRATION

Having broken down the event into manageable parts, you now need to break down each part into its key components and ensure that everything happens to time and on budget. The best way to do this is by having detailed checklists.

For example a venue checklist might look something like this.

Table 13.3 Venue checklist

Item	Description/quantity	Status
Catering: • Breakfast • Coffee/tea/water • Lunch • Bar • Tea • Dinner • Vegetarians/special dietary needs		
Seating plan and layout		
Signage • Branding/logos • Directions		
Staging • Rostrum • Top table		
A/V equipment • Sound • Visual • Lighting • Stage		
Parking • VIP • Others		
Media • Hospitality/interview area • Invites		
Security • Front of house • Main room		
Rehearsal facilities		
On arrival • Welcome • VIP welcome • Signing in • Cloakroom • Lavatories		

This is not by any means a complete list. Moreover this is just for the venue. Checklists also need to be done for all the key elements, from performers through to transportation. If this seems challenging, remember that once you have devised some checklists and developed a style of critical path analysis that you are happy with, it becomes much easier.

But all of these checklists will get you nowhere if you have not ensured that everyone – staff and suppliers included – know exactly what they are supposed to be doing and when. In particular you need to confirm in writing exactly what you expect of external suppliers. For example if you just order 'a car' to pick up your VIP, you cannot really complain if what turns up is not the luxury limo you and your VIP expected. Attention to detail is everything.

HOW TO SOCIALISE EFFECTIVELY

Cultural differences make hard and fast rules on how to socialise problematic. However here are six golden rules for making people feel at ease – not least yourself:

1) *Meet and greet*: What happens when someone arrives at an event can influence how they feel about the rest of the proceedings. Get the signing in and coat-checking dealt with as efficiently and as quickly as possible. Then, if practical, ensure everyone is welcomed, told what to expect from the event, where everything is and what to do next – for example 'take a seat', 'help yourself to coffee', 'the presentations will start in 10 minutes'.

2) *Build bridges*: Ask people questions about themselves – everyone has something to say about themselves. Business questions include 'Is this a busy time for you?', 'You must be very pleased/stimulated by ... ?' 'Where did you work before?' If business is off limits ask them where they live, or what they do with their free time. The Queen of England apparently asks: 'Have you come far?' Listen to their answers, you may pick up something that will enable you to introduce that person to someone with a shared interest ... 'Joseph, this is Mary, she also lives in San Francisco'. If you are doing all the talking you are not being a good host – the guest is the star!

3) *Flatter people*: First and foremost try to remember their name. This is most easily done by repeating it a couple of times as soon as you have heard it. 'Well lovely to meet you Pierre. And, tell me Pierre, how long have you been with ... ?' Then repeat what they have said with some positive affirmation. 'So sales have grown by 50%. That must be very pleasing. Pierre, what do you put it down to?'

4) *Keep off risky subjects*: Topics such as politics, sex and religion are best avoided unless they are highly relevant to the event, and even then should be treated with care.

5) *Network rather than sell*: Often an event is a way to win or grow business, but be careful not to appear to be selling (unless your guests are giving clear buying signals). People like to do business with people they like, so make the human connection first. An exchange of business cards is perfect for this – particularly

in Asia. Once you have someone's card you can follow up later, ideally with an introductory line showing you listened to what they said before pitching into your proposition. 'Dear Abdul, I very much enjoyed meeting you last night and hearing about your son's success at school.'

6) *Watch your body language*: We often give away a lot about how we are feeling by the way we use our bodies. Avoid at all costs standing or sitting with your arms folded across your chest. It looks defensive. Try to mirror the body language of the person you are talking to – it shows empathy.

An eye-catching PR stunt

In September 2010 the international celebrity and pop star Lady Gaga appeared at the high-profile MTV video music awards event in Los Angeles wearing a 'meat dress', an outfit made of slabs of raw meat. The media could not get enough of the startling image. The dress generated a great deal of comment and controversy.[2]

Research this and other eye-catching publicity stunts which have featured in the media. How effective have they been in achieving the PR goals for which they were designed?

---

1 Estimate the cost of a party for 200 members of staff. You have had a good year and the CEO wants to say thank you to everyone. Also consider how long such a party would take from conception, through planning, to completion.
2 Estimate the cost of organising an exclusive dinner for 25 business leaders and politicians at which the well-known author of a controversial new book on management is going to speak.

In small teams take it in turn to organise events – such as guest speakers, film showings, or topical presentations and then critique each event.

A great PR event needs:

- clear strategic thinking about how to realise your objectives (PR events are not just an excuse for a party),
- creativity,
- meticulous administration, and
- confident social skills that are not based on you doing all the talking.

CRISIS MANAGEMENT

INTRODUCTION

Crisis management is probably one of the most controversial areas of PR. It can be about the life and death of an organisation. A badly managed crisis can result in an organisation imperilled, a company out of business, personal reputations destroyed and years of work undermined. On the other hand a well-managed crisis can not only avoid these hazards but can even, in the long term, enhance the reputation of the organisation concerned. Crisis management matters.

LEARNING OBJECTIVES

- Understanding what a crisis is
- Planning for a crisis
- Responding to a crisis

(Note: Since crisis management brings many PR skills to bear, this chapter should be read in conjunction with the following chapters: 7 – PR in the Online World; 8 – Corporate Social Responsibility; 12 – PR Media Skills.)

WHAT IS A CRISIS?

A crisis is an event, accusation or perception that seriously threatens the reputation – and, if not dealt with effectively – the viability of an organisation (or that of a brand or, in some cases, an individual's career).

There are essentially two main types of crisis. The first is what might be called a *real crisis*. Someone has been hurt or even killed. A product has failed in a way that is at best inconvenient to customers or others and at worst damaging. It is this sort of crisis on which we will mainly focus in this chapter.

The second, and sometimes overlapping, type of crisis is a *reputational crisis*. In this instance something happens, or is alleged, that lowers trust, respect and liking for the organisation. Some of the techniques for dealing with reputational crises are covered in Chapter 8 on CSR and Chapter 12 on Media skills. However, much of what is said in this chapter is also relevant.

In groups, write down at least two recent examples of 'real' and 'reputational' crises affecting organisations of any kind. A) Why did they happen? B) How effective was the crisis management? C) What has been the PR legacy of the crisis?

The two main types of crisis can be further subdivided into four categories. These are:

1. *Performance Crises (Fault, Fire and Theft):* This is when an organisation fails to perform properly. Typically examples include when products have to be recalled, accidents and injury occur, laws have been broken or private data has been lost. Simplistically this category can be called *Fault, Fire and Theft*. In some ways this is the easiest category of crisis to deal with in PR terms. Most of these types of crisis can, broadly, be foreseen, even if the timing and circumstances cannot.

2. *Disaster Crises:* These are totally unexpected and virtually impossible to plan for. They include 'one in a million' crises such as a plane crashing into your building or a gunman running amok in your office or store. However, although they may be difficult to plan for, many of the techniques described below, under the heading 'Planning for a Crisis' are relevant.

The events of 9/11 – the terrorist attacks on the USA in 2001 – rank about as high as any disaster crisis can. The biggest of the attacks was of course on the twin towers of the World Trade Centre in New York. As a media savvy modern city New York had crisis management plans in place. The problem was that the designated crisis management centre was within the World Trade Centre complex – proof that crises always involve the unexpected and can be of an unpredictable scale.[1]

3. *Attack Crises:* These occur when someone such as a journalist, disgruntled member of staff or activist is out to get your organisation. They may focus on internal disputes, poor management practice and controversial leaked documents. No-one may have been hurt and no laws may have been broken, but the credibility of your organisation is under attack. In Chapter 12 on media skills we discuss in detail how to deal with attacks from journalists. Similarly Chapter 5 which looks at Internal Communications has some guidance which should reduce the likelihood of attack by disaffected staff.

Attack crises can be particularly difficult for PR staff to prepare for, as they often involve allegations of poor decision-making, unethical behaviour or even criminality on the part of one or more members of the senior management team, up to and including chief executives and corporate chairs. Such allegations, if they turn out to be true (or are seen to be true), can quickly spell doom for even the mightiest organisations. They are sometimes linked to performance crises, which shed light on hitherto hidden aspects of an organisation.

PR people lack the time, resources and expertise (and usually the status) to second-guess all the activities of senior management or everything else that goes on in large organisations, and would not be thanked for trying to do so! So they are often in the dark about such matters until just before they hit the headlines. And yet the biggest corporate crises of recent times had some if not all of these characteristics: think of Enron, WorldCom and numerous banking crises in recent years, including the downfall of Lehman Brothers.

4. *'Moral' Crisis:* Some industries are in the unfortunate position of facing criticism for being in existence. Tobacco companies are one obvious example, but oil companies, mining companies and pharmaceutical companies – and more recently fast food companies – have also come under the spotlight. These are the sort of companies and industries that often seem to have the word 'evil' attached to them, and as the example of fast food indicates, ideas on what constitutes 'evil' can shift over time, so vigilance is required. Whatever such companies do or say someone is going to hate them. Chapter 8 on CSR covers some of the techniques that unloved organisations can use to improve, or at least balance, their image.

 Try to allocate to one of these four categories the crisis you discussed in the previous exercise. Then discuss in what way these different categories of crisis might require different PR approaches.

PLANNING FOR A CRISIS

A crisis is a time of great danger or difficulty. Events suddenly, and usually surprisingly, spiral out of control.

Imagine. Rumour and speculation are rife, the media are banging at the door demanding explanations, staff morale hits rock bottom, and business 'friends' no longer take your calls. The organisation is now in a panic. The boss has locked himself away in his office and is refusing to speak to the media. Investors are withdrawing their money. Journalists have met secretly with members of staff and are now printing anything they are told, even though it is not true. Before long the organisation has collapsed.

This sounds extreme and it is. But it is not impossible. It can and does happen. So what can be done to avoid such a crisis? Indeed, how can it be possible to avoid something that by definition is sudden and unexpected? The answer is through planning.

It may sound like a contradiction in terms but most crises are predictable. Fire, theft and fraud all happen. If they happen they could happen to you. Similarly products fail, accidents occur and employees sometimes behave strangely to customers. We know these things happen because we have read about them, perhaps even experienced them at first hand. As a PR practitioner your task is to try to predict these crises and plan what you would do in the event of them actually happening.

There are six stages in planning for a crisis:

• Scenario mapping
• Response paper writing
• Audience identification
• Crisis team formation
• Staff training
• Crisis manual production

Scenario mapping

The best way of mapping out possible crisis scenarios is to gather a team of people representing each and every part of the organisation and then, with them, try to predict what sort of crisis could occur in each area.

Figure 14.1 shows a simple starting point for a scenario map.

Clearly there are many more possible areas of risk depending on the nature of the organisation. In some cases identifying the risk will prompt immediate action to remove or lessen it. For example you may realise that your financial systems need tightening and that you need to improve the way you check the references on the staff you hire. Or you may decide that you need to install a fire prevention sprinkler system in your factory or increase the fire walls around your computers to reduce the risk of identity theft. But whatever you do you can never eradicate risk altogether. This is why it is essential to develop a response paper for each potential scenario that is identified.

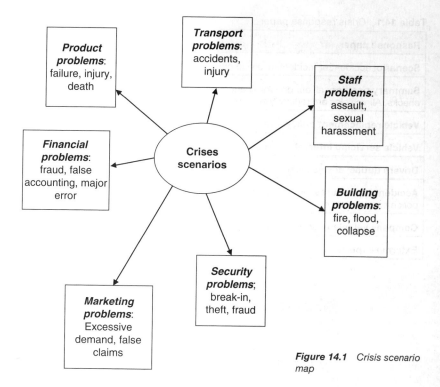

Figure 14.1   *Crisis scenario map*

Response papers

A response paper is, as its name implies, a document that collects all the relevant information on a scenario, including the name and contact details of the person within the organisation responsible for the area, as well as the details of people or organisations that might back you up (allies and ambassadors) or people who might also be involved in the problem (suppliers, competitors and industry associations). It is vital that this information is ready to hand at the time of a crisis.

For example, imagine that you are representing a well-known food retailer and you have just been told that one of your lorries has crashed into a group of school children, injuring four of them. The media are already speculating that the vehicle had not been serviced.

The example below shows an outline response paper for crisis involving a serious vehicle accident.

Table 14.1   Crisis response paper

Response paper
Scenario: accident or incident involving company vehicle
Summary position: all our drivers' licences are checked before employment and are subject to regular spot checks. All vehicles are regularly serviced and replaced.
Vehicle replacement policy: every 100,000 to 150,000 miles or two years
Vehicle servicing intervals: in accordance with manufacturers' recommendations, usually every 6,000 miles
Drivers duties: drivers must carry out weekly checks on fluid leaks, fan belt, tyres, brakes and windscreen etc
Accident procedures: any accidents involving injury to any person and /or third party must be reported to the police immediately etc
Company vehicle expert: Mr xxxxxxx + full 24 hour contact details
External experts/support: this might be the garage or motoring organisation that services the vehicles

 Devise a sample response paper for one of the crisis scenarios shown in the Figure 14.1.

By having a response paper readily to hand you can at least contain the wilder speculation and position your organisation as one that has proper policies while you try to find out what really happened. A point to remember here is that having such policies does not mean they were followed properly, so you should be careful not to claim that something could not have happened: it may have, but at least your company took reasonable measures to minimise the risk.

Having written a response paper for each scenario you now need to map out the audiences you are likely to need to contact in the event of a crisis.

Audience identification

A common mistake in a crisis is only to think about the media as they seem to be the most immediate threat to the reputation of your organisation. In fact there are many other audiences, all of whom can have a major impact on the future of your business.

Listed below are some of the key groups you may need to consider.

Internal audiences

- Senior Management
- Customer-facing staff (i.e. the sales-force, service engineers, delivery staff, receptionists, security)
- Media facing staff (see p. 294)
- Unions and works councils

Staff may quickly become demoralised without information and, even worse, may start feeding information or rumours to the media. All staff need to know if they are allowed to speak to the media: most should not be allowed to do so, but should know how to rebuff media advances politely or refer them onwards. Those trained and allowed to speak to the media need to be kept fully informed as the crisis develops.

External audiences

There are many external audiences who will be concerned:

- Suppliers
- Customers
- Trade/Industry associations
- Investors, financial analysts and banks
- Local communities
- Politicians and government officials (local and national)
- MEDIA

Investors will want to know what is happening to their money. Politicians, if it is a national crisis, may need information so they can make public statements; and if there is a physical hazard local communities will need reassurance. Finally, there is of course the media.

For each of these groups it is also worth devising a plan on how you would contact them in the event of a crisis. Will it be face-to-face, by phone or email? For staff, do you have a system of cascade briefings whereby managers can brief their teams in person? Who will be responsible for keeping the website up to date? All these questions are best answered in advance rather than at the time of the crisis when you will be under enormous pressure and have so many things to do.

Crisis team formation

In the event of a crisis you are going to need a small team of people who can be freed up from their day-to-day work to focus on the crisis while the rest of the staff get on with the vital task of keeping the organisation running as normally as possible. At the heart of the team should be a PR person and a member of senior management with decision-making powers. There should also be a committee secretary to make sure that the administration runs to plan. Depending on the nature of your business you may also need legal and financial experts.

The crisis team should:

- approve all the response papers
- organise the relevant staff training

- decide who can talk to the media
- draw up the contact strategy
- produce the crisis manual

Once a crisis occurs the crisis team will need to co-opt the relevant company experts. These will be the people whose names you have already identified on the response papers.

The crisis committee can be called into session following a request by any committee member or agreed member of the senior management team. For a small crisis it may only be necessary to liaise by phone. However for a major crisis the committee will need to meet in person and a venue, with excellent communication facilities, should be identified at the planning stage.

The committee must also ensure that there is an extensive and up-to-date list of key people's round-the-clock contact details, with back-up individuals identified. Crises have an annoying way of happening outside normal working hours or when key people are absent.

Once the committee is in session detailed notes should be taken, particularly of all media calls, noting the nature of the inquiry, the response given and all actions taken. It is vital to monitor not just the information going out but what is coming in as well.

Finally, do not forget that a crisis may run for 24 hours a day over several days. You will need to plan how you will staff your media-handling operation. A press officer who has been working for 36 hours non-stop is liable to make mistakes.

Staff training

Agreeing who can talk to the media and ensuring they are properly trained in media interview techniques is an important part of the crisis committee's planning role and some tips on this are given later in this chapter.

Almost as important is the training of front line staff such as switchboard operators and receptionists. Unlike most other members of staff they are bound to have some dealings with key external audiences, not least the media. They need to be trained in how to do this and on how to avoid some of the tricks that journalists play when trying to get or make a story. (Recently, now that smoking has been banned in so many places, some journalists have found that sidling up to groups of smokers outside a troubled office or factory is a great way to glean 'unofficial' information!)

One of the most effective ways of planning for a crisis is to simulate one. This can be done by creating an imaginary crisis scenario and then asking a few trusted members of staff to act as journalists. They call into the office asking for a comment on the crisis, the committee meets and the crisis plan swings into action. A good simulation may run over several days. Whatever the scenario, it gets staff used to thinking and working together in a crisis situation. This might seem like a major time commitment but should be viewed as akin to the premium on an insurance policy – it is well worth it compared with the possibility of the plan failing when a real crisis occurs.

Crisis manual

Finally, everything needs to be drawn together in a crisis manual. This should be available online to the committee members, but also needs to exist in hard copy format (imagine if your computer system fails!).

The manual should include:

- all the response papers
- contact details
- media-handling tips
- media enquiry forms

It is best to present it in a ring binder file so that it is easy to update. It should also avoid technical jargon. Everyone from the security guard to the chief executive might have to use it at some point.

The manual should be updated at least once a year. People move on. You do not want to find on the day you have a chemical spillage that your chemicals' expert left two years ago.

So now let us look at what actually happens when the crisis breaks.

DEALING WITH A CRISIS

When a crisis happens there are a number of strategies that should be followed.

The first is to *answer the key crisis questions quickly*. There are always five basic questions that everyone wants to know the answer to. They are:

- *What happened and how?*
- *When did it happen?*
- *Why did it happen?*
- *Whose fault is it?*
- *What are you going to do about it?*

You may not be able to answer all these questions straight away, but as soon as possible you should try to fill the information vacuum that occurs in these situations. Lack of information leads to speculation and speculation, in turn, leads to rumour. This can be disastrous. In the age of the internet a rumour is half way round the world whilst the truth is still pulling its boots on. The key things to say are:

- What happened
- Why it happened
- What you are going to do about it *now* and to stop it happening again in the *future*
- That *you are sorry*

Sorry seems to be the hardest word

Organisations find saying sorry very difficult, particularly because lawyers often warn that saying sorry is an admission of guilt. Saying sorry does not have to be an admission of this kind. For example the injuries caused by your lorry crashing into the school children may be the result of a manufacturer's design fault and nothing to do with your servicing and maintenance. You will still be sorry that one of your vehicles has caused injuries. And if your organisation *is* guilty of a mistake or failure there is no point in denying the fact. It is not just morally wrong but stupid. If it does not come out now that your organisation was responsible it will just come out later and cause you even more reputational harm. There is bound to be a disaffected member of staff who will find out and talk to the media or post it online.

A refusal to say sorry can make an organisation look cold and heartless and do more damage to its reputation than the original accident itself. It takes years to build reputations but they can be destroyed overnight.

The second crisis strategy is to try to *widen the issue and involve others*. For example if the problem is not unique to your organisation you may want to draw in the industry association. This is the usual approach in the event of a moral 'crisis' where it is not just your organisation, but all organisations in the industry that are under attack. For example individual drinks companies and brands seldom respond to the attacks of the anti-alcohol lobby, preferring to form a united front behind the trade or industry association.

Similarly, if the problem lies with a supplier you will obviously need their involvement. This is not passing the buck, though there is a reputational advantage in sharing the problem, but responsible behaviour. If a problem is industry-wide you alone cannot solve it. This is also the case if a problem stems from a supplier's action.

The third strategy is to *recruit allies and ambassadors*. Think about who will support your claims to have proper policies and procedures. Who will vouch for your overall good citizenship even when in a particular instance your organisation's actions have fallen below an acceptable standard or the very *raison d'etre* of your business is under attack? At a time of crisis enemies and detractors are often easier to find than allies. Getting allies and ambassadors on side in advance is time well spent.

Big brands at risk: Pepsi and Coke under attack

The bigger you are the more likely you are to be attacked.

An Indian non-governmental organisation, the Centre for Science and Environment, claimed samples of Coca-Cola and Pepsi products contained harmful levels of pesticides.

The soft drink rivals combined to reject the claims vigorously and were backed by other soft drinks manufacturers who condemned the findings.

'Soft drinks are completely safe,' the Indian Soft Drink Manufacturers Association (ISDMA) said in a statement. Independent tests ordered by the Indian government backed this view.

Some argued that the criticism of Coca-Cola and Pepsi was more about anti-Americanism than proper science. Whatever the truth, it cost the companies a lot of time and money to overcome the crisis.[2]

HANDLING THE MEDIA IN A CRISIS

Journalists want the truth, but usually in the most sensational form possible. You also want to tell as much of truth as you can, but probably do not know exactly what the truth is when the crisis first breaks and the media suddenly call you on the phone or appear at your door.

Before any interview try to identify:

- Who the journalist is and whom they work for
- What they want to know (and what they know already)
- The deadline for the information

Try to get as much information as possible, and try to prepare your answers to the difficult questions that are likely to be asked.

If a journalist calls unexpectedly, just say you are in a meeting but will get back to them as soon as possible. Then get the information you need and prepare your answers.

Whatever you do, *do not*:

- get angry. However rude the journalists is it is not a personal attack,
- try to be funny. Crises are not funny. Smiling is probably not a good idea either; it could make it look as though you are not taking things seriously,
- speak 'off the record', in the belief that you have an agreement with the journalist not to use what you have said. There is no such thing as a true off-the-record agreement. Even if the journalist does not quote you directly, the only reason they are speaking to you is to gather material for the story they are preparing. Anything you say may be used, particularly in a crisis,
- say 'no comment'. Journalists and the public think it means guilty – after all, if you had good news to offer you would not be refusing to reveal it. If you do not know what has happened, admit it but say you are trying to find out and when you will get back to them. Straightforward honesty of this kind is endearing.

(More detailed tips on handling press, radio and television interviews are set out in Chapter 12).

Sometimes during a crisis it will be necessary to hold a press conference.

Press conferences have the advantage of enabling you to speak to a lot of journalists at once. However, they can turn into a feeding frenzy as one journalist's attack follows another. They are also open to hi-jacking by special interest groups or people with a grudge against the organisation. It is better, if you can find the time, to deal with the media on a one-to-one basis.

If you do have to have a press conference, make sure the room is comfortable and well ventilated (see Chapter 13 for details on events management). A hot and uncomfortable journalist is unlikely to be very sympathetic.

Comparing crises

One of the most popular morality tales of crisis management concerns the response of the American pharmaceutical company Johnson & Johnson when it found that some capsules of its popular analgesic, Tylenol, had been laced with cyanide by an unknown culprit, causing a number of deaths. Johnson & Johnson's response included a full product recall. A year later the product had recovered most of its market share.

Johnson & Johnson undoubtedly handled the situation well: indeed in the circumstances anything short of a product recall would have been foolhardy. However its actions went well beyond the remit of any PR person – although doubtless their input was called for. To recover their market position Johnson & Johnson introduced tamper-proof containers, and undertook a major price promotion. People sometimes like to say how crises represent an opportunity, but even in this textbook case the company incurred massive costs.

Tylenol is often contrasted with the how-not-to-do-it example of the Exxon Valdez, an oil tanker belonging to the oil company Exxon (now ExxonMobil, parent company of Esso and Mobil), which struck a reef off Prince William Sound on the Alaskan coast, causing one of the biggest environmental disasters of modern times. Exxon undoubtedly suffered much more devastating criticism than Johnson & Johnson, but was this down to poor PR? It was alleged that Exxon's ship was poorly equipped and its officers were seriously negligent, weaknesses well beyond the power of PR to address, and the situation was entirely different to that of Johnson & Johnson, which seemed to be the victim of a criminal act.

Nonetheless, as a PR textbook commented: 'If the media had captured ... the CEO on the site at Prince William Sound holding an oil-covered bird in his hand and looking as if he were crying, the entire story would be told differently today.'[3]

An online crisis

There is really no such thing as an online crisis. What there are are crises that start online. We discussed in Chapter 7 some of the difficulties of dealing with online attacks. Here we have provided a simple reminder of the key action points for consideration.

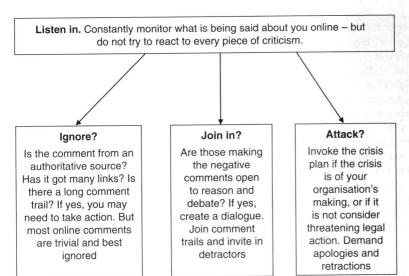

Listen in. Constantly monitor what is being said about you online – but do not try to react to every piece of criticism.

Ignore?	**Join in?**	**Attack?**
Is the comment from an authoritative source? Has it got many links? Is there a long comment trail? If yes, you may need to take action. But most online comments are trivial and best ignored	Are those making the negative comments open to reason and debate? If yes, create a dialogue. Join comment trails and invite in detractors	Invoke the crisis plan if the crisis is of your organisation's making, or if it is not consider threatening legal action. Demand apologies and retractions

Figure 14.2 Online crisis checklist

In conclusion, many PR crises involve PR practitioners in difficult ethical issues. How far are you prepared to go in thwarting journalists who want to know more than your organisation is prepared to tell? How comfortable are you with the core product or service that your organisation offers – for example, alcohol and online gambling which some people regard as improper areas of business activity? How much blame are you prepared to pass on to others?

Within the confines of the law and your own personal ethical code you will have to decide how far you can go along with how your organisation responds to a crisis. Critics of an organisation in crisis will often accuse its PR people and their paymasters of being unethical. What is certain is that a PR practitioner who handles a crisis effectively will earn the respect and gratitude of their boss.

Case study: a real crisis – BP and the environmental disaster in the Gulf of Mexico in 2010

In April 2010 the BP-leased Deepwater oil drilling rig in the Gulf of Mexico exploded. Eleven workers were killed and a huge oil spill spread across the sea, with some reaching the Gulf Coast of the USA. For obvious reasons there was particular concern in the United States, where many people became hostile towards BP and took to referring to the company as 'British Petroleum', a name it had dropped. In the weeks following the accident BP's share price more than halved, there was speculation about BP's ability to pay for the costs of dealing with the oil spill, and some even called into question the future of BP as an independent oil giant. It took five months to seal the leaking well completely, and the clean-up and compensation claims remain to be dealt with. BP, normally a highly profitable company, reported a loss of almost $5bn for 2010, which included setting aside almost $41bn for charges relating to the oil spill. BP stated that it hoped to recover most of those costs from its commercial partners with whom it was working on the rig.

BP's PR early handling of the crisis was widely criticised. BP's then Chief Executive Tony Hayward became the public face of the company, but aroused anger for remarks such as 'the Gulf of Mexico is a very big ocean' and 'there's no-one who wants this over more than I do – I would like my life back'. Significantly – like many senior people in big oil companies – Hayward is a scientist by background. Success in science depends on accuracy, not the emotional resonance of what is said. While it may be technically true that the Gulf is a huge expanse of sea, the first remark sounded insensitive and ignored the real concerns of affected communities. The second remark sounded self-centred – and indeed Hayward attracted even more hostility when he was pictured taking part in a yachting event in Britain during the crisis. These and other PR gaffes had no practical consequences for the oil spill or the clean-up. However they underline how important emotions are in crises of this kind – something politicians and NGOs are normally particularly

good at understanding, whereas many businesspeople do not share, or have not developed, the same instincts.

Throughout the crisis the focus was on BP. Its commercial partners received little coverage. It is also telling that at a later stage in the crisis Tony Hayward, who is British, was replaced as Chief Executive by Bob Dudley, an American who is from close to the Gulf Coast himself.[4]

Questions for further consideration and class discussion

Imagine you are advising BP or a similar large oil company. Applying the lessons of this chapter, outline how you would help them prepare for future incidents of this kind.

As a PR person, what problems would you face in helping a company in such situations? How will you be able to overcome them?

A crisis is something that has the potential to damage or destroy any organisation, brand or individual career.

Careful planning is required well before any crisis appears on the horizon. This includes:

- Scenario mapping
- Response paper writing
- Audience identification
- Crisis team formation
- Staff training
- Crisis manual production

Research and analyse a current or recent crisis and its PR handling by the people and organisation involved. What lessons can be learned?

PART

4

CONCLUSION

CHAPTER 15

PUBLIC RELATIONS: INTO THE FUTURE

INTRODUCTION

Where is PR heading? Is it, as the advertising industry appears to have done already, reaching maturity and now heading for a middle age of uneven health? Will the critics of PR have their day and mount an effective backlash? Or will PR continue to forge ahead, particularly in the new democracies and developing world? And if it does continue to grow, will it follow the currently dominant Anglo-Saxon model or will it take off in a new direction? What shape will the PR industry of the future take? PR has come a long way but has further to go, and its role is being played out against a constantly changing backdrop. In particular the media are changing and face many challenges. This section looks at the way in which public relations is likely to evolve, and how the part it plays in our lives may change.

LEARNING OBJECTIVES

This chapter will enable you to reflect on the way PR is evolving internationally *and* in the part of the world with which you are most directly concerned. It will enable you to reflect on questions such as:

- What will the PR industry look like in coming decades?
- How will political, social and economic change affect PR?
- What impact will changes in the media, including the rise of new, online media, have on PR?
- Will PR's relationship with the other marketing disciplines change – and if so how?
- Which PR specialisms will thrive and why?
- What issues will preoccupy tomorrow's PR people?

❛❛ Increasingly, the marketing world is becoming two-paced or even three-paced, geographically and functionally. Asia Pacific, Africa and the Middle East and Central and Eastern Europe are outpacing the US and the US is outpacing Western Europe; the internet and other new technologies are outpacing network television, newspapers and periodicals.

Sir Martin Sorrell, Chief Executive, WPP Group.[1]

THE GROWTH OF THE PR INDUSTRY

Factors driving growth

In most parts of the world PR is a young discipline. Even in its birthplace, the USA, it is only just over 100 years old. However PR is in demand. Setting aside economic crises (which it has weathered quite well), it has generally enjoyed exponential growth – that is to say it has grown faster – often much faster – than the economies within which it operates. In many of the countries which have emerged in the last two decades from the grip of planned economies and controlled media systems PR is surging forward, even if it is sometimes a little unsteady as it struggles to find its feet.

In our view there are four main drivers of the massive growth in PR which most countries have witnessed:

- *Globalisation.* Once upon a time most people lived in small tight-knit communities, and the pace of change was usually slow. Most sellers knew, or could at least communicate directly with, buyers. Accelerating change, including the industrial revolution and transport improvements, leading to greater volumes of trade at greater distances, made this less and less true. Increasingly mass communication through the media supplemented and took the place of direct communication. It was in this context that the advertising industry took its modern form and PR, as we have seen (see Chapter 1), came into being. Now the information revolution and the development of international marketplaces which service the needs of billions of increasingly prosperous consumers make mass global communications necessary, even if the old Unilever motto, *think globally, act locally,* still seems to hold good. Looking ahead, it is hard to imagine any country or major company which is serious about its ambitions and which does not make use of public relations (even if avoids using the term).

- *Reduced state ownership.* The process that began with President Reagan and UK Prime Minister Thatcher in the 1980s has cascaded around the world as governments have abandoned state ownership of business. After the Berlin Wall came down in 1989 more and more countries decided that the state was an inefficient provider of goods and services. State assets were sold off. Modern management and marketing techniques were introduced. This was good news for PR. State-owned monopolies have a limited need to communicate – by definition their customers have no choice – but the fates of competitive, privately owned businesses are determined by their ability to communicate with many different audiences, including their existing and potential customers. Moreover direct state control of the much of the commercial world was frequently replaced by government oversight and regulation. Concerns about the impact of this on business have meant that businesses increasingly invest in lobbying services (see Chapter 6). Meanwhile the remaining government departments and agencies have had to become more customer-focused and demonstrate value for money – and as a result spend increasing amounts of taxpayers' money communicating. Luckily for PR, it seems extremely unlikely that any major country will return to state ownership and centralised planning. Indeed governments have been at pains to emphasise that their interventions in the banking sector during the financial crisis which began in 2008 were to be temporary. The market economy – and its handmaiden PR – seems to be here to stay.

- *The growth of the media, including the internet and 24/7news.* Organisations have never been under so much scrutiny. In the past angry customers could usually be isolated if not ignored, but today they can band together quickly online and, if they so desire, seek to change or try to destroy those who have upset them. Similarly, rolling news and a general explosion in media channels mean that there are more opportunities proactively to communicate your point of view (but also to be attacked!) than before. All of this is good for PR. Greater volumes of media content have not been accompanied by a matching rise in the number of journalists, making cash-strapped media industries increasingly reliant on PR for 'free' content. And, even as print media sales decline, new forms of digital media are emerging, requiring the skills of a PR practitioner. More media, greater media fragmentation and greater audience segmentation mean more work for more PR people if organisations want to communicate their messages.

- *The death of political philosophies and the rise of single issues.* With the triumph of free market thinking, voters can find fewer and fewer distinctions between different political parties (despite lots of rhetoric to the contrary!). This is reflected in lower levels of participation in traditional political life, although, as we have seen, political parties and governments are increasingly voracious users of PR services themselves (see Chapter 6). Instead people's interest and active support is turning to single issues, such as the environment, world poverty, animal rights and equal opportunities. In each case there are many groups not only trying to further their cause, but often trying to persuade people to support them rather than rival groups. This demands a great deal of PR activity.

So what could hold PR back? The enemies of PR would seem to be state ownership, import tariffs (restricting global trade), and media censorship. At the time of writing the worldwide trend – with some obvious exceptions – is positive for PR. Moreover the relatively free and unregulated way in which PR people operate has been to their advantage. PR can be contrasted with the advertising industry, which fights constant skirmishes with government and others, precisely because advertising will always be high profile and lends itself to regulation. PR firms and PR departments can recruit anyone they like – the judgement is theirs – and can choose how they organise themselves and operate. In this way they have been able to adapt themselves swiftly to meet new needs and challenges in ways that would be difficult if their work was tightly controlled.

PR as an Anglo-Saxon phenomenon

PR may have spread around the world, but it is worth considering why it is more important in Anglo-Saxon cultures than in the capitalist economies of continental Europe or Japan. Of course some form of 'PR' – unconsciously and in other guises – has always been practised in such societies, but there seems to be some catching-up to do with what, in historic terms, is a relatively new American innovation. In general other countries seem now to be moving towards a more Anglo-Saxon use of PR. In considering why PR has flourished so strongly in the Anglo-Saxon world the following factors bear examination:

- *Anglo-Saxon commercial culture* has traditionally been particularly vigorous and competitive – or, in the eyes of critics, ruthless. The emergence of PR in its modern form coincided with anti-trust legislation in the United States, which sought to break up monopolies. In the United Kingdom the boom in PR is associated with the free market reforms of the Thatcher era. PR meets business's need to be assertive and to maximise competitive advantage by making itself heard (and indeed by defending itself) in the marketplace. The huge financial markets – New York, London – of the Anglo-Saxon world place a particular emphasis on PR as they respond instantly to information and opinion, both of which can quickly and sharply influence the value of shares, commodities and currencies. Other countries have moved in this direction, but more hesitantly. Many have traditions of a more consensual approach to business, and the Anglo-Saxon brand of capitalism (with PR as one of its weapon systems) is viewed with some nervousness or even distaste. However, the current evidence in places as far apart as China and France is of a move towards the Anglo-Saxon model, or at least a finessed version thereof.
- *Long traditions of press freedom* in the USA, UK and other Anglo-Saxon countries have also had an impact. Everyone – even the most powerful politicians

and business leaders – cannot be certain that they will be able to say what they want via the press, and, indeed, has to live with a nagging anxiety about what might be said about them and their organisations. Moreover, other forms of news media – from radio and television, to digital media such as blogs – have inherited much of the more confident and combative tradition of the press. PR is an attempt to deal with this uncertainty. In many countries the tradition of media freedom is not as well established, and the media often pull their punches when discussing large companies and political leaders. Once again the world seems to be heading in an Anglo-Saxon direction. There are signs of the media becoming freer and less passive, even (at times) in countries such as China, while French political leaders have found that their media have discovered a new appetite for personal attacks.

- *Opposition parties and powerful pressure groups* supply the media with ammunition and back up the media's role in exercising vigilance. While such parties and campaigning groups exist beyond the Anglo-Saxon world, the tradition is undoubtedly more deeply rooted and stronger in north-west Europe and North America than in much of the European continent or most of Asia. Not only are pressure groups great users of PR resources in their own right, but they also compel the business world and governments to deploy PR resources to counter their campaigns. There are no signs of this trend slowing down, and it is spreading internationally. Indeed it seems likely that as wealth and education grow, often prompting demands for democracy and reform, so will the call for PR.

In 2007 a BBC environment correspondent concluded that activists in India were beating biotech companies and the government in the battle for public opinion over genetically modified food. As a result farmers had been burning their GM crops.[2]

- *Democracy* is of course not unique to the Anglo-Saxon world, but it is particularly well established there, and it takes time – generations even – to establish the deeper characteristics of democratic rule. This implies much more than rule by an elected government. It also involves an unceasing public debate and a clash of ideas, much of which take place in the media and are facilitated by PR people. When countries emerge from dictatorship it can take a while for public debate of this type to become established, and some suspicion and stigma may be attached to any form of persuasion as it is associated with the propaganda of the past regime. For example it has been argued that the notoriety of Nazi propaganda retarded the growth of PR in the post-war German federal republic, as did communism in East Germany. It is notable that now Germany has the biggest PR industry in mainland Europe.

How different is France?

Jean-Pierre Beaudoin, Managing Director, Groupe i&e,
France's top PR consultancy

French society is shaped by history and geography, as is the case for any country. The specificities of France are *centralism*, *colbertism* and *activism*.

Centralism: The Paris area represents 20% of the population on hardly 5% of the territory, and 100% of national decision centres, whether political or economic. And yet, more and more opinion is shaped at the level of the 22 regions, which gain decision power for their own affairs. The PR profession is mostly located in Paris, but there are excellent professionals in the regions, and PR needs, too.

Colbertism[3]: the State has a say in everything. At all levels: national, regional (22), departmental (100) or town (36,000, of which 32,000 have fewer than 2,000 inhabitants). There are laws and regulations on all aspects of daily life, many with an impact on communication as regards health, finance, labour, diversity, the French language, etc ... You cannot be a PR professional of good standard if you disregard the rôle of public authorities.

Activism: the number of associations in France is very high, and a large number of French people are members of associations of all kinds, from sports to culture, to environment, to human rights, etc. This provides for a lively public debate on any subject, and the media pay attention to activist groups of all kinds. Watching public opinion and working with public opinion requires good intelligence on militant life in the public space.

In that context, the French media are economically weak but politically influential. No one so-called national daily (mostly read in Paris) reaches a circulation of 500,000 copies. TV news has the strongest impact but the lowest credibility of all media. The French are good at the internet, and thus more and more hooked into the global trends. But the language remains a strong factor.

The French corporate culture is not prone to resorting to consultants. The French PR agency market is about one fifth the size of the British one, in national economies of comparable sizes.

www.i-e.fr

THE FUTURE FOR PR

Against this background, what is the likely future for the PR industry? This is where any debate must enter the realm of – informed – speculation.

In our view the PR consultancy market in the United States and United Kingdom is now mature. The industry will continue to grow, albeit with economic hiccups along the way, but not at the same spectacular rates witnessed in past decades. There will be changes, but the range and nature of specialist provision will not change dramatically over the next decade, despite claims to the contrary.

Corporate Social Responsibility

One area which firms specialise in – and which may attract new entrants – is corporate social responsibility (CSR), although some of its advocates will continue to give it other names.

As we have seen (see Chapter 8), CSR is a new term – designed to attract more fee income and a place in the boardroom – for what is an old practice. Whether it is about being 'responsible' will remain a moot point as self-interest always comes into play. Indeed there is a danger that PR's claim to 'own' CSR may, given public cynicism about PR, undermine the credibility of some genuinely positive moves by corporations.

We predict that in a few years' time CSR will be talked about less. This will not be because moves to improve corporate citizenship have ceased, but because companies will have realised that trying to ghettoise CSR is counterproductive and creates suspicions. It will also be because they will have come to mistrust PR people who claim to be specialists in CSR, an area of activity which meets none of the criteria we have identified as preconditions for specialist PR activity (see pp. 85–87).

Digital PR

So-called digital PR firms are a more recent band of newcomers. The name is confusing because it refers to neither an audience nor a particular aspect of PR, but instead to a specific communication channel: 'digital media'. It is an example of PR firms seeking competitive advantage by surfing a trend. In our view this will be short-lived. Digital media are vitally important, but, as the main PR consultancies grow accustomed to them, claiming to be 'digital' will become redundant. For PR people digital media are a means to an end, not an end in themselves. It is worth bearing in mind that there are hardly any PR consultancies devoted to other media categories, be they TV or print.

Internal communications

Internal PR is a major force which is here to stay, but we do not predict a major expansion in its practice. As an activity the emphasis will remain in-house – it is, after all, *internal* communications. For a long time consultancy PR people have predicted a surge in internal communications, but it has not happened. The major exception is in emerging economies where modern employment practices are still being learned.

Lobbying

Some have argued that with the growth in regulation by government and international bodies, lobbying or public affairs will become a mainstream PR skill. It is true that generalists will have to develop a better understanding of the political process. However, the obsessive nature of the political world and the peculiarities of political 'animals', together with the importance of tactics other than media relations, mean that lobbying will remain a separate, powerful, but – outside a few key centres of power such as Washington DC and Brussels – relatively small discipline. Lobbying will continue to be controversial, for the reasons we have seen, with negative publicity and – almost inevitably – fresh scandals bubbling up from time to time. It has faced, and will face, much more serious pressure for regulation than almost any other area of PR.

Financial PR

As long as capitalism and the financial and equity markets survive there will be financial PR specialists. Financial markets are peculiarly sensitive to news, opinion and even rumour, and the stakes are so high that companies will always pay a premium to anyone who can influence what is said. Perhaps the benefit of financial PR is more about averting problems than in adding value *per se*.

Healthcare PR

In many parts of the world this is experiencing rapid growth. Pharmaceutical companies understandably expect a return on their enormous investments in research and development, but often have to market their products in a highly regulated environment. This forces them to use highly skilled PR specialists who know the rules, and understand the specialist audiences and the products. Moreover, for obvious reasons, regulation of prescription drugs extends well beyond marketing, and the need to follow and influence such regulations puts a premium on lobbying work. The loose term healthcare PR also can be applied to many non-prescription products, and as these frequently address needs which were hitherto not apparent they are the focus of intense PR (as well as advertising) activity.

Areas of growth

So, if the United States and the United Kingdom are mature markets for PR services, where will the growth be? According to the ICCO (International Communications Consultancy Organisation), agency heads around the world see Central and Eastern Europe, Asia and the Middle East as the clear winners. In terms of sectors they predict healthcare to be the specialisation with the best growth potential, followed by finance, then the public sector and IT, as these markets catch up. This sounds correct to us.

The good news for readers of this book is that the common cry from PR firms around the world is that the biggest obstacle to growth is recruitment. The PR industry simply cannot get enough good people fast enough. One important trend will therefore be continued growth in PR courses, PR training and PR books, with more journalists jumping ship for PR.

WHAT COULD HOLD UP PR?

PR courses are flourishing, but in many countries the industry will be playing catch up for some time. In such places – and it is perhaps the biggest headache for the PR industry worldwide – there is a shortage of adequately trained or suitably experienced recruits. This has an impact on PR's other problem, its image and standing as a business discipline. When so many PR people are young and new to the industry what is gained in terms of energy and enthusiasm is lost in terms of experience and perceived seniority and authority.

> ❝❝ The Chinese market place has more demand than it has supply. It's very hard to find talented people who understand communications in China.
>
> Paul Taaffe, former Global CEO Hill & Knowlton,
> the first international PR consultancy to establish a presence in mainland China.[4]

The other big challenge to PR is its dependence upon the media to get its messages across. The mass media's straitened circumstances may make them more reliant on PR as a supplier of content, but this is no cause for PR triumphalism. The decline of traditional print media in many societies threatens to deny to PR one of its main ways of reaching its publics. Broadcast media fragmentation means that it is becoming harder and harder to reach truly mass audiences via TV and radio. Lurking in the background is a possibility that media which are too reliant on PR may lose their perceived value as third-party endorsers, although there in no evidence of this yet. All the attention is turning to digital PR, but it is far from clear that PR will be in the ascendancy in the online world. Despite plenty of brave talk and salesmanship, PR people often lack the necessary technical and data handling skills and find that other disciplines, including advertising, dominate much of the online territory. The reality is that direct online communication is inherently different from PR's real comfort zone, influencing journalists.

What's in a name?

Public relations people continue to be troubled by what to call themselves. Although the term 'PR' was coined as a polite name to describe what they do, for many the term has become shop-soiled and is avoided at all costs. Those working in NGOs always say they engage in campaigning, not PR or lobbying, and many of those who work in government or the corporate sector prefer to avoid the term PR, often basing their job titles around words such as 'communication'.

Nonetheless we think the title 'public relations' will not be disposed of so readily. All alternatives lack clarity – communications is a hopelessly vague term – and also lack the brand recognition that PR has. It is striking that the big marketing services conglomerates choose to keep using the name to distinguish their PR firms from their advertising agencies and other services – for the sound business reason that it is recognisable to their existing and potential clients.

'Public relations' also has staying power because it is thoroughly institutionalised. Bodies such as the Public Relations Society of America, the Chartered Institute of Public Relations, the Public Relations Consultants Association, the International Public Relations Association and the European Public Relations Confederation are unlikely to change their names overnight – and the same goes for the international trade paper, PR Week. Many training courses and university degree programmes also use the name.

In the end people know that changing the name only changes the wrapping paper. If there are issues that PR people have to confront then they need to do so in other ways.

The three most exciting PR markets in the world

Sally Costerton, Chairman and CEO Europe, Middle East and Africa, Hill & Knowlton

China – PR is moving very fast in China. Practitioners there are dealing not only with a rapidly expanding local Chinese client base, wanting to sell to a vast domestic market but also with increasingly large amounts of 'new' multinationals, wanting to use communications outside China to spearhead and support global expansion.

Africa – Vast opportunities to present African countries and companies with a relevant, compelling view of modern Africa and this will play an important role in attracting international investment.

The UK – defining the next generation of integrated, multi-channel communications reflecting the central role of social media.

www.hillandknowlton.com

Focusing on the areas of PR work which interest you and the places where you might wish to work, try to assess what the future might hold for public relations. In researching the topic, take into account recent developments and what people, both within the industry and beyond it, have to say about the subject.

CONCLUSION

Outsiders often see public relations as being about power, politics and spin, or launch parties and celebrities. Whilst there are elements of truth in these views – as there are in most stereotypes – the reality is that most people in PR work hard, spend a lot of time in the office planning and making preparations, and are employed by useful but unglamorous organisations in the public, commercial or not-for-profit sectors. Only a tiny percentage of PR people spend their time working for celebrities or top politicians. And yet it is true to say that a career in PR can be fast moving, exciting and very fulfilling.

PR at the centre of an organisation

PR people are among the few people in an organisation – the others are the chief executive and the financial director – who are involved in almost everything of significance that happens to it. Be it a new product launch, a public affairs campaign to change the law, a financial merger or takeover, a crisis, personnel changes at the summit of the organisation, or a campaign to win community support…whatever is top of the agenda, the PR team will be involved. Few other jobs offer such variety. One reason PR people may be coming to the fore in modern political life is that in the increasingly technocratic world of modern government and politics they are among the few who span the boundaries of the different specialisations to which others belong. Uniquely they combine a broad knowledge of the key issues in a wide range of areas with vital presentational skills and understanding of the media.

Of course there is a price that sometimes has to be paid. As we have discussed elsewhere PR is not always a well-respected or well-liked industry. Outsiders often see its practitioners as glamorous but manipulative and not always trustworthy. Why is this?

Well, apart from the popular media portrayals of PR on TV and in film as either fluffy or Machiavellian, PR's central position within organisations also places it astride some of the contradictions and dichotomies found in all aspects of life. For example, businesses assert their customers' interests are paramount and then increase prices to please shareholders. They claim they care passionately about the good of society but are happy to see people consume more of their product than is healthy. Government departments promise to spend more on the things we want without increasing taxes. Charities like to say that all their aims are noble but in fact may compete ferociously with rival charities and can be tempted to do what is popular rather than what might be right. Organisations do these things not because they are staffed by liars or people of low principle, but because some of these contradictions are all but impossible to resolve satisfactorily and because they reflect our own dilemmas as voters and consumers. We all want more hospitals without paying more in tax. We want low prices but also want ethical sourcing and manufacturing for the products we buy. We want a greener planet but also want energy consuming cars and overseas holidays.

PR, resting as it does at the heart of organisations and all that they do, has to try to communicate what are at times conflicting aims and objectives. Inevitably, as the messenger and the public voice of the organisation, it may come under attack – not least because there are always groups in society which feel an organisation should not do what it does, or should do it differently. Even bastions of seemingly selfless behaviour and moral rectitude such as churches and hospitals come under attack.

Some in the PR industry hate their public image as not entirely trustworthy manipulators. Journalists get annoyed by the fact that in the morning they may be called by a PR person trying to sell them a story about how great their organisation is, but in the afternoon the same PR may become unforthcoming or even obstructive when the journalist is pursuing an angle which is less favourable to the organisation. Our view is that almost all industries have their stereotypes and it is naive to think PR will be any different, but the very fact that PR comes under attack underlines its importance and centrality. If people like a message they call it a campaign, if they are weary of it they call it PR and if they dislike it they call it spin or propaganda. The frequent use of all these terms demonstrates how PR is central to the marketplace of ideas upon which any democracy and free economy depends. Ironically some of the most frequent users of the term 'PR' as a form of abuse are people in PR roles who are attacking the PR of those they oppose or disagree with!

PR at the centre of society

If PR is at the centre of organisations it is also at the centre of society. Politics depends on PR to communicate its policies and personalities. Businesses depend on PR to create a favourable climate for their activities and to help sell their products. NGOs depend on PR to persuade people to behave in the ways they want and to raise money for their campaigning. Countries depend on PR to help communicate their values and create a good image. Even the media use PR to persuade us to read their words, tune in to their broadcasts and visit their websites. It may be true that finance rivals communication as the essential life support system of any organisation: one can say that money touches on all aspects of organisational life. However, few who work in finance will have the breadth of experience and involvement that PR practitioners enjoy.

PR has not benefited from some of its false claims to virtue, which are at best naïve and at worst provoke derision. PR can serve any cause, good or bad. However PR, in the sense in which we describe it in this book, only thrives in democracies and is, indeed, a symptom of freedom. Dictatorships have little need to refine their skills in media handling, at least within their own borders where they control the media. They make use of persuasive techniques but ultimately rely on coercion. Democracy on the other hand is about persuasion in a competitive marketplace of ideas, and PR plays a key part in the process. (See our book PR – A Persuasive Industry? for further discussion of this.)

Nor is PR all-powerful, as some of its critics and proponents like to claim. Big companies, powerful politicians and well-known celebrities, despite enormous

PR resources, can go from hero to zero almost overnight. Many PR campaigns have little or no impact on the behaviour of the people they are trying to reach and some industries, for example pornography and illegal drugs, thrive, despite having no organised PR and despite enduring huge volumes of negative media coverage. For almost every PR message there is a counter message, either from a competitor or a critic. The fact that not all PR works is right and proper. Not every point of view, product or cause can win.

Asking if PR is good for society – as some do – is a bit like asking if food is good for people. Too much of certain kinds of PR may be bad for us. A balanced diet and healthy scepticism are desirable. Free and independent media through which to consume our PR 'food' are vital. But without PR how would all the groups in modern society argue, debate, inform and try to persuade each other?

PR jobs are relatively numerous, interesting and well-paid because PR is highly valued by all kinds of organisations. And PR is growing apace in almost every country in the world as democracy and free markets take hold.

You are entering a rapidly developing, fascinating, exciting, but sometimes deeply controversial industry. We hope you find it as interesting and enjoy it as much as we have.

- PR's growth has been fuelled by globalisation; a shift away from state ownership of business; the growth and extension of the media, including the online world; and the replacement of political philosophies with single issues.
- The rise of PR was at first particularly marked in the Anglo-Saxon world, but PR is now developing rapidly in other societies.

- The fortunes of particular PR specialisms may wax and wane. PR's role in the field of online communication is not as clear as it sometimes seeks to claim.
- PR is at the heart of modern life and is valued by all sectors of society. It is a symptom of freedom and only really flourishes in democracies or in countries where the state has to some extent relinquished control of the media.

HOW TO GET A JOB IN PR

INTRODUCTION

PR is a very popular career choice, and for a reason. It offers attractive and varied career options, and exciting opportunities for career development. These are highly appealing the world over, so you will not be the only person looking for work experience or applying for a PR job. At least the odds are stacked in your favour. The number of PR jobs is surging ahead in many countries and in others it has remained buoyant in a way that opportunities in other media industries have not – as you will find out when you meet ex-journalists in PR and would-be journalists who have changed tack and are trying to enter the PR industry.

PR is an open industry which is always hungry for new talent. Most of our students have found interesting and enjoyable work all over the world and we want to help you do the same.

LEARNING OBJECTIVE

- To help you get the job you want in PR!

If you have got so close to the end of this book you are probably starting to think seriously about how to get a job in PR. This chapter offers some top tips from us and from some of the most senior people in the PR industry.

In comparison to many careers, it is relatively easy to get started in public relations. No formal qualifications are needed. No years of training. Not even a degree. Moreover, the PR industry continues to show healthy growth rates (particularly in the newer democracies). But the industry's very popularity can make getting a job a competitive task.

To make it easier we have divided the process into four stages. Inevitably, these stages overlap, but we hope you find them useful in planning how to get on in PR.

Preparation: gaining direct or indirect experience, vacation jobs and part-time work, non-academic participation at university, building a bank of references

Even if you have a relevant qualification, the fact remains that CVs, or resumes, can look rather similar. This is a problem for potential employers who can be inundated with them. You may have a degree in PR – and evidence from the PR consultancy Ketchum in America shows that having a PR degree is one of the main indicators of future success – but there are many other people with PR degrees. There are also many PR employers who do not have degrees in PR themselves and remain uncertain of their value. So what can you do? Here are some tips:

- Get as many internships or as much work experience in PR firms and PR departments as possible. This will demonstrate both your experience and commitment to future employers as well as giving you networking opportunities. If you cannot obtain direct experience try to do something related: work in the media, sales promotion, research, advertising, events management, website development or even sales. While media relations is the key element in PR, practitioners also work in related fields. Such experience can impress potential employers.

- If you cannot work in any of the above fields, try to ensure that in any job you do you acquire useful skills. This could include anything from learning about and using the latest office software to dealing with customers, doing the accounts or just working on reception.

- Remember it is not simply paid work experience that employers are looking for. Writing is a key PR skill. Volunteer to write articles for the university newspaper or one of the magazines – print or online – run by many student societies. Employers will be interested to see what you have done and it will give you something to show and to talk about in an interview.

- Specific experience can be useful. If you are interested in corporate PR or public affairs some involvement in the student union, local politics, a pressure group or NGO can be handy. Being involved in events or booking bands could stand you in good stead if you are more interested in consumer or lifestyle PR. All of these things demonstrate to employers that you are a joiner and a doer. Many employers consider what you did at university in your spare time to be as interesting as what you studied.

- If an employer, or even a student with a formal position such as the union president, praises you, ask if you can use them as a referee when applying for jobs. Some positive words in writing are always helpful – plus their agreement to give a reference on the phone if needed. PR is about third-party endorsement. References are the ultimate third-party endorsement. And like any endorsement they have to be earned – they will not just be given regardless.

- Remember that in any job you need to be punctual, reliable, hard working and enjoyable to work with. Coming in late or taking a couple of dubious sick days during a summer job can undermine your chances when it comes to getting a reference for your first proper job. It is worth remembering that 'a reputation for reliability never lets you down'. A poor attendance record in class can also hold you back. If one of your teachers is asked for a reference (it happens!) what would they say if they were asked about your punctuality and reliability? Saying, 'but that was when I was at uni and I got hung-over a lot' is not going to impress. PR is a fun industry but employers still expect you to be in the office on time regardless of how brilliant it was the night before.

Identification: how to research the first approach, how to make contact

Getting a holiday job or internship requires care, attention and a planned and methodical approach. This is even more true for a full-time post.

Use your immediate contacts. Do your parents, other family members or friends work in a business or organisation that might have a job for you?

Attend PR industry events and strike up conversations. Industry organisations and universities often organise such occasions, and trade publications can sometimes provide advance notice of them. If you are studying PR or related subjects there should be opportunities to network and speak to guest lecturers. Don't be shy and stand apart! Remember to try to get people's business cards. Use social media. Follow PR people on Twitter and respond when appropriate. Join LinkedIn. You may be pleasantly surprised to find how keen PR people can be to offer work experience, and how often they are looking for full-time employees: it's a dynamic, opportunistic industry.

If these routes prove fruitless then you need to start researching. In almost every country there will be a trade association for PR consultancies. Their website will usually list the member PR firms, and give links to their own websites. But do not forget most PR jobs are not in consultancy but in-house. Is there a business, charity or NGO you know, or are interested in, which may need PR help? The web is a fantastic research tool.

Once you have identified some target organisations read up about them and, if you can, find the name of the person you should contact. (This is sometimes given in the 'contact us' page on websites, and often there are special pages on organisations' websites which deal with recruitment and work experience.) If you cannot find a specific name for job applications – and in smaller firms and consultancies there often will not be one – find the name of the managing director or the person who is in charge of the area or activity you are interested in. Try to avoid an anonymous 'Dear Sir or Madam' approach.

Having found an organisation and a name, email or phone them (unless they specify that you should write a letter).

When emailing it is usually better to use the person's family name rather than their given name. So Mr Morris not Trevor. If they reply signing off with their first name then you can use their forename thereafter. Try to keep your covering email or letter short and to the point. If you can, make the first paragraph personal and relevant to them. For example: 'I see you have recently won the prestigious PR account for Moroccan Tourism. I am a PR graduate, have undertaken work experience in two travel PR firms and have published several articles on my travel experiences. I would very much like.... ' and then say what you are after – a job, internship or work experience, and when you are available. Don't try to put your whole CV into the letter but only the few points that are particularly relevant to the job and the employer. Concentrate on what matters to the employer (getting good people to work for them) – not what matters to you. And proof – and then proof again – your letter and CV. Grammatical errors and spelling mistakes can consign your application to the trash can in seconds.

Your CV should be pasted on to the bottom of your email rather than sent as an attachment. Some attachments from unknown sources are immediately sent to the 'spam' folder. And, even if they are not, some organisations tell staff not to open attachments from unknown sources to avoid viruses. Moreover scrolling down is easier than opening an attachment – every little thing can help when applying for a job!

The CV itself should be no more than two pages, with the most relevant and most recent experience – including your degree and any relevant work background or special skills – at the top. It should also include full contact details (phone numbers, address and email) at the top. Be careful with what you say under personal interests. Not everyone approves of hunting, likes very religious people or understands why trainspotting is an interesting hobby! One male graduate we know made much in his CV of the fact that he played football to a high level. This might have stood him in good stead with interviewers with an interest in football, but unfortunately he was always interviewed by women – PR is a highly feminised industry – none of whom seemed interested in his sporting prowess.

Once you have sent an email application you MUST check your emails every day and reply immediately if you receive any response. If they email you and do not hear from you for four days they will assume that you are inefficient or do not care.

As an alternative to emailing you can phone, but if so make sure you have an email and CV ready to send immediately if they show any interest. And if you phone, plan what you are going to say – this should broadly be what you might put in your email's opening paragraph.

Be prepared for rejection. Sadly some firms do not even bother to reply to applicants. Do not take it personally. Sometimes it will be because you lack some experience or qualification they are looking for. Sometimes it might just be that the job has already been filled or they have no vacancies. Whatever it is, keep on trying. One of the great things about the PR industry is that there are literally thousands of openings. You will get there in the end.

Presentation: the interview – preparation, arrival and the interview itself

So you have got an interview. What do you do?

There is no excuse, given the wonders of the world wide web, in not knowing about the organisation and indeed the person or people you are meeting. Failure to do some homework shows a lack of initiative and interest. Look at the news releases they have been producing. See what they say about themselves. Use Google to find out what the media have been saying about them. Check the trade press, such as PR Week: if they've featured in it recently you want to be aware of what has been said. Think about the character and culture of the organisation: PR spans some radically different working environments. Try to find out a bit about the background of the people you are meeting – a shared enthusiasm for a particular football team or hobby can be a great ice breaker, and it can also help you avoid putting your foot in it.

Think about a few questions you would like to ask the interviewer. Most people are trained to ask the interviewee – usually towards the end of the interview – if there are any questions they would like to ask. These questions can be about the job itself or the organisation, or both.

Try to dress in a style that suits the organisation that you are visiting. The PR industry operates in so many fields that this can vary considerably. You can often get a feel for what is appropriate by looking at the photographs on their website. If it is an in-house department dress codes may well be influenced by what people wear elsewhere in the organisation, and consultancy staff often dress in a similar style to the kind of clients with whom they spend most time. But as a general rule, tend towards smart rather than casual and avoid flamboyance, high fashion, very high heels, short skirts and visible cleavage. You want a job, not a date!

Arrive about ten minutes early – but not much earlier. If transport or traffic might be a problem set off in good time. (If you arrive far too early go and have a soft drink in a cafe – not coffee as you want to avoid coffee breath. And if you are a smoker have your last cigarette at least half an hour beforehand and then use a mouth spray and apply a little scent or aftershave.)

Arriving late leaves a terrible impression, but if something goes wrong do at least ring to explain you are delayed. Moreover, if you arrive ten minutes early you will be able to gain further useful information. Many organisations have a book of press cuttings in reception, certificates and awards they have won and other useful material. You can even chat to the receptionist if they are not too busy.

Do not sit down in reception unless you know there will be a long wait. Reception chairs are often both low and soft and getting out of them can be ungainly. Much better to remain standing so you can walk forward confidently and shake the hand of the person who has come to meet you. And if it is hot make sure your hand is dry before you shake hands – so do not carry your briefcase in your right hand as it may make it sweaty.

Have a question or observation prepared for the first few minutes such as: 'This is a nice office. How long have you worked here?' Or 'I see from the information in reception that you recently won x award. You must be very pleased.' This may sound like flattery. It is. But we all like a little flattery, provided it is realistic and helps put the interviewer at ease – believe it or not interviewers can be nearly as nervous as interviewees.

You should have thought about what questions they might ask you and have some answers prepared. Why are you interested in them? Why do you want to work in PR? What have you done or achieved that you are proud of? What are you good at? What are you not so good at? This last question is usually asked after it has been established what they are looking for, so you can focus on something that is not key to the job –such as not liking spreadsheets. You can also use a negative as a positive... 'I'm a positive person and sometimes need to be prompted to look at the negative...' in effect saying 'I'm an optimistic go-getter'.

Make sure you are up to date with what is happening in the news. PR is very much about media relations in one form or another. Applicants who appear to be unaware of what is happening in the world, or at least in the sector in which the organisation operates, are unlikely to do well in an interview where many of the questions may well be about your thoughts on topical issues.

Be prepared for some small, on-the-spot tests. PR consultancies often ask interviewees for full-time jobs to write a press release based on some basic information. If you are asked back for a second interview they might even ask you to make a small presentation.

Beware of sounding negative or depressed. Sometimes people who have already had four or five interviews develop a defeatist tone and even posture. It is understandable but needs to be avoided. Imagine success!

At the end of the interview thank your interviewers, ask if there is anything you have not covered that they want to know about and finally ask when and how you are likely to hear if you have got the position. Do not call to chase until the day after they said they would let you know.

If you do not get the job try to find out why. Often they will just say it was very difficult but there was a slightly better candidate. However, sometimes you may get some useful feedback. Although painful at the time, you can then work on improving your chances at the next interview.

If you do get the job read the next section.

Induction: getting started – punctuality, appearance, enthusiasm and being nice to the receptionist and admin people

Getting your first job in PR is a great beginning, but it is only a beginning. First impressions matter.

Be on time – every day.

Be willing and cooperative. You may have plans to be the boss, but if you are asked to make the tea or go to the post office do it, and do it with good grace. The person asking you will almost certainly have to have done the same earlier in their career.

Be friendly to everyone but particularly receptionists and administrative staff. They can make your life much easier if they like you – and make it quite difficult if they do not. (Bosses know that most staff are nice to their face. They find out how nice new staff really are by asking the admin staff.)

Ask questions. If you are asked to do something and you do not know how to, or do not understand, say so. It is less embarrassing than doing the job badly.

Try to socialise after work with other members of staff – but do not let alcohol get the better of you. Remember in the early days people are still forming their opinions about you.

Most PR firms and PR departments are friendly places, but do remember that people are there to do a job and not to look after you. Weaknesses and idiosyncrasies that your lecturers may have tolerated will be less welcome at work – if you produce substandard work you will be harming not only yourself but also undermining the efforts of others. Even typos and grammatical errors can cost money and cause embarrassment. Lateness and absences can throw the plans of others into disarray. Be prepared to work well with people who wouldn't be your first choice of team member, and to work for people with whom you cannot always agree.

Be keen. Volunteer for new projects and jobs. And praise your boss and colleagues. They like praise as much as you do!

Good luck.

With some friends create a brief job description for a post you might apply for.

Draft your CV. Show it to someone who has interviewed people.

Draft a short application letter and show it to someone who has interviewed people.

Rehearse interviews, including your arrival.

Practise the questions an interviewer might ask, including the difficult ones.

Practise the questions you might ask.

Practise being the interviewer...put yourself in their shoes.

TOP TIPS FOR GETTING A JOB IN PR

❝ You must immerse yourself in public relations through reading, placements and 'doing it' as a student, as that will help convince potential employers that you have the commitment they are looking for.

> Professor Tom Watson, Professor of Public Relations,
> The Media School, Bournemouth University

❝ You need to study the craft, get experience wherever you can (try helping out voluntary groups) and then network, network, network.

> Paul Mylrea, Head of Press & Media Relations,
> BBC and President of the CIPR

❝ Getting a job in PR is all about relationships. Get out there and network, on- and offline, and make yourself known on the PR and social media scene.

> Paul Borge, Head Of Digital,
> Consolidated Communications

❝ Get yourself a good work placement. Much better to have a senior experienced mentor in a small company who can give you meaty assignments and good coaching than making tea at a household name company.

> Sally Costerton, Chairman and CEO,
> EMEA, Hill & Knowlton

❝ Be prepared to start at the bottom – keep an eye on which agencies have won new business and write a letter to the head of the agency. Don't email. Send a presentation that is creative and shows you know the media and that agency/ brand. It could be a spoof Q&A from a magazine about you. Something that will capture their attention. What have you got to lose?

> Julian Vogel, Director Modus Publicity /
> Modus Dowal Walker (Top Fashion PR firm)

▲▲ Help potential employers get to know and like you through social media conversations, then dazzle them with a snappy CV and a covering letter that captures your uniqueness.

Simon Cohen, founder and Managing Director, Global Tolerance

▲▲ It might sound heretical, but don't feel you have to do a degree in PR. If you are a good writer, listener and communicator who is prepared to get their hands dirty then read up on the news and apply. And when you go for an interview have at least a couple of examples of PR campaigns you've admired or disliked up your sleeve. I'm amazed how often people don't.

Duncan Burns, Senior Vice President, Hill & Knowlton

▲▲ Be your own PR person. I recruit not only for the skills but also for the personality and the power to persuade. Be persistent but don't over-egg it – the CV has to match the reality.

Karen Myers, Corporate Communications Director IPC Media,
the consumer publisher.

▲▲ Breaking into the industry is not as hard as you might think. Staying in it, is. Possibly even harder. Those who survive and thrive almost invariably have these characteristics: 1. They've studied PR, communications, or marketing at university; 2. If not, they've completed work experience assignments at an agency or within a communications department; 3. They display above-average intelligence, humour and generosity.

David Gallagher, President, Ketchum Pleon

▲▲ Anyone wanting to do PR in France should:

- have a good level of professionalism, as the French profession is good by any standard.
- Understand the local context and how it interfaces with the rest of the world, because that's where non-French professionals bring value.
- Speak, read and write French enough to use at least French and their mother tongue professionally.

Non-French PR professionals are active in France with agencies serving international clients and in the structure of multinational companies needing a national of their HQ country in their local business.

Jean-Pierre Beaudoin, managing director,
Groupe i&e, Paris

NOTES

(Web-based references relate to material available at the time of writing).

CHAPTER 1

1 Theaker, Alison (ed.), *The Public Relations Handbook* (Routledge, 2002), p. 3.
2 www.prsa.org
3 www.cipr.co.uk
4 Quoted in Theaker, Alison (ed), *The Public Relations Handbook* (Routledge, 2002), p. 4.
5 *Absolutely Fabulous*, Series 3, BBC Worldwide DVD 2002, 'Jealous'
6 http://business.timesonline.co.uk/tol/business/law/article1517388.ece.
7 Morris and Goldsworthy, *PR - A Persuasive Industry? Spin, Public Relations and the Shaping of the Modern Media* (Palgrave Macmillan, 2008), pp. 102–103.
8 *Ibid.*
9 Harrison, Shirley, *Public Relations: An Introduction* (Thompson Learning, 2000), p. 10.
10 *Ibid.*, p. 104
11 *Ibid.*, p. 105.
12 *Bridget Jones's Diary* (Universal Studios, 2001, dir. Sharon Maguire, 132 min).
13 Morris and Goldsworthy, *PR - A Persuasive Industry? Spin, Public Relations and the Shaping of the Modern Media* (Palgrave Macmillan, 2008), p. 1.
14 *Ibid.*
15 http://www.prweek.com/go/prcensus/
16 http://www.echoresearch.com/en/imageofpr/
17 http://www.carma.com/research/CARMA%20Executive%20Summary%20-%20State%20of%20the%20PR%20Industry%202005.pdf.
18 Coombs, W Timothy and Holladay, Sherry J, *It's Not Just PR: Public Relations in Society* (Blackwell, 2007).

19 *Absolutely Fabulous* Series 4, BBC Worldwide DVD 2002, commentary by Jon Plowman.
20 *Sex and the City*, HBO, Episode 2.
21 *Ibid.*, Episode 1.
22 *Sliding Doors* (Intermedia Films, 1998, dir. Michael Curtiz, 91 min.)
23 Morris and Goldsworthy, PR - *A Persuasive Industry? Spin, Public Relations and the Shaping of the Modern Media* (Palgrave Macmillan, 2008), p. 13.
24 http://www.gorkana.com/uk/index.php/gorkana-meets-lord-tim-bell/
25 Jacquie L'Etang, *Public Relations: Concepts, Practice and Critique* (Sage, 2009), p. 3.
26 Jacquie L'Etang, Director M.Sc. (full time), University of Stirling. Debate: *PR: A Persuasive Industry? Spin, public relations and the shaping of the modern media. Ethical Space: The International Journal of Communication Ethics*, Vol 6, No 1, 2009, p. 48.
27 *Public Relations in Britain: A History of Professional Practice in the 20th Century* (Lawrence Erlbaum Associates, 2004)
28 (Bodley Head, 2008)
29 (Lawrence Erlbaum, 1992)
30 *Ibid.*, p. 16.
31 *Ibid.*, p. xiv.
32 *Ibid.*, p. 2.
33 (Holt, Rinehart and Winston, 1984)
34 Jacquie L'Etang, *Public Relations in Britain: A History of Professional Practice in the 20th Century* (Lawrence Erlbaum Associates, 2004), p. 5.
35 (Routledge, second edition, 2006)
36 *Lobbyists for Hire* (Dartmouth Press, 1996).
37 *Rethinking Public Relations: PR, Propaganda and Democracy* (Routledge, 2006), pp. xii–xiii.
38 *Ibid.*, p. 169.
39 http://www.timesonline.co.uk/tol/life_and_style/education/article7119993.ece

40 Davies, Nick, *Flat Earth News: An Award-winning Reporter Exposes Falsehood, Distortion and Propaganda in the Global Media*, (Chatto & Windus, 2008), p. 85.

41 Jackall, Robert and Hirota, Janice M., *Image Makers: Advertising, Public Relations, and the Ethos of Advocacy* (University of Chicago Press, 2000), p. 24.

42 Davies, Aeron, *Public Relations Democracy: Public Relations, Politics and the Mass Media in Britain* (Manchester University Press, 2002), p. 179.

43 Davies, Nick, *Flat Earth News: An Award-winning Reporter Exposes Falsehood, Distortion and Propaganda in the Global Media*, (Chatto & Windus, 2008).

44 The Director for the Centre for Investigative Journalism at City University in London has conceded that three-quarters of "investigative reporting" now actually stems from NGOs, with universities also performing an important role (one might add in, alongside campaigning NGOs, their close relations, "Think tanks"): http://ftpapp.app.com.pk/en_/index.php?option=com_content&task=view&id=132103&Itemid=2.

45 Davies, Nick, *Flat Earth News: An Award-winning Reporter Exposes Falsehood, Distortion and Propaganda in the Global Media*, (Chatto & Windus, 2008).

46 This case study is partly derived from Karen S Miller's *The Voice of Business: Hill & Knowlton and Postwar Public Relations* (University of North Carolina Press, 1999). See also www.hillandknowlton.com

CHAPTER 2

1 Stauber, John, and Rampton, Sheldon, *Toxic Sludge Is Good For You: Lies, Damn Lies and the Public Relations Industry* (Constable & Robinson, 2004), p. 22; and Ross, Irwin, *The Image Merchants: The Fabulous World of American Public Relations* (Weidenfeld & Nicolson, 1960), p. 114.

2 http://www.prweek.com/uk/search/article/233327//

3 http://news.bbc.co.uk/1/hi/england/oxfordshire/8339652.stm

4 http://www.sourcewatch.org/index.php?title=Peter_Melchett and bbc.co.uk

5 www.instituteforpr.org

6 Kant, Immanuel, *Groundwork for the Metaphysics of Morals: On a Supposed Right to Lie Because of Philanthropic Concerns*. Translated by James W. Ellington, new expanded edition (Hackett Publishing: Indiana, 1993) pp. 63–68.

7 (Allison & Busby, 2003)

8 Jackall, Robert and Hirota, Janice M., *Image Makers: Advertising, Public Relations and the Ethos of Advocacy* (University of Chicago Press, 2000).

9 Stauber, John, and Rampton, Sheldon, *Toxic Sludge Is Good For You: Lies, Damn Lies and the Public Relations Industry* (Constable & Robinson, 2004), pp. 172–174.

10 http://news.bbc.co.uk/1/hi/talking_point/forum/1604226.stm

CHAPTER 3

1 *Starsuckers* (S2S Productions, 2009, dir. Chris Atkins, 100 min.)

2 *PR Week*, 6.5.2011, Top 150 Consultancies.

3 Research by Centre for Economics and Business Research (CEBR).

4 According to research by UK-based PR search specialist Watson Helsby, 85% of communications directors in the FTSE 100 (Financial Times top 100 quoted businesses) report directly to their CEO.

5 Morris and Goldsworthy, *PR – A Persuasive Industry? Spin, Public Relations and the Shaping of the Modern Media* (Palgrave Macmillan, 2008), p. 123.

6 http://news.bbc.co.uk/1/hi/business/3199822.stm

7 Morris and Goldsworthy, *PR – A Persuasive Industry? Spin, Public Relations and the Shaping of the Modern Media* (Palgrave Macmillan, 2008), pp. 42–45.

CHAPTER 4

1 Moloney, Kevin, *Rethinking Public Relations: PR, Propaganda and Democracy* (Routledge, 2006), p. 135 (based on Bournemouth University data).

2 Corporate Affairs Directors and 'Heads of PR' often have only a 'dotted-line' responsibility for marketing PR as they are not usually seen as experts in the hard-nosed, data driven world of marketing and sales, but more as guardians of corporate reputation, CSR, Public Affairs and financial results. Many in-house and consultancy marketing PR people answer directly to a marketing or brand director, rather than the head of PR.

3 http://www.cim.co.uk/resources/understandingmarket/definitionmkting.aspx

4 There are those that say there are 7 marketing P's ... but 4 will suffice for this book!

5 www.adassoc.org.uk

6 *The Advertising Handbook* (Routledge, second edition, 2002), p. 175.

7 http://news.bbc.co.uk/1/hi/business/3704669.stm

8 http://www.bbc.co.uk/news/business-10952714
9 Harrison, Shirley, *Public Relations: An Introduction* (Thomson Learning, 2000), p. 5.
10 Frill, Chris, *Marketing Communications*, (Prentice Hall, second Edition, 1999), p. 613.
11 *Integrated Marketing Communications*, (CIM Publishing) p. 180.
12 http://www.ourawardentry.com.au/bestjob/, http://news.bbc.co.uk/1/hi/magazine/8037728.stm

CHAPTER 5

1 Olins, Wally, *On Brand* (Thames & Hudson, 2003), p. 75
2 Bunting, Madeleine, *Willing Slaves: How the Overwork Culture is Ruling Our Lives* (Harper Collins, 2004), pp. 109 and 99.
3 http://www.prweek.com/uk/search/article/94936/platform-cruel-kind-increase-profits-want-achieve-effective-internal-communications-canrsquot-always-afford-mr-nice-guy-says-alan-riley/.
4 http://www.bbc.co.uk/news/uk-england-birmingham-12221913, http://www.personneltoday.com/articles/2010/01/20/53750/cadbury-employees-wait-for-news-on-jobs-after-kraft.html

CHAPTER 6

1 http://www.independent.co.uk/news/media/lord-bell-id-do-anything-for-margaret-490592.html
2 http://www.spinwatch.org.uk/-news-by-category-mainmenu-9/173-pr-industry/1117-lord-bell-id-do-anything-for-margaret
3 http://www.timesonline.co.uk/tol/news/politics/article7072367.ece
4 *Public Affairs News*, February 2011, p. 1.
5 *New York Times*, Washington, 28.4.1992.
6 Morris, Trevor, and Goldsworthy, Simon, *Public Relations for the New Europe* (Palgrave Macmillan, 2008), p. 52.
7 http://www.time.com/time/politics/article/0,8599,1874165,00.html
8 http://www.telegraph.co.uk/news/newstopics/politics/8305506/Wife-of-Health-Secretary-Andrew-Lansley-gave-lobbying-advice.html
9 (Simon & Schuster, 1995)
10 http://euobserver.com/9/31186

CHAPTER 7

1 Morris, Trevor, and Goldsworthy, Simon, *Public Relations for Asia* (Palgrave Macmillan, 2008), p. 191.
2 www.borkowski.co.uk/our-heritage/case-studies/bringing-back-wispa/
3 TNS presentation, *PR Week*, 'Global Conference' 24.09.09.
4 http://www.prospectmagazine.co.uk/2010/01/why-the-internet-is-failing-irans-activists/
5 www.alexa.com
6 www.asa.org.uk
7 Echo entry AMEC Effectiveness Awards 2009. http://content.yudu.com/Library/A1irmw/ComunicateMagazine/resources/index.htm?refererUrl=http%3A%2F%2Fwww.yudu.com%2Fitem%2Fdetails%2F103894%2FComunicate-Magazine International-Multi Market
8 http://www.ipa.co.uk/Content/IPA-Social-presentations
9 Morris, Trevor, and Goldsworthy, Simon, *Public Relations for the New Europe* (Palgrave Macmillan 2008), p. 198.
10 http://www.blogpulse.com/
11 TNS presentation, *PR Week*, 'Global Conference' 24.09.09.
12 2008 Middleberger/SCNR Media Survey
13 http://technorati.com/
14 http://www.blogpulse.com
15 http://feedburner.com
16 http://www.sigwatch.com/
17 SEO or Search Engine Optimisation is about trying to ensure that your organisation comes out near the top in any list on a related topic on a search engine. Few people look further than the first page of a search list.
18 http://press.linkedin.com/
19 http://twitter.com/about
20 http://www.blendtec.com/willitblend/
21 http://www.telegraph.co.uk/technology/twitter/5621970/Habitat-apologises-for-Twitter-hashtag-spam.html
22 www.twitalyzer.com
23 http://www.niemanlab.org/2009/04/print-is-still-king-only-3-percent-of-newspaper-reading-actually-happens-online/
24 PR Week Awards 2010
25 TNS presentation, *PR Week*, 'Global Conference' 24.09.09.

CHAPTER 8

1 PR Week, quoted in Morris, Trevor, and Goldsworthy, Simon, *Public Relations for Asia* (Palgrave Macmillan 2008) p. 140.
2 http://www.pcworld.com/article/130390/lenovo_leads_apple_trails_in_green_rankings.html
3 *The Image Merchants: The Fabulous World of American Public Relations* (Weidenfeld & Nicolson, 1960), p. 25.

4 http://www.nottingham.ac.uk/nubs/ICCSR/aboutus.php?c=25
5 http://www.bbc.co.uk/news/uk-england-12318896, http://www.bbc.co.uk/news/business-12013069

CHAPTER 9

1 www.brandchannel.com
2 http://www.prweek.com/news/776215/Exposure-pays-thousands-Kidman-scent-row/?DCMP=ILC-SEARCH
3 http://news.bbc.co.uk/1/hi/uk_politics/8332806.stm
4 http://news.bbc.co.uk/1/hi/world/americas/3106930.stm
5 http://www.bbc.co.uk/bbcfour/documentaries/storyville/mclibel.shtml

CHAPTER 10

1 POSTAR is adapted from P R Smith's SOSTAC planning model – www.prsmith.org
2 A method developed by Peter Drucker.
3 http://www.sexysciencebydita.com/pages/video/
4 Davies, Nick, *Flat Earth News: An Award-winning Reporter Exposes Falsehood, Distortion and Propaganda in the Global Media*, (Chatto & Windus, 2008), p. 85.
5 Jackall, Robert and Hirota, Janice M., *Image Makers: Advertising, Public Relations and the Ethos of Advocacy* (University of Chicago Press, 2000), p. 24.
6 http://www.prweek.com/news/836118/Awards-PRWeek-Awards-2008-finalists/?DCMP=ILC-SEARCH
7 www.travelodge.co.uk
8 http://www.prweek.com/news/156403/EDITORIAL-Cadburys-leaves-bitter-taste-India/?DCMP=ILC-SEARCH
9 *Managing Professional Communications Agencies: How to double your profitability*, Public Relations Consultants Association, 2007.
10 The New York Times, June 2009 (figures from TNS Media, *PR Week*, 'Global Conference' 24.09.09) claimed that the average online visitor spent 4.2 hours a month on its site compared with print users who read it for 26.4 hours per month.
11 http://www.independent.co.uk/news/media/lord-bell-id-do-anything-for-margaret-490592.html
12 www.insightmkt.com/ceo_pr_briefing/findings.asp

13 http://business.timesonline.co.uk/tol/business/industry_sectors/transport/article6900107.ece
14 Adapted from AMEC. www.amecorg.com
15 Kitchen, Philip J. (ed.), *Public Relations: Principles and Practice* (Thomson Learning, 1997), p. 286.

CHAPTER 11

1 A 'pitch' is the meeting at which PR people (usually but not always PR consultants) present their plans and ideas in response to a brief (see Chapter 10). Presenting the plan is called 'pitching'. The term is derived from sales... 'the sales pitch'. It is worth remembering that a lot of PR is about selling – to clients and journalists.
2 This is an adapted version of a copyright document written by Francis Hallawell.

CHAPTER 12

1 According to the Advertising Association's Advertising Statistics Yearbook 2003, in 2002 £12,713,000,000 was spent on display advertising and £4,021,000,000 on classified advertising.
2 Dunn, Jim, *Very Private and Public Relations* (Thorogood, 2008), p. 287.
3 I keep six honest serving men
(They taught me all I knew)
Their names are How and Where and Who
What and Why and When
Rudyard Kipling, journalist and poet.
4 This section draws upon Burchfield, R, *Fowler's Modern English Usage* (Oxford University Press, 2004).
5 *PR Week*, 1.08.08
6 http://www.prweek.com/news/109259/GLOBAL-RANKINGS-2000-INDIA---hot-spot-PR-India-politically-culturally-complex-nation-economic-reform-drives-expanding-market-PR-finds-its-place-fold-Ben-Bold-reports/?DCMP=ILC-SEARCH
7 www.bellpottinger-sansfrontieres.com
8 http://news.bbc.co.uk/1/hi/uk_politics/1823120.stm

CHAPTER 13

1 http://www.prweek.com/news/669694/CAMPAIGN-GW-Travel-adds-class-Trans-Siberian-trip/?DCMP=ILC-SEARCH
2 http://www.bbc.co.uk/news/magazine-11297832

CHAPTER 14

1 http://www.nytimes.com/2001/11/16/nyregion/a-nation-challenged-the-site-workers-shore-up-wall-keeping-hudson-s-waters-out.html

2 http://news.bbc.co.uk/1/hi/world/south_asia/5239758.stm

3 Quoted in Rampton, Sheldon, and Stauber, John, *Trust Us, We're Experts: How Industry Manipulates Science and Gambles Your Future* (Tarcher/Putnam, 2001), p. 116.

4 http://www.bbc.co.uk/news/business-11828093, http://www.bbc.co.uk/news/business-12331804

CHAPTER 15

1 Morris, Trevor and Goldsworthy, Simon, *Public Relations for the New Europe* (Palgrave Macmillan 2008), p. 197.

2 http://news.bbc.co.uk/1/hi/sci/tech/6338377.stm

3 Jean-Baptiste Colbert was the long-serving finance minister to the French king Louis XIV in the seventeenth century. His ideas, which emphasised state intervention in the economy, remain influential.

4 Morris, Trevor, and Goldsworthy, Simon, *Public Relations for Asia* (Palgrave Macmillan 2008), p. 209.

GLOSSARY

Advertorial: An advertisement written and designed in the editorial style of the host medium.

AVEs (Advertising Value Equivalence): A method which measures media coverage by estimating how much it would have cost to buy the equivalent space for advertising (see p. 232).

Below the line: a term sometimes used by people in the world of advertising to describe all other forms of marketing communications activity, including PR (see p. 99).

B2B (Business-to-business): PR activity undertaken with the aim of helping a business communicate with other businesses.

B2C (Business-to-consumer): PR activity undertaken with the aim of helping a business reach consumers.

Brand: A product or company with a recognisable and distinctive identity as opposed to a commodity – for example potatoes or flour sold in plain, unmarked sacks – that has nothing to distinguish it from the competition.

CEO: Chief Executive Officer (sometimes called the Managing Director)

CFO: Chief Financial Officer (Finance Director)

Citizen Journalist: A member of the public – as opposed to a trained, salaried journalist – who uses the internet or blogs to report and comment on current and business affairs. In a similar way members of the public also increasingly provide photographs or film of key events.

Community Relations: PR activity designed to promote relationships between organisations and the communities within which they are based or operate.

Corporate Communications: Although this term is sometimes used interchangeably with PR, properly used it refers to those aspects of PR which focus on the overall reputation of the organisation, rather than, for example, day-to-day marketing objectives.

Critical Path Analysis: A plan of action that determines the optimum sequence in which actions should be undertaken for maximum effectiveness.

CSR (Corporate Social Responsibility): Refers to the increasingly popular idea that businesses have a range of social and environmental responsibilities – to their employees, suppliers, local communities and wider society – and must not only act on these concerns but be seen to act in an accountable way. PR people often play a key role in CSR.

EMEA: Business acronym for Europe, Middle East and Africa.

E-PR: Another name for online PR activity.

FMCG (Fast Moving Consumer Goods): Sometimes called consumer packaged goods. Items which are replaced regularly and hence have a quick turnover. Typically they are relatively cheap. Examples include soap, toothpaste, shaving products and detergents. Global companies such as Procter & Gamble and Unilever produce a wide range of FMCGs.

Front groups: Organisations formed by businesses to mimic NGOs and hence counter NGO campaigns which are seen as threatening their business interests (see pp. 55–56).

Goody Bag: A bag of gifts given to journalists by the host organisation after a press conference or press event. Goody bags are also often given to celebrities and key opinion formers after a PR-organised event.

Horizontal media: Media outlets which cover a wide range of subjects, in contrast to vertical media (see below). Most daily newspapers are horizontal in character.

HR: Human Resources, also known as Personnel.

Integrated Marketing Communications (IMC): The bringing together of all marketing disciplines, including PR, advertising and sales promotion, in a co-ordinated way (see p. 105). Other relevant terms are 'marcoms,' short for 'marketing communications' and 'the marketing mix.' PR used for this purpose is often referred to as marketing PR.

In-house: Term used to describe PR work undertaken within an organisation by its own employees – typically members of its PR department – as opposed to consultancy or agency work.

Internal Communication: Communication targeting the staff within an organisation rather than its customers or other stakeholders. Also called Employee Communication, Employer Branding or, particularly in times of transition, Change Management.

Intranet: An online computer-based communication system or special website only available to those working within an organisation.

IPOs (Initial Public Offerings): The first sale of a business's shares on the financial markets, an occasion which typically requires a great deal of financial PR work.

Lobbying: Any activity designed to influence the actions of government or other bodies which wield law-making, regulatory or similar powers.

Maslow's Hierarchy of Needs: A theory that asserts that societies develop through a number of stages from security, through socialisation, to self-esteem and finally self-actualisation.

Mass Markets: Markets where the product or service is widely available and affordable.

Mass Media: A term used to describe generally available and widely used media such as television, radio and popular newspapers.

Media Monitoring: Examining all relevant media for relevant coverage – of the organisation itself, of its competitors or of relevant issues. Typically this activity, which can be very time consuming, is undertaken by specialist companies which can provide newspaper and magazine cuttings and transcripts or recordings of broadcast material.

M&A (Mergers and Acquisitions): When companies join together or take over other businesses. This forms the basis of a large proportion of financial PR work.

NGOs (Non-governmental organisations): Also known as not-for-profit organisations or even sometimes as the 'third sector.' NGOs are distinct from business and government and include charities and campaigning organisations, such as Greenpeace and Amnesty International, as well as many thousands of less well-known ones.

Not-for-profit sector: Organisations, such as charities and other NGOs, which are not controlled by government and are not driven by the profit motive.

Online Press Office: Facilities for the press, such as press releases and photographs, made available by an organisation, via the Internet.

Pitch: Organisations invite PR firms to pitch for their business, This usually involves 2 or 3 PR firms presenting (pitching) their ideas on how the organisation should do its PR.

Social Networks, Social Media: Commercially hosted internet-based services that allow online interaction between people with shared social interests. Prime examples are Facebook and You Tube.

Spin: A pejorative term used to describe PR when it is seen to have been used to present a very partial view of the truth. People who undertake such work are called Spin Doctors.

Stakeholders: Anyone with an interest in an organisation – for example, its shareholders, employees, customers, suppliers, or the local community.

Third-party endorsement: The concept of an independent person offering a view on something about which someone else may make a decision. In the case of PR the 'third-party' is normally the journalist and the media organisation for which he or she works. Their independent 'endorsement' of, for example, a new product is considered to be worth more than the equivalent amount of paid-for advertising.

Third sector: A catch-all phrase for organisations which are not businesses or government controlled. Generally includes charities, NGOs and voluntary organisations.

Vertical media: Specialist media with a relatively narrow focus – they include, for example, trade magazines which are concerned with a particular business sector or profession, and consumer magazines focusing on particular hobbies and interests such as sport or fashion.

USP: Unique Selling Point or Unique Selling Proposition. A term, derived from advertising, which describes the special quality about a product which singles it out in the marketplace and should be emphasised in all communications with potential customers.

White goods: Household appliances such as refrigerators and washing machines. These are much more expensive than FMCGs (see above) but are replaced much more rarely.

SOME SUGGESTED READING AND SOURCES OF INFORMATION, STIMULATION AND ENTERTAINMENT

Bernays, Edward L., *Propaganda* (Horace Liveright, 1928).

Boorstin, Daniel J., *The Image, or What Happened to the American Dream* (Penguin, 1962).

Borkowski, Mark., *Improperganda: The Art of the Publicity Stunt* (Vision On, 2000).

Burton, Bob, *Inside Spin: The Dark Underbelly of the PR Industry* (Allen & Unwin, 2007).

Campbell, Alastair, *The Alastair Campbell Diaries*, volumes 1–3 (Arrow, 2011).

Campbell, Alastair and Stott, Richard (eds), *The Blair Years: Extracts from the Alastair Campbell Diaries* (Hutchinson, 2007).

Clifford, Max and Levin, Angela, *Max Clifford: Read All About It (Virgin Books, 2005).*

Coombs, W. Timothy and Holladay, Sherry J., *It's Not Just PR: Public Relations in Society* (Blackwell, 2007).

Cutlip, Scott M., *The Unseen Power: Public Relations. A History* (Lawrence Erlbaum, 1994).

Davies, Aeron, *Public Relations Democracy: Public Relations, Politics and the Mass Media in Britain* (Manchester University Press, 2002).

Davies, Nick, *Flat Earth News: An Award-winning Reporter Exposes Falsehood, Distortion and Propaganda in Global Media* (Chatto & Windus, 2008).

Dunn, Jim, *Very Private and Public Relations* (Thorogood, 2008).

Ewen, Stuart, *PR! A Social History of Spin* (Basic Books, 1996).

Fishkin James S., *The Voice of the People: Public Opinion and Democracy* (Yale University Press, 1997).

Fombrun, Charles, *Reputation: Realizing Value from the Corporate Image* (Harvard Business School Press, 1996).

Foreign & Commonwealth Office, *Engagement: Public Diplomacy in a Globalized World*, 2008.

Franklin, Bob, *Packaging Politics: Political Communication in Britain's Media Democracy* (Arnold, 2004).

Gregory, Martyn, *Dirty Tricks: British Airways' Secret War Against Virgin Atlantic* (Warner, 1996).

Grunig, James E (ed.), *Excellence in Public Relations and Communication Management* (Lawrence Erlbaum, 1992).

Grunig, James E. and Hunt, Todd, *Managing Public Relations* (Rinehart and Winston, 1984).

Hargreaves, Ian, *Journalism: Truth or Dare* (Oxford University Press, 2003).

Harrison, Shirley, *Public Relations: An Introduction* (Routledge, 1995, second edition published by Thomson Learning, 2000).

Hobsbawm, Julia (ed.), *Where the Truth Lies: Trust and Morality in PR and Journalism* (Atlantic, 2006).

Hollingsworth, Mark, *The Ultimate Spin Doctor: Life and Fast Times of Tim Bell* (Coronet, 1997).

Jackall, Robert and Hirota, Janice M., *Image Makers: Advertising, Public Relations, and the Ethos of Advocacy* (University of Chicago Press, 2000).

John, Steven, *The Persuaders: When Lobbyists Matter* (Palgrave Macmillan, 2002).

Keeble, Richard (ed.), *Communication Ethics Now* (Troubador, 2008).

Kitchen, Philip (ed.), *Public Relations: Principles and Practice* (Thomson Learning, 1997).

Klein, Woody, *All the Presidents' Spokesmen: Spinning the News – White House Press Secretaries from Franklin D Roosevelt to George W Bush* (Praeger, 2008).

Kunczik, Michael, *Images of Nations and International Public Relations* (Lawrence Erlbaum, 1996).

Lippmann, Walter, *Public Opinion* (George Allen & Unwin, 1922).

L'Etang, Jacquie, *Public Relations: Concepts, Practice and Critique* (Sage, 2007).

—— *Public Relations in Britain: A history of professional practice in the 20th century* (Lawrence Erlbaum Associates, 2004) .

L'Etang, Jacquie and Piezcka, Magda (eds), *Critical Perspectives in Public Relations* (International Thomson Business Press, 1996).

—— *Public Relations: Critical Debates and Contemporary Practice* (Lawrence Erlbaum, 2006).

Marchand, Roland, *Creating the Corporate Soul: The Rise of Public Relations and Corporate Imagery in American Big Business* ((University of California Press, 1998).

Marr, Andrew, *My Trade: A Short History of British Journalism* (Macmillan, 2004).

McNair, Brian, *An Introduction to Political Communication* (Routledge, 2003).

Manning, Paul, *News and News Sources: A Critical Introduction* (Sage, 2001).

Michie, David, *The Invisible Persuaders: How Britain's Spin Doctors Manipulate the Media* (Bantam, 1998).

Miller, Charles, *Politico's Guide to Political Lobbying* (Politico's, 2000).

Miller, David and Dinan, William, *A Century of Spin: How Public Relations Became the Cutting Edge of Corporate Power* (Pluto Books, 2008).

Moloney, Kevin, *Rethinking Public Relations: PR, Propaganda and Democracy* (Routledge, 2006).

Morley, Michael, *How to Manage Your Global Reputation: A Guide to the Dynamics of International Public Relations* (Macmillan 1998).

Morris, Trevor and Goldsworthy, Simon, *PR – A Persuasive Industry? Spin, Public Relations, and the Shaping of the Modern Media* (Palgrave Macmillan 2008).

—— *Public Relations for Asia* (Palgrave Macmillan 2008).

—— *Public Relations for the New Europe* (Palgrave Macmillan 2008).

Miller, Karen S., *The Voice of Business: Hill & Knowlton and Postwar Public Relations* (University of North Carolina Press, 1999).

O'Shaughnessy, Nicholas Jackson, *Politics and Propaganda: Weapons of Mass seduction* (Manchester University Press, 2004).

Palast, Greg, *The Best Democracy Money Can Buy: An Investigative Reporter Exposes the Truth about Globalization, Corporate Cons and High Finance Fraudsters* (Pluto, 2002).

Pimlott, J. A. R., *Public Relations and American Democracy* (Kennikat, 1972; first published 1951).

Pitcher, George, *The Death of Spin* (John Wiley and Sons, 2003).

Pratkanis, Anthony R. and Aronson, Elliot, *Age of Propaganda: The Everyday Use and Abuse of Persuasion* (W H Freeman, 2001).

Ross, Irwin, *The Image Merchants: The Fabulous World of American Public Relations* (Weidenfeld & Nicolson, 1960).

Scammell, Margaret, *Designer Politics: How Elections Are Won* (Macmillan, 1995).

Schudson, Michael, *Advertising, the Uneasy Persuasion: Its Dubious Impact on American Society* (Basic Books, 1986).

—— *The Sociology of News* (W W Norton, 2003).

Stauber, John and Rampton, Sheldon, *Toxic Sludge Is Good For You: Lies, Damn Lies and the Public Relations Industry* (Constable & Robinson, 2004).

—— *Trust Us, We're Experts! How Industry Manipulates Science and Gambles Your Future* (Tarcher/Putnam, 2001).

Taylor, Philip, *Munitions of the Mind: A History of Propaganda from the Ancient World to the Present Era* (Manchester University Press, 1995).

Theaker, Alison (ed.), *The Public Relations Handbook* (Routledge, 2008).

Thompson, John B., *Political Scandal: Power and Visibility in the Media Age* (Polity, 2000).

Trento, Susan B, *The Power House: Robert Keith Gray and the Selling of Access and Influence in Washington* (St Martin's Press, 1992).

Tumber, Howard (ed.), *Media Power, Professionals and Policies* (Routledge, 2000).

Tye, Larry, *The Father of Spin: Edward L. Bernays and the Birth of Public Relations* (Owl Books, 2002).

NOVELS

Buckley, Christopher, *Thank You for Smoking* (Allison & Busby, 2003).

Dezenhall, Eric, *Jackie Disaster* (Thomas Dunne, 2003).

Lancaster, Graham, *Grave Song* (Hodder & Stoughton, 1996).

Larsson, Stieg, *The Girl with the Dragon Tattoo* (MacLehose Press, 2008).

Michie, David, *Conflict of Interest* (Little, Brown, 2000).

Price, Daniel, *Slick* (Villard, 2004).

Priestley, J. B., *The Image Men* (Mandarin, 1996).

Thebo, Mimi, *The Saint Who Loved Me* (Allison & Busby, 2002).

Torday, Paul, *Salmon Fishing in the Yemen* (Weidenfeld and Nicholson, 2007).

Waugh, Daisy, *The New You Survival Kit* (Harper Collins, 2002).

Wilson, Sloan, *The Man in the Gray Flannel Suit* (Four Walls Eight Windows, 2002).

FILMS AND TV

Absolutely Fabulous http://www.bbc.co.uk/comedy/abfab/.

Absolute Power http://www.bbc.co.uk/comedy/absolutepower/.

Bridget Jones Diary (Universal Studios, 2001, dir. Sharon Maguire, 132 min.).

The Century of the Self http://www.bbc.co.uk/bbcfour/documentaries/features/century_of_the_self.shtml.

The China Syndrome (Colombia Pictures, dir. James Bridges, 117 min.).

Days of Wine and Roses (Warner Brothers, dir.Blake Edwards, 113 min.).

Four's a Crowd (Warner Brothers, 1938, dir. Michael Curtiz, 91 min.).

The Hills http://www.mtv.co.uk/shows/the-hills.

In the Loop (BBC Films, 2009, dir. Armando Iannucci, 106 min.).

The Man in a Gray Flannel Suit (20th Century Fox, 1956, dir. Nunnally Johnson, 152 min.).

Phonebooth (20th Century Fox, 2003, dir. Joel Schumacher, 77 min.).

PoweR Girls http://www.mtv.com/ontv/dyn/power_girls/series.jhtml.

Primary Colors (Award Entertainment, 1998, dir. Mike Nichols, 143 min.).

Sex and the City http://www.hbo.com/city/.

Sliding Doors (Intermedia Films, 1998, dir. Peter Howitt, 99 min.).

Spin City http://www.tv.com/spin-city/show/220/summary.html.

Starsuckers (S2S Productions, 2009, dir. Chris Atkins, 100 min.).

The Sweet Smell of Success (Metro Goldwyn Meyer, 1957, dir. Alexander Mackendrick, 93 min.).

Thank You for Smoking (Room 9 Entertainment, 2005, dir. Jason Reitman, 92 min.).

The Spin Crowd http://uk.eonline.com/on/shows/spin_crowd/index.html.

The Thick of It http://www.bbc.co.uk/comedy/thethickofit/index.shtml.

Wag the Dog (Baltimore Pictures, 1997, dir. Barry Levinson, 97 min.).

Waikiki Wedding (Paramount, 1937, dir. Frank Tuttle, 89min.).

WEBSITES

Trade organisations

www.amecorg.com Association of Media Evaluation Companies.

www.cerp.org European Public Relations Confederation.

www.cipr.co.uk Chartered Institute of Public Relations (UK).

www.iabc.com International Association of Business Communicators.

www.iccopr.com International Communications Consultancy Organization.

www.ipra.org International Public Relations Association.

www.prca.org.uk Public Relations Consultants Association (UK).

www.prfirms.org Council of Public Relations Firms (US).

www.prsa.org Public Relations Society of America.

www.warc.com World Advertising Research Center.

Trade websites and papers

www.holmesreport.com.

www.odwyerpr.com.

www.prweek.com.

Critical sites

www.prwatch.org.

www.spinwatch.org.

www.corpwatch.org.

Some examples of PR-related blogs and similar

http://www.edelman.com/speak_up/blog/.
http://www.forimmediaterelease.biz/.
http://www.globalprblogweek.com/.
http://blogs.hillandknowlton.com/blogs/.
http://holmesreport.blogspot.com/.
http://www.thenewpr.com/wiki/pmwiki.php.
http://prstudies.typepad.com/weblog/.
www.strumpette.com.

INDEX